REVELATION
An Introduction and Commentary

REVELATION
An Introduction and Commentary

Homer Hailey

THE WAKEMAN TRUST
LONDON SE1 6SD

Copyright 1992 by
Religious Supply, Inc.
ISBN: 0-8010-4201-1
Library of Congress Catalog Card Number:
78-062441
Printed in the United States of America

Unless otherwise indicated, Scripture quotations are from the American Standard Edition of the Revised Bible, © 1901 by Thomas Nelson and Sons, © 1921 by International Council of Religious Education.

First printing, March 1979
Second printing, October 1979
Third printing, February 1982
Fourth printing, September 1983
Fifth printing, August 1985
Sixth printing, November, 1987
Seventh printing, June 1989
Eighth Printing, June 1992

To my beloved wife
Widna
and to our children
**Roma Luceil (Hailey) Russell
Mary Lois (Hailey) Hoots
Rob Hailey
Dennis Hailey
Carol Ann Hailey
Richard Kirby
Gordon Kirby**

in the sincere hope that this book will give to each an understanding, courage, and zeal to strive earnestly for the heavenly home.

Contents

Foreword 9
Preface 11

INTRODUCTION 15

    I. The Title 18
   II. The Author 20
  III. The Place of Writing 25
  IV. The Date 26
        A. External Evidence 27
        B. Internal Evidence 32
    V. Symbolism 36
        A. Imagery 36
        B. Numbers 41
   VI. Interpretations of the Book 48
  VII. The Theme and Purpose of the Book 51
 VIII. Outline of the Book 53

HISTORICAL BACKGROUND 59

COMMENTARY ON REVELATION* 91

Bibliography 435

*A complete outline of chapters and verses appears on page 53ff.

Foreword

Serious Bible students are aware of the great volume of materials that have been written about the Revelation letter, and the extreme diversity of interpretations which have been made. The extensive use of symbols and the confusion of commentators' views have caused many students to avoid the book almost entirely. Another commentary on the Revelation might bear no particular significance were it not for the unique qualities of the author.

Homer Hailey has given a full fifty years of his adult life to a careful study of the Word of God. This study has grown out of a basic commitment to the Bible as the fully inspired, fully authorative communication from God to man. Mr. Hailey formed a strong attachment to the prophets of the Old Covenant in his early days as a Christian and Bible student. This affection has continued throughout his life, and his work in the prophets has come through in much of his preaching and writing, as well as in his classes at Abilene Christian College (Abilene, Texas) and at Florida College (Temple Terrace, Florida).

Personal friends of Homer Hailey know that he is also unique as a person. Many years ago a bout with cancer which predicted an early death was won with surgery, exercise, diet, determination, and much prayer. Boxing, weightlifting, and disciplined activities have since blessed him with outstanding health. Cheerfulness and optimism are his trademarks, and his quick wit adds an admirable zest. This vibrant love of life is blended beautifully with a kindness and compassion for people.

With all of these qualities contributing, Mr. Hailey has spent many years studying and teaching the Revelation letter, and exploring the thinking of many earlier writers. His insight into the symbolism of the Apocalypse has been enhanced by imbibing the spirit of the prophets he knows and loves. The book benefits from research, from a fair and concise presentation of various views, as well as from the author's insight into the meaning of the text.

Written in a manner to justify his scholarship, Mr. Hailey's work is within the grasp of serious Bible students of any level. Most important, Homer Hailey has brought to the reader an awesome combination of respect for God's Word, careful study, and beauty of expression.

BOB F. OWEN
Temple Terrace, Florida

Preface

Why write another commentary on Revelation? The answer to that question is similar to the answer men give when they are asked why they climb a mountain: The mountain is there, and therefore the challenge to climb it. The Book of Revelation is here, and with it there is a desire to study it and set down in writing one's thoughts which grow out of the study. However, there is this difference: the student and writer of a commentary on Revelation believes he can make a helpful contribution to all who reverently search for truth.

The challenge to write such a book has been before me for a number of years. Finally the book was begun, and now four years later it is being made ready for the public. This commentary is sent forth with the fervent prayer that as one studies Revelation, it may help provide a clearer insight into this beautiful and instructive vision from the Lord to His servant John.

The works of many authors have been consulted, but several have been especially helpful. To these I owe a debt of sincere gratitude, chiefly, Henry Alford, *The Greek Testament*; R. C. H. Lenski, *Interpretation of St. John's Revelation*; Albertus Pieters, *The Lamb, The Woman and the Dragon*; and particularly the classic work of Henry Barclay Swete, *The Apocalypse of St. John*.

In the introduction numerous footnote references will be found, but in the commentary itself these have been limited. Instead, when a quotation has been used, the author's name and the page number of his book are given. The reader may refer to the bibliography for the specific title.

Several abbreviations have been used:

A. & G.: Arndt and Gingrich.
A-N-F: Ante-Nicene Fathers.
C. A. H.: Cambridge Ancient History
E. H.: Ecclesiastical History (Eusebius)

I.S.B.E.: International Standard Bible Encyclopaedia.
ASV: American Standard Version.
KJV: King James Version

Revelation citations are not preceded with the word Revelation (e.g., 2:2). Other books are identified with book and passage (e.g., Isa. 2:22).

In writing a book such as this there are always personal friends whose help has been invaluable and to whom much more is owed than one can ever repay. Chief among these are two to whom I am especially indebted: Mrs. Margie Garrett, Temple Terrace, Florida, whose work in reading and correcting the sentence structure in the manuscript has been of utmost help and which is most deeply appreciated; and Mrs. Ruby Stroup, Tucson, Arizona, who has spent many hours patiently typing and correcting the manuscript, for whose labor of love I am most grateful. I am also indebted to Mrs. Mary Ann Hirt, Tucson, for reading the manuscript for typographical errors; to Mr. Stanley Paher, Las Vegas, Nevada, for reading the material and offering many valuable suggestions; and to Mr. Clair Stroup, Tucson, for checking for accuracy in use and spelling of the Greek words. Also thanks to Mr. Bob Owen, Temple Terrace, Florida, for writing the foreword. Finally, a word of thanks to my esteemed friend, Mr. Herman Baker, and to his excellent company for publishing the commentary.

HOMER HAILEY
Tucson, Arizona

INTRODUCTION

Introduction

Older people can remember with nostalgia their childhood homes in which there was often a special room of mystery. It may have been the parlor or possibly the bedroom of a deceased one. If the parlor, there would be special chairs and a sofa of horsehair covering, a phonograph to be played on particular occasions, pictures of an older generation looking down sternly upon the new generation, a family Bible seldom used except to record births, weddings, and deaths, and a stereoscope which could bring before the viewer's eyes scenes of faraway places.

It is regrettable that in this age of scientific research man desires to uncover all the secrets of the material universe and has largely lost his sense of awe in the presence of the mysterious. No longer do we look at the clouds and, in fancy, see images in their contours, or see ourselves playing upon them and exploring the canyons between. No longer can we close our eyes and in imagination visit the great ice lands of the arctic, imagining ourselves there; or visit the deep woods of the North, chatting with the strong, mysterious inhabitants. Largely, we have lost our love and appreciation for mystery and the mysterious.

In the Bible, God's great temple of spiritual truth, there is one special room filled with mysteries and wonders that fire the imagination to celestial heights and leave us amazed at the grandeur of its portrayal of the spiritual. That room is designated as The Revelation. Man may fathom many of the mysteries of the physical world, coming to an almost complete understanding of them, at least to the point that he loses his sense of awe in their presence. But in contrast, although we can grasp something of Revelation's meaning and use for us, we never cease to stand in amazement and wonder at its mysteries which continue to challenge us.

Patmos, an insignificant rocky island of approximately fifty square miles, lying about twenty-four miles west of the shore of Asia Minor and about seventy miles southwest of Ephesus, has been made immortal by the vision shown John there in the long ago. As we share with him the wonders of that moment in time, we are introduced to the scope of Jesus' ministry and the present glory of His reign. We behold the Lord as He walks among the lampstands, and we listen as He dictates letters to seven churches in provinces of Asia Minor, and we try to grasp the full significance of the picture.

At this point we behold a door opened in heaven, and in the vision revealed to John we see the throne of the universe, and all creation in heaven and on earth doing homage to Him who occupies the throne. Amid the praises of the heavenly beings, one like unto a lamb takes a closed, sealed book from the throne-occupant's hand. John weeps because no one in heaven, on earth, or under the earth is able to open the roll, but he is told that the lion of the tribe of Judah can open it. We look to see a lion, when lo, a lamb takes it and begins to loose the seals. We are filled with awe and wonder at what follows the opening of the seals: Horsemen come forth, each playing a role in the drama before us; souls cry out from beneath an altar for the avenging of a cause for which they have been sacrificed. There follow the terrors of judgment; servants of God receive a seal upon their foreheads, and a great white-robed multitude stands before the throne, serving God day and night.

This scene of such action is followed by a moment of silence in heaven as prayers of the saints are presented before God. Then trumpets in the hands of angels begin to blast, and wonderful and terrible events follow, affecting all nature and the inhabitants of earth. A strong angel cries with a great voice as a lion roars, to which seven thunders respond by uttering their voices. After this John is told to eat a little book, the temple is measured, and two witnesses are put to death because of their testimony about Jesus. But tragedy is turned into triumph when these two are called to come up to heaven. At last the seventh angel sounds his trumpet, and with this the curtain falls on part one. We are excited with what we have seen and heard, but what is it all about?

As the second division of the book opens, we see a radiant woman, arrayed with the sun, with the moon under her feet and twelve stars upon her brow, who is about to bear a child. She gives birth to a man child, while before her stands the devil waiting to devour it. But instead of being devoured, the man child is caught up to God and to His throne and the woman flees into the wilderness. In the vision there follows a great conflict between Michael's heavenly forces on the one side and Satan's diabolical army on the other. In the conflict the dragon, Satan, is cast down to the earth and stands upon the seashore. And, while the dragon stands upon the seashore, a terrible beast arises out of the sea. The beast, who is endowed with Satan's power, throne, and authority, wages war against the woman and her seed. Soon a second beast, who comes up out of the earth, exercising all the power of the first beast, begins an attempt both to deceive and to destroy the servants of God, but succeeds only in deceiving the earth-dwellers. Next, our view is focused on the glorious Lamb of God and a victorious host of 144,000 persons standing with Him on Mount Zion. The second division of this scene concludes with a harvest in which the earth is reaped and is cast into the winepress of God's wrath.

Scene follows scene. Bowls of wrath are poured out upon the earth, resulting in plagues of blood, death, and destruction. A great harlot appears, enticing the earth-dwellers to commit fornication with her; but she is judged and destroyed. Hallelujahs are heard in heaven. All are rejoicing over the fall of the harlot. There follows a great conflict between the beast and his forces and the King of Kings and His forces. The beast and his helper, the false prophet, are cast into the lake of fire. Satan is bound, and saints reign on thrones for a thousand years. At the end of the thousand years Satan is loosed for a little time, during which he makes a final effort to destroy the saints of God. But instead of victory, Satan is defeated and he, too, is cast into the lake of fire.

After the resurrection and universal judgment which follows Satan's destruction in the lake of fire, we see a new heaven and a new earth with God among His people, and His people at home with Him. The picture that follows the judgment is one of a great and glorious city where the inhabitants have all tears wiped away, and who inherit all that is glorious and precious. The whole scene, from first to last, is breathtaking, awesome, and majestic.

Briefly, this is the picture before which we stand in awe, amazement, and wonder. It all seems so fraught with mystery; can we understand its purpose and teaching? Having been written during the latter period of the Flavian dynasty (A.D. 81–96), a period of persecution and suffering for the saints, Revelation's symbolism had a real purpose and message then, and should continue even now to instruct, aid, and encourage God's people. While instructing and encouraging His saints, God was concealing His purpose from the gross and hardhearted unbelievers. God's choice of method in doing this was both prudent and brilliant. We ask, How else could He have instructed and encouraged Christians without playing into the hand of the enemy? This had been His method in ancient times as set forth in Daniel, Ezekiel, and Zechariah. As it had served His purpose in those times long past, it served His purpose no less successfully in John's day. Whether or not we can fathom all the mysterious symbols and signs, the imagery, voices, and actions, we can surely learn something of its message for the people of John's day and its divine instruction for us today. To the task of understanding what we can of its meaning, we set our hand in the writing of this book.

Because of its apocalyptic nature, its imagery and symbolism, and its many allusions to the Old Covenant writings, Revelation has through the centuries had a legion of widely differing interpretations. In the light of these vastly differing views, it ill-becomes any of us to be dogmatic in the positions we take. Recognizing this, I shall strive to present in a modest and restrained spirit what I believe the message to have been and to be, leaving the reader at liberty to agree or disagree.

I. THE TITLE

In our American Standard Version, the text followed in this study, the title is, *The Revelation of John*. In the Greek text it is, *Apokalupsis Iōanou* (in Westcott-Hort, or *Iōannou* in Alford and others). *Apokalupsis* means "an uncovering, a laying bare, making naked" (Thayer). The word is from *apokalupto*, "to uncover, unveil." The book uncovers or unveils through symbols, signs, imagery, and visions the impending persecution facing the church. It seeks to prepare the people for persecution by the revelation which God gave to Jesus Christ to show unto His servants. This apocalyptic method prevents the enemies of God from understanding the message, while making it known to His people. Even so, we must admit that there is much in the book which remains veiled to us.

INTRODUCTION

Apocalyptic writings differ from the prophetic works in substance and form, and yet in both there are predictive and apocalyptic elements. In the prophetic preaching and writing moral issues at hand receive the greater attention, while in the apocalypses the material is more predictive and the extent of subject matter is more inclusive and far-reaching. This latter encompasses a view involving a grasp of world conditions and the global forces at work, looking to the ultimate end which would grow out of these. All nations, forces, and conditions are seen to be under the control of the mighty God. Apocalyptic literature flourished during a time of some great national crisis when a formidable enemy threatened the life of the people—a time of trial and stress. This type of writing is characterized by symbols in dreams and visions, in actions and consequences, instructing and encouraging the people under such conditions. The Spirit chose this method to reveal the struggles of God's people with heathen forces and the victory of His cause and kingdom over these worldly powers. An inspired writer of an apocalyptic book might assume the role of both prophet and apocalyptist.

In nearly all aspects of truth the genuine gives rise to the counterfeit or imitation. The uninspired writers of these imitation works strove to imitate the genuine in both the prophetic and apocalyptic elements. Beginning about 200 B.C. and continuing to near A.D. 200, apocalyptic literature became common among the Jews, being patterned largely after the writings of Daniel. The pseudo-apocalyptic literature, like the genuine, is characterized by "visions" in which the writer claims to see God acting on behalf of His people and against their enemies. The uninspired writings of this category which were accepted and esteemed by the people of the period in which they were written were known as the Apocrapha. Those which were rejected are described as pseudepigrapha.

The three genuine apocalyptic books of the Old Covenant, which were inspired by the Spirit of God, are Daniel, Ezekiel, and Zechariah. The only one of the New Covenant is the Revelation of John, henceforth referred to as Revelation. In these canonical books both the apocalyptic and prophetic elements are strongly evident.

Daniel and Ezekiel spoke and wrote during the period of the great and powerful Babylonian Empire, when God's people were either being carried into the Babylonian captivity, or were already there

(605–539 B.C.). Zechariah prophesied during the Persian rule and power, after the return of the remnant of Israel from Babylon (520 B.C. to an indefinite date). The three wrote to instruct the people of God, to encourage them in a time of extreme hardship, and to prepare them for further severe trials. These continued even to the days of Antiochus of Syria and to the period of the Roman persecution. Through the study of the three ancient writings and John's Revelation, the people of God can find instruction and encouragement even to the end of time. As will be pointed out later, Revelation was written during the days of the strong and indomitable Roman Empire to inform Christians what was happening and would happen, and to encourage them to persevere while suffering at the hands of the Jews and Romans, and to assure them of ultimate victory under Christ. All four writers of these genuine apocalyptic books manifest a broad grasp of world affairs and events, and by the Spirit of God give assurance to the suffering saints that God's overruling providence brings ultimate judgment and destruction to the heathen persecuting powers, and victory and glory to God's kingdom. Their style is dramatic and awe-inspiring.

II. THE AUTHOR

Four times in Revelation the author refers to himself as John (1:1, 4, 9; 22:8). The question is whether the writer was an unknown prophet named John, a presbyter who lived at Ephesus, or the apostle John, who wrote as an apostle and prophet. It is true that the writer nowhere refers to himself as an apostle, but external evidence (the voice of tradition) and internal evidence point to John the apostle, the author of the Gospel and three epistles which bear his name, as the author of the Apocalypse.

It is true that the writer refers to his message as "prophecy," and thus identifies himself as a prophet. John speaks of his writing as "the words of the prophecy" (1:3), "the words of the prophecy of this book" (22:7, 10, 18), and "the words of the book of this prophecy" (22:19). Having received the revelation set forth in the first part of the book, John was instructed by a voice from heaven to take a little book out of an angel's hand and eat it, for "thou must prophesy again over many peoples and nations and tongues and kings" (10:11). John is further identified as a prophet when an angel sets himself forth as a fellow-servant with the writer and with the writer's brethren, "the prophets" (22:9). Without controversy, these passages clearly point to the author as a prophet. But does it follow that he is an apostle as well?

Although a few relatively early writers raised the question of authorship, the apostle John's composition of Revelation was never seriously questioned until modern nineteenth-century liberal criticism. Many critics have attempted to associate the book with a certain "John the presbyter," who is supposed to have lived, died, and been buried at Ephesus. The evidence offered by these critics is weak and most unconvincing, as will be pointed out.

Space permits only a brief summary of the external and internal evidence in support of the apostle John as the writer of the book. It will probably be acknowledged by all students of the subject that of the two bodies of evidence, external and internal, the external—the voice of early writers—is the stronger and more convincing. In this commentary a lengthy and involved discussion of "John the presbyter" and "John the apostle" would be out of place. Let it suffice our purpose to present as briefly and concisely as possible the testimony of the early church writers who considered John the apostle to have been the writer.

Justin Martyr (A.D. 110–165) in his *Dialogue with Trypho the Jew* (LXXXI) says, "There was a certain man with us, whose name was John, one of the apostles of Christ, who prophesied by a revelation," and then refers to the thousand years, the resurrection and the judgment of Revelation 20.[1]

Irenaeus (A.D. 120–202), who had heard Polycarp, a disciple of John the apostle, wrote in his *Against Heresies* (IV. xx. 11), "John, also the Lord's disciple... says in the Apocalypse," and then quotes profusely from that book.[2] Having thus identified him as "the Lord's disciple," Irenaeus says later: "In a still clearer light has John, in the Apocalypse" revealed certain things, which the writer proceeds to discuss (V. xxi. 1).[3]

---

[1] *The Ante-Nicene Fathers*, vol. I, p. 240. Henceforth referred to as A-N-F.
[2] Ibid., pp. 491–492.
[3] Ibid., p. 554.

Clement of Alexandria (A.D. 153-217) in his treatise, *Who is the Rich Man that Shall Be Saved?* (XLII), writes of "the apostle John" who "returned to Ephesus from the isle of Patmos" after "the tyrant's death." The tyrant is unnamed.[4]

Tertullian (A.D. 145-220), sometimes called "the Father of Latin Christianity," a voluminous writer, wrote five books *Against Marcion*. In book III. xxv, Tertullian writes of the Jerusalem let down from heaven. He quotes Paul, who called it "our mother" (Gal. 4:26), and he says, "the apostle John beheld" it, referring to Revelation 21:2.[5]

Origen (A.D. 185-254), in *De Principiis*, says, "According to John, God is light" (I. II. 7), unquestionably referring to the apostle John. Then later he says, "Listen to the manner in which John [the John whom he had quoted above] speaks in the apocalypse" (I. II. 10).[6] Surely, Origen knew only one John who wrote Scripture, and that was John the apostle.

Hippolytus (A.D. 170-236), in his *Treatise On Christ and Antichrist* (36-42), identifies the writer of Revelation as John the apostle when he says, "Tell me, blessed John, apostle and disciple of the Lord, what didst thou see and hear concerning Babylon?" and then quotes chapters 17, 18.[7]

Victorinus (who died in the persecution, A.D. 303), bishop of Petau, wrote the earliest known commentary on Revelation, only a fragment of which has survived. Commenting on 10:3 he says, "And by his voice John gave his testimony in the world . . . because he is an apostle."[8]

Surely, such an array of testimony from these early writers can lead to but one conclusion: John the apostle was God's servant whom He used to give to His church this marvelous and fascinating book.

The earliest church writer and teacher to question the apostolic authorship of Revelation was **Dionysius** (A.D. 200-265), Bishop of Alexandria. Dionysius was a strong anti-millenarian or anti-chiliast. In his zeal against the thousand-year theory in vogue among some teachers at that time, Dionysius took the position that Revelation was

---

[4]Ibid., vol. II, p. 603.
[5]Ibid., vol. III, p. 342.
[6]Ibid., vol. IV, pp. 248, 250.
[7]Ibid., vol. V, pp. 211, 212.
[8]Ibid., vol. VII, p. 353.

not written by John the apostle. Of what value this position was to his view on the millennium is not clear. He confessed that he did not understand the Book of Revelation. Although he admitted "that it was the work of some holy and inspired man," he further stated, "What John this is, however, is uncertain." He was "of opinion that there were many persons of the same name with John the apostle," especially in Asia, and mentions John Mark specifically. He concludes by saying, "I think, therefore, that it was some other one of those who were in Asia. For it is said that there were two monuments in Ephesus, and that each of these bears the name of John."[9] But this proves nothing, for he had already said that there were many persons in Asia named John; and further, he rests his conclusion on hearsay. Though interestingly and ably set forth, his entire discussion does not affect the testimony of the above writers, and moreover, fails to identify any particular person as the author of Revelation.

The argument for a "John the presbyter" instead of "John the apostle" as the writer of Revelation seems to rest primarily on a statement from Papias (A.D. 70–155), who is reputed to have written five books, of which only a few scant fragments have come down to us. But the passage relied upon for this argument (that "John the presbyter" is separate from John the apostle) seems to have been misread by those who use it. Papias wrote, "If, then, any one who had attended on the elders came, I asked minutely after their sayings, —what Andrew or Peter said, or what was said by Philip, or by Thomas, or by James, or by John, or by Matthew, or by any other of the Lord's disciples." He identified these apostles as *elders,* which is not surprising since the word was used as a term of respect for an older person or to designate an older or past generation (I Tim. 5:1; Heb. 11:2; et al.), as well as applying to overseers of the church (I Peter 5:1; Titus 1:5; et al.). Papias continued by saying, "which things Aristion and the presbyter [elder] John, the disciples of the Lord, say." In this he does not identify Aristion as an elder, but distinguishes him from the presbyter John, thus identifying this John as the John of the seven apostles whom he identified as elders or presbyters.[10] But if it could be proved that Papias

---

[9]Ibid., vol. VI, pp. 82, 83. See also Eusebius, *Ecclesiastical History,* Bk.VII, chap. 25, pp. 297–301. Henceforth referred to as E. H.
[10]*Ante-Nicene Fathers,* vol. I, p. 153.

is writing of two men by the name of John, an apostle and a presbyter (and this cannot be deduced from the text), it still does not follow that this John the presbyter wrote Revelation. The evidence for a John the presbyter as writer of Revelation is practically nil.

Now a word on the internal evidence for the apostolic authorship. A close look at the book reveals that there is a wide difference between the Greek of the Gospel and First John and the Greek of Revelation. This difference, it is claimed, argues for a separate writer for the latter book. There are various answers given in explanation for this stylistic difference, which I leave for the Greek scholars to discuss. One possible answer is that in giving to the church a book that is different from all others, God set forth the book using a different language style. To one who believes that the writer was under the inspiration and guidance of God's Holy Spirit and that he spoke through or by the Spirit (1:10; 2:7, 11, 17, 29; 3:6, 13, 22; 4:2; 14:13; 22:17), this difference in speech is of little concern. The language was chosen by the Spirit. The Spirit was to teach the apostles (John 14:26) and guide them into all truth (John 16:13); when the Spirit came they spoke "as the Spirit gave them utterance" (Acts 2:4), "not in words which man's wisdom teacheth, but which the Spirit teacheth; combining spiritual things with spiritual words" (I Cor. 2:13). We see, then, that the Spirit chose the language. This line of reasoning carries little weight with the modern liberal critic, but it should satisfy the believer.

The use of certain words found in John's accepted writings—the Gospel and I John—and Revelation point to identity of authorship. The first of these that connects the three is the identity of the Son as "the Word" (*logos*): "the Word was God" (John 1:1; cf. v. 14); "the Word of life" (I John 1:1); "The Word of God" (Rev. 19:13). Only in these three books is Jesus identified as "the Word."

Another word peculiar to these three works (with three exceptions: Luke 11:22; Rom. 3:4; 12:21) is *nikaō*, "to overcome" or conquer. Jesus used it of Himself (John 16:33); John used it seven times in I John, and it occurs seventeen times in Revelation. In each instance in Revelation it is used of Christ and the saints overcoming as in the Gospel and I John, with two exceptions, that of the saints being temporarily overcome by the enemy (11:7; 13:7).

A third word occurring especially in these three books, and forming a connecting tie, is "true" (*alēthinos*). The only other writings in which this word is found are Luke 16:11; I Thessalonians 1:9; Hebrews 8:2; 9:24; 10:22. The word occurs eight times in the Gospel of John, four times in I John, and ten times in Revelation. The peculiar use made of the word in the three writings points strongly to a common authorship.

A fourth word found only in the Gospel of John and Revelation is *arnion*, "lamb." Jesus used it of His tender disciples (John 21:15), and in Revelation it occurs twenty-eight times of Jesus and once of the earth-beast, "who had two horns as a lamb" (13:11). The kindred word *amnos*, "lamb" (discussed more fully in the commentary), is used twice by John in the Gospel, both times referring to Jesus (John 1:29, 36). *Amnos* is not used by the writer of Revelation; he uses only *arnion*. *Amnos* is used to translate Isaiah in Acts 8:32, and by Peter of Christ's blood "as of a lamb" (I Peter 1:19). The reference to Jesus as a lamb in the Gospel and Revelation adds some weight to the evidence for oneness of authorship.

One must confess that if he were dependent solely on internal evidence his case would be weak; but with the abundance of traditional evidence for the apostolic authorship and the almost total absence of evidence for another, his case stands on much firmer ground than does that of the presbyter theory. In either case, the believer comes back to the position that the book is God's revelation, given by His Spirit through whomever He may have used as His penman. Most students, however, accept John the apostle as the Lord's instrument to write the book. For a thorough and more detailed presentation of the external and internal evidence on the subject, the student is referred to Henry Alford's *Greek Testament*, to which I am indebted for many suggestions offered above.[11]

III. THE PLACE OF WRITING

The question has been posed by some whether the book was written on Patmos at the time of the revelation to John or after his return to

---
[11]Vol. IV: 198–239.

Ephesus. The question is answered in the text itself. The writer was instructed by a voice saying, "What thou seest, write in a book *and send it* to the seven churches...." The voice then specified Ephesus as one of the churches to receive the book (1:11). John was further instructed, "Write therefore the things which thou sawest, and the things which are, and the things which shall come to pass hereafter" (1:19). Each of the letters to the seven churches begins with instructions to write to the angel of the particular congregation (chaps. 2—3). When John heard the seven thunders utter their voices, he "was about to write," when instructed not to (10:4). Three times following this John is told to write (14:13; 19:9; 21:5). This evidence clearly reveals that John wrote from Patmos where he received the message and from where it was sent to the churches.

IV. THE DATE

Scholars have periodically debated the date for John's receiving and recording the revelation, but the choice usually lies between the time of Nero, A.D. 64–68, and the time of Domitian, A.D. 91–96. However, there are a few who place the date of writing between these two, possibly under the rule of Vespasian or about A.D. 70, the year Jerusalem was destroyed. A formidable array of illustrious names who defend the Neronian date could be set over against an equally reputable and scholarly host of defenders of the Domitian date; but this array of names would not resolve the question. After considering arguments for each of the positions, I believe that the weight of evidence favors the late date, A.D. 91–96, though there are some strong, but inconclusive, arguments for the Neronian date.

Determining the exact date of composition is not as essential as recognizing the purpose of the book. By studying the historical background of Revelation (see pp. 59–90), we learn that there was a series of persecutions, and thus the book served to encourage the saints during the entire period. The book was written not only for the Christians in distress during the time of Nero or Domitian, but also for those in "the great tribulation" (7:14), which continued with periodic interruptions and intermittent intervals of anxious and apprehensive peace for a period of 249 years, from A.D. 64 to 313. This background of the development of the Roman attitude offers strong supporting evidence for the later date. Philip Schaff, who accepts and defends the earlier date, has said of John's exile to Patmos and the disputed date, "External evidence points to the reign of Domitian, A.D. 95; internal evidence to the reign of Nero, or soon after his death, A.D. 68."[12] Schaff favors a date between Nero's death (June 9, 68), and the destruction of Jerusalem (August 10, 70).[13] I am not only persuaded that the external evidence strongly favors the Domitian date but am also convinced that the internal evidence lends itself with equal strength to the same conclusion.

A. External Evidence

1. Conditions Set Forth in Acts

The early spread of the Christian faith in the first century was nothing short of phenomenal. Before the end of the era following the Pentecost of Acts 2, Christians and churches existed throughout the Roman world, even as far east as ancient Babylon. Paul could say that in his day the gospel had been preached "in all creation under heaven" (Col. 1:23).

The earliest opposition to the preaching of Christ's gospel came from the Jews (Acts 8:1-4; 12:1-19; 13:50-52; 14:2; et al.); the early clashes with the Roman power were not from religious opposition but from economic considerations. In Philippi Paul and Silas were arrested, beaten and cast into prison for curtailing the income of certain men. They had cast out a spirit of divination from a maiden whose soothsaying had brought much gain to her masters (Acts 16). When Paul was at Ephesus, trouble arose over the loss of business by the makers of silver shrines to a goddess. However, Paul maintained friendly relations with certain Asiarchs of the city (Acts 19). There is no evidence of opposition to Paul and his work from the heathen priests of the city.

---

[12]Schaff, *History of the Christian Church*, vol. I, p. 427.
[13]Ibid., p. 834.

2. Nero's Persecution

Conservative scholars are generally agreed that Paul spent two years in Rome, probably A.D. 61-63, awaiting his trial before Nero. Also, it is generally agreed that Nero released Paul and allowed him to continue his travels and work in the gospel. This indicates that up to this time there had been no imperial opposition to Christians and to the church; however, all this was to change with the great fire in Rome, A.D. 64. Nero cast about for an escape from the accusation that he himself caused the fire and found his way of escape in the Christians. At this point it is profitable to take a second look at the charge made against the Christians by Tacitus, who said they were "a class hated for their abominations. . . . An immense multitude was convicted, not so much of the crime of firing the city, as of hatred against mankind."[14] The execution must have been extremely brutal, for the historian says that the persecution was so severe that from among the populace "there arose a feeling of compassion" for the Christians; "for it was not, as it seemed, for the public good, but to glut one man's cruelty, that they were being destroyed."[15] Three points stand out clearly: the Christians were hated for abominations not specified; they were charged with firing the city, the truth of which charge Tacitus seemed to doubt; and their conduct, in sharp contrast to Roman society generally, made them appear to hate mankind. It seems clear that although the Christians' religion was involved, the persecution was not a war against their religion *per se*. Nero's approach passed through two stages: first, he sought to divert suspicion from himself as the cause of the fire; and second, he persecuted the Christians on the charge of hostility to society. The conduct of Christians did not fit in with Roman social customs, and so they were considered enemies of the Roman society. They were charged with using magic because of their power over people and over their own lives. Consequently, they were inflicted with the punishment that was imposed on users of magic and Nero soon dropped the charge of incendiarism.

At this point two questions are raised. Did Nero's persecution extend beyond Rome into the provinces? And did the Emperor issue an impe-

---

[14]*Annals*, XV. 44.
[15]Ibid.

rial edict or proscription against Christians? There is no solid evidence that Nero's persecution extended beyond the city of Rome itself. The two earliest writers to assert clearly that it extended beyond Rome are Sulpicious Severus and Orosius (both ca. A.D. 400). Schaff admits that Severus gives his account "mostly from Tacitus."[16] William Ramsay also says that Severus' account of the Neronian persecution is founded on Tacitus, and quotes Severus as saying in almost the words of Tacitus, "This was the beginning of severe measures against the Christians. Afterwards the religion was forbidden by formal laws, and the profession of Christianity was made illegal by published edicts."[17] But were formal laws making Christianity illegal by published edicts issued by Nero, or did they come later? It seems clear from the correspondence between Pliny and Trajan (see pp. 75f) that even at this time (A.D. 111-113) there had been no formal edict; for if there had been such an edict issued, Pliny would have known what to do. It seems therefore, as pointed out by Ramsay, that Nero's principle was an unwritten law by which the governors of the provinces judged Christians. This means that punishments inflicted were administrative and not judicial.[18] If Severus depended on Tacitus for his information, and Tacitus says nothing about "formal laws" and "published edicts," it follows that these laws and edicts came through later emperors. Therefore there seems to be no other interpretation of Severus' statement, "Afterwards the religion was forbidden by formal laws, and ... made illegal by published edicts." Nero allowed Christians to be charged with offenses which were social or moral, rather than criminal. By this practice Nero set a precedent which became an unwritten law, respected and followed by later emperors and used against Christians by the magistrates of the provinces.

Ramsay points out the time element in Nero's reign between A.D. 64 and 68 as another factor in the evolving of the attitude towards the Christians and in the development of fixed laws. The persecution which began in 64 was interrupted, if not ended, by Nero's departure from Rome to Greece in 66. He returned to Rome in 68 just in time to

---

[16]Schaff, vol. I, pp. 384, 389.
[17]William M. Ramsay, *The Church in The Roman Empire*, p. 243, quoting Severus, *Chron.* II.29.
[18]Ibid., p. 258.

learn of the revolt that led to his death a few weeks later.[19] This is not to say that persecutions ceased completely, for Paul was put to death during this period; but it does mean that persecution by Nero abated. There seems to have been insufficient time during this brief period for the development of a fixed pattern and a basis of opposition to the faith.

From the available evidence, it appears that Nero's persecution was not aimed at the annihilation of Christianity, that it did not extend beyond Rome, and that he issued no formal edict against the Christians. This indicates that the attitude toward the Christians was not finally determined under Nero, but that the formal laws and edicts mentioned by Severus developed under emperors who followed Nero. State action against Christians developed in the empire within the period between A.D. 70 and 96; but even during this period, there seems to have been no imperial edict of proscription from any emperor completely outlawing Christianity.

3. Domitian's Persecution

There can be no doubt that Nero's policy was continued by Vespasian and Titus, but there is no record of a direct confrontation with Christians by either of these rulers. However, under Domitian, who was motivated by fear of conspiracy and by his insatiable desire for divine honors, the policy against any freedom of the individual or any opposition to despotism was carried to extreme. Ramsay thinks this policy against philosophic interests "did not originate in mere capricious tyranny," but that the opposition to Christians was political. The action was against the church as an organized unity.[20] Domitian sought to restore the Roman cultus and encouraged worship of himself as lord and god.[21] This reverence for the gods and the emperor was considered proof of loyalty to the empire; a refusal to pay this homage was considered sacrilege and treason. From Domitian's point of view the issue was political; from the Christian's point of view it was religious. In either case the lines were drawn, and the conflict was to be long and bloody for the saints.

---

[19]Ibid., p. 244 (footnote).
[20]Ibid., pp. 273-275.
[21]Seutonius, *Domitian*. 13.

The difference in the attitudes of Nero and Domitian toward divine honors and worship of themselves appears quite marked, and the harsh attitude of Domitian argues strongly for the later date of Revelation. Upon being declared emperor, Nero forbad statues to himself of solid gold and silver.[22] However, Tacitus does mention a bronze statue of the emperor that was melted in a fire.[23] Seutonius says, "He despised all religious cults except that of Atargatis, the Syrian Goddess," to whom he sacrificed three times a day.[24] Although Nero reveled in the plaudits of the populace and accepted worship as a god, he seems to have been somewhat restrained at deification by the general principle "that divine honors are not paid to an emperor till he has ceased to live among men."[25] And since Nero loved life, he was in no way anxious to join the ranks of the deceased deities. In sharp contrast to Nero's disposition, Domitian avidly courted the worship of himself by the people and wanted them to look upon him as a god. This disposition of Domitian and the spirit of his reign fits much better into the tenor of Revelation than the attitude of Nero. As will be pointed out in the section on internal evidence, the whole theme of Revelation is that of a terrific conflict and struggle of moral and spiritual forces; truth and loyalty to Christ are pitted against religious error and loyalty to a great ruling power.

4. Early Writers

A few quotations from early church writers will conclude the external evidence for the later date. Irenaeus (A.D. 120–202), writing of John, who beheld the apocalyptic vision, said, "For that was seen not very long since, but almost in our own day, toward the end of Domitian's reign."[26] Clement of Alexandria, writing near the end of the second century (ca. A.D. 193), simply identifies John's release upon the death of an emperor, saying, "For when, on the tyrant's death, he returned to Ephesus from the isle of Patmos."[27] He does not name

---

[22]Tacitus, *Annals*, XIII. 10.
[23]Ibid., XV. 22.
[24]*Nero*, 56.
[25]Tacitus, *Annals*, XV. 74.
[26]*Against Heresies*, V. 30. 3, A-N-F. I. p. 559 f.
[27]*Salvation of a Rich Man*, 42, A-N-F. II. p. 603.

"the tyrant," but according to Eusebius (below), tradition held the tyrant to be Domitian. In his *Commentary on the Apocalypse*, Victorinus, who was martyred in the persecution of Diocletian (A.D. 303), comments on 10:11, "When John said these things he was in the isle of Patmos, condemned to the labor of the mines by Caesar Domitian. There, therefore, he saw the Apocalypse."[28] Commenting later on 17:10, he says of the seven heads, "One remains, under whom the Apocalypse was written—Domitian, to wit."[29]

Eusebius holds to the Domitian date, but acknowledges that his evidence rests on tradition. In writing about the persecution under Domitian (book III. 17), he continues in the next chapter, "In this persecution, it is handed down by tradition, that the apostle and evangelist John... was condemned to dwell on the island of Patmos."[30] This testimony rested on that of Irenaeus, quoted above. Eusebius continues, saying, "It was then also [under Nerva] that the apostle John returned from the banishment in Patmos, and took up his abode in Ephesus, according to the ancient tradition of the church."[31] He refers to the same again in chapter 23; and in book V. 8, he refers again to Iranaeus' testimony. The force of this evidence is challenged by some, but it appears that those who reject it have failed to sustain their objection.

B. Internal Evidence

1. The Letters to the Seven Churches

The general condition prevailing when John wrote fits the period of Domitian better than that of Nero. It was definitely a period of general tribulation shared by John and the brethren to whom he wrote (Rev. 1:9). In these letters we detect a marked difference of condition and attitude in the congregations from that revealed in the letters of Paul and Peter.

---

[28]*A-N-F*. VII. p. 353.
[29]Ibid., p. 358.
[30]*E. H.*, III, 17, 18.
[31]Ibid., III. 20.

a. To Ephesus (2:1-7). To the Corinthians Paul writes of men "who are false apostles, deceitful workers, fashioning themselves into apostles of Christ" (II Cor. 11:13). These were not necessarily claiming to be apostles, but they were fashioning themselves into such by lying and deceitful teaching. However, at Ephesus men were laying claim to apostleship; they "called themselves apostles" (Rev. 2:2), indicating a fuller development of the concept. The charge against the church at Ephesus was, "thou didst leave thy first love" (Rev. 2:4). This is a decided change from that existing at the time Paul wrote to the church at that place (ca. A.D. 62), commending "the love which ye show toward all the saints" (Eph. 1:15). It is true that this changed condition which developed between the time of Paul's letter and Jesus' letter in Revelation could have evolved within a decade, but it is not likely. However, by the time lapse of a generation or two it could easily have happened. The influence of the Nicolaitans over the church at Ephesus and Pergamum (2:6, 15) developed only after Paul's day, and this is a strong point in favor of the later date.

b. To Smyrna. In writing to the church at Smyrna (2:8–11), Jesus refers to "the blasphemy of them that say they are Jews, and they are not, but are a synagogue of Satan" (v. 9). The destruction of Jerusalem and the temple did not diminish the Jews' hatred for Christians, but rather intensified it. It is said that even in the year A.D. 155, when Polycarp was condemned to death by burning, those who gathered the wood and fagots for the pile did it with great haste, "the Jews especially, according to custom, eagerly assisting them in it."[32] The expression, "according to custom," says much.

c. To Pergamum (2:12-17). This city was a center of emperor worship, "where Satan's throne is... where Satan dwelleth" (v. 13). As pointed out above, this worship was more intense in the period of Domitian's reign than during Nero's. It seems also that Peter's prophecy of teachers of corruption who would appear was now being fulfilled. The apostle had warned that as there had been false prophets among Israel, so also there would arise among the churches false teachers who would bring in destructive heresies, even denying the

---

[32] *The Martyrdom of Polycarp*, chap. 13, A-N-F. I. 42.

Master who had bought them (II Peter 2:1). Peter continues his description of these false teachers saying that when they would come they would act after a certain pattern, "having followed the way of Balaam, the son of Beor, who loved the hire of wrong doing" (v. 15). These teachers of Peter's prophecy were now active in the church at Pergamum, along with the Nicolaitans, who seem clearly to have been related to the "Balaamites" in their erroneous and lascivious teaching.

d. *To Thyatira* (2:18-29). Thyatira had its Jezebel, a false prophetess who likewise fits into the pattern of Peter's prophecy. These seem to be steeped in "the deep things of Satan, as they are wont to say" (v. 24), influenced by the paganism of that stronghold of emperor and pagan idol worship. This condition is far removed from that found in the letters written prior to A.D. 68.

e. *To Sardis* (3:1-6). The church at Sardis had a name that it lived, "and thou art dead" (v. 1). In spite of this condition, it had a few names that had not defiled their garments (v. 4). This indicates the necessity for a lengthy period during which such a state of spiritual lethargy could develop.

f. *To Philadelphia* (3:7-13). This congregation was situated in a city which also had its synagogue of Satan, but they of this church would prevail over these fleshly Jews who made up this unholy assembly (v. 9). There was an hour of trial which was to come upon "the whole inhabited earth" (v. 10). This trial grew out of the attitude which developed after Nero and which expanded into the political-religious war extending from the days of Domitian through Diocletian, to the edict of Constantine.

g. *To Laodicea* (3:14-22). The church at Laodicea is the only one of the seven which had not one thing to commend it; it stood in a class by itself. In his letter to the saints at Colosse Paul indicates that the church in Laodicea was then an active group (Col. 4:13). He sent salutations to the brethren there, and requested that the Colossian letter be read to them at Laodicea and that their letter be read to the Colossians (Col. 4:15, 16). It would surely have required more than a decade for the church at Laodicea to depart so completely from its earlier acceptable status that there was nothing about it to be commended.

2. The Souls Underneath the Altar (6:9-11)

The cry of the souls underneath the altar, as "they cried with a great voice saying, "How long, o Master, the holy and true, dost thou not judge and avenge our blood on them that dwell on the earth?" (v. 10), seems to indicate impatience or restlessness at the long delay in vindicating martyred Christians' blood by avenging their death. This group of martyrs would include those of Nero's persecution and any in the interval between. But those crying out are admonished to be patient, for the avenging would come when the martyrs who follow should have fulfilled their course (v. 11).

3. The Beast out of the Earth (chap. 13)

An argument made for the early date based on the 144,000 being Jews after the flesh, who were numbered while the nation still dwelt in Judea, is dealt with in the commentary (7:4). Another argument made for the pre-Domitian date is that when John was told to measure the temple it was still standing (11:1, 2). This also will be considered in comments on the text.

One commentator identifies the beast out of the earth (13:11ff.) as the Roman emperor's subordinate rulers in Palestine, sent out by the emperor to execute his will in the land of the Jews. According to that writer's contention, the signs and wonders of the earth-beast were deceptions and machinations worked by the provincial rulers who served as persecutors to deceive the people in Judea, just prior to the destruction of Jerusalem.[33] But this beast is later called "the false prophet" (16:13; 19:20), which identifies him with false religion, emperor worship, and paganism, backed by the sea-beast, the Roman power (13:12; 14:11). This will be discussed more fully in the commentary. However, instead of supporting the early date, the view of the religious significance of the earth-beast, acting by the authority of the sea-beast, the Roman power, is one of the stronger internal proofs for the later date. When we reach the later period of Domitian's rule, the conflict between faith and paganism had become a war to the death.

---

[33]Foy E. Wallace, Jr., *The Book of Revelation*, pp. 295-298.

From Domitian's point of view it was political; from the Christians' it was religious.

V. SYMBOLISM

A. Imagery

As was characteristic of the apocalyptic books of the Old Covenant and pseudo-apocalyptic books of later years, the Book of Revelation abounds in imagery, symbols, and signs. Most of the imagery is symbolic; however, a portion is not. Some of the images and symbols are explained; some are left veiled or semi-veiled. The unexplained portions force the interpreters to rely upon their own judgment, or the judgment of others, for conclusions, applications, and explanations. As would be expected, expositors are not united in their views. Therefore, each interpreter must reach his conclusions in the light of his understanding of the total revelation of God.

One is cautioned to be careful to avoid explaining each aspect of a symbol. Neither should he look for literalism in the symbols, for some are grotesque when viewed literally. Symbols, signs, and images are used to express ideas; one must look *through* John's particular vision, with its symbols and images, and strive to grasp the idea in the mind of God as He revealed it to John the writer.

Many of the symbols and images are rooted in the Old Covenant writings; therefore, a familiarity with the older Scriptures will prove extremely helpful to the student in arriving at an understanding of the message. However, the Holy Spirit through John changes or uses these to suit His own immediate purpose and aim. Though an understanding of the Old Covenant symbolism will be helpful, one must strive to see the application being made by John, for some of the imagery and symbols he uses are completely new—they are peculiar to the need at hand.

John's signs, symbols, and imagery are drawn from all realms: the heavenly, the spiritual, and the material universe. One is amazed at how all these are woven so intricately into the fabric of this book and its message. Without claiming that the list is complete, we here present a summary of the persons and forces dealt with, and the realms from which they are drawn:

1. Deity

God, the occupant of the throne of the universe, is revealed as a sparkling white diamond (jasper) and as a dazzling and precious ruby (sardius) (4:3). Jesus is a lamb (5:6), the lion of the tribe of Judah, the root of David (5:5), and the bright and morning star (22:16). The Holy Spirit is seven Spirits, seven lamps of fire, and seven eyes which are the seven Spirits of God (1:4; 5:6). These are symbols conveying characteristics of God.

2. *Spirit Realm*

The scope of the book and its imagery embraces heaven, hades, and the lake of fire. It includes a great red dragon, a serpent (Satan), angels, demons, unclean spirits, and souls. Great beasts are woven into the picture, one out of the sea and the other out of the earth. The scope also includes death and the resurrection, and gives to these a role of great importance.

3. *Natural World*

Symbols and imagery are drawn from practically every realm of the natural world, from geology to astronomy: reference is made to the sun, sun-rising, the moon, stars, day and night, air, earth, sea, great waters, rivers, fountains, clouds, lightning, thunder, earthquake, great winds, hail, a rainbow, fire, smoke, brimstone, wilderness, and an abyss. All of these pass before the eyes of the reader, some serving as stagesetting, others conveying an idea or bearing a message to be learned.

4. *Earthly Kingdoms*

Kings of earth, princes, captains, bondmen, freemen, rich and poor, the great and servants all play a role in the intense drama being enacted before us. Our interest and understanding are challenged by

INTRODUCTION 38

references to nations, thrones, diadems and victory crowns, keys, a rod (or scepter) of iron, great swords, two-edged swords, slaughtering swords, a bow, a prison, and the winepress of judgment.

5. *Culture and Society*

Great armies sweep across the stage before us, clashing in deadly combat and ultimately suffering defeat and destruction or winning victory. Chariots, armor, wars, clashing of forces, plagues, fears, suffering, and mourning all have a role to fill. Also drawn into the scene are the bride and groom, marriage and the marriage supper, lamps, voices, the thief, and a woman in childbirth. We may add to these measuring reeds, doors of admission, and doors through which we see and behold. All help to complete the theme.

6. *Religion*

Prophets, priests, altar of sacrifice, golden altar, lampstands, sacrifice, blood, incense, synagogue, sanctuary, temple pillar, ark of the covenant, and trumpets—each of these fills an important place in the scenery, symbolism, and imagery of the marvelous divine cinema which we are permitted to watch and hear. In contrast to the symbols of divine worship stand the symbols of the heathen. These act in opposition to the true, seeking to seduce the faithful: idols and images, things sacrificed to idols, false prophets, sorcery, and false teachers (Balaam, Jezebel, and the Nicolaitans).

7. *Locales*

Places familiar to the readers of John's book are flashed upon the screen, each conveying an idea: Egypt, Babylon the Great, the Euphrates, Sodom, Mount Zion, Harmageddon (Mount Magedo), the great city, the holy city, and the New Jerusalem for the new heaven and new earth. Some would endure and some would be destroyed; all had a message to impart.

8. *Persons*

Individuals from various walks of life move across the stage, each telling a story conveying an idea or revealing a truth: a radiant woman arrayed in the sources of light (the sun, moon, and stars), a man child born to her, virgins, a wife, a queen, a great harlot and her daughters, and paramours who have committed fornication with the harlot. There are also children, servants, Balaam, Jezebel and Gog and Magog (in Ezek. 38:2, Gog *of* Magog) bearing symbolic lessons to be learned.

9. *Attire*

Much can be determined about character or station in life by manner of dress. The attire of the persons in this divine revelation suggests ideas and contributes to our understanding of truth. Kingly-priestly garments, white robes, fine linen, sackcloth, purple and scarlet are all appropriately worn by those described.

10. *Physical Anatomy*

The anatomy of man comes in for its place in the vision and drama of the great unveiling of Christ and spiritual truth: the head, hair, forehead, eyes (and tears), ears, mouth, tongue, teeth; the heart, blood, reins (kidneys or loins), belly, hands, and feet. Each is observed, though the part named may play an insignificant role or merely be supplementary.

11. *Vegetation and Agriculture*

In this particular realm of creation, the writer introduces and uses both life's essentials and its luxuries: wheat, barley, grapes, wine, olive trees, oil, figs, honey, spices, trees, wood, palms, grass, and wormwood. The sickle, reaping, harvest, vintage, and winepress are also part of this complex whole.

12. *Mineral Kingdom*

Man has always prized minerals, metals, and precious stones because of their intrinsic beauty and value. These, likewise, find a place in the seer's vision: gold, silver, brass, sea of glass, precious stone and precious stones, white stone, jasper, sardius, emerald, pearls, and others, whose identity appears uncertain.

13. *Animal Kingdom*

In these symbols the greatest and the lowest animals, those friendly and useful to man, and those that appear otherwise, play a part: the lion, bear, leopard, calf (or ox), lamb, horses of various colors, flying eagles, vultures, wild beasts bristling with horns, locusts, scorpions and their stings, serpents, frogs, sea creatures and "every created thing." All these pass before our eyes in some meaningful and instructive way.

14. Social Intercourse: Trade and Commerce

Our prophet again draws from a well of human experience and activity to emphasize his message: ships, merchants, shipmasters, sailors, mariners, tradesmen, craftsmen, millstones, coins, goods, and balances used in trade.

15. Literature

The elements of literature are drawn into the picture. John is told to "write in a book." He writes of a book written within and on the book, of a little book, the book of life, seals, alphabet (alpha and omega), and numbers (which will be considered separately). All spoke some symbolic message and conveyed some essential idea.

16. Music and Musical Instruments

The spectacular pageant depicting the divine drama of life and its forces would be incomplete without music. Music, both vocal and instrumental, has played an emotional role in the story of good and evil, and in the spiritual, physical, and psychical life of the human family. Trumpets blast, harps, flutes, and choirs fill the auditorium with music and singing, as we sit enthralled with what we see and hear. Minstrels, harpers, flutists, and trumpeters fulfill their roles before us. Great music like the sound of mighty waters and voluminous thunders resound from the heavenly choirs and earthly performers. Hallelujahs are shouted in heaven; a great multitude responds with the same paean of praise, while the smoke of defeated forces rolls upward forever. Hearts tremble or rejoice at the sound of the music, depending on its nature and the character of the hearer.

17. Pharmacists

Even the pharmacist and his science are introduced and employed as men are told to make for themselves eyesalve with which to anoint their eyes, as their own "homemade" remedies fail.

18. Time and Eternity

Finally, that period of duration known as time becomes part of the symbols of the seer. Various periods are designated: half an hour, one hour, a third part of a day, three days and a half, ten days, twelve hundred and sixty days, forty-two months, a thousand years, and day and night. And then beyond time there is forever and forever.

What an array of symbols describing Creator, creatures, and forces, to teach us and to challenge our study of things spiritual and eternal!

B. Numbers

Throughout the Bible numbers are used both to indicate literal quantity and to represent an idea. As the reader was warned against literalism in the use and interpretation of symbols and imagery in the Revelation, so must he exert care in interpreting the numbers found in the book. In learning the use or significance of something, one may be told plainly what its use is, or he may learn by observing the use made of it. If told plainly that something is a sign or that it signifies a certain truth, there is left no question in the reader's mind. But if not specifically declared, the symbolic sense, if there is a symbolic significance, must be determined by the use made of the object considered. It is from the use made of numerical figures that we are to determine any symbolic significance. This may not be totally satisfactory, because it appears inconclusive, but to this writer there is no other alternative. Space forbids a thorough or involved study of the subject. In this introduction we shall deal only with numbers which will assist in an understanding of Revelation.

In Revelation the numbers three, four, seven, ten, twelve, and multiples of some of these have special significance. Throughout the book the following numbers are found: one-fourth, one-third, one-half, one, two, three, three and a half, four, five, six, seven, (eight is not found, though "eighth," "ninth", etc., are found in a sequence), ten, twelve, forty-two, one hundred forty-four, six hundred sixty-six, one thousand, one thousand two hundred, one thousand six hundred, seven thousand, twelve thousand, one hundred forty-four thousand, one hundred million, and two hundred million. The fractions, one-fourth, one-third, one-half, are used in a symbolic or figurative sense to designate a minor part of the whole under discussion.

One is used primarily to designate a single unit, or one out of several. At other times it is used symbolically, as "one hour." In its symbolic use it may represent unity or oneness in an order, as "these [ten] have one mind" (17:13).

Two may designate a definite number, as "two woes" to come out of a total of three (9:12); or it may be used as a symbolic number, as "forty and two months" (11:2). From its use in other portions of Scripture, as well as in Revelation, two seems to suggest strength, and is so used symbolically: e.g., "Two are better than one... if they fall, the one will lift up his fellow... if two lie together they have warmth" (Eccles. 4:9–11). The law required the testimony of two or more witnesses as a minimum to convict one of a crime (Deut. 17:6; 19:15; II Cor. 13:1). This principle probably explains why Jesus sent out His disciples "two and two" (Luke 10:1). The witnesses who prophesied in sackcloth were two in number; these were the two olive trees and the two lampstands that stand before the Lord (Rev. 11:3-4).

The number *three* seems to have had special significance from the earliest times. The number three occurs hundreds of times in Scripture in reference to persons and things both sacred and secular, to time, and to incidents or events. Just a few of these references will suffice.

In the creation there was God, the Spirit of God, and the Word of God ("God said," Gen. 1:3). Noah had three sons, Shem, Ham, and Japheth (Gen. 5:32). The three patriarchs are thought of as Abraham, Isaac, and Jacob. Daniel had three Hebrew friends who were carried with him into Babylon and who were cast into the fiery furnace (Dan. 3:23). Daniel prayed three times each day (Dan. 6:10, 13). Esther urged the Jews to fast for her three days and three nights (Esther 4:16). Peter denied the Lord three times (Matt. 26:69ff.), and then confessed his love for Him three times (John 21:15–17). The three apostles, Peter, James, and John, were with Jesus on three special occasions: the raising of Jairus's daughter (Luke 8:49ff.), the transfiguration (Matt. 17:1f.), and the night in Gethsemane, the sacred place of pryaer (Matt. 26:36ff.). The sheet which Peter beheld while in a trance, filled with all manner of creatures, was let down from heaven three times (Acts 10:16). Paul thrice petitioned the Lord on behalf of his thorn in the flesh (II Cor. 12:8). Jesus endured a threefold temptation (Matt. 4) and the avenues through which the lusts of our own temptations come are three (I John 2:15–17). The three persons of the Godhead were present when one of their number was baptized (Matt. 3:13–17); the three are associated in name at the baptism of all believers since the issuing of the Great Commission (Matt. 28:18–20). Over and over the number three is used in reference to time: three hours, three days, three weeks, three years. The classic and most important use of the number to believers is the resurrection of our Lord on the third day.

Considering its use throughout Scripture, three appears to have been "symbolic of a complete and ordered whole." As all completeness and fullness in the absolute are found in God or the Godhead, it is only natural that men should come to think of it as the divine number, the number of deity. However, this point should not be pressed beyond the bounds of Scripture. The number is found some ten times in Revelation, but it does not occur nearly so often as four and seven.

Four is found often throughout Scripture, in both the Old and the New Covenants. Amos is the earliest of the writing prophets to use the number four in a symbolic sense. In his prophecies against six heathen nations surrounding Israel and Judah, and against these two latter kingdoms also, he begins each message with, "For three transgressions... yea, for four...." As three indicated completeness, four suggests that the transgressions have gone beyond the fullness of God's patience—they have run the cup over. In later prophetic writings one reads of "the four corners of the earth" (Isa. 11:12), and "the four winds from the four quarters of heaven" (Jer. 49:36; for "four winds" see also Ezek. 37:9; Dan. 7:2; 11:4; Zech. 2:6; Matt. 24:3; Mark 13:27). Daniel, who lived most of his life in the kingdom of Chaldea, repeatedly saw kingdoms and judgments in series of four. The great image of Nebuchadnezzar's dream was interpreted to represent four notable world kingdoms (chap. 2). In his own dream Daniel saw four winds break forth upon the great sea, followed by four terrible beasts coming up out of the sea. One of the beasts had four wings upon its back and four heads (chap. 7). These represented the same four kingdoms that were symbolized in Nebuchadnezzar's dream.

Ezekiel, who in some ways resembled his contemporary, Daniel, frequently used the number four: "four living creatures," "four faces," "four wings," "four sides" (1:5–8), "four wheels" (10:9), "four sore judgments" (14:21; cf. Jer. 15:2–3), and "four winds" (37:9). Zechariah, associated with Daniel and Ezekiel as apocalyptic writers of the Old Covenant, likewise saw many series of four in his visions and revelations. He saw "four horns" (1:18) and "four smiths" (1:20), and he spoke of the "four winds of the heavens" (2:6). From between two mountains he saw coming forth "four chariots" drawn by horses of "four colors" (6:1–2). These four chariots were "four spirits," or winds (6:5).

After finding the number four so often in the three Old Covenant apocalyptic books, one is not surprised to find it standing out prominently in Revelation. Four living creatures play an important role throughout the book. There are "four angels," "four corners of the earth," "four winds of the earth" (7:1), four horses coming forth as the first four seals are opened (6:1–8), and "four horns [some MSS omit the four in this passage] of the golden altar" (9:13). Four is used often with other numbers: twenty and four elders, a hundred and forty and four cubits, and one hundred and forty and four thousand.

From its use throughout Scripture it becomes apparent that "four" is the number symbolic of the world or creation. A consideration of the passages indicated above justify this conclusion.

In some instances *five* seems to have had symbolic value. It is half of ten, as in Matthew 25:2 there were five wise and five foolish virgins. The "five loaves" from which Jesus fed the multitude are mentioned by all four writers of the Gospels, apparently to indicate the small quantity. It is in this connection that Paul writes of speaking "five words with the understanding" (I Cor. 14:19). In Revelation John seems to use the number five as a symbol of a short but definite period, as when he speaks of the locusts hurting men for five months (9:5, 10).

The number *six* is used only twice in Revelation. First, it refers to the wings of the living creatures about the throne (4:8), and second, it is used in triplicate, 666, as the number of the beast (13:18). The six wings would be three pairs, possibly used to indicate the speed with which these carried out the will of the throne occupant. The symbolism of the number 666 will be discussed in the commentary.

Without question, *seven* is the most outstanding number in this

INTRODUCTION

book. The number occurs scores of times in the Old Covenant, often with symbolic significance. But it is in the Book of Revelation that it stands out most prominently, occurring twenty times more in this book than in all other books of the New Covenant combined.

In his combinations of seven, John mentions seven churches (four times[34]), seven spirits (four times), seven lampstands (five times), seven stars (five times), seven lamps of fire (one time), seven seals (two times), seven horns (one time), seven eyes (one time), seven angels (nine times), seven trumpets (two times), seven thunders (three times), seven thousand slain (one time), seven heads (five times), seven crowns (one time), seven last plagues (four times), seven golden vials (three times), seven mountains (one time), and seven kings (two times). The book uses the number "seven" fifty-four times, designating seventeen groups of seven plus the seven thousand slain.

It is worthwhile to note how the number seven is used in the rest of the New Covenant: "seven other spirits" (Matt. 12:45), "seven loaves" (Matt. 15:36), "seven baskets" (Matt. 15:37), "seventy times seven" (Matt. 18:22), the Sadducees' hypothetical problem of "seven brothers" who, in succession of age, married the same woman and died (Matt. 22:25–28), seven servants to minister at table in the early church (Acts 6:3), "seven nations" (Acts 13:19), "seven sons" (Acts 19:14), and "seven days" (Acts 20:6; 21:4, 27; 28:14).

From its repeated use in Scripture, we observe that almost beyond question "seven" stands as the numerical symbol of the complete or perfect. If it is correct that three is the symbolic divine number and four the symbolic world or creation number, then a proper combination of these would be perfection, completeness, and fullness. However, there is no indication that the importance of the number seven is derived from the three plus four idea, although in Revelation a clear division of some of the sevens falls into a three plus four or a four plus three pattern.

Ten appears many times in both covenants, and it seems to have

---

[34]*Englishmen's Greek Concordance of the New Testament.* Englishmen's Greek New Testament and Berry's Greek New Testament Interlinear omit *seven* in 1:11. However, many authorities add it.

been from ancient times a "favorite symbolic number, suggestive of a rounded total, large or small, according to the circumstances,"[35] a complete number. Further, its use in Revelation of "ten kings," "ten horns" and "ten diadems" appears to indicate fullness of power or rule; therefore, it is the power number. Multiples of ten, thousand, one hundred forty-four thousand, and larger numbers indicate fullness to a superlative or unlimited degree.

From its numerous appearances in both Covenants, and its close relation to persons forming the foundation of the Hebrew and Christian economies, *twelve* is thought to be the religious number, bearing a symbolic religious idea or concept.

In the Old Covenant the twelve sons of Jacob became the fathers of the twelve tribes of Israel. Then there were the twelve precious stones on the breastplate of the high priest, representing the twelve tribes (Exod. 28:15-21). Twelve cakes of showbread were in the holy place of the tabernacle (Lev. 24:5). At the dedication of the altar of the tabernacle, twelve princes brought gifts. Among these were twelve silver platters, twelve silver bowls, and twelve golden spoons. At this dedication the animals for the burnt offering were twelve bullocks, twelve rams, twelve he-lambs and twelve male goats (Num. 7:78-87). Later, Solomon's brazen laver rested upon the backs of twelve oxen (I Kings 7:25). Twelve graven lions stood "on the one side and on the other" of the king's throne (I Kings 10:20). This is only a sampling; over and over the number twelve is used in relation to people, worship, and families of the ancient nation.

In the New Covenant, the activities of the twelve apostles, and the twelve thrones on which they were to sit, judging the twelve tribes of Israel, are given predominance. Along with these significant uses of the number twelve, Jesus was found teaching in the temple at the age of twelve years (Luke 2:42), twelve baskets of fragments were gathered up (Luke 9:17), and James addressed his epistle to the twelve tribes scattered abroad (James 1:1).

In Revelation, twelve thousand from each of the twelve tribes are numbered for a total of one hundred forty-four thousand. The radiant

---

[35]*International Standard Bible Encyclopaedia*. Chicago: The Howard Severance Co. 1937. Vol. IV, p. 2162. Henceforth referred to as I.S.B.E.

woman has on her head a crown of twelve stars (12:1). The celestial city has twelve gates, which are twelve pearls inscribed with the names of the twelve tribes of the children of Israel, guarded by twelve angels (21:12, 21). The twelve foundations of the city are twelve precious stones, and on them are the names of the twelve apostles (21:14, 19f.). The city itself is portrayed as a cube measuring twelve thousand furlongs in length, breadth, and height. The wall about the city is one hundred forty-four cubits high, a multiple of twelve times twelve. As a symbolic number, as suggested above, it seems to point to a religious or spiritual idea.

One other number needs to be considered, *three and a half.* This number and its equivalents are used several times in Revelation. Each time the number is used throughout the Bible, it is used of trial, hardship, and testing.

Jesus and James speak of the three years and six months (three and a half years) of the drought in Elijah's day as a time of no rain and great famine over all the land (Luke 4:25; James 5:17). Here the number three and a half is associated with trouble and hardship.

Daniel writes of the time when "the fourth beast" would "speak words against the Most High" and "wear out the saints of the Most High," and the saints would "be given into his [the beast's] hand until a time and times and a half a time" (Dan. 7:25). The "time and times and a half a time" are three and a half, as will be pointed out presently. This was a period of great oppression for the saints. The prophet later uses the same expression as a period of breaking in pieces the power of the holy people (12:7). Again the three and a half is symbolic of a period of persecution and affliction. The prophet also points to the cutting off of the sacrifice and oblation, another period of trial, "in the midst of the week" (9:27), which would be after three and a half days. In each instance the three and a half designates a time of persecution, hardship, and calamity.

"Three and a half" and equivalent periods are used several times in Revelation, and each time they are associated with a period of oppression. The two witnesses were overcome and slain, and their bodies were left unburied in the streets for three and a half days—during which time the world rejoiced over their death (11:9, 11). This was a period of grief and humiliation. A period of three and a half years is introduced by the seer in association with persecution, trials, and oppression. The holy city would be trodden under foot forty and two months—three and a half years (11:2). The two witnesses would prophesy for twelve hundred and sixty days—the same period of three and a half years—then be put to death (11:3, 7). This, likewise, is a period of opposition. The woman who gave birth to the man child was forced to flee into the wilderness for twelve hundred and sixty days— three and a half years—where she was providentially cared for (12:6). This same period is referred to as "a time, times, and a half a time" (12:14), being identical with the twelve hundred and sixty days of verse 6. Both indicate a time of opposition, oppression, and persecution by Satan. This also sheds light on Daniel's use of the expression, "time and times and half a time," and shows it to mean three and a half years. Additional evidence for this conclusion is provided when it is said of the beast, "there was given to him authority to continue forty and two months," three and a half years (13:5). This is the beast that made war against the saints and overcame them (13:7). A parallel study of Daniel 7 and Revelation 13 reveals the identity of Daniel's fourth beast and John's beast out of the sea; both represented the Roman Empire. Also, such a study points out that Daniel's "time and times and half a time" is equivalent to John's "forty and two months"; both are three and a half years. In every instance where three and a half is used, it is used of a time of oppression, opposition, trial, or persecution.

This fact leads to the conclusion that, just as seven is the symbolic number for fullness, completeness, or perfection, so three and a half, a broken seven, is the symbolic number for a period of trial, persecution, famine, and oppression. The number is used in each instance symbolically, not literally.

VI. INTERPRETATIONS OF THE BOOK

Because it is an apocalypse employing numerous symbols, signs, and visions, it is inevitable that the Book of Revelation has many schools of interpretation. Each student must reach his own conclusions, and adopt a method of interpretation commensurate with his understanding of the date of writing, the purpose for which the book was written, and his own understanding of the nature, purpose, and application of prophecy in general. The various schools of interpretation briefly summarized below vary widely in assigning meaning to the symbols and events of the book.

A. The **Futurist** position holds that the book reveals the conditions and events which will immediately precede the second coming of Jesus. This view is held in some form by millenarians generally. This school of interpreters contend that the first three chapters of Revelation applied to conditions in the churches of John's day and were directed especially to them, but that chapters four through nineteen point to the time just prior to Christ's final advent. They hold that when He returns He will establish His "Millennial Kingdom" here on earth, sit upon the throne of David and reign for a thousand years. After the thousand years Satan will be loosed for "a little time" or "season" in which he will gather the nations together against the saints; he will then be cast into the lake of fire. The final judgment then takes place, followed by the eternal state of the just and the unjust. Many different schools of thought exist among millenarians as to the nature and character of the millennium and the final state of the saved and the lost. In connection with this view two questions should be raised: (1) What meaning or encouragement could this view have had to a suffering people of John's day? and, (2) How is one to know when he is in the period of time just prior to Christ's coming, covered by chapters 4—19? The position is exceedingly speculative and gives rise to numerous false interpretations of Scripture.

B. The **Continuous Historical** view holds that the book is a forecast of the church's history and fortunes from John's day to the end of time, and thus some parts of the book have been fulfilled and some parts have not. This view finds in Revelation the rise of the papacy and the Roman Catholic Church, Mohammedanism, the Reformation, and other historical movements within the general church concept. This interpretation likewise would have no meaning for the suffering saints of that day, and it also leads to exegeses as speculative and uncertain as does the futurist view.

C. The **Philosophy of History** advocates see in the book symbols representing forces at work rather than specific historical events and persons which these symbols signify. These forces are seen as moral and spiritual, good and bad, righteous and sinful, which are at war in a deadly conflict. In this conflict, good is victorious over evil. This view has more to recommend it than do the first two; however, it seems to overlook certain historical settings which gave birth to the book, and which it was intended to deal with. The view falls short in too many areas.

D. The **Preterist** position holds that the book was written for the people of John's day and was fulfilled in that general period. Some hold that the book was written before the fall of Jerusalem and was fulfilled in that event. Others hold that it was written later and fulfilled in the conflict with the Roman Empire and power. There seem to be two sides of the preterist position which vary concerning the value and application of the book to the people of today. One side gives it little worth or application to the present; the other gives it more.

E. The **Historical Background** advocates see in Revelation a book written for the people of that day, set in a definite historical background and fulfilled in the events of the first two or three centuries. These advocates differ from some preterists in that they see in this background and series of historical events and conflict a very definite message for all time.

The view held by this writer could probably be called an "eclectic" position, a combination of some aspects of all five views, especially the latter. The book has a concrete setting in a definite period of history and deals with very real problems faced by Christians of the period. Diverse figures symbolize powerful moral and spiritual forces involved in a violent clash in which the forces of God are ultimately triumphant. By their faith and steadfastness to Christ and to truth, the saints of that day found encouragement and gained the crown of victory. The particular instruments through which the satanic forces and powers of John's day warred against the saints have long since fallen. But the message of that defeat continues to instruct and encourage God's people today and will always sustain them when they face similar conflicts. The book makes no specific reference to historical events to come, such as the rise of the papacy, Mohammedanism, the Reformation, and other significant events. But in dealing with the forces of Satan and falsehood of the period, it reveals the principles of victory through righteousness and truth and the ultimate failure of all that is false. The forces and principles of truth are divine and will always prevail over the forces of error. Some of the prophecies are yet to be fulfilled; examples of these are the passing of the present order, the resurrection, the judgment, and the final reward and punishment of the righteous and the wicked. Consequently, some futurist aspects of the book are to be recognized.

VII. THE THEME AND PURPOSE OF THE BOOK

The grand theme of Revelation is that of war and conflict between good and evil resulting in victory for the righteous and defeat for the wicked. The verb *polemeō*, "to make war, to fight," is found six times in Revelation and only once elsewhere in the New Testament. The noun *polemos*, "make war on someone" (A. & G.), is used nine times in the book and nine times in the remainder of the New Testament. The conflict is spiritual, not carnal or military. In this book God flashes upon His screen of revelation a panoramic view of a gigantic spiritual struggle between God and His forces set against Satan and his forces. Satan uses the Roman power to back and support paganism and social worldliness, while God uses His victorious Christ to strengthen and lead His faithful saints and exercises His righteous judgments to overcome and defeat Satan and his powers. It is a war to the death for one, and eternal victory for the other.

The message of the book is an assurance of victory and triumph—the triumph of truth and righteousness for the saints who hold the truth, and the defeat and ultimate destruction of Satan along with his followers and helpers. Jesus Christ came into the world confessing Himself to be the Christ and claiming to be the Son of God. These claims had to be proved. They were tested when He was put to death and were verified by His triumph over death in the resurrection. Jesus taught that the kingdom was at hand, and the apostles preached it as an established reality, affirming that the saints were in it. As Jesus and His claims had to be tested so did this claim concerning the kingdom of God have to be proved and verified. The claim of its divine origin and character and its ability to endure was tested by Satan's effort to destroy the church. It proved to be the spiritual kingdom of prophecy when it emerged from the conflict victorious, with saints sitting on thrones reigning with Christ. It was proved to be the kingdom that could not be destroyed, the one that would stand forever. Its message is "Victory through faith!"

The purpose of the book is to reveal through symbols the nature and character of the great conflict breaking forth between forces mentioned above. God and His throne are in absolute control of His universe, and His Son, the Lamb and King, is carrying out His divine purpose to its ultimate and glorious end. The book is designed to encourage Christians to be faithful in the face of all opposition and persecution, regardless of how terrible the onslaught might be. Its message and purpose were not for that period only, but they extend to all who have lived since the dark days of that terrible ordeal, and to all who shall face such in the future. The book gives assurance that in every spiritual and moral conflict Christ gives victory to the steadfast in faith and life.

One key word of the book is *nikaō*, to overcome or conquer, which is used seventeen times. Rewards are on the basis of overcoming (chap. 2, 3), which is made possible by the power of God and the victory of Christ. The conquerors overcame "because of the blood of the Lamb, and because of the word of their testimony; and they loved not their life even unto death" (12:11); and these that overcome shall inherit that which God has provided for the victors (21:7). Someone has said, "The Revelation has all the appeal of a fairy story in which the bad dragon is beaten, and the beautiful lady is saved."[36]

Three helpful rules for studying and interpreting the book are here suggested:

What did the book mean to the people of that day to whom it was written? Any interpretation that omits or overlooks this point is invalid. This approach involves (1) some understanding of the conditions under which the saints lived, and (2) the spiritual needs of the hour, which were: revelation and instruction of Christ's present rule, and encouragement and assurance of victory in the midst of trials.

A second help is an understanding of the Old Testament, particularly the prophets and especially the prophets Ezekiel, Daniel, and

---

[36] Charles Frederick Wishart, *The Book of Day*, p. 4.

Zechariah and their use of symbols and signs. If one does not have an acquaintance with these, he should try to acquire some knowledge of them, or be directed by one who has made such a study. It is variously estimated by students of Revelation that the book contains from two hundred sixty to more than four hundred allusions to the Old Testament; but it is acknowledged by all that there is not a single direct quotation from it. In giving to the church a revelation of truth in visions and symbols, there would necessarily have to be some divine basis on which to interpret the message. The total Old Testament revelation and the writings of the New Testament is that basis. As God showed to John vision after vision and allowed him to hear voice after voice, the Holy Spirit directed him in recording these. The visions and message of the voices were so patterned after the revelations God had made known through the centuries that these writings become our guide and basis of interpretation. The Spirit uses symbols and revelations of the past without slavish duplication of them, but uses them as they serve God's present purpose in providing this New Testament apocalypse.

A third rule is that all interpretations must be consistent and harmonious with the total teaching of the remainder of the New Testament. There must be no conflict or contradiction between the two. When these three simple rules are kept in mind and followed, the careful student will find a rich reward and blessing from his study and will not be led astray and become lost in the quicksands of error.

VII. OUTLINE OF THE BOOK OF REVELATION

Part One

Conflict and Judgment Within and Without the Church
Chapters 1—11

Chapter 1. Christ Among the Lampstands 95
    The Superscription, vv. 1–3 95
    The Salutation, vv. 4–7 97
    The Seal, v. 8 103

John's Charge to Write, vv. 9–11 104
The Vision: Christ's Majesty and Glory, vv. 12–16 108
The Charge to Write, vv. 17–20 112

Chapter 2. Letters to the Churches 117
Introduction to the Letters 117
Ephesus, vv. 1–7 119
Smyrna, vv. 8–11 125
Pergamum, vv. 12–17 129
Thyatira, vv. 18–29 134

Chapter 3. Letters to the Churches, Continued 143
Sardis, vv. 1–6 143
Philadelphia, vv. 7–13 148
Laodicea, vv. 14–22 155

Chapter 4. The Throne Scene 164
The Throne of God the Almighty 165

Chapter 5. The Lamb and the Book 174

Chapter 6. The Opening of the First Six Seals 186
The First Seal, vv. 1–2 187
The Second Seal, vv. 3–4 189
The Third Seal, vv. 5–6 190
The Fourth Seal, vv. 7–8 192
The Fifth Seal, vv. 9–11 194
The Sixth Seal, vv. 12–17 196

Chapter 7. An Interlude 200
Sealing the 144,000, vv. 1–8 200
The Victorious Multitude, vv. 9–17 206

Chapter 8. The Seventh Seal and the First Four Trumpets 214
The Seventh Seal: Prayer and Response, vv. 1–5 214
The First Four Trumpets, vv. 6–12 217
The Eagle: Herald of Woes, v. 13 223

Chapter 9. The Beginning of the Woes 225
The First Woe, vv. 1–12 225
The Second Woe, vv. 13–21 233

Chapter 10. The Angel and the Little Book 241

INTRODUCTION

Chapter 11. The Vision Continues 249
The Measured Temple and the Two Witnesses, vv. 1-13 249
The Third Woe—The Seventh Trumpet, vv. 14-19 261

Part Two

War and Victory!
Chapters 12—22

Chapter 12. The Woman and the Dragon 267
The Woman, the Dragon, the Man Child, vv. 1-6 267
The Great Spiritual War, vv. 7-12 272
Persecution of the Woman, vv. 13-17 278

Chapter 13. The Two Wild Beasts 282
The Beast Out of the Sea, vv. 1-10 282
The Beast Out of the Earth, vv. 11-18 292

Chapter 14. Righteous Judgment 300
The Lamb and the 144,000 on Mount Zion, vv. 1-5 300
Angels' Messages and a Voice of Warning from Heaven, vv. 6-13 ..306
Twofold Vision of Harvest and Vintage of the Earth, vv. 14-20 312

Chapter 15. The Seven Bowls of Wrath 318
The Seven Angels Introduced, vv. 1-8 318

Chapter 16. The Bowls of Wrath Poured Out 325
Bowls Involving Nature, vv. 1-9 326
Bowls Involving the Moral and Political, vv. 10-21 332

Chapter 17. The Infamy and Fall of Babylon 341
The Babylon Harlot Identified, vv. 1-6........................342
Explanation of the Mystery of the Woman and the Beast, vv. 7-14..349
Further Identification of the Harlot, vv. 15-18 355

Chapter 18. The Fall of the Harlot 358
Heaven's Decree: "Fallen is Babylon," vv. 1-8 358
Lament of the Earthlings over Babylon, vv. 9-19 363
The Voice of Rejoicing, v. 20 368
The Silence of the Tomb, vv. 21-24 369

Chapter 19. Victory 373
  Hallelujahs of Victory, vv. 1–10 373
  The Warrior-King: Defeat of the Two Beasts, vv. 11–21 380
    A. The Warrior-King Revealed, vv. 11–16 381
    B. The Angel's call to "The Great Supper of god," vv.17–18 386
    C. The Decisive Battle and Defeat of Evil, vv. 19–21 387

Chapter 20. The Thousand Years and the Final Judgment 389
  The Thousand Years, vv. 1–10 389
  The Final Judgment, vv. 11–15 399

Chapter 21. The Eternal Glory 404
  "All Things New," vv. 1–8................................... 404
  The New Jerusalem, vv. 9–27 410
    A. Exterior of the City, vv. 11–21 411
    B. Interior of the City, vv. 22–27 417

Chapter 22. The New Jerusalem, continued 420
    C. Its Life, vv. 1–5....................................... 420
  Conclusion: The Divine Witness, vv. 6–21 424

HISTORICAL BACKGROUND

Historical Background

A brief look at the historical situation into which Christianity was born and cradled, and into which the early saints carried the gospel should be helpful in one's appreciation of the message of Revelation. The coming of Christ and His kingdom had long been the theme of Israel's prophets. The Jews were looking for a messiah who would deliver the nation from the tyranny of the heathen Gentiles and restore the glory of David and Solomon—yea, one who would lead them to glory far surpassing that of any preceeding period of their history. When He came, Rome ruled the world, and Judaea was only a small province of that great and far-flung empire.

Jesus disappointed the Jewish expectations; and so they rejected and crucified Him. Although many Jews accepted the Christ and His gospel in the years immediately following the resurrection, they gradually became bitter enemies of the newborn faith. The faith of the gospel was to have been universal; their prophets had foretold this, but the Jews could not accept the Gentiles apart from the law and circumcision. This led to a diminishing number of Jews who accepted Christ and His gospel, and the church was soon composed almost exclusively of Gentiles.

For more than seven centuries Rome had been developing from a miscellany or group of tribes and city-states in northern and central Italy—Etruscans, Sabines, Latins, Umbrians, Samnites and others—into a world power that surrounded the Mediterranean Sea. Its territory extended from Britain and Spain in the west and present day France and Germany in the north to the Euphrates in the east and Egypt and North Africa in the south. Rome awed the world; its power seemed infinite, unlimited.

Many years before the coming of Christ the religions and philosophies of the east had been making inroads into Rome. Foreign deities were being accepted by the emperors as "allies" to the Roman world conquest and were being blended or fused with the Roman deities. This process removed religious differences and tended to unify those who came to Rome from the provinces. The educated had little, if any, faith in the gods as divine entities or beings; however, religion held a deeply-ingrained power and influence in the hearts and over the lives of all. The rites and rituals were enthusiastically and solemnly practiced.

Within the century before Christ's birth, the growing acceptance of the emperors as divine was a far more powerful religious force. This, no doubt, could be traced to the oriental influence of identifying rulers with deities. More will be said later about the development of emperor worship as the various rulers are considered. Accepting emperors as divine and rendering homage to them sprang from a sense of patriotism and loyalty to Rome and the emperor. The state was personified in its head. Regardless of how base, cruel, and immoral some of these emperors were, their position related them to deity; the worship of these expressed a deep-seated desire and longing of the human soul for a relation to the divine and supreme power.

Rome's goal was to dominate the world; she built an empire based on force, an empire whose rule was absolute. All within her domain had to be loyal to the emperor and to Rome; this loyalty found expression in offering or burning incense to the image of the emperor. In contrast, Jesus came to build a universal empire based on love, righteousness, and truth—a kingdom not of this world (John 18:36). As its King, He required absolute and undivided loyalty to Himself and His Father as the one and only God. Divine honors could not be divided between God and emperor; and so the clash between Christians and Roman paganism was inevitable. Any worship of the emperor and state, "Rome and Augustus," and the worship of God and Christ, were utterly incompatible.

Yet Christians considered themselves loyal to the emperor and to the Roman state. Jesus the King had said, "Render unto Caesar the things that are Caesar's" (Matt. 22:21), and the two apostles, Paul and Peter, had taught them to "be in subjection to the higher powers" (Rom. 13:1), to "pray for kings and all that are in high place" (I Tim. 2:1-2), and, "Be subject to every ordinance of man," both to kings and governors as sent by the king (I Peter 2:13-14). The true disciple strove to do all this. The clash which came, a war to the death, was not over

HISTORICAL BACKGROUND

disregard for Roman law or treason toward the ruler of Rome, but over religious loyalty.

The century before Christ saw the empire torn by strife and civil wars, which resulted in the collapse of the old city-state form of government. This was replaced by the development of an imperial rule that would endure for four or five centuries. The wars produced wretched conditions in the east; taxes, plundering, and a broken and depressed spirit left that section a shambles. Possibly this helped prepare the way for the gospel, "for the people despaired of this earthly life and sought consolation in religion and philosophy which held out the possibility of a better life—beyond the grave."[1]

Out of these civil wars Julius Caesar (ca. 102-44 B.C.), an able general, statesman, and author, emerged victorious. Caesar never assumed the title *king*, but maintained that of *imperator*, usually reserved for generals in the field. His rule was short-lived, from 48 B.C. to March 15, 44 B.C., when he was assassinated by a group led by former associates, Brutus and Cassius. Caesar had many ambitious plans for Rome, all of which were cut short by his untimely death. With him began the imperial nature of Rome's rule. Our interest in Caesar, however, is religious. In life he had the audacity to present himself as a god, and upon his death he was deified by the loyalists in the senate, 42 B.C.

With the death of Caesar the empire was again plunged into civil war. There was a power struggle between Octavian Caesar (nephew and adopted son of Julius) and Mark Antony on the one hand, and Brutus and Cassius on the other. Octavian and Antony defeated Brutus and Cassius in battle at Philippi, 42 B.C., following which both defeated men committed suicide. Antony's infatuation for Cleopatra, Queen of Egypt, and her arrogance led to war between Octavian and Antony and Cleopatra. The forces of Antony and Cleopatra were defeated at the Battle of Actium, in western Achaia (Greece), in the year 31 B.C., after which Antony and the queen committed suicide. This left Octavian the undisputed master of both East and West.

The rule of Octavian is dated from 31 B.C., following the Battle of Actium, to A.D. 14. In 27 B.C. he assumed, or had bestowed upon him

---

[1]M. Rostovtzeff, *Rome*. p. 156.

by the senate, the title Augustus, which "signified the possessor of superhuman Increase, the 'augmented' and sanctified. The same term had of old been applied to temples and sacred objects,"[2] implying that such gods "were 'augmenters' and creators of something different and better.... Thus the title was conferred upon Octavian as the restorer and 'augmenter' of the state, and as the man invested with the highest authority."[3] He was the first to use the term *Princeps*, which instead of meaning "*a* leader" had come to mean "*the* leader."[4] It is felt by many historians that the empire was built by the genius of Augustus. He was a man of tremendous intuition and leadership ability. He set himself to the task of transforming Rome from the narrow confines of the city-state to its position as ruler of the world. He gave himself relentlessly to the task of building the empire, reforming the laws, and giving peace to a war-weary world. And in spite of many selfish, irrational, and incompetent rulers who followed Augustus, the empire was able to experience the golden age of her history in the first and second centuries, A.D.

Augustus seemed at first to be reluctant to receive divine honors. However, he allowed temples to be built and altars erected in his honor in the provinces, but he discouraged this being done in Rome. Nevertheless the concept of divinity, the worship of Rome and Augustus, which began in the provinces, spread rapidly. Temples were erected, high priests appointed, sacrifices offered, and public games celebrated in a most solemn manner. These religious festivals and provincial organizations acted as a sacred bond between province and empire and encouraged the religion of the state.[5] Even while he lived, the statue of Augustus was placed in the vestibule of the Pantheon of Agrippa, where it "was associated with the images of the supreme gods of the temple itself."[6] After his death he is referred to repeatedly by Tacitus as "the Divine Augustus."[7] One was in no way bound to this worship only, but rather could worship any or all gods if he so chose. The

---
[2]Michael Grant, trans. *Tacitus—The Annals of Imperial Rome*. Baltimore Penguin Books. 1968. Key to Technical terms, p. 402.
[3]Rostovtzeff, p. 166.
[4]Grant, p. 407.
[5]Abbi Duchesne, *The Early History of the Christian Church*, p. 7.
[6]Rostovtzeff, p. 190.
[7]Tacitus, *Annals*, 1.10, 11, et al.

63 HISTORICAL BACKGROUND

worship of Rome and Augustus was a symbol of loyalty to the state. With the deification of Julius Caesar and the acceptance of the title or name "Augustus" by Octavian, the groundwork for emperor worship was now solidly laid. With temples and altars dedicated to Rome and Augustus throughout the provinces and with his deification and status in the city of Rome, it was easy for the incompetent rulers who followed to establish firmly the cult of emperor worship.

At the death of Augustus his adopted stepson, Tiberius, became successor to the throne and ruled from A.D. 14 to 37. Tiberius was the son of Livia, the third wife of Augustus, who influenced Augustus to adopt this son of her former marriage. This means that Tiberius was emperor because of his mother's marriage and not because of his own merit or right. His reign is described by historians as "that of a wise, intelligent stateman with a strong sense of duty."[8] Rostovtzeff says of him, "Tiberius was a competent general of the old Roman type—strict, methodical, and sincerely devoted to his country; and he showed the same virtues as a statesman and ruler."[9] Seutonius[10] and Tacitus[11] paint a very ugly picture of Tiberius' moral character in later life, but this view is considered overly severe by some modern critical writers. Seutonius says the emperor "abolished foreign cults from Rome, particularly the Egyptian and Jewish," removing the Jews of military age to unhealthful regions and expelling those too old or too young.[12] Tacitus gives the number of those conscripted into the army as four thousand.[13] Though hated and maligned, Tiberius proved to be the best of the four Julio-Claudian emperors who succeeded Augustus.

Tiberius seems to have been embarrassed at the suggestion that he was a "god." However, "all prayers were addressed to Tiberius.... They [the Senators] raised their hands to the gods, to the statue of Augustus, and to the knees of Tiberius, when he ordered a document to be produced and read."[14]

Caligula ruled from A.D. 37 to 41. The first eight months of his

---

[8]Angus, "Tiberius," I.S.B.E., vol. V, p. 2979.
[9]Rostovtzeff, p. 194.
[10]Seutonius, Tiberius, 42–67.
[11]Tacitus, Annals. I.4, 6.
[12]Seutonius, 36.
[13]Annals II.85.
[14]Ibid., I.11.

reign were characterized by moderation and consideration for the people; but after an illness he became mentally unbalanced. He is thereafter described as one of the most cruel and debased of men. He assumed the role of a god, and "insisted on being treated as a god—sending for the most revered or artistically famous statues of the Greek deities (including that of Juppiter [sic] at Olympia), and having their heads replaced by his own."[15] "He established a shrine of himself as God, with a priest, the costliest possible victims, and a life-sized golden image, which was dressed every day in clothes identical with those he happened to be wearing."[16] Caligula offended the Jews by commanding his statue to be set up in the temple at Jerusalem, but he died before the order could be carried out.[17] After ruling for three years, ten months, and eight days, this insane tyrant was murdered by two guards.

Claudius, who reigned from A.D. 41-54, was the uncle of Caligula. He is described as weak in body and will, but he did show a traditional Claudian devotion to duty and patriotism. He was first controlled by his wife, Messalina, in whose hands he is said to have been "a mere puppet." Finally he was persuaded to put her to death, only to become the victim of another vicious and conniving wife, Agrippina, his niece. Agrippina's supreme desire was to get the infamous Nero, her son by a former marriage, on the throne. Persuading Claudius to adopt Nero, she planned and effected the death of Claudius, thus paving the way for her son to become ruler.

Claudius restored the Jews' rights and privileges which had been granted them by Augustus but taken away by Caligula.[18] Also, he gave Agrippa, grandson of Herod the Great, the Palestinian kingdom formerly controlled by his grandfather.[19] However, the numerous Jews in Rome did not fare so well. Luke tells us that "Claudius had commanded all the Jews to depart from Rome" (Acts 18:2), but gives no reason for the edict. Seutonius says, "Because the Jews at Rome caused continuous disturbance at the instigation of Chrestus, he expelled

---
[15]Seutonius, *Gaius Caligula*, 22.
[16]Ibid.
[17]Josephus, *Antiquities*, XVIII, 8:2-9.
[18]Josephus, *Antiquities*, XIX, 5.
[19]Ibid., chap. 6.

them from the city."[20] Apparently "Chrestus" is a confused spelling of "Christus," and refers to the Christ. It may be assumed from this that the Jews were making disturbances over the Christ and with Christians at this time, probably A.D. 51 or 52.

Nero, who succeeded Claudius, his great-uncle and father by adoption, ruled from A.D. 54 to 68. His mother, Agrippina, a scheming and ruthless woman, played an important role in his life. Nero is of special interest to our study because of his persecution of Christians and his relationship to the question of the date of Revelation.

The first five-year period of Nero's reign was moderate and characterized by good government at home and in the provinces, but he was increasingly influenced by Agrippina, his mother, who tried to dominate his life. Fearful of Brittanicus, his half-brother and rightful heir to the throne, Nero had him killed, and later he had both his wife, Octavia, and his mother put to death. Tacitus insinuates that Nero's jealousy of Seneca and Burrus, his tutors and counselors of earlier years, caused him to have Burrus poisoned, and to demand that Seneca take his own life.[21] Scores of Rome's outstanding citizens were put to death by Nero. His life was filled with crimes and immoralities of every conceivable character, with vanity and arrogance, and with waste and extravagance which added taxes and misery to the oppressed peoples, threatening the empire with bankruptcy.

Nero enjoyed having the populace sacrifice to his image, and would have had the people think of him as a god. Merle Severy says in *Quest for Our Golden Heritage*, "In the entry [of Nero's Golden House] stood a guilded-bronze colossus of Nero as sun god, taller than the Statue of Liberty."[22] As the end drew near, Nero found himself too cowardly to take his own life and could find no one to do it for him. Finally, upon learning that a terrible death was decreed for him by the senate, he put a dagger to his throat, and with the help of his scribe his life was brought to an end.[23]

Nero is remembered primarily for the great fire at Rome in A.D. 64

---

[20]Seutonius, *Claudius*, 25.
[21]Ibid., XV. 60–64.
[22]*Greece and Rome, Builders of Our World*. Washington: National Geographic Society, 1968, p. 21. See also Seutonius, *Nero*, 31.
[23]Seutonius, *Nero*, 49.

and for his persecution of Christians following that great conflagration. The fire broke out in the section of the city containing shops stacked with flammable wares. Immediately the fire began to spread, smoke spiraled heavenward, and the wind carried the flames from section to section until the whole city was a roaring inferno. In many places people were trapped; in others they trampled one another trying to find escape or refuge from the flames. It is reported that when the fire was finally brought under control or had burned itself out, half the city was totally destroyed and half of the remainder badly damaged.

Nero was at Antium at the time of the fire, but he returned to Rome as the flames approached his own home. The populace began to seek a cause for the fire (which in all probability was accidental). Because of Nero's depraved conduct, the people began either to blame him directly, for giving the order, or indirectly, for bringing upon the city the wrath of the gods. All his efforts to throw off suspicion and accusation failed, and he had to find a scapegoat. The Christians were at hand to satisfy this need.

Tacitus says, "Consequently, to get rid of the report, Nero fastened the guilt and inflicted the most exquisite tortures on a class hated for their abominations, called Christians by the populace." The historian proceeds by telling of the crucifixion of "Christus" under Tiberius, at the hands of Pilate, and of the spread of "the mischievous superstition" to Rome. Christians faced persecution because of their failure to follow in the general stream of Roman society and their opposition to the moral standards of the day. In the eyes of Tacitus, their unity and their faith in Christ as King made them a threat to the Roman goal of world power and unity.[24] It is clear from his writings that Tacitus himself did not believe that the Christians were guilty of incendiary action, but he does reflect a hatred for and an ignorance of Christ and Christians.

In the context of his discussion of the great fire, though not in direct association with it, Seutonius says, "Punishments were also inflicted on the Christians, a sect professing a new and mischievous religious belief."[25] Schaff says of the persecution: "It was, however, not a strictly religious persecution, like those under the later emperors; it originated in a public calamity which was wantonly charged upon the innocent

---

[24]Tacitus, *Annals*, XV.44.
[25]Seutonius, *Nero*, 16.

Christians."[26] Although not strictly a religious persecution, as Schaff correctly maintains, the religion of the Christians was involved; it so antagonized the Romans that it gave Nero the outlet he sought. In contrast, it seems clear from the internal evidence that the persecution under Domitian dealt with in Revelation was religious.

Did Nero's persecution extend beyond Rome into the provinces? Many historians think not, or at least they consider the evidence meager. If one is to judge by the testimony of heathen writers and their silence concerning the provinces, it appears that the persecution was confined to Rome. Gibbon, and Milman (who edited the 1945 edition of Gibbon's history), confine the persecution to Rome, having found no evidence for its extension beyond the city.[27] Philip Schaff, who defends the earlier date for the writing of Revelation and leans toward the view that the Neronean persecution extended beyond Rome, admits that the persecution was not religious but that Nero used it to divert attention from himself. Also, Schaff admits that the earliest evidence for its extending beyond Rome is that of Orosius (about A.D. 400) and Sulpicious Severus (also about the same year)[28] each of whom depended upon Tacitus and appeared rather late to prove the point. There seems to be no reason for assuming that Nero sought the destruction of Christians throughout the empire; he looked for an escape from the finger of accusation for a crime charged against him and found it in the Christians at Rome. Evidence does not indicate that the persecution extended beyond Rome at this time. It probably gave excuse to the local magistrates throughout the provinces to give vent to their wrath upon the hated Christians, but their persecution was not by a decree of Caesar.

Coleman-Norton quotes Sulpicious Severus (Chron. II.29.3): "Also, afterward by issued laws that religion was forbidden, and by openly published edicts it was not lawful that a Christian exist";[29] and Tertullian (A.D. 145–220) says, "You [Roman rulers] sternly lay it down in your sentences, 'it is not lawful for you to exist.'"[30] If Nero issued an edict for the provinces, no such edict has survived, but the

---

[26]Schaff, *History of the Christian Church*, Vol. I, p. 378.
[27]Edward Gibbon, *Decline and Fall of the Roman Empire*, I:605.
[28]Schaff, p. 389.
[29]P. R. Coleman-Norton, *Roman State and Christian Church*, Vol. III, p. 1179.
[30]A-N-F. Vol. III, Apology, chap. 4, p. 21.

persecution of Christians in Rome did pave the way for Christianity's becoming an "illicit or forbidden religion" in the empire.

The death of Nero marked the end of the Julio-Claudian line of emperors. During the following two years three men were raised to the throne, only to be put to death shortly thereafter. The first of these was Galba. He was of a noble and affluent family and, as the administrator of a province, he had distinguished himself in justice, discipline, and bravery. But when he became emperor by the power of the sword, his conduct made him very unpopular. Seutonius says that "he outraged all classes at Rome," especially bringing upon himself the hatred of the army that had elevated him to the throne.[31] After ruling for six months, Galba was murdered by a party of assassins from among the cavalry.

Otho, the second of the three, had joined Galba in the revolt against Nero, but he actually had his eye on the royal robes himself. As conditions worsened under Galba, Otho made plans to overthrow the ruler and have himself declared emperor. Seutonius says that it was he who dispatched the troop of cavalry to murder Galba.[32] Elevated by his soldiers, Otho reigned only a short while. The army in Germany under Vitellius swore allegiance to their commander instead of to Otho. Upon learning this, Otho set out to meet Vitellius in battle. Defeated in the battle, he committed suicide at thirty-seven years of age, having ruled only ninety-five days.

Vitellius, a favorite of three emperors, Caligula, Claudius, and Nero, was then declared emperor by his army. His immoral conduct of earlier years did not improve when he became emperor. Seutonius says of him, his "ruling vices were gluttony and cruelty."[33] He imposed himself and his requests on others by demanding banquets at tremendous costs to his hosts and gave extravagant feasts himself. "His cruelty was such that he would kill or torture anyone at all on the slightest pretext—not excluding noblemen who had been his fellow-students or friends."[34] Within the year his soldiers revolted against him and swore allegiance to Vespasian. When Vespasian's advance guard entered the

---
[31]Seutonius, *Galba*, 16.
[32]*Otho*, 6.
[33]*Vitellius*, 13.
[34]Ibid., 14.

HISTORICAL BACKGROUND

city and found Vitellius, they murdered him, dragged his body to the Tiber and threw it in the river. Vitellius was fifty-six years of age at the time of his death and had reigned less than a year.

Vespasian, the first of the Flavian emperors, ruled from A.D. 69–79. Before his elevation to the throne he had proved himself a capable leader and general in the army, and Nero had entrusted him with the conquest of Judea. Returning to Rome to claim the throne, he left his son Titus to complete the conquest of Jerusalem. According to Josephus' account, the siege and fall of the city occurred with terrible suffering and humiliation heaped upon the recalcitrant Jews. The city fell in August, A.D. 70, after a heroic, though futile, effort on the part of the Jewish nation. Vespasian and Titus shared in the elaborate triumph given them at Rome in the following year.

Vespasian restored peace to the empire; and except for having to put down a few border uprisings on the outskirts of his domain, he was able to give himself to the business of state. He is described as "a wise, strong, sober ruler."[35] He sought the restoration of the principate as devised by Augustus. Seutonius speaks well of him, charging him with having only the one serious fault of avarice. However, the historian throws the mantle of charity over this fault by pointing to the emptiness of the treasury as demanding the need for stringent means of supplying the national need.[36] The emperor died a natural death in June, A.D. 79. There seems to have been no direct confrontation between Vespasian and the Christians.

Titus succeeded his father, Vespasian, but ruled for only two years (A.D. 79–81). He followed in the steps of his father in the attempt to reestablish the state, especially its finances which had been so completely depleted by the madness of Nero and the civil wars of A.D. 68–69. He proved to be a very mild and popular ruler, and under his rule the amphitheater at Rome, begun by his father and later called the Colosseum, was completed and dedicated, A.D. 80. It is thought by some that his death was caused by poisoning by his brother, Domitian, though there seems to be little evidence for this.

Vespasian's second son, Domitian, became emperor in A.D. 81, the

---

[35]C. K. Barnett, *The New Testament Background: Selected Documents*, p. 18.
[36]Seutonius, *Vespasian*, 16.

year of his brother's death, and ruled until A.D. 96. The first few years of his reign were commendable. Seutonius says that at the beginning of his reign he governed in an even manner, "that is to say, his vices were at first balanced by his virtues. Later, he transferred his virtues into vices, too."[37] Seutonius does not believe that Domitian was evil-minded at first but that he was driven to greed by lack of funds and to cruelty by fear of assassination. In fact, Seutonius speaks well of Domitian's restraint and conduct in the early years of his reign, but this was not to last.[38] In Domitian the spirit of Nero was reincarnated and soon his cruelties and crimes knew no bounds. Men of nobility were put to death on the slightest pretext; crimes of the basest sort were perpetrated. He was consistently discourteous and presumptuous. His vanity and arrogance are well expressed in the salutation with which he would have his letters begin, "Our Lord God instructs you to do this!" and "Lord God" became his regular title both in writing and conversation.[39] Images dedicated to him had to be of gold and of a certain weight. "All this made him everywhere hated and feared."[40] Domitian was conscious of the feeling towards him and lived his last months in constant fear and dread of death. Finally a conspiracy was formed, and he was slain by the steward of Domitilla, his niece. He died at the age of forty-four, A.D. 96, ending the reign of the Flavians; two were good rulers and one a tyrant.

Upon his death the senators had his images torn down and smashed, "decreeing that all inscriptions referring to him must be effaced, and all records of his reign obliterated."[41] This may account for the scarcity of historical proof or information of the persecution beyond Rome. Concrete evidence of this has been revealed in recent excavations at Jerash, in Jordan. In removing the bank of dirt and debris from the east wall of the south theater built by the Romans, two beautiful Greek inscriptions of the dedication of the theater were discovered. In each of these the title of Domitian is the same, but in both his name has been erased.[42]

---

[37]Seutonius, *Domitian*, 3.
[38]Ibid., 9.
[39]Ibid., 13.
[40]Ibid., 14.
[41]Ibid., 23.
[42]American Schools of Oriental Research. Newsletter No. 4. October, 1974.

HISTORICAL BACKGROUND

What was the extent of Domitian's persecution of saints in Christ, and what juridical evidence do we have that he issued a special edict against them? Coleman-Norton says that our knowledge of his persecution "rests chiefly on literary and archeological evidence."[43] In his letter to the Corinthians Clement excuses his tardiness in writing "to the sudden and successive calamitous events which have happened to ourselves,"[44] which indicates persecution in Rome at that time. Eusebius charges Domitian with cruelly persecuting the Christians in and out of Rome, punishing many by exile.[45] He relates the story of the tyrants having called two kinsmen of the Lord to appear before him; but upon examination he released them, being convinced by "the hardness of their hands" that they were poor laborers, and not competitors to the throne.[46] It is believed that the real reason Domitian had his cousin, Consul Titus Flavius Clemens, put to death and Clemens' wife, Flavia Domitilla, banished to the island of Pandateria, was that the two were Christians.[47] In connection with this, Schaff says Domitian "treated the embracing of Christianity as a crime against the state."[48] The archeological evidence for this further persecution of Christians is found in the catacombs within and in the environs of Rome.[49]

With respect to worship of the emperor in Asia, Kidd says, "The worship for which Domitian thus hungered was nowhere rendered with such readiness as in Asia."[50] Asia was one of the most prosperous provinces of the empire. At the time of Domitian it had been a Roman province for more than two hundred years. Under the republic, Asia had suffered much at the hands of the Roman magistrates who sought to fill their own personal coffers at the expense of the provinces. The

---

[43]Coleman-Norton, p. 1179.
[44]A-N-F, Vol. I, p. 5. The date of Clement's letter to the Corinthians is uncertain. If early, then in A.D. 68 or shortly thereafter; but if not at that time, then about A.D. 97. The editors of the Edinburgh Edition, Roberts and Donaldson, place the date about A.D. 97. With some reluctance A. C. Coxe, editor of the American edition who added the notes and prefaces to volume I, accepts the date toward the close of Clement's life.
[45]Eusebius, *E. H.*, Book III, chap. 17.
[46]Ibid., chap. 20.
[47]B. J. Kidd, *A History of the Church*, I:72.
[48]Schaff, Vol. II, p. 44.
[49]Kidd, I:73.
[50]Ibid., p. 74.

people therefore welcomed Augustus as a savior, for emperor worship had long been in vogue in the East. It was therefore easy for Augustus to see the value of the altars and temples to "Rome and Augustus," and use it to his advantage. This imperial cult would provide a basis for unity between Rome and the provinces and for an expression of loyalty to the emperor. The cult was overseen and directed by the "Commune" or "Common Council" in the province; however, details regarding representation in the "Commune" have been lost. Members of this group are mentioned one time in the New Testament as being friends of Paul (Acts 19:31).[51] Under Domitian, when Christianity had attained greater recognition in Asia, the conflict between Christians and the imperial cult quite naturally and inevitably became more pronounced, and from the Christian's viewpoint, incurred greater religious persecution than before.

For the two and a half centuries following Domitian, the empire was ruled by both good and bad emperors. Only those who affected the fortunes of the church will be touched upon here. To an extent, Rome was tolerant of the conquered peoples. The ancient religions of the people were tolerated and their rites allowed to be practiced so long as they did not interfere with the interests of the state. At first Christianity was looked upon as a sect of Judaism which Rome permitted to continue. But when rapidly spreading Christianity began to take root and become strongly entrenched in the hearts of many Roman subjects, Rome's attitude changed. It was a number of years before Rome came to recognize that there was a difference between Judaism and Christianity, though Rome seemed never to have understood Christianity. Rome's gods were national, and in her eyes universal; she could brook no rival. Christianity stood in direct opposition to these claims of Rome, for it claimed to be the one and only true religion. In the light of this conviction, the Christian could neither worship the pagan deities nor accept the divinity of the emperor. This brought an inevitable religious conflict between the two which really began under Domitian. Persecution inevitably followed.

Some historians count ten principal persecutions, others count

---

[51]For a discussion of emperor worship and the Commune see Ramsay, *The Letters to the Seven Churches in Asia*, pp. 92–113; Kidd, Vol. I, pp. 74–75; Swete, *Apocalypse of Saint John*, lxxxvi–xc.

fewer than ten. Some of these persecutions, however, were not comparable to others. Coleman-Norton lists the following ten rulers and dates of the ten most severe persecutions of Christians: (1) Nero, 64; (2) Domitian, 96 (these two have been considered); (3) Trajan, c. 100–113; (4) Aurelian and Commodus, c. 161–185; (5) Septimius Severus and Caracalla, c. 202–213; (6) Maximinus I, 235–238; (7) Decius and Gallus, 249–252; (8) Valerian, 251–260; (9) Aurelian, 274–275; (10) Diocletian, Maximian I, Galerius, and Maximinus II, 303–313. But for only some of these are found imperial ordinances indirectly quoted.[52]

Domitian's successor, Nerva, who ruled from A.D. 96–98, was a most humane and considerate ruler who loved justice and devoted his time during this short reign to restoring order in the empire. He showed great moderation in government and had a number of laws passed which were of great benefit to the masses, especially to the poor. He rejected or rescinded some of the intolerable laws of Domitian's period including the exiling of people for political "crimes," and allowed those who had been exiled to return to their homes. Tacitus observes that under Domitian many of Rome's noblest ladies were exiled and made fugitives by the emperor.[53] Eusebius says the tyrant "punished vast numbers of honorable men with exile," including the apostle John, for according to tradition John was condemned to dwell on Patmos.[54] Schaff points out that Nerva "recalled the banished," and refused to treat the confession of Christians as a political crime.[55] Eusebius continues by saying that it was at that time, under Nerva, that John was released from Patmos and returned to Ephesus. However, he acknowledges that what he says of John's release was according to tradition.[56] This circumstantial evidence indicates that exile or banishment was a practice of Domitian, but there is no evidence that such exile occurred under Nero. (This seems to strongly favor the later date under Domitian over the early date under Nero.)

The following summary of Roman rulers and their attitude toward

---

[52]Coleman-Norton, p. 1179.
[53]*Agricola*, 45.
[54]Eusebius, *E. H.*, III, 17, 18.
[55]Schaff, Vol. II, p. 45.
[56]Eusebius, *E. H.*, chap. 20.

the Christians is included so that the reader may have a clearer grasp of the struggles and strivings of God's people against great odds. In reviewing the history of this period one feels a closer empathy with the Christians as he acquires a more complete picture of the persecutions, trials, and victory which followed the decade in which Revelation was written.

Trajan, who reigned from A.D. 98–117, is recognized by historians as one of the very best, if not the best, ruler Rome had. He had many virtues as a military genius, a statesman, and a far-sighted administrator who was thoroughly conscious of the problems that faced the empire. He was, however, wholly ignorant of the nature of Christianity. Indeed, a lack of understanding of the basic tenets and goals of this new and rapidly spreading religion appears to have been a weakness of all Roman emperors. This is understandable when one considers the religious background of these rulers and their concept of deity and the gods. The deities were looked upon as protectors and providers of the empire and were to be worshiped and revered as such even though they were abstractions, unseen and unfelt. Since the days of Augustus, all the emperors had come to be looked upon as saviors and benefactors. In them the people found something tangible and personal, and they deified them as worthy of worship and sacrifice.

Though Tiberius was none too lovable, Angus quotes ancient writers who spoke of him as "the common Benefactor of the world," and "God visible"; to the Alexandrians he was "our God Caesar." An ancient inscription declares of the insane and base Caligula: "The world knows no limit to its joy, and every State and people has turned eagerly to gaze on the face of the God as if now the happiest age had dawned on mankind." An altar dedicated to Nero in A.D. 67 reads, "to Nero God, the deliverer forever." In the Greek eyes Trajan was "God, the invincible Son of God."[57] It is little cause for wonder that the emperors reared in such an atmosphere could not understand Christianity.

Nero had looked upon and treated Christianity as a *religio illicita* (an unlawful religion). W. H. C. Frend points out that what one sees in Nero's action "is a brutal application of police administra-

---

[57]S. Angus, *The Religious quest of the Graeco-Roman World*, pp. 27–28.

tion...not the beginning of a policy launched by an edict." He further contends that Nero's persecution was confined to Rome and was not extended to the provinces.[58] This attitude of Nero had set a precedent which lasted until the middle of the third century, and even then was set aside only temporarily.[59] Persecutions in the second century were sporadic and were generally stimulated by mobs who hated the Christians and their faith. It was not until the third and fourth centuries that persecutions were universal in application, and even then they were not continuous.

Correspondence between Trajan and his younger friend Pliny throws light on the relationship of the Christians to the empire and the attitude of the emperor toward the Christians. In September, A.D. 111, Trajan appointed Pliny legate to Bithynia. Immediately after arriving there Pliny traveled through the province from west to east visiting the various cities (A.D. 111-113). During these visits, he met with the question of the Christians' attitudes toward sacrifice to the emperor and the images of the national deities. Having never before come face to face with this question concerning the Christian faith and not knowing how to cope with it, Pliny, as was his custom when he was in doubt, wrote a lengthy letter to his superior asking for guidance in the matter.

The letter reveals a number of important points: (1) Pliny had never been present at an examination of the new sect, and consequently he knew neither the ground on which to begin the investigation nor the penalty to mete in such cases. (2) He raised questions as to whether a pardon should be granted to those who would retract and deny Christ, and whether an individual should be punished for bearing the name Christian, or for the crimes associated with the name. (3) He had proceeded in the trials by asking the individuals if they were Christians, and by warning them of the penalty if guilty. If the person persisted in confessing his faith, he was asked the question a second and third time; and if he continued to persist, he was led away for execution on the grounds of obstinacy and stubbornness. (4) Pliny testified to the large number of Christians throughout the province as he wrote of the "widespread and increasing variety" of the charges. He seemed dis-

---

[58]W. H. C. Frend, *Martyrdom and Persecution in the Early Church*, p. 166.
[59]Kidd, Vol. I, p. 233.

mayed at the large number of persons of all ages and sexes who were implicated. (5) He also understood that no genuine Christian would deny the Christ and burn incense to the gods. (6) The legate described the worship of the Christians as meeting before dawn to sing, to bind themselves with an oath to abstain from theft, robbery, and adultery, to commit no breach of trust and to deny no trust committed to them. They would then disband and meet later to partake of a harmless kind of food. However, they had given up this latter practice when Pliny made known to them the emperor's edict banning such practices. (7) He confessed that the temples to the heathen deities had been almost deserted, but he believed many could be reformed and led back to their ancestral worship.

In his reply, Trajan (1) commended the course followed by Pliny, admitting that it was impossible "to lay down a general rule to a fixed policy." He further advised (2) that the Christians should not be hunted out; (3) but if brought before the court they should be punished; and (4) if one denied he was a Christian and offered prayers to the gods, he should be pardoned. (5) The emperor further ruled that anonymous charges must play no part in any accusation.[60]

Several interesting factors are brought to light from this correspondence: (1) Though practice had made it seem so, there had been no general edict issued proscribing the Christian religion, and though Trajan's letter was not intended to pronounce one, for all practical purposes it did. From Nero's time Christianity had been considered a *religio illicita* which if confessed must be punished. (2) Each case was determined on its own merit or demerit. (3) The Christians were not to be sought out. This in itself was an admission that Christians were not criminals; for if they had been ordinary criminals, the emperor could not have advised as he did. This answered Pliny's question: the crime was in the name Christian and not in acts as crimes associated with their religion. (4) The decree forbidding anonymous testimony or charges was to the Christians' benefit. In the light of these considerations it is clear that neither the emperor nor those who followed him were inclined to push the matter of searching out and punishing Chris-

---

[60]Pliny: *Letters and Panegyrecus*. Vol. II. Book X. 96.

tians. This put Trajan in the unsavory position of accusing and punishing subjects as criminals while not seeking them out as such.

During Trajan's reign, A.D. 115, there was a general Jewish uprising that engulfed most of the Hellenistic world. The Jews had cruelly slain many Gentiles, but when the revolt was crushed by Trajan's army in A.D. 117 the repression was as merciless as had been the Jewish uprising. In the minds of the Romans the Christians were still too near Judaism to escape completely this retribution; consequently, many Christians suffered during this period. But even though Trajan was a noble ruler, many faithful leaders among the Christians in the provinces suffered martyrdom.

Sixteen years after the revolt of the Jews under Trajan there was another uprising of the nation during the reign of Aelius Hadrian (A.D. 117-138). During a visit to Palestine in the year 130, Hadrian decided to rebuild Jerusalem, intending to make it a pagan city. This enraged the Jews and contributed to the Jewish uprising and rebellion (A.D. 132) led by Simon Kosba, whom the Jews called *Bar Kochba*, "The Son of the Star." The rebellion was completely crushed by the forces of Hadrian (A.D. 135) who left Judea prostrate, mercilessly slew a half million Jews, and sold thousands of others into slavery.

During this period the Jews added their measure to the sufferings of the Christians by persecution, as indicated by Justin: "In the Jewish war which lately raged, Barchochebas, the leader of the revolt of the Jews, gave orders that the Christians alone should be led to cruel punishment, unless they would deny Jesus Christ and utter blasphemy."[61] After the rebellion was crushed, the city of Jerusalem was rebuilt, renamed Aelia Capitolina (honoring the emperor Aelius Hadrian), and declared to be a pagan city. A temple dedicated to the Roman god Jupiter was erected on the site of the ancient temple to Jehovah, and the Jews were forbidden on penalty of death from entering the city. Little is known of Jerusalem from that time until the period of Constantine (A.D. 307-337), who made it possible for both Jews and Christians to enter the city.

Under the reign of Hadrian the lot of Christians was somewhat eased

---

[61] Justin Martyr, *Apology* I, 31, A-N-F, I. p. 173.

by the disposition and attitude of the emperor, although their legal position remained the same. In responding to the Proconsul of Asia, Caius Minucianus Fundanus, who requested help in dealing with Christians, the emperor stated: "If anyone bring an accusation against any of these men [Christians] out of mere calumny, you proceed against the fellow in proportion to his criminality and inflict severer penalties."[62] In the emperor's response three points stand out: (1) Trajan's policy continued to remain in force, (2) the magistrates were not to persecute the Christians because of popular clamor and prejudice, and (3) heavy penalties were to be imposed on false accusers. However, in spite of Hadrian's position toward Christians, there were a number of well-authenticated martyrdoms recorded under his reign.

During this period the development of the Christians' status in the empire did include differentiation between Jews and Christians. It seems that the emperor and his advisors made the distinctions that had not been clearly drawn before.

Antoninus Pius (A.D. 138-161) is remembered for his clemency toward his subjects and for lenient administration of the existing law. Both secular historians and Christian apologists bear testimony to his benign and humane spirit. He is described as a conservative, religious, and high-minded ruler. As a statesman he let the law take its course; as a religious man he was devoted to the worship of the national gods and was himself worshiped during his lifetime. Pius had little sympathy toward the Christians, for, in his view, they represented a secession from the religion of the state.

While little or no encouragement was given to those who wanted to denounce Christians, Christian communities remained illegal societies.[63] Under the reign of Antoninus Pius many Christians were martyred, among these was Polycarp, an aged bishop and teacher of the church in Smyrna. Eusebius seems to place his martyrdom during the reign of Marcus Aurelius,[64] but Stevenson defends the date (February, 156) under the reign of Pius.[65] For a detailed account of the trial

---

[62]Kidd, I:241.
[63]Frend, p. 255.
[64]Eusebius, E. H., Book IV. 13-15.
[65]J. Stevenson, A New Eusebius, p. 25.

and martyrdom of Polycarp see Stevenson,[66] or the account in the letter from the church at Smyrna to the church at Philomelium.[67]

Under the reigns of Antoninus Pius and Marcus Aurelius (A.D. 161-180) the Jews were restored to their pre-130 A.D. privileges. Once again Judaism was recognized as a *religio licita* (lawful or legal religion), but the Jews were confined to narrow geographical limits. Wherever they could, the Jews stirred up trouble against the Christians, even joining the pagans against them. Their bitterness against the Christians was demonstrated at the trial of Polycarp as they joined with the pagans in crying out for the death of the aged saint; and when it was determined that he should be burned at the stake and the wood was being gathered for the fire, "the Jews as usual showed themselves specially zealous in the work [of collecting the wood]."[68]

Marcus Aurelius Antoninus (A.D. 161-180), the Stoic philosopher who followed Pius on the Roman throne, is described by T. R. Glover as a man "who had almost a morbid horror of defilement from men and women of coarse minds,—a craving too for peace and sympathy; he shrank into himself, condoned, ignored."[69] In spite of whatever good qualities he may have had as a man and ruler, Aurelius persecuted Christians. He saw in them disloyalty to the state; their stubborn, unwavering faith was a strong contrast to his own wavering mind. It was of great importance to the Romans that the gods should be honored, for they believed this necessary to the well-being of the state. In the Romans' view, Christians were atheists because they did not believe in the gods and would not worship them. Aurelius' disposition toward Rome and Roman law, and the Christians' contempt for death and scorn for the worship of "Rome and Augustus," made the emperor bitterly opposed to those who held to the religion of Christ.

The imperial policy was now departing from the somewhat tolerant attitude of Trajan and Hadrian. Christians were being sought out for persecution, especially in the period A.D. 166-178, even though recantation still carried with it pardon and escape from death. Kidd quotes

---

[66]Ibid., pp. 18-24.
[67]A-N-F. Vol. I. pp. 37-44.
[68]Stevenson, p. 22.
[69]T. R. Glover, *The Conflict of Religion in the Early Roman Empire, p. 200.*

Lightfoot as saying, "The persecutions under Marcus Aurelius extended throughout his reign. They were fierce and deliberate. They were aggravated, at least in some cases, by cruel tortures. They had the emperor's personal sanction."[70] Aurelius was killed on the field of battle, A.D. 180, but the persecutions lasted on into the reign of his son, Commodus. The full weight of public opinion was behind the persecutions.

This period produced many apologists among the Christians, but they failed in their efforts to show the Christians' loyalty to Rome. Among the number of apologists martyred under Aurelius was Justin Martyr who, with five of his friends, was brought to Rome for trial. Here the six were tried before the prefect Rusticus, who earnestly endeavored to persuade the six to deny Christ and burn incense to Caesar. The attempt was to no avail, and they were taken out and beheaded.[71]

In the years following the death of Marcus Aurelius, 180–235, the Christians were gaining power and respect; and in spite of the character of Commodus, son of Aurelius (180–192), many fair-minded judges presided over courts before which Christians were tried. Commodus is described as "a second Nero or Domitian, he recalls the worst rulers of the Julian and Claudian dynasties."[72] He neglected administration and military affairs to spend "his life in continuous debauchery and in gratifying his morbid passion for the gladiator's art."[73] His reign was a repetition of the mad tyranny of Caligula and Nero. The absorption in his own lusts and passions left little time for Christians; however, there were martyrdoms in those milder days.[74] Commodus was murdered Dec. 31, A.D. 192.

Actually during this period (A.D. 180–235) the faith was expanding and becoming fixed as one of the main religions of the Roman Empire. However, the rivals of Christianity were also prospering. The

---

[70] *Kidd*, pp. 249–250.
[71] *For an account of Justin's trial and martyrdom see* A.N.F., vol. I. 305–306, or Stevenson, pp. 28–30.
[72] Rostovtzeff, p. 266.
[73] Ibid.
[74] Eusebius, *E. H.*, V. 21.

period of the Severi (A.D. 193-235) saw devotion to the imperial cult undiminished in the capital or in the provinces.[75] The official religion of Roman gods still dominated religious life and bound together local and regional patriotism into a single loyalty to the empire. To the majority of Roman subjects the greatness of Rome was personified in the emperor. He stood as mediator between the subjects and the gods who represented their guarantee of peace and security.[76]

At the death of Commodus (A.D. 192) the empire was again thrown into a state of civil war. After a brief rule of two emperors, each of whom was murdered in conspiracy of the soldiers, Septimus Severus (A.D. 193-211) was placed on the throne by his army. Through the years 195-200 as well as from 208-212, there were sporadic persecutions of the Christians. They were looked down upon as the very lowest members of society and were always subject to short-lived persecutions according to the whims of the individual governors. But their zeal never waned, and because of their ardor and activity the government became alarmed, fearing that the conversion of individuals might lead to the desertion *en masse* from the official religion of the empire. In an effort to check this widespread conversion to Christianity the emperor Severus issued an edict in 202, in which "under heavy penalties he forbad people to become Christians."[77] This persecution seems to have been stimulated by severe earthquakes in Asia Minor, for which Christians were held responsible. At this time popular fury blazed up against the Christians.[78] In his proscription of Christians the emperor also included Jews, forbidding that any citizen should embrace the Jewish faith.[79]

This was the first official persecution by edict; it was aimed at new converts, and reversed the regulation of Trajan that Christians "are not to be sought out."[80] Also, this was the first coordinated move against

---

[75]W. H. C. Frend, p. 305.
[76]Ibid., p. 310.
[77]Kidd, p. 337.
[78]Hans Lietzman, *Cambridge Ancient History*, XII. P. 520. Henceforth referred to as C.A.H.
[79]Coleman-Norton, p. 1180.
[80]Kidd, p. 347.

Christians. The saints suffered greatly in all the major cities, Carthage, Alexandria, Rome, Corinth, and Antioch, where they were burned, beaten, and beheaded. Persecution seems to have been especially terrible in Rome.[81] The mere profession of Christianity was their sin, not crimes of wickedness against the emperor or society.

There were four of the Severan emperors: Septimus Severus (193–211), an able ruler in spite of his persecution of Christians: Caracallo (211–217), noted for his brutality; Heliogobulus (218–222), noted for his debauchery; and Alexander (222–235), noted for his wisdom and justice in the affairs of government. The reign of Alexander Severus was followed by a period of collapse in the empire, a period of confusion in which the sword seated and unseated emperors at will. Anarchy reigned; the country was ruled by the military. Taxation, plunder, and stagnation of literature and art characterized the third century. Between 235 and 285 A.D. there were twenty-six Roman emperors; and only one of them died a natural death.[82]

Maximin (Maximinus) (235–238), Decius (249–251), and Valerian (253–260) declared open war against Christianity. Rostovtzeff says, "Again and again, with feverish activity, they persecuted not only individuals but the whole society in the persons of its chiefs and rulers."[83] Maximin was an enemy to the senate, the middle class, and the Christians. He hated his predecessor, Alexander Severus, with a passion and began his persecution by executing those of the former emperor's court and household along with others whom Alexander had favored. The persecution began with the execution of the church leaders, but eventually it was extended to include other Christians. The emperor attempted to revive paganism throughout the provinces, demanding that all men, women, and children partake of the sacrifices and libations to the gods.[84] The persecution was especially severe in Cappadocia where the Roman aristocracy regarded the Christians as potential revolutionists and where the provincial mobs found in them ready scapegoats, blaming them for a severe earthquake and other natural disasters. However, persecutions for these natural calamities

---

[81]Frend, p. 321.
[82]Rostovtzeff, p. 269.
[83]Ibid., p. 303.
[84]Eusebius, *E. H.* IX. 4.7.

HISTORICAL BACKGROUND

came not from the emperor, but from the governor of the province, "a bitter and terrible persecutor."

Gaius Decius was proclaimed emperor in September, 249, and reigned until near the end of 251. Among the several difficult tasks which confronted him was that of restoring traditional Roman discipline. In his effort to achieve some measure of success in meeting his problems by uniting all forces to his aid, he called for all to worship the titulary gods. It was probably this desire to consolidate the empire by a return to the traditional Roman virtues and customs that moved him to persecute Christians, for he saw in them a potential danger to all that was Roman. The negative disposition of the Christians towards Rome and her cults, their refusal to worship Roman deities, aroused among the people a widespread hostility to the church.

Soon after coming into office Decius issued a royal edict against the Christians.[85] Though the content has been lost, we do know that the edict "was the signal for a persecution which, in extent, consistency and cruelty, exceeded all before it... and was the first which covered the whole empire."[86] Decius seemed determined to exterminate the Christian religion; his severe means were vigorously applied. The office of censor was revived and entrusted to the senator Valerian, who was commissioned to correct all abuses, whether in the senate, government, or elsewhere.[87] This first edict was directed primarily against the bishops and other high church officials; it called for all to join in sacrifices and homage to the titular gods of the empire.

This was followed by a second edict that called upon all—men, women, and children—to taste meat offered in sacrifice and to pour out a libation to the gods. The penalty for refusal was death, and a commission was appointed in each city to enforce the emperor's decree. When a person yielded to the demand to sacrifice, a certificate was given him stating his residence, sex, and occupation and certifying that he had sacrificed. If he would not yield, he was tried before the proconsul; if he continued to profess his faith, in an effort to break down his constancy he was tortured, subjected to imprisonment,

---
[85]Eusebius, *E. H.* VI. 41.
[86]Schaff, II. 60.
[87]Duchesne, p. 267.

HISTORICAL BACKGROUND 84

exiled, stripped of his property, or threatened with death. If these failed, he was put to death. The persecution did not seek to make martyrs, but instead its purpose seems to have been to destroy the church: (1) by destroying the organization through an attack on its leaders, and (2) by making apostates, so that the prestige of the church would suffer and decline.[88] In the conflict many apostatized; but to their credit and eternal glory, many stood firm and endured the terrible sufferings inflicted upon them. The persecution slackened with the death of Decius on the field of battle (June, 251).

Though some say hundreds and others say thousands, only God knows for sure how many were martyred in this great persecution. The church had become weak during the long peace from the days of the Severi, and many persons of wealth had been attracted to it. Though many died for the faith, there was "wholesale defection" which presented a problem to the church when the persecution was over.[89] The testings of the short but sharp persecution of Decius did much to purge the church of those whose convictions were weak. One outstanding difference is detected between this persecution and those before: the sympathy of the Roman people seems now to be for the Christians, whereas formerly it had been against them.

The first several years of the reign of Valerian (255-260) are described by Eusebius as peaceful for the church. The emperor is described as "kind and friendly toward the pious."[90] However, about midway in his reign he turned against the Christians, fiercely persecuting them. There is divided opinion on the reason for the sudden change in attitude and conduct. Frend guesses it was the wealth of some Christians who had taken refuge in the church; Eusebius says the emperor was influenced by his minister, Marcianus, who hated the faith and wished to destroy it.[91] Along with these reasons, a probable third is the feeling that Christians stood in the way of the old Roman desire to restore the unity of the empire, now being harassed by barbarian invaders.

[88]Coleman-Norton, p. 1181.
[89]Hans Lietzman, C.A.H., XII., p. 521.
[90]E. H., VII., p. 10.
[91]Ibid.

The first edict of Valerian (A.D. 257) was mild; the emperor sought to stay Christianity without bloodshed. During this time Cyprian, leader of the church in north Africa and bishop of the church at Carthage, was tried and sent into exile. The second edict of the emperor (A.D. 258) was much more severe, imposing the death penalty. Martyrdoms followed; Cyprian was again tried and this time he was beheaded (258).[92] Decius had tried to force the Christians to become apostates to the faith, but Valerian sought to destroy the church, its hierarchy, its worship, and its property. Valerian's persecution seems to have been more severe in the west than in the east, where sympathy for the Christians was stronger. The persecution continued unabated during the year 259, but was brought to an end when Valerian was captured in battle with the Persians (260) and later slain.

Valerian's son, Gallienus (253-268), had been co-ruler with his father for seven years, and he became sole ruler upon the death of Valerian. The new emperor soon issued an edict (which has been preserved by Eusebius) restraining the persecution of Christians.[93] This act of Gallienus restored the right to worship and to maintain cemeteries to Christians, both of which were very important to them.

Christianity was now declared to be neither outside the law nor against it.[94] The edict introduced a peace for Christians which would last for a period of nearly forty years, during which the church grew numerically—though many compromises were made with the world and human doctrines. Gibbon says that the prosperity of the period "was far more dangerous to their [the Christians'] virtue than the severest trials of persecution."[95] By the time of Diocletian's rule the spiritual condition of the church confirmed the observation of Gibbon.

The final persecution against Christians, executed by the emperor Diocletian and his co-rulers, Maximian, Galerius, and later, Maximin II, was so severe that it made all previous persecutions fade into the

---

[92]For an account of the rescript of Valerian's second edict, and the trial and martyrdom of Cyprian, see Stevenson's *A New Eusebius*, pp. 259-262.
[93]*E. H.*, VII. 13. See also Stevenson, pp. 267-268.
[94]A. Alfoldi, *C.A.H.*, I., p. 207.
[95]Gibbon, I., p. 633.

background. Diocletian was declared emperor by his army September, 284, and reigned until he abdicated the throne May, 305, and was succeeded by Galerius, his son-in-law and the Caesar at the time.

A new order of rule was introduced by Diocletian. Soon after his selection as emperor he turned to Maximian to fill the role of Caesar. Then on April 1, 286, Maximian was appointed joint Augustus with Diocletian and Galerius and Constantius were selected as Caesars to work with the two Augusti. The rule of various portions of the empire was distributed among the four, but Diocletian maintained the chief rule among them. Under him the imperial authority became absolute.[96] The senate lost almost all its power, and at the same time the primacy of Italy was ended. Milan, the headquarters of Maximian, replaced Rome as the capital of Italy; Trier, in Germany, was the base of Constantius' rule in the west; Nicomedia, in Bithynia, was made the capital of Diocletian; and Sermium, in the province of Ponnonia, was the adminstrative center for Galerius.

Apparently, the persecution did not begin immediately upon the ascension of Diocletian and his co-Augusti; in fact, it seems that in those early years they did not break the religious truce which had been preserved since Gallienus. However, in spite of Gallienus's edict, Christianity was not yet recognized as a *religio licita*.[97] Eusebius says it was in the nineteenth year of Diocletian's reign that the persecution broke out.[98]

Describing the church before the persecution, Eusebius states that Christians enjoyed freedom, held high offices in government positions, were excused from sacrificing, and possessed spacious buildings. But he also describes the internal condition of the church as corrupt and filled with hypocrisy, avarice, and hatred. The believers were almost ready to take up arms one against another.[99] There were many Christians in Diocletian's household and court. His wife and daughter were exceedingly friendly to the faith, and it is probable that they were Christians.[100]

---

[96]See Gibbon, I. chap. 13, for a discussion of the governmental changeover.
[97]N. B. Baynes, *C.A.H.*, XII., p. 655.
[98]*E. H.*, VIII. 2.
[99]Ibid., 1.
[100]Kidd, p. 513.

HISTORICAL BACKGROUND

Space does not permit a thorough discussion of the possible causes of the persecution, and Diocletian appears to have opposed it. Suffice it to say that Galerius was a bitter enemy of the church and possessed an implacable hatred for it. Many historians feel that he was the moving force behind the edicts. It must be remembered that in the Roman mind peace and prosperity depended on popular worship of and reverence for the traditional gods of Rome. The Romans believed that these were still the forces which preserved the universe and the empire.[101] However, the greatest barrier between the Roman and the Christian was the worship of the emperor. To the Roman such sacrifice was a tribute of respect to the ruler of the Roman world, but to the Christian it was the very essence of idolatry. Faith in the gods was on the decline, but the Romans were not ready to accept Christianity as an alternative. Gibbon thinks Diocletian may have been moved by fear of the church's opulence, its organization (as an entity within the state), its government by its own laws and magistrates, and its independent treasury. He also thinks that the church's rejection of the gods and the institutions of Rome were probable contributing factors.[102]

Along with these factors, another enemy had appeared on the scene in the person of Porphyry, the "prophet of the great persecution," who was an able writer and a bitter enemy of Christianity.[103] His weapon was the pen. He wrote voluminously, with telling force against the whole Christian system, and for many years his writings were the chief source of material for opponents of the faith. Finally the time had come for a showdown. Roman paganism, ingrained in the popular mind, and Christianity could not endure side by side—one had to go. The conflict would be a long and bitter one, fought to the death of one and victory of the other. By this time the fight was inevitable.

Feelings mounted in the provinces; pressures increased; soldiers who refused to sacrifice were discharged, given corporal punishment, and returned to civil life deprived of certain privileges and rights. By 301 the handling of this problem was developing into a persecution.

During the winter of 302–303 Diocletian and Galerius spent much

---

[101]Frend, pp. 480–481.
[102]Gibbon, I., p. 641.
[103]Frend, pp. 480–481.

time together at Nicomedia where it is thought that Galerius tried to persuade the emperor to issue the edict of persecution. After counseling with his leaders, who approved persecution, and appealing to the oracle of the Milisian Apollo, Diocletian decided in favor of persecution and issued the edict in February, 303. The persecution began in Nicomedia. Since the emperor opposed bloodshed, at first the Christians' buildings were destroyed, their property confiscated, Scriptures burned, and those of honorable station were debased and degraded; but torture and bloodshed soon followed.[104]

Two fires which broke out in the imperial palace, falsely blamed on the Christians by Galerius, inspired the second edict against them.[105] There is strong suspicion and evidence that the fires were set by Galerius himself so that the Christians might be blamed. This second edict was directed especially against the clergy, the church leaders, demanding that they be delivered in chains to the authorities and imprisoned until they were compelled to sacrifice. The third edict, issued December 303, commanded the release of those who would sacrifice, "but to lacerate with myriad tortures those who would not."[106]

The fourth edict was issued in the spring of 304 during a severe illness of Diocletian. It is uncertain whether it was issued by Maximian or Galerius, but most historians ascribe it to Galerius. The most severe edict issued up to this point, it called for a general persecution. All men, women, and children were to offer a libation or suffer the penalty of death. Needless to say, many refused and were put to death.

In May of 305 Diocletian and Maximian abdicated as Augusti, whereupon Constantius and Galerius were hailed as Augusti. Severus and Maximin II were appointed Caesars. Maximin, the cousin of Galerius, was equal to him in cruelty and even surpassed him in inventing means of torture. Likewise Galerius is described by Lactantius as one of the basest and cruelest of all persecutors, both of Christians and Pagans.[107]

The fifth edict against the Christians came in the spring of 306, in

---
[104]*E. H.*, VIII. 2.
[105]Ibid., VIII. 6. See also Lactantius, *On The Death of the Emperors*, A-N-F., Vol. VII., p. 306.
[106]Coleman-Norton, p. 1183.
[107]Lactantius, 21, p. 309.

the form of a letter from Maximin calling upon everyone, regardless of sex or age, to sacrifice at the temples under the supervision of the magistrates. "This instruction reinforced the two-year-old ordinance, which had been permitted to lapse, or represented a periodical check on backsliders."[108] The punishments were grievous and severe.

The sixth of the series of edicts of the ten-year period was again issued by Maximin in the autumn of 308. It called for the rebuilding of pagan temples and altars and decreed once again that all should be forced to sacrifice and do homage to the deities. All were compelled to taste the sacrifices, and it was also ordered that every article for sale in the markets should be defiled with the libations (blood or wine) of heathen sacrifices. Guards, whose duty it was to pollute those that had been cleansed, were placed before the baths.[109] This was actually an effort on Maximin's part to revive paganism.

In the year 311 Galerius was smitten with an incurable disease[110] similar to that of Herod (Acts 12:23). Tormented by "raging pain," and realizing that death was near he sought to make some atonement for his misdeeds by publishing an edict of toleration toward the Christians, suspending the persecution.[111] This was a great victory for the saints; and although more persecutions were to come, a battle had been won and the scent of victory was in the air. A long stride toward religious liberty had been achieved. Soon after issuing the edict Galerius died (311). Maximian had died shortly before him (310) and Diocletian died in 313.

Maximin ignored the edict of toleration issued by Galerius, and in the fall of 311 began a final effort to destroy Christianity. This persecution was executed with such vigor and ferocity that it was probably the most severe of all, climaxing the entire period from Nero to Constantine. Both Eusebius and Lactantius describe in bitter and painful terms the horror of the execution of the edict and the terrible sufferings of the Christians, an unbelievable outrage by men upon fellow human beings.[112]

---

[108]Coleman-Norton, p. 1185.
[109]Eusebius, *The Book of Martyrs*, ch. 9.
[110]Lactantius, 33, p. 314.
[111]For a copy of the edict see Lactantius, chap. 34 (p. 315), Stevenson, p. 296, or C. A. H. XII., p. 672.
[112]Eusebius, *E. H.*, VIII. 10, 14, et al.; Lactantius, 36 (p. 316).

HISTORICAL BACKGROUND 90

In the year 313 Maximin was defeated in battle against Licinius, emperor of the east, and according to Lactantius, some time afterwards he took his own life, dying a terrible death.[113] Shortly before the defeat of Maximin, Maxentius was defeated by Constantine, the son of Constantius, in a battle fought at the Milvian bridge just north of Rome. With the defeat of Maxentius in the west and Maximin in the east, Constantine and Licinius became the sole rulers of the Roman Empire. After Constantine's victory, the two men met at Milan and drew up what is known as "the Edict of Milan," the first document of its kind in the annals of human history. The edict, which had far-reaching effects, granted universal religious toleration; and though it did not outlaw paganism, it did grant men the right to choose their own religion and the deity whom they would worship. The ten-year battle had been a long, hard, murderous one, but it had now been won for Christianity and the cause of Christ. Christianity had become a *religio licita*.

The conflict between Christians and Jews began in the early days of the faith. As Christianity spread, so did the war against it. Magistrates of the provinces were influenced to persecute the church in their various cities. Wave after wave of persecutions came until finally there was an all-out war between the faith of Christ and the paganism of the Roman Empire.

An enlightening statement from Coleman-Norton will close this section: "Of the 249 years from the first persecution under Nero in 64 to the final peace under Constantine I in 313, it is estimated that Christians endured persecution about 129 years and enjoyed toleration about 120 years. But this calculation must be qualified by the circumstances that even in the periods of comparative peace Christians were ever exposed to pagan prejudice and hatred not only in Rome and in Italy, but also in the provinces, and that doubtless sporadic and spasmodic deletion of Christians occurred not seldom before magistrates, who, if conscientious officials, obeyed the existing enactments and ordered the execution of Christians thus denounced."[114]

---

[113]Lactantius, 49, p. 321.
[114]Coleman-Norton, p. 1188.

COMMENTARY ON REVELATION

PART ONE
Chapters 1—11

CONFLICT AND JUDGMENT WITHIN AND WITHOUT THE CHURCH

CHAPTER 1
Christ Among the Lampstands

THE SUPERSCRIPTION
vv. 1-3

v. 1. "The Revelation of Jesus Christ, which God gave him to show unto his servants, even the things which must shortly come to pass: and he sent and signified it by his angel unto his servant John." "The Revelation of Jesus Christ" is the title that John gives to his book. Revelation, a translation of *apokalupsis*, means an unveiling, removing the cover from something. Although the word appears eighteen times in the rest of the New Testament, where it is used to describe divine things hitherto unknown but now being revealed by the Holy Spirit (I Cor. 2:10), and to describe the understanding by saints (Eph. 1:17), it occurs only here in the Book of Revelation.

The question may be raised, Is this a revelation from Jesus Christ or a revelation in which Christ was both the recipient and the giver? While scholars differ on the answer, the next phrase, "which God gave him to show unto his servants," indicates that it is a divine revelation given to Christ as the recipient of the message, which He in turn gives to His servants; it is a revelation which Jesus makes. The book is also a revelation of Jesus Christ in His present glory, rule and executor of judgment. It unveils the struggles through which the church was destined to pass and its ultimate triumph and victory under Christ. "Which God gave him," makes God the ultimate source and author of the revelation.

Throughout the Gospel of John, Jesus claims that what He did and taught was from the Father (John 5:19; 6:38; 7:14-17; 8:28; 12:48-50; 14:23-24, et al.). The whole of God's eternal plan originated in His mind, was carried out by Christ and was revealed by the Holy Spirit (I Cor. 2:6-10; Eph. 1:9-10 et al.); this final phase of the revelation is also from God. This revelation was given unto Christ "to show unto his servants." The things to come were to be made known to God's bondservants—the redeemed. The revelation was committed to them for safekeeping and for their comfort and encouragement.

"Even the things which must shortly come to pass," clearly refutes the futurist view that John was writing about things to transpire immediately prior to Jesus' second coming. On the contrary, he is writing of things in the near future—the crises through which the saints were soon to pass. He repeatedly affirmed this imminence of the things to come, saying: "for the time is at hand" (v. 3), "the things which must shortly come to pass" (22:6), and again "for the time is at hand" (22:10). The Revelation begins and closes with an assurance of immediacy of things to come, even though the book does deal with the final judgment and the new order of things beyond the judgment, which were in the distant future and are yet to come (20:11; 21:8); but the major portion of the revelation pertained to things at hand, events soon to transpire.

"He sent" points to Jesus to whom the revelation was given and through whom it was made known. "Signified (*sēmainō*) it," means that the revelation was to be delivered as expressed by signs (*sēmeian*). To the apostle John all wonders or miracles were "signs"; he used the word repeatedly in his Gospel. The reader must interpret the signs and determine the divine message intended for the people to whom it was addressed, and the meaning for us today. The word "sign" appears seven times in the book and is one of twenty-nine words that John uses seven times in the Revelation. "By his angel" signifies the immediate heavenly messenger from Jesus to "his servant John." "His servant" identifies John as a fellow-servant with the rest of God's servants.

v. 2. *"Who bare witness of the word of God, and of the testimony of Jesus Christ, even of all things that he saw."* John here affirms that he fulfilled his mission by bearing the witness which was entrusted to him. "The word of God" in this instance refers not to his past witness to truth set forth in his Gospel and epistles, but "even of all things that he saw," thus pointing to that which God and Christ were now giving him, both in vision and in word. These things which he saw would be made known when they were read in the churches. In the past God's Word had revealed and called for action (John 1:1-5); here also it reveals and calls for responsive action by the servants.

v. 3. "Blessed is he that readeth, and they that hear the words of the prophecy, and keep the things that are written therein: for the time is at hand." "Blessed," that is, happy or fortunate, is used here the first of seven times John uses the word in this book (1:3; 14:13; 16:15; 19:9; 20:6; 22:7, 14). "He that readeth" refers to a reader in the public assemblies. "He," the reader, is singular, while "they that hear" is plural. Apparently John provided only one copy of the book (v. 11) which was to be read publicly in each congregation. The public reading of Scripture in assemblies was a practice adopted from the Jewish synagogue meetings (cf. Luke 4:16). Doubtless few early Christians could read well, and each congregation probably selected the best reader, who would be considered fortunate or happy to have this privilege. Likewise a blessing is pronounced on those who heard the Word read. Hearing embraces more than mere listening to what is being said; it involves hearing with a view to doing. Jesus said, "If ye know these things, blessed are ye if ye do them" (John 13:17); and James had stated the principle simply, "But be ye doers of the word, and not hearers only, deluding your own selves" (James 1:22). The blessing lies in accepting and doing that which one hears.

"The words of the prophecy" identifies the message as inspired, a revelation from God through the Spirit, for the prophet was a mouth of the Lord, an inspired teacher (see Eph. 3:5; II Peter 1:21). "And keep the things that are written therein" confirms the above conclusion that to hear involves keeping, abiding in, and doing that which is revealed. "For the time is at hand," provides strong motivation for obedience in keeping the things heard, for the things to be revealed—the woes, the fears, the battles, and the hope—were in the near future.

THE SALUTATION
vv. 4-7

v. 4. "John to the seven churches that are in Asia: Grace to you and peace, from him who is and who was and who is to come; and from the seven Spirits that are before his throne." The writer needed no further introduction or designation of identification, for as "John" he was well known as the apostle who had labored among the churches of Asia for many years. Asia was the western province of modern Asia Minor, the richest of all Roman provinces. "The seven churches" introduces us to the first use of the symbolic seven, a number that will occur in some manner fifty-four times in the book. It is not to be concluded that there were only seven churches in the entire province, for there were also Troas, Colosse, Hierapolis, and possibly others. Seven is the "perfect" number, symbolizing completeness or fullness, and these seven are selected by the Lord as congregations which possessed the qualities characterizing various congregations throughout history. Combinations of these conditions are present in any church of the Lord today.

"Grace to you and peace" is a typical salutation of New Testament letters. It is found in all of Paul's letters (with a slight variation in I and II Timothy) and in both letters by Peter. John uses it in II John. It was by grace, God's unmerited favor, that they of the churches had been redeemed; and it was by the same favor that they were now God's servants destined to win the crown of victory. "Peace" denotes "the spiritualized, Christian form of prosperity; security, soundness; salvation [which ideas are] associated with the word from the very earliest use... no doubt... colored... by the consciousness of the peace of reconciliation existing with God" (Hastings, IV, p. 160). More than friendly intercourse, it includes positive well-being and general security. This peace, a gift from Christ (John 14:27; 20:21), follows the provisions of the divine grace.

"From him who is and who was and who is to come," clearly points to the eternal Father. Lenski thinks this divine name does not reproduce the Septuagint translation of the Hebrew *Yahweh*, "I am" of Exodus 3:14 (p. 39), while Pieters says it is an amplification of the name given by God to Moses on that occasion (p. 81). Pieters translates it, "The Being, the Was, the Coming" (ibid.), while Lenski would have it "The Being One and the Was One and the Coming One." The definite article (*ho*) precedes each of the nouns, "the was, the is, the is to come." However, in translating the Greek, it is clear that the name was intended to designate the Father's eternity. "Such a title of the Eternal Father stands fitly among the first words of a book which reveals the present in the light both of the past and of the future" (Swete, p. 5).

"The seven Spirits" (see also 3:1; 4:5; 5:6) balances the "seven churches," and is another use of the symbolic seven. Jesus and the apostles spoke always of *the* Holy Spirit, singular; there is one Spirit as there is one God and one Lord (cf. Eph. 4:4–6). The seven should be thought of symbolically and not literally; "the seven Spirits" symbolize the sevenfold perfection, completeness, and universality of the Spirit's working. It is doubtful that John is referring to Isaiah's description of the Spirit which was to be upon the Messiah, for there the prophet describes the Spirit of Jehovah in three descriptive couplets, making six characteristics instead of seven (Isa. 11:2). Probably Zechariah's reference to "seven" is more to the point. He describes the seven eyes upon the stone set before Joshua the high priest (Zech. 3:9), and the seven eyes which should rejoice at the completion of the temple by Jehovah's Spirit, which are "the eyes of Jehovah, which run to and fro through the whole earth" (Zech. 4:6, 10). Perfection, completeness, and universality of the Spirit's working seem to be the symbolic significance of the "seven." The seven Spirits are described as before the throne of the Lord, ever ready to carry out His purpose and will.

v. 5. "*And from Jesus Christ, who is the faithful witness, the firstborn of the dead, and the ruler of the kings of the earth. Unto him that loveth us, and loosed us from our sins by his blood.*" "And from Jesus Christ," completes the triune concept of the Godhead. Grace and peace come from or by the three, since all share in man's redemption by grace and provide the peace which follows. The Christ is mentioned last because the Book of Revelation deals particularly with His place and glory. He is presented in a threefold executive position of prophet, priest, and king. As prophet He is the "faithful witness." He came into the world that He should bear witness to the truth (John 18:37); and John said, "What he hath seen and heard, of that he beareth witness" (John 3:32). In confirmation of this, Jesus claimed, "My witness is true" (John 8:14). He was a faithful witness before the people as He taught, before the Jews when falsely accused by them, and before Pilate when on trial. His witness to the being and character of God, to the purpose and redemptive plan of God, and to the truth of God is complete.

"The firstborn of the dead" points to His resurrection, a birth from earth's womb which held Him for a few short hours (cf. Col. 1:18). In another passage He is "the firstfruits of them that are asleep" (I Cor.

15:20). In this triumph over death He brought "to nought him that had the power over death, that is, the devil," and was thereby able to deliver all who through fear of death had been subject to bondage (Heb. 2:14-15). In His temptation, sacrifice, and victory He qualified Himself to become a merciful and faithful high priest for us before God (Heb. 2:16-18).

From victory over death He ascended to God's right hand where He became "the ruler of the kings of the earth." The Roman rulers who had crucified Him were now his subjects. These rulers of the earth are the kings of the unregenerate world; they are not the subjects of His spiritual kingdom. God thus fulfilled His promise, "I also will make him my firstborn, the highest of the kings of the earth" (Ps. 89:27). What consolation this would be to suffering saints to know that their king is ruler over their persecutors! His faithfulness to truth, His victory over death, and His exaltation to the position of highest of earth's potentates would guarantee their own victory. Alford quotes DeWette as saying, "That which the tempter held forth to Jesus, Matt. 4:8, on condition of worshipping him, He has now attained by the way of his humiliation unto death: viz. victory over the world. John 16:33" (Alford, p. 550).

The doxology follows: "Unto him that loveth us, and loosed us from our sins by his blood." His love, demonstrated in His sacrificial death, procured our redemption. The KJV reads, "and washed us from our sins," but "loosed," of the ASV, is preferable. Being loosed from sins which alienated and separated them from God, the redeemed are now delivered from sin's condemnation and power, maintaining fellowship with God while walking in the light and being kept clean from sin by Christ's blood (I John 1:5-7).

v. 6. *"And he made us to be a kingdom, to be priests unto his God and Father; to him be the glory and the dominion for ever and ever. Amen."* Being loosed from sins and brought into fellowship with the Father, the redeemed now become the kingdom of God, the new spiritual Israel. As Israel was set free from Egyptian bondage and became a new kingdom and priests unto God (Exod. 19:5-6), so the redeemed, set free from sin's bondage by the blood of Christ, became a new nation (kingdom) under Christ. Based on later manuscript evidence, the word "kingdom" is preferable to "kings." Collectively, the redeemed are a kingdom; individually, they are priests. The kingdom of Old Testament prophecy and of Jesus' preaching was now a reality. John was in the kingdom (1:9), those purchased with blood are the kingdom (5:10), and the saints at Colosse had been "translated into the kingdom" (Col. 1:13). Rather than being established at Christ's second coming, the kingdom will be delivered up to God at that time (I Cor. 15:24).

This spiritual kingdom made up of priests serving and glorifying Christ's Father stands in contrast to Caesar's kingdom which was of the earth. As the theme of Revelation is developed, the conflict between the two stands out. The kings of two worlds had met in Pilate's hall to determine the issue of truth and falsehood (John 18); so now the two kingdoms must meet in a decisive contest over the same principles. As an individual, the priest's function is to offer spiritual sacrifices to God (I Peter 2:5), sacrifices of praise, the fruit of lips (Heb. 13:15), having first presented his body as a living sacrifice, holy and acceptable to Him (Rom. 12:1).

"Glory" carries with it the basic idea of brightness, brilliance, and splendor. It has two principal meanings, "(1) honor, praise, good repute; (2) that which by exciting admiration brings honor or renown" (Hastings, III, p. 451). These ideas characterize the word when applied to God or Christ: to Christ be this splendor, honor, praise, admiration, and renown due such a one. In the New Testament the word "dominion" (from *kratos*) is translated "strength," "power," "might" except in the several doxologies where it is translated "dominion" (I Peter 4:11; 5:11; Jude 25; Rev. 1:6; 5:13), meaning rule or sovereignty. (The one exception is the doxology in I Tim. 6:16, where it is translated "power.") Christ's receiving the kingdom and glory and dominion fulfills Daniel's vision in which, looking from heaven's viewpoint, the prophet saw one like unto a son of man coming on the clouds of heaven and being brought before the Ancient of Days where "there was given him dominion, and glory and a kingdom" (Dan. 7:13-14). As foretold by the prophets Christ now has this kingdom, glory, and dominion; these are His "for ever and ever." At the end of the present age He will deliver up the kingdom (kingship) to God the Father, and will Himself become subject to the Father (I Cor. 15:24-28). But in some way not revealed to us His dominion will continue even in eternity.

On "for ever and ever," it may be observed that *aiōn* (Eng. aeon or eon) describing an age, a period of time, or an indefinite period of time, always appears in Revelation in the double plural (*eis tous aiōnas tōn aiōnōn*). "This combination of the double plural seems to be peculiar to the New Testament" (Thayer), and indicates unending or unlimited duration. This phrase of the double plural appears twelve times in Revelation with the article and once without it (14:11). It is used of Christ's dominion (1:6) and of His present unending life (1:18). It appears five times in the doxologies, four of God (4:9, 10; 7:12; 11:15), and once of God and the Lamb (5:13; and though occurring in the KJV in 5:14, it is omitted in the ASV). It is identified with God in an angel's oath (10:6) and with Him in the bowls of His wrath (15:7). The phrase describes the smoke of the torment of those who worship the beast and his image (14:11, article omitted), the smoke of Babylon's destruction (19:3), and the smoke of the devil's and his helpers' torment (20:10). Finally, it is used of the eternal reign of the saints beyond the judgment (22:5) in contrast to the reign of a thousand years (20:4). "Amen" expresses certainty, and was used "to adopt as one's own what has just been said" (Hastings, III, p. 53).

v. 7. *"Behold, he cometh with the clouds; and every eye shall see him, and they that pierced him; and all the tribes of the earth shall mourn over him. Even so, Amen."* "Behold" focuses attention on what follows. "He cometh with the clouds" points to His coming to judge and execute. Although this passage includes His second coming (cf. Acts 1:10-11) and the great judgment of that hour, it also includes the idea of His coming on clouds in all judgments before that great event. The idea of coming on clouds or a cloud was also used to describe Jehovah's coming against Egypt (Isa. 19:1; Ezek. 30:3; 32:7), and the judgment against His own people (Ezek. 34:12). Jesus promised that He would come "on the clouds of heaven" in judgment against Jerusalem (Matt. 24:24-30; Mark 13:24-30). So now He would come against the Romans, and ultimately He will come to judge all. He said repeatedly, "I come quickly" (2:16; 3:11; 22:7, 12, 20), indicating that at a time ripe for judgment He will come to judge the forces of evil and to defend His own people (14:14-20). The expression "He cometh with the clouds" points to the final coming and judgment but also includes all His comings against His enemies before that time, for all judgment has been given unto the Son (John 5:22).

"And every eye shall see him, and they that pierced him." Only the apostle John used Zechariah 12:10 to describe the action of the Jews against Jehovah in nailing His Son to the cross (John 19:37). That heinous crime is still before the apostle's eyes as he writes the Revelation; those that pierced Him shall look upon Him as also shall all who have crucified Him afresh, or who have persecuted Him by persecuting His church (see Acts 9:4; I Cor. 15:9). Every knee shall bow and every tongue shall confess Him as Lord (Phil. 2:10-11); for those who rejected Him, the confession will be to the glory of God and to their own damnation. "And all the tribes of the earth shall mourn over him," including Jews, Romans, and Greeks who shared in His rejection and crucifixion, standing in opposition to His cause; they shall all mourn over Him. "Mourn" indicates the beating of the head or breast in lamentation, suggesting a condition of utter hopelessness. "Even so, Amen," combines a Greek word, translated "even so," with its Hebrew equivalent, "Amen," which gives a double endorsement to the pronouncement.

THE SEAL
v. 8

v. 8. *"I am the Alpha and the Omega, saith the Lord God, who is and who was and who is to come, the Almighty."* The salutation and introduction reach a climax with the seal, "I am the Alpha and the Omega." These are the first and last letters of the Greek alphabet, indicating God's fullness and completeness, His all-inclusiveness. "Saith the Lord God, who is and who was and who is to come, the Almighty." It is difficult to determine whether the speaker is the Eternal Father or the glorified Christ. Commentators are almost equally divided between the two interpretations; however, the evidence favors the Father as speaker. As the speaker, He would be attaching His seal of approval to the authenticity of the Revelation and personally endorsing the message as originating with Him. He declares His completeness and then asserts His eternity and His almighty power as the all-ruler. He is complete, eternal, and almighty; therefore, what is being done through the Son is of and from Him. However, the speaker might well be the Son, for He is the fullness of Godhood or deity (Col. 2:9), and shares in the attributes, deity, and totality of the Father (Heb. 1:3). If it is the Father who speaks, He speaks only here and in 21:5ff. (See further comments 4:8).

JOHN'S CHARGE TO WRITE
vv. 9-11

v. 9. "I John, your brother and partaker with you in the tribulation and kingdom and patience which are in Jesus, was in the isle that is called Patmos, for the word of God and the testimony of Jesus." John introduces himself by name for the third time. He identifies himself with those to whom he writes and claims a kinship by calling himself "your brother and partaker with you in the tribulation and kingdom and patience which are in Jesus." In his relationship to Christ he was a slave, but in his relationship to the saints he was a brother. "And partaker" indicates a sharer or joint-participant with someone in something. Here the writer shares with his brethren "in the tribulation and kingdom and patience" in Jesus. Tribulation (*thlipsis*) is "a pressing together (as of grapes), squeezing or pinching" (I.S.B.E.), hence a crushing as of grapes or grinding as of wheat. Jesus had forewarned His disciples that such would be their lot when He said, "In the world ye have tribulation"; then He added the comforting assurance, "but be of good cheer; I have overcome the world" (John 16:33). The apostle Paul had urged the saints to be faithful, assuring them "that through many tribulations we must enter into the kingdom of God" (Acts 14:22). Tribulation had been the lot of the church from its beginning, but it was now breaking upon the saints with an increasing intensity that would cover a period of more than two hundred years (see introduction and historical background). John was a partaker with them, which meant there was a link of sympathy between him and all Christians.

"And kingdom" (see under v. 6). Here was the focal point between the tribulation and patience. Through many tribulations they would enter into the fuller and richer blessings of the kingdom, but these blessings would become theirs through patience. "Patience" is steadfast endurance, through which one obtains perfection in the faith (James 1:4). Such endurance is constantly urged in the New Testament letters, as when Paul links the two words urging the Romans to be "patient in tribulation" (Rom. 12:12).

"Which are in Jesus." These three, tribulation, kingdom, and patience, were all in and by Him. Those out of Him were spared the tribulation, for they were not in the kingdom. Those in Him were in the kingdom and were the persecuted; it was they who would find the power to continue steadfast. If the kingdom did not already exist by the time of this writing, this statement carries little if any meaning. In using the human name "Jesus," John related the persecuted sufferers with Him in His earthly life and trials.

John "was in the isle that is called Patmos," a rocky and uninviting island located about seventy miles southwest of Ephesus, about forty miles from Miletus, and twenty-four miles from the shore of Asia Minor. The island is ten miles long and, at its widest point, six miles across. The sea almost pinches it off at one place, forming a harbor. Moffatt, relying upon Pliny (*Historia Naturalis* IV. 12, 23), says the Roman authorities sometimes banished criminals to this island. Eusebius, relying on traditions of his day, says John was condemned to exile on Patmos during the reign of Domitian (*E. H.*, III, p. 18).

"For the word of God and the testimony of Jesus." The statement is a simple one, but it is difficult to know what John means. Three views are held: (1) He was on Patmos to preach to the people in an evangelistic effort; (2) He was there as a prisoner because of his preaching and the testimony he had borne in Asia; (3) He was there for the specific purpose of receiving the revelation being given him.

Unless there are undiscovered grounds for accepting the first interpretation, it can be eliminated because of the insignificance and location of the island. John's care to identify Patmos as an isle indicates that it was not as well known as other New Testament places specifically identified. The third position lacks any real evidence to sustain it, therefore is rejected.

Three arguments are suggested in behalf of the second view: (1) John identified himself with the saints to whom he was writing as a partaker in the tribulation. This would account for his being in exile, since exile was a part of the tribulation. (2) The parallel language in the use of the phrase "the word of God and the testimony of Jesus" in 6:9 and 20:4, although in different contexts, confirms the view that John was on Patmos for the same cause suffered by these saints:

1:9 *dia ton logon tou Theou kai dia tēn marturian Iēsou*
for the word of God and for the testimony of Jesus
6:9 *dia ton logon tou Theou kai tēn dia marturian ēn eichon*
for the word of God and for the testimony which they held
20:4 *dia   tēn marturian Iēsou, kai   dia*
(for/on account of) the testimony of Jesus, and (for/on account of)
ton logon tou Theou
the word of God.

It seems clear that John was on Patmos for the same cause that the souls of the slain were under the altar (6:9), and that the victorious souls were on thrones (20:4). Tribulation was the cause for all three. (3) Finally, there is the evidence of tradition from the earliest writings that John was banished to exile as a part of the tribulation (see introduction and appendix).

v. 10. *"I was in the Spirit on the Lord's day, and I heard behind me a great voice, as of a trumpet."* "I was in the Spirit," does not mean that John was in a spirit of worship or meditation or under the spell of a self-imposed ecstasy, but that he was under the power or control of the divine Spirit. A parallel to John's experience is found in Ezekiel (Ezek. 3:12, 14; 8:3; 11:24; 37:1; 43:5) where by the Spirit the prophet was shown wonderful things of God. So now through the Spirit John saw and heard the things recorded in chapters 1—3. A second time John claims the same control by the Spirit when he is shown the awe-inspiring vision of heaven and the marvelous events that followed (4:1).

"On the Lord's day," occurring only here in the New Testament, clearly refers to the first day of the week. The Lord had been raised on that day (cf. Luke 24:1, 13, 21, 46), the Holy Spirit came on the first day (Acts 2:1), the Jewish festival Shavuot (Pentecost) always came on the first day of the week (Lev. 23:15, 16). Since the church began on

Pentecost, the first day was the birthday of the church. The early church met on that day to eat the Lord's supper (Acts 20:7), and believers were taught to lay by of their means on that day for the support of others (I Cor. 16:1-2). "The Lord's day" is not to be confused with "the day of the Lord," used often in both testaments. This latter expression always refers to a day of judgment and retribution; "the Lord's day," indicates the first day of the week. The following use of *Kuriakos* may help to explain John's point: *Kuriakos*, "belonging to the Lord, the Lord's" (A. & G.), is used only here, *Kuriakē hēmera*, "Lord's day," and in I Corinthians 11:20, *Kuriakon deipnon*, "Lord's supper." The day was the Lord's day, the supper was the Lord's supper. The Lord's supper was observed on the first day of the week (Acts 20:7). Surely the Lord's supper was observed on the Lord's day, and if so, it must follow that the Lord's day was the first day of the week. The Lord provided this new name for a new day on which new religious service was observed.[1]

"And I heard behind me a great voice, as of a trumpet." Why the voice sounded from behind John is not revealed; a parallel to this is related by Ezekiel, who heard behind him "the voice of a great rushing" (Ezek. 3:12). Jehovah's revelation of the law at Sinai had been introduced with the voice of an exceeding loud trumpet (Exod. 19:16, 20). The voice which John heard was *as* a trumpet, meaning that it was loud and clear; the Deity was about to speak and reveal. Through-

---

[1]The ante-Nicene writers who wrote after John followed a consistent pattern in considering "the first day," "the Lord's day," the "resurrection day," and the day of meeting, Sunday, as identical. Ignatius (30–107 A.D.) writes, "Let every friend of Christ keep the Lord's day as a festival, the resurrection day, the queen and chief of all the days (of the week)" A-N-F, I, p. 63). Justin (110–165 A.D.), writing of the day on which the saints met for worship identified it as "Sunday . . . the first day . . . and Jesus Christ our Saviour on the same day rose from the dead" (I, p. 168). *The Teaching of the Twelve* (120–190 A.D.): "But every Lord's day do ye gather yourselves together, and break bread" (VII, p. 381). Clement (153–217 A.D.), writing agonist Gnostics, identifies the Lord's day with the resurrection, saying, "He, in fulfillment of the precept, according to the Gospel, keeps the Lord's day . . . glorifying the Lord's resurrection" (II, p. 545). Tertullian (145–220 A.D.) identifies "the Lord's day" as "every eighth day" (III, p. 70). *Constitution of the Holy Apostles* (250–325 A.D.): "And on the day of our Lord's resurrection, which is the Lord's day, meet more diligently" (VII, p. 423); and "on the day of the resurrection of the Lord, that is, the Lord's day, assemble yourselves together, without fail" (ibid. p. 471).

out musical history the trumpet has been used for a fanfare, an announcement or a call to attention. The Romans used trumpets extensively for these purposes. Scholars are divided in their views as to whether the voice was Christ's or His angel's. Because of what is said in verse 1, "He sent and signified it by his angel unto his servant John," some have concluded that the voice John heard was that of an angel. But because of whom John saw when he turned to look and because it was Jesus who spoke later (vv. 17-20), others contend it was the voice of Jesus. It was probably the angel who attracted John's attention and spoke that which follows in verse 11. But Jesus is definitely the speaker in verses 17-20.

v. 11. *"Saying, What thou seest, write in a book and send it to the seven churches: unto Ephesus, and unto Smyrna, and unto Pergamum, and unto Thyatira, and unto Sardis and unto Philadelphia, and unto Laodicea."* John is to write what he sees and hears. He probably wrote on a papyrus roll, which has been estimated to have been approximately fifteen feet long, depending on its width. It seems likely that John wrote at the time of the revelation and not at some later time. He apparently made only one copy which was to be read in each congregation. Although each church probably made its own personal copy, this is not stated. "The seven churches" (see under v. 4) symbolically represents all churches of the Lord. The phrases "I am Alpha and Omega, the first and the last," and "in Asia," found in the King James version, are omitted as part of the American Standard Version because there is not sufficient textual evidence to include them. The location of these seven churches form an irregular circle. Beginning at Ephesus and going north to Smyrna and Pergamum, the traveler would turn southeast to Thyatira, Sardis, Philadelphia, and Laodicea, before completing the circuit by returning westward to Ephesus. Each city will be discussed briefly as it is introduced in chapters two and three.

THE VISION: CHRIST'S MAJESTY AND GLORY
vv. 12-16

v. 12. *"And I turned to see the voice that spake with me. And having turned I saw seven golden candlesticks."* Impelled by natural instinct

CHRIST AMONG THE LAMPSTANDS 1:14

John turned to see the voice (the speaker) that uttered the loud, clear sound. As he turned, a glorious vision burst upon his sight—seven golden candlesticks, or lampstands. Gold was the metal used in the vessels of divine service. The tabernacle in the wilderness had been lighted by a single stand of seven lamps located on the south side of the holy place. Solomon's temple multiplied this number by ten, five on one side and five on the other before the Holy of Holies. In John's vision there are seven stands; each light is an individual pedestal. Whereas there was formerly one lampstand with seven lamps standing on a common base confined to one location, there are now seven separate stands suggesting the independence of each stand or church, separated by distance but bound together by a common faith and Head. The unity of the church is "in Him" who is in the midst of the congregation and who holds the seven stars in His right hand (v. 16). The purpose of the lampstand is to support and provide light; if it gives no light its purpose disappears. In the same way, when a congregation fails in its mission of providing spiritual light, it will be removed.

v. 13. "*And in the midst of the candlesticks one like unto a son of man, clothed with a garment down to the foot, and girt about at the breasts with a golden girdle.*" The lampstands formed a circle, with the glorified Christ in the center. The churches are inseparable from their Head; He moves among them as their king and high priest, beholding and knowing every facet of their life and conduct, giving counsel and leadership in time of need and comfort in affliction. He upholds all things and in Him all things adhere (Heb. 1:3; Col. 1:17). He is the controlling force and sustaining power in all congregations. "Clothed with a garment down to the foot, and girt about at the breasts with a golden girdle," are signs of high rank and office, an oriental mark of dignity. In considering the dress of the high priest of the Old Covenant (Exod. 28:39), one is unable to find indication of priestliness in the dress described here. The seven angels of 15:6 are similarly arrayed, indicating the high rank of their position.

v. 14. "*And his head and his hair were white as white wool, white as snow; and his eyes were as a flame of fire.*" One thinks immediately of Daniel's description of the Ancient of Days, but there is a significant difference. In Daniel's vision the Ancient of Days is described as having raiment "white as snow, and the hair of His head like pure wool"

(Dan. 7:9); whereas in this passage the glorified Christ is portrayed as having His head and hair as white as wool or snow. Since the wool is described by John as white, the apostle relates the one described here to the Ancient of Days. The white wool signifies the purity and holiness with which the Lord's head is crowned, and does not necessarily indicate His antiquity or eternity, though this could be a secondary meaning.

"And his eyes were a flame of fire," penetrating and burning deeply into the heart and soul of every congregation and member thereof, discerning the thoughts and intents of each. These eyes can flash with the fire of wrath and righteous indignation as in the days of His flesh (Mark 3:5); but also they can glow with love (Mark 10:21), tender pity, and compassion (Luke 22:61). The fiery eyes may also express the fierce and tireless energy of God.

v. 15. "*And his feet like unto burnished brass, as if it had been refined in a furnace; and his voice as the voice of many waters.*" The word for "burnished brass" (*chalkolibanō*) is used in the New Testament only here and in 2:18. The exact metal is unknown, but it is thought to be a mixture of metals similar to brass or bronze (Swete). Concerning the word itself Swete says, "The expression is due ultimately to Ezekiel 1:7, where the Hebrew is similarly rendered by the LXX." (See also Dan. 10:6). Although the metal may be undetermined, the lesson is clear. When the Lord comes in judgment with feet glowing as though fired in a furnace, aglow as if still in the crucible, He is able to tread under foot and turn to ashes all that His feet touch. The passage is reminiscent of God's promise made to His saints, "and ye shall tread down the wicked; for they shall be ashes under the soles of your feet" (Mal. 4:3).

"And his voice as the voice of many waters," reflects the thought of Ezekiel 1:24; 43:2, and of Daniel 10:6. His voice roars as the voice of ocean breakers exploding upon the rocky shore, with the terror of billows crashing in a storm, or as the thundering cataract of the mighty Niagara as its waters roll relentlessly on—powerful, strong, resolute. This seems to be the meaning here and in 14:2 and 19:6. On the other hand that same voice can be soft and tender, speaking "comfortable words" (Zech. 1:13), even as a mother comforting her little ones (Isa. 66:17); "He will speak peace unto his children" (Ps. 85:8).

v. 16. "*And he had in his right hand seven stars: and out of his mouth proceeded a sharp two-edged sword: and his countenance was as the sun shineth in his strength.*" The right hand suggests majestic power and strength (Ps. 110:1; Heb. 1:3, 4). These stars are as jewels strung together, lying across His hand (for a discussion of the symbolic meaning of stars see v. 20). Whatever the stars symbolize, they are under His protection and control. "And out of his mouth proceeded a sharp two-edged sword." The *rhomphaia*, said to have been of Thracian origin, was longer and heavier than the *machaira*, the short sword generally carried by Roman soldiers. Outside the Revelation *rhomphaia* occurs only once (Luke 2:35), where the word is used metaphorically as an instrument of anguish. In Revelation it is always used figuratively. It occurs twice in judgment against the church (2:12, 16), and twice in judgment against the world (19:15, 21). Once it refers to the slaughtered saints, slain by their enemies with such a sword (6:8). The sharp "two-edged sword" finds its equivalent in "the rod of his mouth" and "breath of his lips" in Isaiah (11:4); but it is not the word of the gospel inviting men to salvation, although the total word is spoken of as a two-edged sword that judges, discerns, and convicts (Heb. 4:12). In the passage before us the "two-edged sword" out of His mouth indicates the Lord's readiness to judge and do battle, to declare and wage war.

Opsis, translated "countenance," is used only by John: in this instance, and twice in the Gospel where it is translated "appearance" (7:24) and "face" (11:44). Here it may refer to His total appearance (the view held by Lenski and some commentators) or his face only (held by Moffatt and others). A. & G., thayer, and Vine prefer "countenance." Swete sees in the description the glory of the ascended Christ anticipated in the transfiguration, where "his face did shine as the sun" (Matt. 17:2). In either case, whether the word refers to His face or His whole appearance, its brilliance was as the sun, not hidden by the slightest cloud, but shining in all its brightness and splendor, revealing the effulgence of the divine light and glory.

John had said of Him in His earthly appearing, "In him was life; and the life was the light of men. And the light shineth in the darkness; and the darkness apprehended [or overcame] it not" (John 1:4-5). As the source of life and light, He now reigns in the totality of Godhood, providing the light of life in its fullness. He is now before us as the glorified Christ; a priest and king, absolute in holiness, His eyes penetrating to the most remote recesses of the soul, His voice striking terror to His enemies or speaking comfort to His own. With His countenance shining unclouded in the light of His divine being, He is ready to judge and do battle against His enemies as He defends and protects His own.

THE CHARGE TO WRITE
vv. 17-20

v. 17. "And when I saw him, I fell at his feet as one dead. And he laid his right hand upon me, saying, Fear not; I am the first and the last." Overcome by awe and fear at the sight which he beheld in the vision, John collapsed *as* one dead, falling into a swoon. Prophets before him had been overcome by similar experiences. When he beheld the vision of Jehovah's throne, Isaiah cried, "Woe is me! for I am undone" (Isa. 6:5). Ezekiel, seeing the vision of Jehovah's chariot, fell upon his face (Ezek. 1:28). And Daniel, too, at the sight of Gabriel in a vision shown him fell upon his face, "fainted and was sick certain days" (Dan. 8:17, 27). On another occasion he said, "When I heard the voice of the words, then was I fallen into a deep sleep on my face, with my face toward the ground" (10:8-10). Such visions seem to have had a strenuous physical effect on the beholders. But the conquerer of death and the ruler of the universe, in an act and word of tenderness, "laid his right hand upon me saying, Fear not, I am the first and the last." Only His enemies shall experience terror at His presence; wherefore let those who are His have no fear at His appearance but let them find assurance and peace before Him.

The expression "first and last" is found three times in Isaiah and three times in Revelation. In assuring Judah of His absolute Godhood whereby He was able to drive out His enemies and redeem His people, Jehovah had said, "I am the first and the last" (Isa. 41:4; 44:6; 48:12). And now the glorified Christ uses the same expression of Himself three times, thereby identifying Himself with the power and everlastingness of the eternal God (1:17; 2:8; 22:13).

v. 18. "And the Living one; and I was dead, and behold, I am alive for evermore, and I have the keys of death and of Hades." "And the Living one," continues the thought of verse 17. Jesus here appropriates to Himself another divine title. In the Old Covenant "the living God" and "Jehovah liveth" occur repeatedly to describe the Supreme One who lifts His hand and says, "I live forever" (Deut. 32:40). Oaths were taken before Him as the people would swear, "as Jehovah liveth" (Jer. 5:2; cf. Matt. 26:63). Likewise in the New Testament the Father is "the living God" (e.g. Matt. 16:16), who is not the God of the dead, but of the living (Luke 20:38). Jesus identified Himself as being "the life" (John 14:6), having this same life in Himself (John 5:26), and John claimed that this life in Him is the light of men (John 1:4).

"And I was dead, and behold, I am alive for evermore." From the day He came into the world death had ever been before Him, and it had been especially foreshadowed by His baptism, which in fulfilling all righteousness would ultimately lead to the cross. Now that He had been once offered in death, and had proved His claim to be "the life" by His resurrection from the dead, death no more had dominion over Him (Rom. 6:9). He is now alive, to die no more; for it is appointed unto men only once to die (Heb. 9:26-27), and this He had done.

The word *key* or *keys* is never used literally in the New Testament but is always used figuratively or symbolically, as "the keys of the kingdom of heaven" (Matt. 16:19) or the "key of knowledge" (Luke 11:52). It is used four times in the Revelation, twice of Christ (1:18; 3:7), and twice of angels who have the key of the abyss (9:1; 20:1). The "key" or "keys" as used in the New Testament implies power and authority, either inherent or delegated by one to another. Each time a key is claimed or used, it implies the exercise of power from without, or which may be used to open from the outside. In this instance "keys" is plural, indicating His power over both death and Hades. *Hades* is the equivalent of the Hebrew *Sheol*. The two words are used in the two testaments to designate the abode of the dead; literally, Hades means "the unseen." The ASV transliterates the word "Hades," reserving the word "hell" (*Gehenna*) for the state or place of the wicked beyond the judgment. The KJV use of "hell" for both *Hades* and *Gehenna* has been confusing. Death claims the body, which returns to the dust; and Hades claims the spirit, which, after death, is in the realm of the unseen. The two, death and Hades, are joined together in 6:8, where

Hades is personified as following death; both give up the dead at Christ's appearing, and both are cast into the lake of fire at the judgment (20:13, 14; see comments, 6:8). Jesus here claims the power over both; when He shall speak the word, both death and the unseen realm will give up their prisoners (John 5:28–29; for a discussion of Satan's defeat by Christ see comments under 12:6–12.)

v. 19. *"Write therefore the things which thou sawest, and the things which are, and the things which shall come to pass hereafter."* Although there may be a question who the speaker is in verse 11, there is no question who speaks here: It is "the first and the last, and the Living one," the glorified Christ. What is said in verse 11 is here reinforced by the authority of Him who conquered death and now rules. "The things which thou sawest" would be the things which John had seen to this point. "And the things which are," points to the conditions and state of the churches (chaps. 2, 3); and "the things which shall come to pass hereafter," looks to that which would follow these conditions (chaps. 4ff.). However, this interpretation cannot be held too strictly, for the things revealed in the seven letters blend into and also point to things which were to come. John was to write what he had seen, what presently was, and what would come to pass.

v. 20. *"The mystery of the seven stars which thou sawest in my right hand, and the seven golden candlesticks. The seven stars are the angels of the seven churches: and the seven candlesticks are seven churches."* The writer returns to what had been introduced in verses 12 and 16. "Mystery (*musterion*) stands for rites and truth which must be closely guarded by those who possess them" (Hastings, IV, p. 49); "primarily that which is known to the initiated" (Vine). In the New Testament the word *mystery* describes the purpose and plan of God for human redemption, formulated in His own mind after the counsel of His will, closely guarded by Himself and neither known nor understood by man until revealed and made known by the Lord. The word is used once by Jesus concerning the kingdom (Matt. 13:11; Mark 4:11; Luke 8:10), and twenty times by Paul, especially in Romans, I Corinthians, Ephesians, and Colossians. The apostle to the Gentiles used the word to teach that the purpose of God, unknown by man until it was fulfilled in Christ and the Church, was now revealed by the Holy Spirit through the apostles and prophets, God's specially selected agents. John uses the word four times: once in this passage referring to the stars in His right hand and the lampstands, once referring to the "Mystery of God, according to the glad tidings which he declared to his servants the prophets" (10:7), and twice of the harlot and the beast who carried her (17:5, 7). The word does not imply the idea of "the mysterious," that which cannot be understood by man, but refers to that which can be understood only when the meaning is revealed to the initiated by the Holy Spirit through the apostles and prophets. John and those to whom he was writing were about to be initiated into an understanding of something that otherwise they could not know.[2]

Notwithstanding the fact that Jesus here reveals something—makes known a mystery—great diversity of opinion exists as to who or what the seven angels are. The word *astēr* (star) is used both literally and figuratively the ten times it occurs in the rest of the New Testament. In Revelation it is used symbolically each time it appears. A kindred word, *astron*, found four times in the New Testament, is never used by John. A brief look at angels generally may help our understanding of angels as symbolized by the stars. In the Old Covenant, Haggai speaks of himself as Jehovah's "messenger" (Heb., *angel*, Hag. 1:13); Malachi speaks of the priest as "the messenger [Heb., *angel*] of Jehovah" (Mal. 2:7), and of the forerunner of the Messiah, John the Baptist, as the Lord's "messenger" (*angel*, Mal. 3:1; cf. Matt. 11:10). In these instances the word is used to describe men. In the Book of Daniel both the Persians and the Jews had their "prince," the Jewish prince being Michael, an angel (Dan. 10:13, 21; cf. Jude 9). The writer of Hebrews says the Lord makes His angels "winds" and "his ministers a flame of fire" (Heb. 1:6f.), and that in their nature they are "ministering spirits" (Heb. 1:14). In the Gospels, Acts, and Epistles there are angels of the Lord (heavenly), angels of the devil, and human messengers, who are servants either of God or of Satan. In Revelation "angel" or "angels" is used seventy-six times: it refers to heavenly servants of the Lord who minister to Him (sixty-two times), angels of the church (eight times),

---

[2]For a discussion of the origin of *musterion* and its Hebrew use in the LXX, and of the numerous mystery religions among the heathen, see Hastings *Dictionary of the New Testament* IV, p. 49-62.

Michael and his angels (once), the dragon and his angels (once), the angel of the bottomless pit (once), the waters (once), fire (once), and winds (once).

At this point our concern is to identify the angels of the churches. Various explanations have been offered, several of which are here summarized: The angels are (1) men sent to John to inquire of his state (Scofield); (2) angels who stand for and are responsible for the church's spiritual state (Mauro, Moffatt); (3) chief pastor, bishop, or the entire eldership of each church (Barnes, Ellicott, Hendriksen, Hinds, Lenski, Summer, Tenney, Trench); (4) powers, character, the history and life of the church (Ramsay); (5) the heavenly counterpart of the churches, the spiritual counterpart of human individuals (Alford, Caird); (6) symbolic representation in which the *active* (as distinguished from the passive) life of the church finds expression (Milligan, Roberson); (7) the spiritual character, inward state or prevailing spirit, of the church itself (Barclay, Erdman, Pieters, Plummer, Swete, Wallace). This last has stronger supporting evidence. Since the lampstands are the churches—the supporters of the light—viewed externally, the stars may well represent the inward life or spirit of the congregations addressed by Jesus. This position seems to be confirmed by the letters themselves; Jesus addresses each letter to "the angel of the church ... ," and concludes with the appeal, "He that hath an ear, let him hear what the Spirit saith to the churches." Whoever is addressed is to hear; the angels are addressed; the churches are to hear. It follows that the angels are that part of the church addressed which is to hear; this would be the spirit or active life of the churches.

CHAPTER 2

Letters to the Churches

INTRODUCTION TO THE LETTERS

In reading the letters to the seven churches one is impressed with the total absence of any collective organization of the congregations. There is no form of hierarchial oversight, either by an individual or a college of individuals. Each congregation is a separate unit completely independent of all the others. There is no intimation of congregational fellowship or of instruction for one church to withdraw from another because of immoral conditions; neither is there any instruction to faithful individuals to withdraw themselves from unfaithful members and form a new congregation. The command from the Lord is to change the sinful condition before a little leaven leavens the whole lump (1 Cor. 5:6) and the lampstand is removed. The time may have come when the faithful had to withdraw themselves and begin anew, but concerning this point the text is silent. Christ is the Head; He addresses each church individually. They were bound together by a common faith, spiritual life, and goal, and not by an ecumenical union or by an ecclesiastical hierarchy. Each church was to read what was said to the others, and each hearer was to take heed to the total that was said. The principle which regulated one regulated all.

From the internal evidence of the letters there appears to have been five distinctive threats to the spiritual life of the churches in Asia: (1) Paganism in general and emperor worship in particular; (2) Jewish harassment; (3) the temptation of materialism and lawlessness under the form of the doctrine of the Nicolaitans, Balaam, and Jezebel, any of which would lead to compromise; (4) loss of zeal or love—spiritual weariness; and (5) lukewarmness, indifference, or indecision. Succumbing to any one of these would be fatal to the spiritual life of the churches and would extinguish the light supported by the lampstand.

In all seven letters, there are three expressions which challenge attention. (1) "I know"... "thy works" (Ephesus, Thyatira, Sardis

Philadelphia, Laodicea), "thy tribulation" (Smyrna), "where thou dwellest" (Pergamum). The variations are due to differing circumstances. The One in their midst knows all about each church and each one that makes up the church; nothing is hidden from His eyes, "but all things are naked and laid open before the eyes of him with whom we have to do" (Heb. 4:13). Whether it be works, tribulation, or extremely trying surroundings that test the faith of His saints, He knows! (2) "He that overcometh" is laid down in each letter as the basis of reward. *Nikaō*, to overcome or be victorious, is a favorite word with John. Of the twenty-eight times the word occurs in the New Testament, it is used twenty-four times by John: once in the Gospel when Jesus said He had overcome the world (John 16:33), six times in I John, referring to the saints overcoming, and seventeen times in Revelation. In this letter he uses "overcome" as the basis of the Christian's reward, of Christ's overcoming and of Christians' overcoming by Him, and of the beast's overcoming the saints (two times, 11:7; 13:7). The saints overcome by Christ's blood, by faithfulness to their own testimony, and by loving not their life even unto death (12:11); he who overcomes inherits the glory of heaven (21:7). But the fearful— cowards who yield under pressure—will have their part in the lake of fire (21:8). (3) A third phrase found in each of the seven letters is, "He that hath an ear, let him hear what the Spirit saith to the churches." This gives emphasis to the universal application of the message. (4) A fourth expression found in all but the letter to Smyrna is "I come."

A careful analysis of the letters leads to the conclusion that all conditions ever to be found in a congregation of the Lord's church at any time in history may be found, at least in principle, in one or more of these seven churches. This makes the letters practical and worthy of study for all time.

It is interesting and worthwhile to note that each church took on characteristics of the city in which it was located, a tendency of religious bodies and congregations since that time. The early church gradually imbibed the spirit of Rome and slowly patterned its organization after that of the empire. This spirit and organization is clearly visible in the Roman Catholic church. National influence is also detected in the Lutheran and Calvinist churches that originated in medieval Europe. America gave birth to a new spirit in religion, a more independent search for truth and a disposition to debate principles considered vital. But as the American spirit has changed in its political ideals and social views, a parallel change can be detected in American religious bodies. Social work and emphasis has come to dominate American churches, while attention to doctrine and conviction on matters of faith has waned. A general breakdown in national morals is reflected in churches everywhere. The tendencies and weaknesses observed and condemned in the early church are being repeated today, and the Revelation should serve as a warning to the church today against conforming to the world.

A general pattern is followed in each of the letters: (1) The letter begins with a salutation to the particular church addressed. (2) The salutation is followed by a self-designation of the divine author in which He uses one or more of the descriptions found in chapter one (there is an exception, however: the self-description to the church at Philadelphia is not found in chapter one). Altogether these descriptions make up a total picture of the speaker, just as the description of the seven churches reveals a complete concept of the church. (3) The Lord praises what can be commended in the particular church addressed; only the church at Laodicea has nothing to approve. (4) The speaker condemns what is wrong or contrary to His standard for the church. Two churches, Smyrna and Philadelphia, have nothing to condemn. The remaining four, Ephesus, Pergamum, Thyatira, and Sardis, contain a mixture of the commendable and the condemnable. (5) Warnings and threats follow. (6) The speaker gives exhortations to faithfulness and (7) promises of blessings or rewards. This outline is not always followed absolutely, but it covers the general pattern.

EPHESUS
vv. 1-7

v. 1. "To the angel of the church in Ephesus write: These things saith he that holdeth the seven stars in his right hand, he that walketh in the midst of the seven golden candlesticks." For "angel of the church," see comments, 1:20. Ephesus was located in west Asia, near the sea, at the mouth of the Cayster River. Though not the capital, it was the chief city of the province. River silt has so filled the ancient harbor that the ruins of the city are now four to six miles inland.

Ephesus derived its greatness from two sources, commercial trade and religion. It was the chief commercial city of the province, and the center of the mother goddess worship of western Asia. The goddess was known to the Greeks as Artemis and to the Romans as Diana. Ephesus boasted a theater that could accommodate 24,500 persons, and the great temple to Diana, which was one of the seven wonders of the ancient world. After years of archeological research the ruins of the temple were discovered in 1877 by J. T. Wood. The platform on which the temple stood was 418 by 239 feet, and the temple itself was 342 by 163 feet and had over one hundred columns supporting its roof (Kraeling, p. 447).

On his third preaching tour Paul spent between two and three years in the city laboring night and day to establish the church there (Acts 20:31). Demetrius the silversmith testified to the influence of Paul's preaching when he said that it was felt throughout almost all Asia (Acts 19:26). The churches in Colosse, Hierapolis and Laodicea were probably the fruit of his work in Ephesus. Paul left Timothy in that city on two occasions to correct certain false teachers (I Tim. 1:3f.). Tradition says that after Paul's death the city became the home of John for many years. Paul's letter to the Ephesians commends the faith and love of the saints there, and generally Jesus' letter to the church at Ephesus is laudatory. The church was commended for its sound orthodox faith and works; its one criticism was of a waning love. That love, however, could be revived; it was not dead! The special letter was a part of the whole book (1:11) and was to have been read by all. "These things saith he that holdeth the seven stars in his right hand, he that walketh in the midst of the seven golden candlesticks." This self-designation of the Lord is from 1:12, 16, 20. His right hand which holds the stars indicates His power to determine the destiny of each; "in the midst" portrays His presence among all the churches.

v. 2. "*I know thy works, and thy toil and patience, and that thou canst not bear evil men, and didst try them that call themselves apostles, and they are not, and didst find them false.*" "I know," from *oida*, to have fullness of knowledge, to know perfectly, is found in the seven letters. There follows a list of seven commendable qualities of the church at Ephesus, all fully known to the Lord; nothing is hidden. "Thy works" is said of five of the churches. Works may be either good or bad; here they appear to be good. "And thy toil and patience"; toil, indicating strenuous or wearying labor, is accompanied by patient enduring under such trying circumstances. Three times Paul connects toil with "travail," thereby indicating painful effort (II Cor. 11:27; I Thess. 2:9; II Thess. 3:8). Strenuous painful toil endured with patient steadfastness brings forth commendation and praise from the Head and king. "And that thou canst not bear evil men," that is, they could not bear in their midst the company of evil men who were morally or ethically base in their character. This attitude toward evil men is commendable; if they will not be transformed, let them be transferred. "And didst try them that call themselves apostles, and they are not, and didst find them false." A city of such prominence as Ephesus, located on a world thoroughfare, was bound to get its share of false teachers, even men claiming to be apostles. In an age when we pride ourselves in tolerance and compromise, this attitude might appear bigoted and intolerant. Bigoted, no; intolerant, yes, but an intolerance commended by the Lord. Churches would do well today to follow such a course with their intellectually oriented teachers and leaders who pervert truth and make boastful claims for their own human wisdom. John approved the practice of proving all spirits (I John 4:1). The test of an apostle would be his ability or inability to perform miracles—these which were the credentials of apostleship (II Cor. 12:12).

v. 3. *"And thou hast patience and didst bear for my name's sake, and hast not grown weary."* "And thou hast patience," commended above (v. 2), means that they persevered under tests and trials, remained steadfast under the strain and stress of labor for the Lord, and were unwavering in their vigorous opposition to false teachers. These manifold trials and tests prove faith which develops steadfastness, and steadfastness leads to perfection and completeness (James 1:2-4). "And didst bear for my name's sake." Enduring for His name's sake and for His glory makes bearing of the trials and tests of faith commendable. It was not a self-serving patience which sought the glory of men. "And has not grown weary." A trait of human nature is the tendency to grow faint under hard work and pressures from without. How often in the advancing years of life do men and women who formerly were diligent in serving the Lord retire from the Lord's work with the plea, "I carried the load in my younger years; I am now passing the work on to those in the vigor and strength of that age." But is there ever a time to grow weary, to retire and let others bear the brunt of battle and carry the load that should be mine? No, never!

v. 4. "But I have this against thee, that thou didst leave thy first love." In spite of the seven commendations enumerated above, there is one thing that had to be corrected; they must revive the first love which they had left. Though the Lord had only one criticism, any point short of the perfection demanded by God of His people must be overcome and corrected. Love was still there, as demonstrated in the things commended; but the "first love" was lacking. We are not told specifically what that first love was. Alford thinks it is as the conjugal love of the newly married bride; but there is a question as to how that love had been expressed. Was it the love demonstrated in the burning of books of magic and mighty growth of the Word of the Lord (Acts 19:19-20)? Was it love such as had been manifested toward Paul in their sorrow at his leaving them (Acts 20:36-38)? Or was it the love shown one for another in the early years of the church, commended in his letter to them (Eph. 1:15)? It may have been one or a combination of all these. Perhaps this loss of an early fiery devotion can be accounted for by the fact that the congregation was now in the second or third generation of its existence. This is always a dangerous period in the life of a church. At such a point the youthful fire of discovery and the enthusiasm of a glorious anticipation of future hopes too often begin to diminish.

v. 5. "Remember therefore whence thou art fallen, and repent and do the first works; or else I come to thee, and will move thy candlestick out of its place, except thou repent." "Remember therefore whence thou art fallen"—the point at which they had left their first love. That first love could yet be revived and experienced as at the first, if they would recognize what had happened. It is the same with congregations today. Repentance is a change of mind, or will when the human will submits to the will of God. There comes a time in the life of every church when it should take a fresh inventory of its whole life and disposition, reminding itself again of the day when it mounted up with wings as eagles, ran without weariness, walked without fainting, and renewed its strength in the Lord (Isa. 40:31). This change of will demands action: "And *do* the first works." The way to revive love is by action, obeying God in love.

Next comes the warning, "or else I come unto thee and remove thy candlestick out of its place, except thou repent." This coming against the church would not be in sudden wrath; it would be removal (*kineō*) of the lampstand in which the church would be discontinued (Vine). The lampstand's purpose or place was to uphold and dispense light, but without the motivation of true love it fails in its purpose and therefore no longer has a right to exist. A demand for repentance is repeated; the verdict is, "Repent or be removed." Ramsay, however, interprets the removing to express a change in local position. The cooling of their enthusiasm must be corrected; but if it cannot be achieved among themselves, the church will be removed to another place (*Letters to the Seven Churches*, p. 243-44). There is insufficient evidence to support this view.

v. 6. "*But this thou hast, that thou hatest the works of the Nicolaitans, which I also hate.*" The criticism that the church has left its first love is followed by further commendation. "But [which complements the 'but' of v. 4] this thou hast, that thou hatest the works of the Nicolaitans, which I also hate." At times it is difficult for us to separate the persons committing works or deeds from the deeds themselves. Both the church and the Lord hate the works, the practices of the Nicolaitans, *not* the Nicolaitans. Under the Old covenant, Jehovah, who loved righteousness, expressed Himself as hating the abominations and memorials to false gods among the heathen (Deut. 12:31; 16:22), all workers of iniquity (Ps. 5:5; Prov. 6:16-19), the wicked lovers of violence (Ps. 11:15), the empty feasts of His own people (Isa. 1:14; Amos 5:21), the mistreatment of one's neighbor, and the taking of false oaths (Zech. 8:17). Jehovah anointed His Messiah—the Christ—because He, too, loved righteousness and hated iniquity (Ps. 45:7; Heb. 1:9). His people must follow this divine pattern, for with the same intensity that one loves he also hates. The child of God who does not hate wickedness does not love righteousness, however strongly he may boast of his love.

Little is known about the Nicolaitans. Several traditions exist and numerous theories have been suggested regarding their origin and doctrines, but these have not been established factually. The

Nicolaitans were probably a sect of the Gnostics, but history is silent as to their actual origin, peculiar doctrines, and ultimate fate after the Revelation. We do know that they flourished at Ephesus and Pergamum.

v. 7. *"He that hath an ear let him hear what the Spirit saith to the churches. To him that overcometh, to him will I give to eat of the tree of life, which is in the Paradise of God."* This command to hear is repeated in each of the seven letters. The charge is reminiscent of Jesus' words, "He that hath ears to hear, let him hear," repeated after explaining that John the Baptist was Elijah (Matt. 11:15), and after relating the parable of the sower (Matt. 13:9; Mark 4:9; Luke 8:8), and following the interpretation of the parable of the tares (Matt. 13:43), and after the parable of the lamps (Mark 4:23), and after stating the exacting demands of discipleship (Luke 14:35). Hearing necessitates an ear for spiritual truths; some have such an ear (Matt. 13:16), whereas others' ears have grown dull (Matt. 13:15). Hearing is personal and individual, involving an acceptance of and compliance with that which is said. Each is to hear what the Spirit said to all the churches. Though Christ is the speaker, the Spirit in John reveals and records the message.

"To him that overcometh" is the third saying found in the seven letters (see Introduction to the Letters, pp. 117f.). In the first three letters this exhortation follows "hath an ear to hear," and in the last four it precedes the phrase. "To him will I give to eat of the tree of life, which is in the Paradise of God," is a reward promised to the overcomer, the conquerer. What man lost by sin in the Garden of Eden, where apparently the fruit of the tree of life signified fullness of life and immunity to death (Gen. 3:12-24), is now restored in Christ to him that overcomes sin, who is to enjoy all the fullness of life implied by the expression (Rev. 22:2). The word "paradise" is thought to be of Persian origin, denoting the parks of Persian kings and nobles. The word is found a number of times in the Septuagint, but only three times in our English translations. Jesus used it of that place or realm into which He and one of the malefactors on the cross would be after death (Luke 23:43); Paul identified it as "the third heaven" unto which he was caught up and where he heard unspeakable words not lawful for him to utter (II Cor. 12:2, 4). Here the Spirit says it is the place of the tree of life, which is the full possession of the victorious saints in their final redeemed state (Rev. 22:2). From this it follows that Paradise is the garden of life where the redeemed will join God to enjoy the fullness of eternal life and glory for ever.

SMYRNA
vv. 8-11

v. 8. "And to the angel of the church in Smyrna write: These things saith the first and the last, who was dead, and lived again." Smyrna was located between thirty-five and forty miles north of Ephesus on a rather long gulf possessing two excellent harbors, one small and the other much larger. It was second only to Ephesus in exports, and like its sister city, was the terminus of a road from the east. Noted especially for its beauty, the city was surrounded by rolling hills and groves of trees, and contained well-paved streets leading past stately buildings and temples. Its acropolis on Mount Pagas gave the appearance of a crown, which became the symbol of the city. Smyrna allied herself to Rome early in the period of Roman conquest, and as a result enjoyed an almost unbroken career of prosperity. As an expression of her fidelity to Rome, the city erected a shrine to Roma, the Roman goddess, as early as 195 B.C.; and under the reign of Tiberius (A.D. 14-37) Smyrna was chosen as the site for a temple to Tiberius. The city claimed to be the first city in Asia: first in beauty, first in literature, first in loyalty to Rome. The origin of the church in this city is unknown; this is the only mention of the city or church in the New Testament (1:11; 2:8).

Because Smyrna claimed to be first and would brook no rival, Jesus introduces Himself with the designation, "These things saith the first and the last, who was [became] dead, and lived again" (cf. 1:17f.). His primacy must be universally recognized; Smyrna would have to revise all her ambitious claims. The Lord's victory over death and His present position should inspire confidence within a church that was about to suffer imprisonment and tribulation even unto death.

v. 9. "I know thy tribulation, and thy poverty (but thou art rich), and the blasphemy of them that say they are Jews, and they are not, but are a synagogue of Satan." As the Lord knew the works of the church at Ephesus, so also He knows the crushing and grinding lot of the church in Smyrna; nothing is concealed from His sight. And having suffered as they are beginning to suffer and will suffer, even unto death, He can now give them compassion and can succor them in these trials (Heb. 2:18; 4:15). The poverty of these commendable saints, against whom the Lord brought no criticism, was no doubt from two sources: (1) they came from the poorer class, and (2) their loyalty to Christ would bring them into direct conflict with the paganism of this heathen city. But their poverty was offset by a far greater wealth than silver and gold; they were rich in faith and favor with God and in all the attendant blessings of glory that belong to the heavenly citizenship. Their treasure was in heaven (Matt. 6:20), which is the true riches of life (Luke 16:11) that cannot be touched by the world.

Added to the tribulation and earthly poverty of this church was the blasphemy and strong opposition from the Jews. Blasphemy is "any contumelious speech, reviling, calumniating, railing" (Vine). The Jews in the flesh had rejected the Christ and His teaching while He was on earth and crucified Him, and had driven many saints out of Jerusalem. They had persecuted His apostle to the Gentiles from city to city and even now in Smyrna were blaspheming His name and His saints and were stirring up the Romans against them. Jesus had charged those Jews who would seek to kill Him as being children of the devil (John 8:44); and now these kinsmen in Asia were following the same pattern: they are a synagogue belonging to Satan. The true Jews, God's Israel, are those who are circumcised in heart (Rom. 2:28-29), who worship by the Spirit of God and glory in Christ Jesus (Phil. 3:3). These Asian Jews were everything but this. The word "synagogue" belonged to the Jews, and is used in the New Testament of their meeting place (with one special exception when Luke speaks of the breaking up of the synagogue or assembly, Acts 13:43). In contrast, the word "church" belonged to the Christians. Only once is "synagogue" used of Christians, and in that instance it refers to their meeting place and not to them as a body of God's people (James 2:2). The blasphemy, reviling, and sneering at the Christians by the Jews was a work of Satan through his emissaries.

v. 10. *"Fear not the things which thou art about to suffer: behold, the devil is about to cast some of you into prison, that ye may be tried;*

and ye shall have tribulation ten days. Be thou faithful unto death and I will give thee the crown of life." The saints are urged to allay their fears and not to retreat from the tribulation, the blasphemy of the Jews, and the poverty being brought upon them. For He who became dead is now alive and able to give victory over every obstacle, even death. "About to suffer" indicates that the church was just entering into a long period of Roman persecution, which was being introduced by Domitian and would extend to the days of Constantine (A.D. 313). The tribulation would be severe, but the Christians at Smyrna are admonished not to fear what would be imposed upon them. As Lenski observed, it is easy to write about such matters while sitting in a pleasant study, surrounded by modern comforts and favorable circumstances of life, but it would be quite another thing to practice this admonition in the face of suffering and the threat of death.

"*Behold, the devil is about to cast some of you into prison.*" The real enemy, the devil, accuses the brethren (12:9–10), sifts them as wheat (Luke 22:31), oppresses by physical suffering (Acts 10:38), and as a roaring lion seeks whom he may devour (I Peter 5:8). He is the archenemy of God and man, but is destined ultimately to be cast into the lake of fire (20:10). Through certain Jews he would rouse the pagan populace to cast the saints into prison. "Prison" here is best understood as a general word for arrest, trial, fine, exile, or death, whatever should be their lot. "That ye may be tried," does not refer to a legal trial, but either to the testing of their faith to the fullest extent or to the tempting by Satan to sin by denying the Lord under test. Although the general use of the word used here (*peirazō*), test or try, is most often used of tempting to sin, there are important exceptions (John 6:6; Acts 16:7 [assayed]; II Cor. 13:5; Heb. 11:17, 37; Rev. 2:2; 3:10). The word generally used for "try" or "test" is *peirasmos*. Both are used in 3:10. Scholars differ over which way the word is used here. The idea of testing of faith is preferable, for when faith is tested the devil's moment to tempt one to deny the Lord is at hand.

"And ye shall have tribulation ten days" is neither a literal time period nor a reference to ten major persecutions by Roman emperors. Rather, the Lord speaks of a full and complete period, which may be long or short, that would come to an end. "The trial might be prolonged, but it had a limit known to God" (Swete); "a period which can be measured; that is, which comes to an end" (Ramsay, *Letters*, p. 275). "Be thou faithful unto death," is an admonition to hold to the faith and not deny the Lord, even to the point of dying for the faith. The Lord is not saying "until you die," though this is required; but He is saying accept death rather than recant. Modern day Christians may not be called upon to die for the faith, but they must have the spirit of willingness to die.

"And I will give thee the crown of life." A crown of flowers was worn by the pagan worshiper (Ramsay), a crown adorned the patron goddess, as indicated on the coins of the city, and the city had a crown of buildings on the crown-shaped acropolis of Mount Pagos. But all of this would fade away. In contrast, the faithful Christian would be given a crown of life. Paul calls it "an incorruptible crown" (I Cor. 9:25), "the crown of righteousness" (II Tim. 4:8), James, "the crown of life" (James 1:12), and Peter, "the crown of glory that fadeth not away" (I Peter 5:4). The crown here promised by the Savior sums up and includes all of these. In the New Testament two words are used for crown; *stephanos* occurs in all but three references; in these *diadēma* is used of the Dragon, the Beast, and Christ (Rev. 12:3; 13:1; 19:12), symbolizing rule or royalty over a particular realm. The crown (*stephanos*) was worn by athletic and military victors, by the populace during festive seasons, and by the bride on nuptial occasions; it was thus the festive or victory crown. Scholars differ as to whether the crown in this instance is to be considered a diadem, a crown of royalty, or a victory crown. Trench and others believe that it is a royal crown offered by the Lord, since we reign with him. Others believe it is the crown of victory. A study of the word as it is used throughout the New Testament leads to the conclusion that it is the festive crown of victory, given to the saint in honor of his triumph over tribulation and death.

v. 11. *"He that hath an ear, let him hear what the Spirit saith to the churches. He that overcometh shall not be hurt of the second death."* Whatever is expected of and promised to the church in Smyrna applies to all churches then and now. "He that overcometh shall not be hurt of the second death," is a most appropriate promise to the church that is entering into a period of severe tribulation. There are only two alternatives, the crown of life—eternal life—or the second death. Later John specifies the "second death" three times: over the victor it has no power

(20:6); it is defined as the lake of fire (20:14) and the destiny of the wicked (21:8). It is the equivalent of Gehenna fire, used by the Lord in describing the end beyond the judgment of all who live in rebellion against Him and His Father. Compare with verse 7.

PERGAMUM
vv. 12-17

v. 12. "And to the angel of the church in Pergamum write: These things saith he that hath the sharp two-edged sword." Pergamum was built on a large conical hill overlooking a broad and fertile valley about thirty miles north of Smyrna, and fifteen miles inland from the sea. In 190 B.C., with Roman aid the Pergamenians expelled Antiochus III, king of Syria, from the city; at his death, in 133 B.C., king Attalus III bequeathed Pergamum and his entire kingdom to the Romans. Pergamum became the royal city of Asia and served as the political capital of the province for more than two centuries. Beautiful state buildings adorned the acropolis of Pergamum, a city which boasted a library of two hundred thousand volumes, the largest outside of Alexandria in Egypt. The city gave its name to "parchment" (*pergamena*), a writing material made from skins of various animals and developed by the Pergamenians when they could no longer secure papyrus from Egypt. As early as 29 B.C. a temple dedicated to Roma and Augustus was erected in the city as the first and, for a time, the only temple of the imperial cult in all Asia. It was followed by a second temple to Trajan and a third to Severus. The city had the distinction of being three times named temple-warden of the state religion, before the honor was transferred to Ephesus. Besides the imperial cult there were four patron deities of the city, Zeus and Athena of Greek origin and character, and Dionysus and Aesculapius (sometimes spelled Asclapius), both of Asian origin. Aesculapius, honored as the god of medicine and healing, was worshiped under the emblem of a serpent and had a large temple outside the city dedicated to his honor. A part of the extensive ruins shown the traveler today is referred to as "the hospital."

Christianity in Pergamum was confronted with three distinct types of pagan religion: popular Asiatic, cultured Greek, and official Roman. Official Roman or emperor worship was far more political than religious, and in the time of Domitian it was made a test of loyalty to the state (Hastings, IV. p. 167). On "the two-edged sword" see comments on 1:16. The sword, recognized by the Romans as the symbol of authority and judgment, belongs to Christ and not to Rome.

v. 13. "I know where thou dwellest, even where Satan's throne is; and thou holdest fast my name, and didst not deny my faith, even in the days of Antipas my witness, my faithful one, who was killed among you, where Satan dwelleth." As He knows the works of the church in Ephesus and the tribulation of the church in Smyrna, so the Lord knows the oppressive conditions under which the church in Pergamum has to live and the obstacles it faces. He encourages each to be of good cheer, for He, not Rome, wields the sword. The significance of "Satan's throne" and its location in Pergamum is better understood when one considers that it was the political capital of the province and the seat of pagan deities and emperor worship. All these elements combined to produce a heavy and oppressive Satanic atmosphere deserving of the title which the Lord bestows upon it. It is uncertain whether the designation was derived from its being the political capital and the center of emperor worship, or from the fanatical worship of Aesculapius, or the martyrdom of Antipas, or a combination of all these. Probably a combination of all these was the real cause, with emperor worship being predominant. In Smyrna persecution came chiefly from the Jews, but here it was prompted by an imperial and pagan source.

"And thou holdest fast my name, and didst not deny my faith," is a strong commendation to a church amidst such surroundings, for opposition seems to surround His name. The Christians had been willing to suffer for it and had held fast the name "Lord Christ," refusing to confess "Lord Caesar," even at the threat of death. The name stands for all that Jesus is: His deity, authority, and Lordship over God's entire universe. "My faith" would be the sum of doctrine which He revealed, "the faith once for all delivered" (Jude 3; cf. Col. 1:22f.). The church did not deny the name or faith of Jesus, "Even in the days of Antipas, my witness, my faithful one, who was killed among you, where Satan dwelleth." Nothing more is known of Antipas, this beloved martyr of the Lord, than what is said here. He had been faithful to what he had seen and heard about Christ Jesus and true to the name and to the faith. It is doubtful that he was the only one who had suffered death for the faith at this time, for "even in the days" looks back to a period prior to John's writing. He is likely the first among a list of martyrs who had suffered for the name. "Among you" suggests that he was a member of the congregation there, though it is possible that he lived elsewhere and was brought to Pergamum for trial where he was readily accepted by the Pergamum church which stood by him. His death was probably at the hands of the magistrates, but it could have been by a lawless mob, because there was popular opposition to Christians and hatred for the name. "Where Satan dwelleth" would be a most appropriate expression for the place of such strong opposition.

v. 14. *"But I have a few things against thee, because thou hast there some that hold the teaching of Balaam who taught Balak to cast a stumblingblock before the children of Israel, to eat things sacrificed to idols, and to commit fornication."* "But I have a few things against thee" introduces that which is condemned by the Lord. "Few things" stands in opposition to the great commendations. No doubt these whom He is about to introduce are a small minority of the church; but knowing the danger of even a little leaven, this condition cannot be tolerated. "Because thou hast there some that hold the teachings of Balaam, who taught Balak to cast a stumblingblock before the children of Israel, to eat things sacrificed to idols, and to commit fornication." When Israel came to the border of Moab and Balaam found himself unable to curse the people of God for Barak, king of Moab (Num. 23, 24), he counseled Barak to send forth the daughters of Moab and entice the men to join them in their lascivious worship (Num. 31:16). By this means he achieved what he could not otherwise accomplish. Balaam's compromise proved fatal; the doctrine of compromise is one of Satan's most lethal weapons. The teachings of Balaam are summed up under three headings: (1) He taught Balak to cast a stumblingblock before the children of Israel. A "stumblingblock," from *skandalon*, indicates that part of a trap on which the bait is placed, which when disturbed causes the trap to spring, ensnaring the victim. Thus by his advice Balaam set a trap before the children of Israel, causing many to perish. Whether or not they were conscious of it, certain ones in the church at Pergamum were setting a trap that eventually would ensnare the entire church if not corrected. Compromise is always a death-trap to saints in Christ. (2) "To eat things sacrificed to idols" involves not simply eating meat as discussed by Paul (I Cor. 8—10), but actual participation in the idolatrous worship itself, making some compromising excuse for a completely untenable practice. (3) "And to commit fornication," describes what was often a part of the pagan ceremony. Although "fornication" frequently refers to idolatry, here it probably means the act itself.

Those who followed the teachings of Balaam and compromised with idolatry would gain some favor with the pagan society by demonstrating to their heathen neighbors that they were not fanatical extremists. Following the doctrine in practice would be a compromise for hire, gaining some favor or reward from the world, as had Balaam (II Peter 2:15; Jude 6). But it would have been fatal to the church for this to have gone unrebuked and uncorrected. There is no point at which the church can tolerate compromise or wink at sin when the name and faith of the Lord Jesus are involved.

v. 15. "*So hast thou also some that hold the teaching of the Nicolaitans in like manner.*" Though some eminent scholars hold that Balaam and the Nicolaitans are identical, John's introduction of the Nicolaitans with "also" and "in like manner" argues for two separate groups. They may have had much in common, but they appear to have been two distinct parties. There is so little known about the Nicolaitans and their doctrine that it is difficult to conclude anything with certainty. The church at Ephesus hated the Nicolaitans' works; the church at Pergamum had taken a compromising position toward their teaching. Only a few at Pergamum accepted this teaching while, if the followers of Jezebel were of this sect, the church in Thyatira was greatly influenced by it. To accept the teachings of Balaam or the Nicolaitans would be as futile as attempting to serve Christ and pagan Rome at the same time.

v. 16. "*Repent therefore; or else I come to thee quickly, and I will make war against them with the sword of my mouth.*" Jesus cannot tolerate the sin of compromise within His church, therefore the command, "Repent, or else." The command is to the whole church. Those yielding to the seductive teachings of Balaam must repent of the sin itself, while the church must repent of its lax attitude toward the compromising spirit and take a firm stand against it. The church cannot afford to tolerate such a disposition as manifested by these few. A compromising disposition is a weakness of the present generation, and the fruits are seen on every hand. The alternative is not pleasant to anticipate. The swift coming of the Lord will be to make war against the church by executing judgment against the unfaithful, compromising children of God. Such coming had been introduced in 1:8, and the sword in 1:16 and 2:12. As Balaam had been slain by the sword of those whom he sought to curse (Num. 31:8), so these would be executed by Him whom they would make a curse by reducing His teaching to the status of philosophy or carnal religion. The judgment was complete, for neither the Nicolaitans nor the Balaamites left documents or institutions behind.

v. 17. "He that hath an ear, let him hear what the Spirit saith to the churches. To him that overcometh, to him will I give of the hidden manna, and I will give him a white stone, and upon the stone a new name written, which no one knoweth but he that receiveth it." The Lord's "hidden manna" stands in contrast to the things sacrificed to idols (v. 14). In this manna there is an unmistakable allusion to the manna given the children of Israel in the wilderness, a pot of which was to be kept before Jehovah for a memorial throughout their generations (Exod. 16:31, 33; Heb. 9:4). Kept either within or before the ark of the covenant (cf. Exod. 16:33; I Kings 8:9; Heb. 9:4), it was hidden from view. Jesus says He is the true manna from heaven, and to eat of that bread is to live (John 6:33-35, 50-59). It is "hidden" as was Jesus' teaching to the twelve concerning His death and resurrection (Luke 18:34), and as were the things which belong to peace hidden from the eyes of the Jews (Luke 19:42) but were later seen and understood by all who had eyes to see. Likewise the treasures of wisdom are hidden in Jesus (Col. 2:3), but revealed in truth and to be found by those who search for them. Also, our life is "hid with Christ in God" (Col. 3:3), to be made fully known when He shall be manifested (I John 3:2). Even so, the saint who overcomes and eats the true bread, manna hidden from the worldly compromisers, has a taste of the heavenly gift, the good Word of God and the powers of the age to come (Heb. 6:4-5). He thus has a foretaste of the fullness of eternal life which shall be his as he eats of the tree of life in the garden of God (Rev. 22:2).

"And I will give him a white stone, and upon the stone a new name written, which no one knoweth but he that receiveth it." Interpretations and applications of "the stone" are legion. (For various views see Alford, and for a lengthy discussion of the problem see Ramsay, *Seven Letters*, and Trench, *Seven Churches*.) The word "stone" is from *psēphos*, "a small, worn, smooth stone; pebble." It is said that in ancient courts of justice the accused were condemned by black pebbles and acquitted by white (Thayer). The word occurs only twice in the New Testament, here and in Acts 26:10. In the latter passage Paul is recorded as saying, "I gave my vote [literally, my pebble of voting] against them." There is probably some analogy between what Jesus said and a practice of that day understood by the churches addressed, but lost to us.

In Revelation, white is the color of holiness and purity, and is also the heavenly color. It describes the head and hair of Christ (1:14), the garments worn by the elders (4:4), the horse on which Christ goes forth to conquer (6:2), the cloud (14:14), a second horse on which He sits followed by a heavenly army arrayed in white linen riding on white horses (19:11, 14), and the throne of judgment (20:11). Saints walk with Him in white (3:4, 5, 18) and martyrs are arrayed in white (6:11), as are those coming out of the great tribulation (7:9, 13).

The white stone pertains to this heavenly relationship, though the meaning is not clear, unless it indicates total acquittal. The "new name" is known only to him who receives it. One's name stands for all that he is; a new name would indicate all that he is in his new relationship to Christ, as proved by his overcoming to be totally trustworthy. The permanence of this new relationship is preserved by his name being engraved on stone. Only each individual knows who and what he is, whether he is strong or weak, and what he has done, whether good or bad. The new name denotes the totality of this newness and relationship.

THYATIRA
vv. 18–29

v. 18. "And to the angel of the church in Thyatira write: These things saith the Son of God, who hath his eyes like a flame of fire, and his feet are like unto burnished brass." Although not so important as other cities in the province, Thyatira was a wealthy city, located in the northern part of Lydia, near the border of Mysia, on the Lycas River. The city was approximately forty miles southeast of Pergamum, about midway between the two once-royal cities of Pergamum and Sardis. The city had been in Roman hands since 190 B.C., and was included in the province of Asia. No acropolis adorned the city, for it lay in a valley and was surrounded by gently sloping hills. The city had no temple to the emperor. The chief deity of the city was Tyrimnos, who was identified with the Greek sun god Apollo, and in whose honor games were held at various intervals. A goddess of less importance was associated with Tyrimnos in the Thyatiran pantheon. A temple dedicated to Sambethe was also located at Thyatira. At this shrine there was a prophetess who claimed to utter sayings of this deity which were imparted to the worshipers and accepted by them as oracles. This prophetess seems to have had her counterpart in Jezebel of Pergamum.

As an important trade and manufacturing city, Thyatira was noted for its purple dye and dyed garments. Scholars believe the important dye was of a Turkish-red color, made from the madder-root which abounded in the vicinity. The city was also known for its trade-guilds, which were probably the basis of the problems found in this church. Evidence has been found for a number of various guilds; Ramsay lists wool workers, linen workers, makers of outer garments, tanners, leather workers, dyers, bakers, slave dealers, and bronzesmiths (*Seven Letters*, p. 325).

This is the lengthiest of the seven letters, no doubt because of the nature of the problem there. Nothing is known of the origin of the church in Thyatira; it is mentioned only here in Scripture. The earliest contact with anyone from the city is found in Acts 16:11-15. Paul's first convert on European soil was Lydia, a seller of purple of the city of Thyatira, whom he baptized in a river just outside the city at Philippi. It has been conjectured that Lydia returned to her home in Thyatira and became responsible for the church there, but there is no evidence for this conclusion.

The title "Son of God" occurs only here in Revelation; similarly, however, the overcomer is related to God as His son (21:7). This title is a summation of the total description of Jesus in chapter one, to which there may be a reference in 1:6. The other two aspects of His self-designation are from 1:14f. (see comments on this passage). The word *chalkolibanō* (burnished brass), found only here and in 1:15, was no doubt understood and used by the coppersmiths of the city, though its exact meaning is no longer clear. The Son of God's eyes flash with indignation as they penetrate with piercing insight into the corruptness of the prophetess' false teaching; His feet are ready to trample and burn to ashes all who yield to her seductions.

v. 19. "I know thy works, and thy love and faith and ministry and patience, and that thy last works are more than the first." As was said to the church in Ephesus, so here nothing is hidden from Him who walks among the lampstands; all works are known. The words and works of Christ were redemptive (Matt. 11:2-6; John 17:2-4); those of the apostles were evangelistic (Acts 14:26; 15:38). The works of the saints were good deeds for the benefit of others (Acts 9:36, 39; II Tim. 3:17), and their teaching to the end of building the church through works of spiritual ministering (Eph. 4:12). The church's faithfulness in works is known to Jesus.

"And love and faith and ministry and patience." Love is generally given priority in John's writings, though faith (*pistis*, which is not found in his Gospel), is not omitted in Revelation (2:13, 19; 14:12). Paul usually reverses the order, with faith preceding love when the two are used together (Philem. 5 is an exception). Love motivates action in ministering, i.e., in rendering service (John 14:23, 24), whereas faith is the basis of patience, i.e., steadfast endurance under all testing, temptation, and opposition. "And that thy last works are more than the first." Ephesus had let its first love wane and languish while Thyatira had kept its love aflame. This continuously burning flame of love and enduring faith had led to the increase of works. Even today such love and faith will keep a church active in its works for the Lord.

v. 20. "But I have this against thee, that thou sufferest the woman Jezebel, who calleth herself a prophetess; and she teacheth and seduceth my servants to commit fornication, and to eat things sacrificed to idols." What a disappointment, that it was necessary to mar such an excellent commendation with a sharp word of condemnation. The first question confronting us is, Was the "woman Jezebel" an individual, or a name given by the Lord to a segment of the church that tended to lead the whole body astray after idolatry, as did the Jezebel of old? A second question is, Was her teaching identified with the Nicolaitans or Balaam, or was it a third type of error which crept into the churches? In answer to the first question, though either is possible, it is more likely that there was in the church at Thyatira a woman of great leadership ability by whom the people were being greatly influenced. Her prototype for whom she is named was the daughter of Ethbaal, king of the Sidonians, who led her husband Ahab to serve Baal (I Kings 16:31). She cut off the prophets of Jehovah (I Kings 18:4) and encouraged idolatry by feeding the prophets of Baal and the Asherah (I Kings 18:19). Her sins were summed up as "the whoredoms and witchcrafts" of Jezebel (II Kings 9:22).

In answer to the second question, our ignorance of the Nicolaitans makes it difficult to know whether or not she was identified with them. It is probable that the three, Nicolaitans, Balaam, and Jezebel had similar characteristics but with differences that distinguished them as separate parties. A third question may be posed as to what extent she and her followers shared in the commended works (v. 19). No doubt much of the influence of this Jezebel and her followers was derived from sharing in these works. The two women of Thyatira mentioned in New Testament Scripture, Lydia and Jezebel, share some characteristics in common—leadership, good works, and activity—but they are totally different in character.

Where would Jezebel's teaching and practice find a ready response? In this city of guilds, each had its social festivals, embodying strong pagan religious elements. Members of the guilds were probably her most devoted adherents. Wishing to keep his employment or promote his business, the Christian would feel impelled to maintain membership in the guild of his profession. But could he maintain membership in a guild and be true to Christ? It is likely that Jezebel taught a compromising position just here, telling the saints that membership could be maintained while ignoring the religious aspects of such societies and their activities. But the Christian continued to be faced with the immoral associations of their festivals, and there could be no compromise when faith or morals were involved. This became the issue. Followers of Jezebel succumbed to the temptation, yielding to pressures and sinning against the Lord.

Today many Christians are faced with a similar question regarding labor unions. The Christian has to decide whether the association calls upon him to participate in conduct contrary to the teaching and faith of Jesus. If no principle is violated, there is no wrong; if a principle is violated, there can be no compromising of that principle. At this point the Christian may have to choose between his faith and his job, between Christ and Jezebel.

The fornication condemned by the Lord was probably spiritual (idolatry) rather than physical, although it could have been the latter, inasmuch as it often accompanied pagan festivals. The committing of fornication and eating things sacrificed to idols, whether literal or symbolic, sums up the consequence of Jezebel's teaching and influence. The church "suffered" (allowed, permitted, tolerated) her to continue, offering no opposition. This was Jesus' criticism of those who stood aloof from her teaching but said nothing. Not only must one have no fellowship with the unfruitful works of darkness, but he must reprove them (Eph. 5:11).

v. 21. "And I gave her time that she should repent; and she willeth not to repent of her fornication." God's longsuffering in giving her time was now exhausted. Her obstinate resistance even surpassed the flagrancy of the immorality she had introduced and encouraged. Time given to repent, which should be recognized as opportunity for salvation, is too often taken as indifference on God's part. "Because sentence against an evil work is not executed speedily, therefore the heart of the sons of men is fully set in them to do evil" (Eccles. 8:11). To reject God's gracious offer and call to repentance is to despise "the riches of his goodness and forbearance and longsuffering" intended to bring one to repentance (Rom. 2:4). "She willeth not to repent"—she did not want to change. Repentance, a change of mind, is subject to the will of the individual. This Jezebel was not the last to follow such a pattern.

v. 22. "Behold, I cast her into a bed, and them that commit adultery with her into great tribulation, except they repent of her works." The exclamation "behold" arrests attention. With the expiration of God's longsuffering and time for repentance, judgment must follow. In contrast to the luxurious couch of sin on which she had led others to share in her wicked teachings and practice, she would be cast into a bed of pain and affliction which inevitably follows sin. Those who had shared her couch of sin must now share with her the consequences of great tribulation that follows. It is not that she has the bed and they the tribulation, but the bed into which she and they are cast is a bed of great tribulation. However, there is yet opportunity to escape: the averting of the bed of tribulation is conditional, "except they [you] repent of her works." The works had their origin in Jezebel's teaching, but the church had either shared in the teaching or had failed to oppose it; in either case unless they repented, they would share in the inevitable judgment. To cast, from *ballō*, does not indicate violence, but rather "cast... into a bed" refers to one who is forced to lie on a bed of sickness (Matt. 8:14; 9:2-5 et al.).

v. 23. *"And I will kill her children with death; and all the churches shall know that I am he that searcheth the reins and hearts: and I will give unto each one of you according to your works."* Her spiritual offspring, those who had been begotten of her, succumbing to her influence and practicing fully what she taught, would perish in some signal manner by the Lord. These "children" would be distinct from those who had been influenced but had not completely yielded to her wiles; these latter could repent. We now have (1) Jezebel, the source of the trouble, (2) her children who had been brought completely under her teaching, and (3) her victims who had been influenced, but who could yet be redeemed. These last would be cast into the bed of tribulation, but not be "killed with death" as would she and her children. Through the experience of this church, every Christian should realize the consequence of such compromising behavior. The lesson is for all time. Sin cannot be condoned nor compromise tolerated without the fearful consequences of such a disposition. For Jesus, who has eyes like a flame of fire, searches beneath the surface and sees every secret disposition.

"Reins," is defined literally as kidneys, but figuratively it is "the seat of the deepest emotions and affections of man, which God alone can fully know" (I.S.B.E.), "the movement of the will and affections, and by heart, the thoughts" (Swete). Whatever the distinction between "reins" and "heart" may be, the thought is that the discerner of hearts sees the whole inner man: emotions, affections, will, mind, and thoughts of each. The address now becomes personal, individual, "I will give unto each one of you." Each stands alone before God, personally responsible for his inner being and outward conduct. "Works" here are not only the outward deeds, but also include the inner thoughts and purposes of the heart. The heart is the workshop in which the deeds of life are wrought (Matt. 15:19).

v. 24. *"But to you I say, to the rest that are in Thyatira, as many as have not this teaching, who know not the deep things of Satan, as they are wont to say; I cast upon you none other burden."* Instead of seeking for "the deep things of God," searched out by the Spirit and revealed through the apostles (I Cor. 2:10), these heretics looked for "the deep things of Satan." Does the Lord call their teaching "the deep things of Satan," or does the sect itself speak of these things as such? The Lord recognizes their teaching for what it is—of Satan. He had called certain Jews a "synagogue of Satan" (2:9), emperor worship as the throne of Satan (2:13), and now He charges the teachings of Jezebel and her followers as being "the deep things of Satan." It is probable, though not definite, that this was a sect of the Gnostics, for "deep" and "profound" were favorite words with them. Apparently, the sect taught that in order to know and meet Satanic doctrine and life one should know by experience what they are, for the experience would not affect the spirit but only the flesh. Peter had forewarned against such teachers and their teaching when he said, "For, uttering great swelling words of vanity, they entice in the lusts of the flesh, by lasciviousness, those who are just escaping from them that live in error" (II Peter 2:18; cf. also Jude 16). However, no one has to murder in order to know what it is, or commit fornication to understand it.

"I cast upon you no other burden" than of moral character and keeping the faith. This phrase is reminiscent of the apostolic encyclical drawn up in Jerusalem and sent to the churches in which it seemed good "to lay upon you [Gentile Christians] no greater burden than these necessary things," to abstain from Gentile heathen practices of idolatry and immorality (Acts 15:28–29). The Lord never lays upon anyone a greater spiritual demand than that which is within his reach.

v. 25. *"Nevertheless that which ye have, hold fast till I come."* The Lord continues the thought introduced above, and instructs the believers to hold to the moral life required to keep the faith. "Till I come" leaves the time and manner of coming indefinite. The Lord refers not to His final coming, but as in the other five letters, He speaks of a coming to aid the church or to judge it.

v. 26. "And he that overcometh, and he that keepeth my works unto the end, to him will I give authority over the nations." The Lord is addressing those that overcome the Jezebel threat and keep His works by doing what He has commanded. "Unto the end," from *achri telous* (also in Heb. 6:11), is stronger than *heos telous*, used by Paul (I Cor. 1:8; II Cor. 2:13), and means "*even* to the end." There is no place to slow down, digress, or give up in the service of Christ. "Authority over the nations" is continued in v. 27.

v. 27. "And he shall rule them with a rod of iron, as the vessels of the potter are broken to shivers; as I also have received of my Father." This verse is clearly associated with Psalm 2, where the Father raised the Son to sit on the throne by divine appointment (vv. 6–7). To the Son was given the nations (Gentiles) for an inheritance over which He should rule with a rod of iron, smashing and destroying them at His discretion (vv. 8–9; see also Ps. 110:5–6; Isa. 11:4; Mic. 5:15; Rev. 1:5; 12:5; 19:15). Now to him that overcomes and keeps His works, the Lord shares that rule with Himself. This is evident by such assurances as "they [those purchased out of the earth with His blood] reign upon the earth" (Rev. 5:9–10); and, "they that receive the abundance of grace and of the gift of righteousness reign in life through the one, even Jesus Christ" (Rom. 5:17). Both Christ and Christians sit and reign, and they shall until the last enemy, death, is destroyed. Christ now sits at the right hand of God where He shall sit until His enemies are put under His feet (Heb. 1:3, 13). The last enemy to be abolished is death (I Cor. 15:25–26). Therefore, His sitting and reigning are coextensive: as He sits now He reigns now. The sitting and reigning of Christians is parallel to that of Christ. They have been raised up and made to sit with Christ (Eph. 2:6), and they reign with Him in life on the earth (Rom. 5:17; Rev. 5:9–10). Therefore their sitting and reigning are likewise coextensive. The reign is not a "millennial reign" of the future, but a reign now as the overcomer partakes of the power of Christ which He received of the Father (Matt. 28:18; Eph. 1:20–23), and by that power the evil of the nations (Gentiles) is smashed by truth. It is a spiritual rule through the triumph of the Gospel and the cause of Christ over all forces.

v. 28. "And I will give him the morning star." The many explanations of the morning star that have been suggested testify to the difficulty of a positive interpretation. The meaning seems to be that as the morning star, one of the brightest in the heavens, heralds the approach of dawn and a new day, so Christ here promises that He will give to the conquerer a new day; the night is almost over. In prophecy the star that should arise to smite the territory of its enemies and break all the sons of tumult, was also identified as a scepter, indicating royalty (Num. 24:17). Jesus identifies Himself as "the bright, the morning star" (Rev. 22:16), and surely it is He who fulfilled the prophecy referred to above. In these promises the overcomer rules with Him over the heathen, sharing with His royalty and enjoying the assurance of dawn and a new day, for the night will pass away.

v. 29. "He that hath an ear, let him hear what the Spirit saith to the churches." "He that hath an ear... ," see comments under 2:7. Beginning with this letter the order of "he that hath an ear" and "he that overcometh," is reversed. In this and the following three letters "he that overcometh" precedes "he that hath an ear." However, there seems to be little significance in this change of order.

CHAPTER 3
More Letters to the Churches

SARDIS
vv. 1-6

v. 1. *"And to the angel of the church in Sardis write: These things saith he that hath the seven Spirits of God, and the seven stars; I know thy works, that thou hast a name that thou livest, and thou art dead."* Sardis, the capital of ancient Lydia, was a little more than thirty miles south-southeast of Thyatira, lying at the foot of Mount Timolus and about three miles south of the Hermus River. Among the oldest and most renowned cities of Asia Minor, Sardis was built on a smooth, almost perpendicular rock hill that provided a natural citadel, inaccessible from three sides and easily protected on the fourth. Rising fifteen hundred feet from the plain below, the hill overlooked the wide and fertile Hermus Valley. Sardis had long been a capital city; the kings who ruled from it were noted for their life of wealth, splendor, and luxury. They were also known for their tendency to become soft and weak. Ramsay says of the city, "It was more of a robber's stronghold than an abode of civilized men" (*Seven Churches*, p. 354). From this capital, Croesus, whose name became synonymous with wealth, had ruled over Lydia in the sixth century B.C. Cyrus, king of the Persians, took the city from him in 549 B.C. Tradition says that a soldier found a crevice in the rock hill up which he led a band of soldiers to the summit, taking the city by surprise. About 330 years later (218 B.C.), Antiochus the Great took the city in the same way; thus the city had twice been surprised and taken as "a thief in the night."

The city's patron deity was Cybele, a nature goddess, but there were altars and shrines to other deities worshiped by the people. This city along with eleven others was destroyed by a terrible earthquake in A.D. 17. It was rebuilt with help from Emperor Tiberius, of Rome, who contributed heavily out of the national treasury and also remitted taxes for five years (Tacitus, *Annals* 2. 47). When the seven letters were written, Sardis was a city with a past but no future. Swete says, "The church perhaps encountered in Sardis no special danger to her place; but the atmosphere of an old pagan city, heavy with the immoral tradition of eight centuries, was unfavorable to the growth of her spiritual life" (p. lxiv). James Strahan sums up the similarities between the church and the city under four particulars, all of which help is to understand the letter: (1) Each had a name that it lived, but was dead. (2) Each fulfilled none of its works; both would promise but fail to execute. (3) With each it was watch, or be surprised as by a thief; Sardis had been caught napping each time it was taken. (4) It is implied that the garments of the church had been defiled with immorality, for which the city was noted (Hastings, IV. 458).

The church in this city seems not to have been plagued with emperor worship; neither was it disturbed by the Jews or the Nicolaitans, though Nicolaitan influence might have been present. Only this church and the one in Laodicea seem not to have had outward or inward foes to combat, but they both had internal conditions to overcome. As set forth in the condemnation of verse 1, the greatest obstacle this congregation had was the influence and character of its history recast in its people. Viewed externally the church looked peaceful and acceptable, possibly a model church, but from the Lord's point of view it was spiritually dead.

"These things saith he that hath the seven Spirits . . . and the seven stars." In 1:4 the seven spirits are before the throne (see comments) where they are ready to carry out the divine mission; here Jesus has the seven, ready to act as He directs. The "seven stars" are in His hand (see comments, 1:20). If, as suggested, the stars represent the spirit or inner life of the churches, then the Holy Spirit, the energizing, life-imparting, directing power of God has the ability to revive this "dead" church if it be willing. He is able to bring this church from the present state of death back to a full and complete state of life.

The "name" indicates the church's reputation, the esteem in which it is held from without. This church has the reputation of being alive, but the Lord sees it as it actually is—dead. Apparently this church, like the one in Ephesus, had begun with enthusiasm and a burning zeal for Christ and truth, but now it was dying of "dry rot" (Lenski), an internal deterioration. As the widow who gives herself to pleasure "is dead while she liveth" (I Tim. 5:6), so this church had sunk into spiritual inactivity, possibly to the level of the world, while yet maintaining an outward impression of love and piety. This describes many churches today that have a reputation of soundness and activity, but inwardly are decaying and dying.

v. 2. *"Be thou watchful, and establish the things that remain which were ready to die: for I have found no works of thine perfected before my God."* The exhortation "be watchful" should have struck a responsive chord in the heart of every Christian in Sardis, for twice their city had fallen because of negligence and carelessness (see above under v. 1). Also, constant vigilance and watchfulness had been an urgent exhortation of the Master, "Watch therefore; for ye know not on what day your Lord cometh" (Matt. 24:42f.; Luke 12:39f.). Eternal vigilance is the bulwark of the faith and safety of the saints. But even beyond vigilance, the "things that remain," whether works or persons, must be firmly established. There was yet a sufficient degree of faith and characteristics of a church to recognize it as Christ's; all was not lost, though the church stood on dangerous ground. There was yet a flicker of life that could be fanned into flame: and though the fire had cooled to a few coals that were fast becoming ashes, so long as there was that flicker of light there was hope. Similarly Paul had urged the church at Ephesus to "awake, thou that sleepest, and arise from the dead, and Christ shall shine upon thee" (Eph. 5:14).

The Lord had found no works of this church perfected before God. To perfect (from *pleroō*) means "bring to completion, finish something already begun" (A. & G.). Christ here brings a broad and sweeping charge against the church at Sardis. This church may have been strong in the beginning, but it had been quick to waver and falter under the weight of its own inability to persevere. Part of the problem may have been that there was no strong opposition, for meeting vigorous opposition develops character.

"Before my God"—the expression "my God" used by Jesus is found only in John's writings, providing additional evidence that the apostle John wrote both the Gospel bearing his name and the book of Revelation.

v. 3. *"Remember therefore how thou hast received and didst hear; and keep it, and repent. If therefore thou shalt not watch, I will come as a thief, and thou shalt not know what hour I will come upon thee."* We know nothing of the origin of this church, but the fact that the Lord wants them to remember *how* they had received and heard indicates that it had begun in a special, if not a glorious way; they had heard and readily received. As the church in Ephesus was to remember from whence it had fallen and recover its stance, so the church in Sardis was to remember its beginning and in the memory and stimulation of that joyous beginning *perfect* the demands of the message so readily received.

"And keep it," hold fast to the end, let it not slip from your grasp. "And repent," the church was to turn from the lethargy and deathlike condition into which it had fallen.

If the church does not watch, the Lord "will come as a thief," in an unsuspected hour. The coming in this instance, as other "comings" in the seven letters, has no reference to His final coming, but refers to His coming in judgment upon the enemies, or for discipline of or aid to the particular church. In the final return of the Lord, He is coming whether or not anyone watches and repents. "As a thief," used often of the Lord's coming, indicates that he will come in secrecy, unannounced and when least expected. "And thou shalt not know when I come upon thee." Men in the spiritual stupor which characterized this congregation were in no condition to determine the hour; they could not read the handwriting on the wall. Churches in the torpor of death are always blind to their own condition.

v. 4. "*But thou hast a few names in Sardis that did not defile their garments: and they shall walk with me in white; for they are worthy.*" Finding a few with undefiled garments is like finding an oasis in a wind-blasted desert, or a refreshing shower in the midst of drought. The "few names" reveal that there were yet some who had remained spiritually alive and who testified to the truth that all could have been so. It is comforting to learn that in a church of spiritual corpses the Lord sees and knows the congregation as individuals and is mindful of each as a personal entity. "That did not defile their garments," indicates that not all of this church's faults were sins of omission, or a failure to do; there was also the active sin of worldly defilement. To defile one's garments is to pollute the life that has been cleansed by the blood of Christ. Defilement is a failure to keep "oneself unspotted from the world" (James 1:27); it grows out of failure to hate "even the garment spotted by the flesh" (Jude 23).

These few who had not defiled their garments "shall walk with me in white; for they are worthy." Only the living walk; the dead are inert. Walking with the Lord indicates fellowship, oneness, mutual agreement; for, "shall two walk together, except they have agreed?" (Amos 3:3). These walk with him in a victory procession as Paul points out, "But thanks be unto God, who always leadeth us in triumph in Christ" (II Cor. 3:14). White is the symbol of purity (Isa. 1:18; Dan. 12:10), and of joyfulness and festivity (Eccles. 9:8–9); it is the heavenly color (see comments, 2:17). Therefore to walk with him in white is to walk with Him in purity and holiness (which are put on in baptism), which make for a joyous heavenly relationship. "For they are worthy" expresses the Lord's estimate of these few. These are accounted worthy because of their redemption in Christ through His blood, an act of divine grace, and because of their life and works, a walk of personal faith.

v. 5. *"He that overcometh shall thus be arrayed in white garments; and I will in no wise blot his name out of the book of life, and I will confess his name before my Father, and before his angels."* To him that overcomes the Lord promises a threefold reward: (1) "He shall thus be arrayed in white garments." "Arrayed" is from *periballō*, "to throw around, put round, to put on or clothe oneself" (Thayer). The Christian's holiness or purity is at best imperfect in this life, but in heaven God will clothe him with perfect purity, with all the glory that the word "white" implies. (2) "And I will in no wise blot his name out of the book of life." The phrase "book of life" occurs seven times in the New Testament; once in Philippians (4:3), and six times in Revelation (3:5; 13:8; 17:8; 20:12, 15; 21:27. In 22:19 the greater evidence is for "tree of life"). The "book of life" is distinguished from "the books" in 20:12, 15 (see comments there); and though designated by other terms, is implied in both the Old and New Testaments (Luke 10:20; Exod. 32:32–33; Dan. 12:1; Mal. 3:16 et al.). From various passages it appears that the Jews kept a register of their citizens, which was a book of the living (Isa. 4:3; Ezek. 13:9; Neh. 12:22f.). From this register the name was removed at death. God's book is a "book of life," made up of the names of the righteous (Ps. 69:28), a book of remembrance of those who feared Him and thought on his name (Mal. 3:16). Others, whose names once may have been there but who had sinned against Him, would have their names blotted out (Exod. 32:32f.). The name of the one who overcomes will not be blotted out, but will be found there when the books are opened at the judgment. The strong implication is that the names of the spiritually dead will not be found there, for these will have been erased. (3) "And I will confess his name before my Father, and before his angels." Not only will the conqueror's name be in the book of life, but it will also be confessed by the Lord before the entire heavenly host, the Father and all the angels (cf. Matt. 10:32f.; Luke 12:8f.). In the same way that the graduating student has his name called before the faculty and audience when he receives his diploma of graduation, so the faithful one will have his name called as he receives the victory crown of life. But for those whose names are not found in the book there will be a complete denial by the Lord (Matt. 7:23; Luke 13:27).

v. 6. "He that hath an ear, let him hear what the Spirit saith to the churches." See comments, 2:7.

PHILADELPHIA
vv. 7-13

v. 7. "And to the angel of the church in Philadelphia write: These things saith he that is holy, he that is true, he that hath the key of David, he that openeth and none shall shut, and that shutteth and none openeth." Philadelphia was located on the Cogamus River, a tributary to the Hermus, twenty-eight miles southeast from Sardis. The city was named after its founder, King Attalus II Philadelphus, of Pergamum (159–138 B.C.), who was a great admirer of his brother and predecessor, Ecumenes II. Out of this affection the king named the city Philadelphia, meaning "brother loving" or "brother lover." The city was founded primarily to spread the Greek civilization and culture eastward and was therefore from its beginning a "missionary" center. Although the city was successful in advancing various aspects of the Greek culture and language (to the point that the Lydian tongue ceased to be spoken and the Greek became the language of the country), there is no indication that the Greek spirit took the place of the Anatolian (Ramsay, *Seven Churches*).

Because it was located on a main trade route from west to east, the city became an important and wealthy trade center. The vicinity about the city was especially conducive to grape growing, which made it famous for its fine wines. This gave prominence to Dionysus, the Greek god of the vine and of wine, and made this the chief pagan cult of the city. Philadelphia had so many temples and festivals to the pagan deities that it was often called "Little Athens" (Hastings). However, opposition to the church and Christians stemmed from wealthy Jews who had a beautiful synagogue in the city and who seemed to have flourished there. There is no solid evidence that the saints were openly persecuted by the Jews, but they were opposed by them in every possible way.

Along with eleven other cities in the area, Philadelphia was destroyed by the terrible earthquake in A.D. 17, and, like Sardis, was rebuilt with the help of Tiberius with funds from the national treasury. In gratitude for this help, the name of the city was changed to Neocaesarea (New Caesar). Later under Vespatian, its name was changed again to Flavia, but neither name caught on with the people. For a number of years the people were kept in terror by the continual tremors that plagued the area, and because of this fear much of the populace lived in huts in the adjacent countryside outside the city.

Jesus' introductory self-designation set Himself forth in contrast to situations found in the city. "These things saith he that is holy, he that is true, he that hath the key of David, he that openeth and none shall shut, he that shutteth and none openeth." As "the holy" (*ho hagios*) Jesus identified Himself with the absolute holiness of God, who throughout the Old Covenant repeatedly claimed that He is the Holy One and that all pertaining to Him is holy. In Christ is set forth the ideal demanded by God of absolute separation from the profane and sinful. "The true" (*ho alēthinos*), "true, dependable, genuine, real" (A. & G.), is used to declare an attribute of the Lord in opposition to "them that say they are Jews, and they are not, but do lie" (v. 9). In opposition to Jewish claims, Jesus is the true, the real, the genuine Messiah in whom is realized the total consummation of promise and expectation in the Jewish prophets. This word "true" (*alēthinos*), a favorite with John, is used by him twenty-two of the twenty-seven times it appears in the New Testament. In his writings Jesus is the "true light" (John 1:9), "the true bread" (John 6:32),·"the true vine" (John 15:1), "the true God" (I John 5:20), and "the faithful and true witness" (Rev. 3:14).

Having "the key of David" identifies Him with the rule and throne promised to David's seed. "Key" is a symbol implying power and authority. The "key of the house of David" was laid upon the shoulder of Eliakim, to whom was committed certain governmental powers to open and shut (Isa. 22:22). These powers were entrusted to him, who was an anti-type of Christ, but to Christ they belong by right. For upon His shoulders belongs the government which pertained to the "throne of David" and His "kingdom" (Isa. 9:6, 7), which was given to Him as "the Son of the Most High" to "reign over the house of Jacob for ever" (Luke 1:32f.). Jesus now claims this supreme power and rule. The "key," singular, includes His total rule in all realms: in heaven and on earth (Matt. 28:18), over "angels and authorities and powers" (I Peter 3:22), over the church (Eph. 1:20–22), over the kings of the earth (Rev. 1:5), and over death and Hades (Rev. 1:18). This strikes at the foundation of all Jewish claims to the contrary (and all millennial claims today). The Jews of that day may have claimed the power to shut the doors of the synagogue to all who confessed the name of Christ and to declare the terms by which all were admitted into the fold; but it is Jesus who opens what none other can shut and who shuts what none other can open. The way into heaven is opened by Him who is "the holy, the true," and the door is shut to all whom He determines unworthy or outside the Way.

v. 8. "*I know thy works (behold, I have set before thee a door opened, which none can shut), that thou hast a little power, and didst keep my word, and didst not deny my name.*" The word "door" (*thura*) is used literally only in Acts; otherwise its use is metaphorical. A "door of faith" had been opened to the Gentiles (Acts 14:27); to Paul "a great door and effectual" was opened at Ephesus (I Cor. 16:9), a door for the gospel at Troas (II Cor. 2:12). Paul sought the prayers of the church in Colosse for an open door for the Word in his work elsewhere (Col. 4:3). In these instances the door indicates opportunity, an opening through which a goal could be achieved. In like manner Jesus had opened a door of opportunity in Philadelphia which none could shut. As the city had been built on the borders of Mysia, Lydia, and Phrygia as an open door for the spread of Greek civilization, so now the Lord had opened a door of evangelism to the church in that city. Its position gave it a special opportunity and challenge. None would be able to shut that door, for He who held the key of power had declared it open.

Three qualities possessed by the church which would enable it to take advantage of the opportunity are now set forth. (1) "I know... that thou hast a little [or, little] power." Plummer omits the parentheses making the passage read, *"Because* thou hast a little power, and hast made good use of that little, I have given thee an opportunity of which none shall deprive thee" (P. C.). Whether its power was small because of its few members, or because of its economic status in comparison to other, wealthier groups in the city, or because of the lowly social order out of which its members had been called (cf. I Cor. 1:26), that church's power was sufficient to achieve Christ's purpose. As it had been with the ancient heroes of the faith, who "from weakness were made strong" (Heb. 11:34), so it could be with this church. (2) "And didst keep my word." Under some unrecorded trial of faith the church had kept His Word, standing fast, being "true" as was their Lord. The keeping of His Word is a test of love for Him and His Father (John 14:23f.), while to deny His Word is to reject Him, and to reject Him is to reject His Father (Luke 10:16). (3) "And didst not deny my name." As the Word is to be in the heart and kept by obedience, so the name is to be revered and confessed always (Rom. 10:8-10; Phil. 2:9-11). To deny His name under pressure from external forces is to fall away; it is to crucify Christ afresh (Heb. 6:6). The Philadelphian saints had stood fast.

v. 9. "Behold, I give of the synagogue of Satan, of them that say they are Jews and they are not, but do lie; behold, I will make them to come and worship before thy feet, and to know that I have loved thee." The true Jew was one inwardly, who had been circumcised in heart, in the spirit, whose praise was of God (Rom. 2:28f.). He was a Christian who worshiped by the Spirit of God, gloried in Christ Jesus and had no confidence in the flesh (Phil. 3:3). The Jews in the flesh boasted that they were the true Israel, the people of God. Those who did forsake this fold for Christ were looked upon as traitors and deserters worthy of death. The Jews' fierce hatred for the Christians made them an antonym to the name Philadelphia. Like the Jews in Smyrna, they were a synagogue of Satan, and their claim to spiritual superiority was a lie. In Jesus Christ, "the holy, the true," the bearer of "the key of David," was realized the true Messiah and God's Israel; if these Jews would be willing to listen and learn and to see in Him the fulfillment of their own prophets, they would become what they falsely claimed.

The Lord's promises to make the Jews come and worship before them raises a question. Does this say that through the providence of God and the faithful preaching of the gospel by the church the Jews would be converted to Christ? Or will the promise be fulfilled by those of the synagogue of Satan who come to recognize the true power of the church but do not obey the truth? Scholars are divided over the answer; the construction of the statement makes either possible.

In view of the disposition and spirit of the Jews and the continual hardening of their hearts as the church came to be comprised of Gentiles, the latter seems the more probable. At that time, many Jews who did accept the faith, actually accepted their own concept of what it should have been and became Judaizers, striving to combine the law and the faith. Within twenty years from the time of this letter Ignatius (A.D. 30–107) wrote to the Philadelphians warning them in vigorous terms to beware of such teachers (Phil. 6. A-N-F I. 82–83). Whereas the Jews hated them, in this victory "they shall know that I have loved thee."

v. 10. *"Because thou didst keep the word of my patience, I also will keep thee from the hour of trial, that hour which is to come upon the whole world, to try them that dwell upon the earth."* "The word of my patience" is not the word exhorting or commanding to be steadfast, but the endurance of Christ, "that patience which belongs to me" (Moffatt), that which is manifested in Christ (cf. II Thess. 3:5); Christ's own endurance out of which His Word grew. "I also will keep thee from the hour of trial, that hour which is to come upon the whole world [inhabited earth], to try them that dwell upon the earth." As the saints in Philadelphia have kept the word of His patience, so Christ will keep (*tēreō*, protect) these from the hour of trial. "Hour" is here used of a season, a period of trial. "From the hour of trial," from out of the midst of (*ek*); "but whether by *immunity from*, or by *being brought safely through*, the preposition does not clearly define" (Alford). The question seems best determined by the context: the trial that was to come upon the whole inhabited earth was to test "them that dwell upon the earth."

The word *earth* (*gē*) occurs 81 times in the course of the book and is used in numerous ways. It is frequently used as metonymy for the realm or world of unregenerated men. This use will be pointed out in various places where the redeemed are distinguished from "them that dwell upon the earth," earthlings or earth-dwellers. The church will have its trials which test faith, but it will be kept from trials which would affect the earthlings, the world of the unregenerated. Those of the world, those in conflict with Christ and His church, will be, in this instance, the ones tried.

v. 11. "*I come quickly: hold fast that which thou hast, that no one take thy crown.*" The final or "second" coming is not in view; for, although he repeats "I come quickly" three times in Chapter 22 (vv. 7, 12, 20), He also says of the things written in the book, they "must shortly come to pass" (22:6) and "the time is at hand" (22:10). The New Testament writers did not believe or teach that the Lord was to return immediately, as is sometimes charged by modern writers, but taught clearly that His ultimate coming was not "just at hand" (II Thess. 2:1-3). When He would come He would come as a thief, unannounced (3:3); but when needed He would come quickly. There are constant and continual comings of the Lord to aid His people and to judge the oppressing world.

"Hold fast that which thou hast," which is an open door, His Word, a little power, steadfast endurance, and an assuring promise from the Lord. Hold each of these fast; keep hold of what you have. The promise of keeping these safe (v. 10) implies and imposes continuous steadfastness by the saints. "That no one take thy crown" (the crown of life, 2:10) away from you. The thought does not concern itself with gain to the taker, but with loss to the loser. The crown may be forfeited by any individual who grows careless, complacent, self-satisfied, overconfident, or who neglects opportunity and duty. There is no criticism against this church, but there is the warning that such an exalted position may become the very cause of stumbling; "wherefore let him that thinketh he standeth take heed lest he fall" (I Cor. 10:12). To forfeit the crown is to lose eternal life. The doctrine that a redeemed child of God cannot so act as to be lost is here clearly denied.

v. 12. *"He that overcometh, I will make him a pillar in the temple of my God, and he shall go out thence no more: and I will write upon him the name of my God, and the name of the city of my God, the new Jerusalem, which cometh down out of heaven from my God, and mine own new name."* In each of the seven letters as the writer draws to the close he changes from addressing the church collectively to addressing the individual. So here, the individual who overcomes is promised a reward; the victory and reward are personal. Making one a pillar emphasizes the thought of permanence rather than support, as indicated by the assurance, "and he shall go out thence no more." If more than this is intended it must be determined by the meaning of "temple": the temple (*naos*, sanctuary) may be the church (I Cor. 3:16; II Cor. 6:16; Eph. 2:21), or it may be heaven, the sanctuary of God. On this point there are differences of opinion. If it is the church, then as a pillar one gives stability and support to the church by his character and life; this would be involved with the thought of permanence. There are two arguments against this view: (1) As long as one is in the flesh he can lose his crown (v. 11); he can go out of the temple if he so wills. (2) The word temple (*naos*) is used sixteen times in Revelation, and except for 11:1, 2, where almost certainly it is used of the church, it always refers to the heavenly temple, unless this passage is another exception. It seems to follow that the promise is of permanence in the heavenly temple of God, where neither earthquakes nor violence can ever destroy or cast out. John's saying, "I saw no temple therein" (21:22), does not invalidate the above conclusion, for the whole of heaven is one eternal temple and he who overcomes has a permanent place in it.

Each individual was to have inscribed upon him a threefold name which would denote possession and relation: (1) The name of God the Father, to whom the individual would now belong in a permanent and fixed way. However, others who are upon the earth, the church militant, are also sealed unto Him (7:2; 9:4; 14:1). (2) The name of the New Jerusalem identifies the victorious saint as a citizen of the heavenly city, made ready as a bride adorned for her husband (21:2). The old Jerusalem had been destroyed for over twenty years, the new (*kainos*, new in kind) is the city of the true Israel. With its name written upon him the conqueror has the right to enter by the gates into the city (22:14). This city stands in contrast to "the great city," the symbol of the world (11:8, see comments). (3) Christ's own new name, likewise new in kind, "the name written which no one knoweth but he himself" (19:12), identifies the victor as sharing the glory which is Christ's. This name summarizes all that He is, even beyond that which is known or comprehensible to us while in the flesh. "When Christ . . . shall be manifested, then shall ye also with him be manifested in glory" (Col. 3:4); and "we know that, if he shall be manifested, we shall be like him; for we shall see him even as he is" (I John 3:2). The Christian shares in Christ's victory, wears His own new name and enters into an eternal relation with Him as His bride, to abide with Him for ever.

v. 13. "He that hath an ear, let him hear what the Spirit saith to the churches." This is all we know of this good church. The Scriptures are silent as to its origin and place among the churches. It stands out as one of the two that deserved no censure or condemnation. It was a church (1) with opportunity, (2) of victory, (3) that was kept safe, (4) that attained to that sought by David, a permanent place in the temple of God (Ps. 27:4), and (5) whose faithful members were given the name which belongs to God, His city, and His Christ. Truly, this was a glorious church!

LAODICEA
vv. 14-22

v. 14. "And to the angel of the church in Laodicea write: These things saith the Amen, the faithful and true witness, the beginning of the creation of God." Laodicea was between forty and fifty miles southeast of Philadelphia and more than ninety miles east of Ephesus. One of the three cities located in the Lycus valley, it was eleven miles west of Colosse and six miles south of Hierapolis (Col. 4:13). The city was founded by Antiochus II, a Seleucid king (261-246 B.C.), who named it after his wife, Laodice. Originally built as a strong garrison on the strategic eastern trade route, Laodicea became a center of Hellenic culture, reaching its peak of importance and wealth when Asia was made a Roman province in 190 B.C. The native religious cult was that of Men Karou, identified as Zeus by the Hellenists of the city.

Laodicea was also a center of imperial worship, receiving the coveted recognition of the temple-wardenship.

A famous school of medicine, located thirteen miles from the city, strongly influenced its religious life, for all aspects of life were tied in with religion. This school developed an eye medicine known as Phrygian powder, which became widely used and added fame to Laodicea. The district surrounding the city was famous for a special breed of sheep that produced a soft, glossy-black wool, used to make highly prized and widely sought garments. The city became a noted banking center, which together with its trade brought great wealth to the community, making it one of the wealthiest cities in the world of its day.

When the city was destroyed by an earthquake in A.D. 60, its independent and self-sufficient people refused help from Rome, rebuilding with their own resources. Many Jews were attracted by the city's affluence and trade and made it their home. The city's easy and opulent life made it an appealing retirement center for the wealthy. Because retired persons often conclude that they have served their purpose and reached their goal in life, they consequently become lukewarm to the issues facing society. Ramsay describes Laodicea as a city of no extremes, a city that had no peculiar characteristics unless this lack of peculiar characteristics was its peculiar characteristic. These qualities that distinguished the city were also reflected in the church.

The origin of the church in Laodicea is unknown. It is assumed, however, from Luke's statement, "All they that dwelt in Asia heard the word of the Lord, both Jews and Greeks" (Acts 19:10), that the church had its beginning during Paul's stay in Ephesus. It is possible that Epaphras may have been the first to preach there since he was from nearby Colosse (Col. 1:7; 4:12f.). It appears that Paul wrote a letter to the church in Laodicea (Col. 4:16), but the letter has been lost, unless the Ephesian letter is the one mentioned.

"Amen," from a Hebrew word meaning "to be firm or steadfast" and a verb meaning "to prop," is akin to the Hebrew word "truth" (cf. Isa. 65:16, Heb. "Amen" translated "truth"), and was intended to express certainty. In writing of the promise of God, Paul says that in Christ is the "amen," the certainty of these promises (II Cor. 1:20). The word is used as a proper noun only here, and as His name it guarantees all that He says. In the synoptic Gospels Jesus often used the word translated "verily" to introduce His teaching, finding in it the proper guarantee of His own authority and the absolute faithfulness of His message. In the Gospel of John the word is doubled, "Verily, verily," probably for emphasis. This name, "Amen," gave fixity to Christ's purpose and character; this the Laodiceans lacked.

Jesus had been introduced as "the faithful witness" (see comments, 1:5), and as "the faithful and true witness" His testimony is absolutely trustworthy. As the supreme and rightful critic of the church and the absolutely trustworthy one, His criticisms and warnings should be heeded. In Him is fulfilled in the highest sense all that belonged to a witness, of which, according to Trench, three things are necessary: (1) He must have first-hand knowledge of that to which He testifies and must have seen with His own eyes that to which He attests; (2) He must be competent to reproduce and relate this for others; and (3) He must be willing to make this known faithfully and truthfully (Ramsay, *Seven Churches*, p. 256). Jesus completely fulfills these essentials.

The wording of the phrase, "the beginning of the creation of God," allows two interpretations: (1) in the passive sense, Christ is a created being, the first of God's creation; and (2) in the active sense, Christ is the source of all created beings and things, the active agent of God in creation. The Scripture clearly attests that the latter is the true meaning. In the beginning God created, but the Word was the means, "God said" (Gen. 1:1–3), which involved His Word. This Word was with God in the beginning, and was God, i.e., deity, through whom all things were made that have been made (John 1:1–3). "He was in the world and the world was made through him" (John 1:10). This is further attested by Paul who likewise affirmed that in Him were all things created and that He is before all things (Col. 1:15–17). If all created things were made through Him and He is before all things, then it follows that Christ could not have been at the same time the Creator and the created. If the idea is accepted that Christ was created and yet it is affirmed that He is the Creator then He created Himself! This reduces to an absurdity the idea of His having been created. God is the designer and creator of all things in the sense that they originated in His mind and are expressions of His will (4:11), but Christ is co-eternal with the Father and is the active agent of all that has been created. In the Book of Revelation the Son is identified with the Father as being equal in deity and eternity, for "every created thing" in all realms of creation praise Him as being worthy of blessing for ever (5:13).

v. 15. "I know thy works, that thou art neither cold nor hot: I would thou wert cold or hot." The Lord knows the works of this church, the whole course of its life is before Him; nothing is hidden, and it was neither cold nor hot. Cold, from *psuchros*, "cold or chilled, chilly," occurs only twice in the New Testament, once literally of "a cup of cold water" (Matt. 10:42), and here metaphorically (vv. 15–16) of Christ's evaluation of this church's spiritual condition. Hot, *zestos* (from *zeō*) occurs only here and means to boil, be hot, fervent. Apollos is spoken of as being "fervent [*zeō*] in spirit" (Acts 18:25), and in a like use of the word Paul urges the Roman saints to be "fervent [*zeō*] in spirit serving the Lord" (Rom. 12:11); the church in Laodicea was neither chilled nor fervent. When the Lord says "I would thou wert cold or hot," He expresses not a wish but a deep regret at this condition (Trench). Jesus is not saying He wished that they were cold in that they had never come under the power of the gospel, but rather by contrast He is giving emphasis to their lukewarmness. It is nevertheless true that a person who has once tasted and experienced the good and then grown indifferent to it is hard to bring back (cf. Heb. 6:4–6; II Peter 2:20). But even if being cold meant openly antagonistic and opposed to Him and His work, this verse indicates that at least belief is something to be earnest about.

v. 16. "So because thou art lukewarm, and neither hot nor cold, I will spew thee out of my mouth." Lukewarm (*chliaros*, one of the various forms of *chliō*) means "to become warm, liquify, melt" (Thayer). Here the word is used metaphorically to express a condition that produced nausea. A hot or cold beverage might refresh; but a tepid, insipid, lukewarm liquid produces only nausea and vomiting. As Israel went in to possess the land of the Canaanites, Jehovah warned the people that they defile it not, but keep the law, "that the land vomit not you out also . . . as it vomited out the nation that was before you" (Lev. 18:28; 20:22). The Lord's threat to the Laodiceans is even more serious than that to Israel; for it is the Lord, not the land, that vomits them out in His abhorance of their condition, separating them from Himself as the nations had been separated from their land for ever.

In passing from cold to hot one passes through a temporary lukewarm state; but the condition here was becoming permanent. As Moab and the people of Jerusalem had "settled on their lees" and were worthy of being cast out, so had these. They had said in their heart, "Jehovah will not do good, neither will he do evil" (Jer. 48:11f.; Zeph. 1:12). However there is yet hope for these in Laodicea; they can do something about their condition if they will. Literally the Lord says, "I am about" (*mellō*, cf. 2:10, "about to suffer") to spew you out of my mouth. He then makes an earnest plea for a change on their part so that the fervent spirit and relationship may be restored.

v. 17. *"Because thou sayest, I am rich, and have gotten riches, and have need of nothing; and knowest not that thou art the wretched one and miserable and poor and blind and naked."* Here is the cause and consequence of their lukewarmness; this church, deluded in its self-sufficiency, was reaping the fruits of harvest. It need not be concluded that the entire congregation was made up of wealthy people, though no doubt there were wealthy ones among them. It may have been composed of a smug "middle-class" group that had so imbibed the spirit of their city that they had become totally complacent. There was no real need for God; they were satisfied.

The picture well describes many congregations today: they possess material prosperity, they engage in "projects" that use finances but which express no real spiritual zeal. They develop a "teaching program" more formal than productive of true inward development. They enjoy a comfortable building and a respected social position in the community, and live in worldly enjoyment that requires neither sacrifice nor effort. They feel sufficient within themselves. Such a church can point to these externals and boast, "See how the Lord has blessed us," but such boasting is reminiscent of Ephraim who said, "Surely I am become rich, I have found me wealth; in all my labors they shall find in me no iniquity that were sin" (Hos. 12:8), and of the Pharisee who was perfectly satisfied with himself as expressed in his complacent prayer to God (Luke 18:11f.). In reality, every man is ever an unprofitable servant, dependent on God in every way and for every thing (Luke 17:10).

Spiritually this church was in a deplorable condition. As the church in Smyrna was the "poor rich" church, this congregation was the "rich poor" one. Jesus uses one article and five adjectives to describe its spiritual plight; "the wretched one" (*talaipōros*), which is the same word used by Paul to describe the pitiable condition of one dependent upon his own resources for deliverance under the law—"Wretched man that I am!" (Rom. 7:24). "And miserable" (*eleeinos*) is another word occurring only twice in Scripture; here, and by Paul to describe one who has hoped in Christ only in this world but with no hope beyond, literally, "more miserable" than all (I Cor. 15:19). "And poor" (*ptōchos*), is said of one reduced to begging or to a state of dependence on others for support. "And blind," is used metaphorically by Paul of those who are spiritually blind (Rom. 2:19), and by Peter to describe one who lacks the spiritual graces of growth, who is blind to his own condition, "having forgotten the cleansing from his old sins" (II Peter 1:9), which is here used to describe the same condition of the Laodiceans. "And naked" (*gumnos*), describes the soul without the heavenly habitation (II Cor. 5:2f.), not having on the "holy array—beauty of holiness" required by the Lord (Ps. 110:3), and divested of any covering before Him. This is the pathetic picture of a church long since gone, but replaced today by many from the same mold.

v. 18. *"I counsel thee to buy of me gold refined by fire, that thou mayest become rich; and white garments, that thou mayest clothe thyself, and that the shame of thy nakedness be not made manifest; and eyesalve to anoint thine eyes, that thou mayest see."* The Lord's description of the church's spiritual state is followed by an earnest exhortation, "I counsel thee"—the advice of a friend—"to buy of me gold," indicates that this gold could come only from the Lord, for all spiritual riches are from above, which would compensate for their spiritual poverty. The true riches are spiritual; faith proved by fire, tested in the crucible of trials and found genuine (I Peter 1:7), and the "treasures of wisdom and knowledge," like a casket of jewels, are to be found only in Him (Col. 2:3). But to obtain these one must dispose of that on which he has set false value in this life, his own self-sufficiency, and buy these true riches of Him (cf. Matt. 13:44-46). The Laodiceans are also urged to buy white garments that they may clothe themselves, that the shame of their spiritual nakedness be not made manifest. White is the symbol of holiness (see comments, 2:17; 3:4), and is possibly used here in contrast to the glossy-black garments for which Laodicea was noted. As of the gold, so also the white garments can be provided only by Christ. Without the wedding garment, which appears from the parable of the wedding feast to have been provided by the king, the presumptuous guest who did not have one on was cast out (Matt. 22:11f.). "Buy" is used metaphorically, for no one can literally buy salvation, righteousness, or white garments.

Although the people would be urged to come and buy without money and without price (Isa. 55:1f.), yet there is a price to be paid. The price in this instance is the exchanging of a self-imposed righteousness for that which Christ has provided in Himself. Only those who put on Christ in baptism (Gal. 3:26f.) and maintain the righteousness of God in Him (II Cor. 5:21), shall be properly clothed and not have their spiritual nakedness exposed to the world.

Eyesalve with which to anoint their eyes that they may see is also another absolute necessity. Blind to their own faults and to their materialistic and worldly interests, these church members needed divine enlightenment that they might see their pitiable condition. If they would but give heed they could obtain this help. The apostle Paul had long since taught the lesson that "the things which are seen are temporal; but the things which are not seen are eternal" (II Cor. 4:18), a lesson needed by this church and by all since.

v. 19. "*As many as I love, I reprove and chasten: be zealous therefore, and repent.*" Christ's chastening and correction of His saints stems from His deep affection for them. Instead of *agapē*, the broader and more inclusive word for love which relates to the will (indicating an intelligent and purposeful principle by which we live and act in relation to God and man), Jesus uses the warm and affectionate *phileō* (love). The word *phileō* expresses affection and emotion which one holds toward another. In spite of this church's attitude toward Him, the Lord yet has a tender and affectionate feeling for it. "As many" extends the feeling and promise beyond the immediate church making it include all who need correction, at that time and now. "I reprove," correct, discipline because He loves. The word implies a rebuke that carries conviction even to the extent of punishing if necessary, though the idea of punishment is not inherent in the word. To "chasten" implies correction and training of the moral and spiritual part of the person's life, leading to the eradication of faults and sins.

Chastening and reproof by the Lord should not be regarded lightly or shrugged off, but neither is it so depressing that it should cause one to faint (Heb. 12:5). "Be zealous therefore, and repent," is a call for immediate repentance, and a constant and continuous zeal for the Lord. The divine purpose of reproof and chastening is to turn people from sin, and its success depends on the spirit in which the discipline is received. This objective had not been obtained in the Laodicean church, but it had to be manifested now; however, it could be realized only if the attitude was changed by repentance. With this change the church would be no longer lukewarm but would become what the Lord desired it to be.

v. 20. *"Behold, I stand at the door and knock: if any man hear my voice and open the door, I will come in to him, and will sup with him, and he with me."* Here is a picture of the Lord seeking admittance into the life of this spiritually indifferent church from which He had been excluded. The knocking expresses His effort through the Word to be admitted. The knocking is not one thing and His voice another; this is clear from what follows. "If any man hear my voice and open the door, I will come in to him, and will sup with him, and he with me." The Savior never forces admission but seeks entrance by the willing disposition of the individual. His effort and the necessary willingness and action of the saints is clear testimony to the freedom of the human will to choose or reject the divine call. As He knocks, He identifies Himself that there may be no misunderstanding concerning who seeks entrance. To hear His voice is more than to hear a sound; it is to understand the message and acknowledge the Guest who would enter. On the road to Damascus Paul's companions heard "the sound" (marginal, Acts 9:7), but "heard not the voice" (Acts 22:9), that is, they understood not the message; Paul both heard and understood. To hear and open the door is to give heed to Christ's Word and accept His entrance into the heart. To "sup" is to dine with Him in spiritual communion and fellowship, which to the Oriental meant close confidence and affection. Supping with Him now is a foretaste of the glory to be shared with Him in the eternal home. The Lord knocks today as He seeks admittance into the heart and life. To those who reject the divine One the time will come when these shall knock, but it will be too late; the answer of finality will be, "I know not whence ye are; depart from me, all ye workers of iniquity" (Luke 13:25-27).

v. 21. "*He that overcometh, I will give to him to sit down with me in my throne, as I also overcame, and sat down with my Father in his throne.*" As in the other six letters, the promise of reward is to the overcomer. Christ's victory was the cross through which He overcame the world (John 16:33), brought to naught Satan's power over sin and death (Heb. 2:14), and led captivity captive; that is, He led captive that which for so long had held man in its captive power (Eph. 4:8). He now sits on the right hand of the majesty on high (Heb. 1:3), on His own throne (Heb. 1:8f.), which is the throne of God (Heb. 12:2). The redeemed sit with Him in this spiritual realm (Eph. 2:6), reigning with Him in life (Rom. 5:17; Rev. 5:9f., see comments 2:26f.). The one who overcomes is promised a place with Him on this throne of His Father and Himself. Paul assured Timothy that as we died with Him we shall live with Him, and as we endure we shall also reign with Him (II Tim. 2:11f.). The similarity between Jesus' statement here and Paul's in the letter to Timothy raises the question as to whether they are speaking of a present sitting and reigning or of the eternal reign in heaven (22:5). It seems that each is speaking of our present sitting and reigning with Him. The faithful share with Him in this life and His victory over sin and in His reign in righteousness, and shall also share in the reign for ever and ever in eternity (22:5).

v. 22. "*He that hath an ear, let him hear what the Spirit saith to the churches.*" Although the promise of this letter is to the church in Laodicea, it is all-inclusive. All who overcome reign with Him as they share in His life, suffering, and victory.

CHAPTER 4
The Throne Scene

In chapter one the scope of Christ's ministry and His present glory were revealed. As King and Priest He holds the destiny of the churches in His hand as He walks among the congregations. The conflict involving tribulation, which John shared with the saints, was also introduced. Following this introduction of Jesus, John stood with Him among the churches beholding their conditions, problems, and possibilities of victory through their Lord (chaps. 2 and 3). John heard and wrote the Savior's words of commendation, condemnation, warning, and promise of reward to those who would overcome. Though variously expressed, the reward is victory over the enemy now and eternal life hereafter. In the letters, the conflict of the church with the forces of evil within and without and the grounds of ultimate victory of the faithful were clearly set forth. The question now is, What shall be the fate of God's enemies and of His people? The following chapters tell of the fierceness of the conflict and the final outcome.

However, before describing the conflict which was already beginning and which would grow in intensity, God draws aside the curtain of heaven and gives to John, and through him to His persecuted saints, a vision of the throne and majestic court of the Ruler of the universe. Let the reader of Revelation always bear in mind that what John sees is a vision in which symbols are pictures of ideas. In the rest of the New Testament truth is imparted to the mind, but in Revelation it is communicated to the eye. Truth that had been preached and written by apostles, prophets, and evangelists is now emphasized in pictorial action.

An evening spent watching the movie, "The Longest Day," will leave the viewer shaken by the horrors of war as could no amount of newspaper and magazine copy. Books and maps of Bible cities may be read and studied for years, but seeing the sites and ruins of ancient Philippi, Ephesus, Pergamum, Patmos, Salamis, and others makes vivid the grandeur and power of ancient Rome as no words can possibly do. As one reads Revelation let him imagine himself seated in a great theater on Patmos watching a pageant of truth and error in deadly conflict, with God directing and Christ leading the forces of truth and right while the devil champions the cause of falsehood and sin. As scene follows scene, the reader must not become bogged down in efforts to interpret and apply stage settings and incidentals to the point of missing the overall theme and lesson of the book. He must watch, listen, and strive to learn what God, the author of the script, is revealing in His spectacular drama of the ages. To the literalistic mind, lacking the power of imagination, Revelation will forever be a sealed book; to the speculative and visionary mind the book will provide fuel to inflame far-fetched assumptions and conjectures which totally miss the truth. But to the mind prepared by the rest of the Bible for reality in picture and action, impressions of truth will be made that give strength for victory in every conflict of life.

This vision of the great heavenly throne scene (chaps. 4 and 5) introduces the two major sections of the book (chaps. 4—11 and 12—21). God on the throne amidst exalted living creatures and the redeemed is the central figure of chapter 4. The Son as the Lion of the tribe of Judah, the root of David, and a Lamb slain but living is the central figure of chapter 5. Only He is worthy to take the sealed book out of God's right hand, loose the seals, and carry out the purpose of God to its consummation. Amid the praises of the heavenly beings, the redeemed, and all creation, He takes His place at the right hand of God, the Almighty. As the saint beholds this wondrous scene and catches its spirit, he is prepared to face persecutions, tribulations, and even death if need be. He is strengthened in the assurance that the great God and His victorious Son rule in every realm of creation and that through them he can be victorious under any circumstance and in any earthly conflict. Therefore let the devil and his forces charge the citadel of Zion with assault after assault. The faithful saint, in his faith and the strength of the Lord, has nothing to fear, for ultimately victory is his!

THE THRONE OF GOD THE ALMIGHTY

v. 1. "After these things I saw, and behold, a door opened in heaven, and the first voice that I heard, a voice as of a trumpet speaking with me, one saying, Come up hither, and I will show thee the things which must come to pass hereafter." "After these things" introduces a new aspect of the message following that which had begun at 1:1. It does not imply that the revelation was being made to John in parts, separated by intervals of time; for it seems to have been one continuous unfolding of the divine disclosure. John uses the phrase to introduce new and emphatic points, as here, 7:1, 9; 15:5; 18:1; 19:1; 20:3. The "door opened in heaven" is the third door brought into view thus far. There was the door of opportunity set before the church in Philadelphia (3:8), the door of the human heart in the letter to the Laodiceans (3:20), and now the door of heaven opened for the admission of John into heaven (in the vision), and the revealing of God's throne to His saints.

In former times Jehovah had opened "the windows of heaven" to pour out the flood in judgment (Gen. 7:11), had promised to open them to pour out a blessing upon Judah (Mal. 3:10), and had opened "the doors of heaven" to pour forth the manna upon Israel (Ps. 78:23f.). He opened the heavens to reveal a vision to Ezekiel (Ezek. 1:1), to send the Holy Spirit upon His Son (Matt. 3:16), to reveal the glory of His Son (John 1:51; Acts 7:56), and to assure Peter of His acceptance of the Gentiles (Acts 10:11). And now John beholds "a door set open," not its being opened (Alford), to admit him into the divine presence that he might see that portion of heaven relevant to God's present purpose. The voice John heard is probably the voice of the same unidentified heavenly speaker of 1:10 (see comment, 1:10), who invites him to enter through the open door from where he can behold coming events. Since these events would affect the inhabitants of earth—the saints of God and the sinners of Satan—but be controlled from heaven, the seer would be able to understand and make known from the viewpoint of both heaven and earth.

v. 2. *"Straightway I was in the Spirit: and behold, there was a throne set in heaven, and one sitting upon the throne."* John had been "in the Spirit" from the beginning (1:10, see comments). But now that he is to behold and write of even greater things, those of heaven, he repeats the formula, "Straightway I was in the Spirit." Probably there is no difference in the degree to which he was controlled by the Spirit at either time. At the first he was able to see and hear the things given to him, but now in vision he is lifted up to heaven itself where he beholds "a throne set in heaven, and one sitting upon the throne." This is the first of many scenes to be impressed upon John's attention; the throne and its occupant is the subject of this chapter. The word "throne" is used seventeen times in chapters 4 and 5, emphasizing its importance. It would be futile to speculate upon the number seventeen, although it is a combination of seven, the perfect number and ten, the power number, indicating the perfection and power of the throne of the universe; if there is any significance to this special number it is unknown.

The throne might be visualized as semicircular, placed against a further wall of the great judgment hall (Pieters, p. 109), or perhaps as square, with steps leading up to it making it approachable from all directions and with the angels and all other creatures surrounding it in circular manner (Hendriksen, p. 102). Lenski refrains from attempting a description of any kind on the grounds that the reality of heaven is inconceivable to us now (p. 170). We must be content to think of the throne as symbolizing the infinite rule of Jehovah.

v. 3. "And he that sat was to look upon like a jasper stone and a sardius: and there was a rainbow round about the throne, like an emerald to look upon." Unlike Ezekiel who described the throne-occupant of his vision "as a likeness as the appearance of a man" (Ezek. 1:26), John portrays no form, but describes what he sees as two brilliantly flashing gem-like stones of resplendent beauty. Nowhere in Revelation is God described as having human form; however, the Son is referred to twice as one "like unto a Son of Man" (1:13; 14:14). God must be thought of in terms of Spirit, character, and attributes. The jasper stone is variously described by writers both ancient and modern; but from John's description of the holy Jerusalem, "having the glory of God," and her light being "like unto a stone most precious, as it were a jasper stone, clear as crystal" (21:11), it is probably the sparkling white diamond. Although it is difficult to determine exactly, the sardius is thought to have been a stone of fiery red color. If these deductions are correct, the jasper stone is probably descriptive of God's holiness and righteousness, and the sardius is a symbol of His justice in the divine judgments. This conclusion is justified by the psalmists who said, "Righteousness and justice are the foundations of his throne," from which proceeds "livingkindness and truth" wherein walk the people who know the joyful sound (Ps. 89:14-15); and before which foundation of righteousness and justice goes a fire that "burneth up his adversaries round about" (Ps. 97:2-3). These qualities of the divine character, righteousness and justice, seem to be symbolized in the two stones.

The rainbow around the throne was "like an emerald to look upon." The emerald is described as a stone of beautiful "velvety" green color, and it appears in John's vision as a halo about the throne. It is thought by many to represent the mercy of God; but the uncertainty of its significance is indicated by Swete as he says, "It *may perhaps* represent the mercy which tempers the revelation of the Divine Majesty" (p. 68, italics mine). If these suggestions are correct, these verses describe the holiness and righteousness of God's character, "dwelling in light unapproachable" (I Tim. 6:16), and the justice of His divine judgments encompassed and tempered by His infinite mercy.

v. 4. "*And round about the throne were four and twenty thrones: and upon the thrones I saw four and twenty elders sitting, arrayed in white garments; and on their heads crowns of gold.*" Twenty-four "thrones" (*thronous* or *thronoi*) conveys the idea better than "seat" (KJV), although the word does indeed denote seats of authority, power, or rule, which are in some way associated with the great central throne, the seat of God's mighty power and dominion. These are "round about" the throne, indicating a position beyond the rainbow. Before attempting to identify the twenty-four elders, it should be observed that they are arrayed in white garments and wear golden crowns. White is the heavenly color, representing holiness (see comments, 2:17); only those arrayed in "the beauty of holiness" (Ps. 110:3) are permitted to worship in the divine presence. The golden crowns are victory crowns (see comments, 2:10). In holy array, wearing crowns of victory, and sitting on thrones, they reign with the almighty God and His Christ (cf. Eph. 2:6; Rom. 5:17; Rev. 5:10).

But who are they? These seem not to be angels, as thought by some, or ministers of the Word, as suggested by others; certainly they are not figures drawn from Judaistic tradition. The number twenty-four suggests a combination of the twelve patriarchs of the twelve tribes of Israel and the twelve apostles, thus representing the redeemed of both covenants now united through Christ. Verily, those of the Old Covenant received the inheritance through Christ (Heb. 9:15) as do also Jews and Gentiles since Christ (Eph. 2:16), and "that apart from us [Christians] they [the faithful under the Old Covenant] should not be made perfect" (Heb. 11:40). All are redeemed, made perfect, and receive the inheritance in and through Christ. This view seems to be further confirmed by the victorious throng who sing the song of Moses and the Lamb (15:3), thereby combining both groups into one and acknowledging their redemption as being from God.

v. 5. "And out of the throne proceed lightnings and voices and thunders. And there were seven lamps of fire burning before the throne, which are the seven Spirits of God." These mighty phenomena symbolize the divine power, majesty, and glory which are intensely awesome to the beholder. When Jehovah descended upon Mount Sinai to meet with and address His people, He came in the midst of thunders and lightnings and the voice of a trumpet; and when Moses spoke, Jehovah responded by a voice (Exod. 19:16–19). These also symbolize His manifestation in judgment against the enemies of His chosen ones as He thunders, utters His voice, and sends His lightnings to discomfort them (Ps. 18:13–14); by these the enemies are scattered (Ps. 144:6). Here and in other places where this combination of "lightnings and voices and thunders" appears (8:5; 11:19; 16:18), it symbolizes the majesty and power of God in the exercising of judgment upon the ungodly.

The word translated "lamp" is more properly translated "torch," as it is in John 18:3. (On the "seven Spirits" see comments, 1:4.) As torches, the Spirit can be sent wherever the throne occupant wills. Since they are torches and not lamps and are closely related to the thunders and lightnings of judgment, Milligan concludes that, "As they burned before the throne [they] sent out a blazing and fierce rather than a calm and soft light" (p. 68), indicating strong, robust activity. But, in contrast to the terror generated by the thunder and lightning of judgment, the Spirit instructs, illuminates, and comforts (cf. Acts 9:31); thus comfort is mingled with terror.

v. 6. "And before the throne, as it were a sea of glass like unto crystal; and in the midst of the throne, and round about the throne, four living creatures full of eyes before and behind." This majestic scene is enhanced by the description of a glassy sea before the throne upon which shimmers in reflection the sparkling glory of the jasper and sardius, symbolic of Him who sits upon the throne. Many and varied have been the explanations of this symbol; some of them are exceedingly fanciful. (For a list of these see Plummer, *Pulpit Commentary*.) Note that the sea is "before" the throne, not under it as if the throne rested upon it. Lenski makes an interesting argument for its representing the providence of God, transparent and lucid, clear as crystal. It seems more probable, however, that the sea of glass before the throne indicates the transcendence of God and marks the differential between creature and Creator, between believer and God. This differential will ever exist in time, and the saints' approach to God and His throne must be accomplished as through the fire before one can sing the victory song (15:2). But when the present order shall have passed away and the saints are at home with God, the sea is no more (21:1); for we shall be like Him (I John 3:2).

The King James translation "beasts" is admitted by all to be unfortunate. These are not "beasts" (*thērion*), wild beasts (cf. 13:1, 11, etc.), but "living creatures" or "living beings" (A. & G.), (*zōan*, from *zōē*, life). For a fuller discussion of these "living creatures" see under verse 8 below. These are distinguished from the angels (5:11) and from "every created thing" that praises God and the Lamb (5:13f.). Their being "full of eyes before and behind" indicates ability to see in every direction, thus maintaining total insight of God's creation; nothing escapes their gaze.

v. 7. "*And the first creature was like a lion, and the second creature like a calf, and the third creature had a face as of a man, and the fourth creature was like a flying eagle.*" It cannot be determined with certainty whether the form of each is different or whether only the faces are diverse. Swete seems to have suggested an explanation for the four faces which presents the fewest difficulties when he said, "The four forms suggest whatever is noblest, strongest, wisest and swiftest in animate nature." These qualities are combined in the living creatures to carry out the divine purpose.

v. 8. "*And the four living creatures having each one of them six wings, are full of eyes round about and within: and they have no rest day and night, saying, Holy, holy, holy, is the Lord God, the Almighty, who was and who is and who is to come.*" A study of Isaiah's "seraphim" (Isa. 6:2-3) and Ezekiel's "cherubim" (Ezek., chaps. 1 and 10) will be helpful, though not decisive, in interpreting John's living creatures, for John's use of figures and symbols is independent. Isaiah's seraphim have six wings; Ezekiel's cherubim have four; John's living creatures have six as do Isaiah's seraphim. Ezekiel's cherubim have four faces each; John's living creatures have one face each. Isaiah's seraphim worship and praise Him who sits upon the throne; Ezekiel's cherubim go forth as burning coals, as flashes of lightning to carry out the divine will in the execution of judgment, providing the coals of fire to be scattered over the city. John's living creatures praise God day and night (4:8); they usher in the four horsemen (6:1-8); one of these give the seven bowls of wrath to the seven angels (15:7); and they are among those who commend God's judgment against the harlot, saying, "Amen; Hallelujah" (19:4). From this it may be concluded that they either represent spiritual forces of God used to carry out His divine purposes, or are a special order of heavenly beings, probably the highest and closest to the throne, who serve God's majestic will. The latter view is preferred. As they share in His holiness so they share in His judgment against sin. Being "full of eyes round about and within," the four see not only all that is external but also all that is within themselves. Man and earthly creatures must have rest to survive, but these "have no rest day and night." They maintain constant vigil over all God's creation. Their song is one of praise to the eternal Father, whose attributes are absolute.

The phrase "Holy, holy, holy is the Lord God," probably does not embrace the "trinity" concept, but rather it indicates the use of the divine thrice holy to express the perfect and absolute holiness of God. "The Almighty," occurring only once in the Epistles (II Cor. 6:18) and nine times in Revelation, always refers to God the Father. This conclusion is sustained by its use in 1:4 (see comments) and in 19:15 and 21:22 where it definitely refers to the Father as distinguished from the Son. As the Almighty He exercises sovereignty over His creation, has all might and power, and is the All-ruler, the provider of all things spiritual and material. He reigns supreme (11:17; 19:6), is King of the ages (15:3), executes judgments (16:7), wars against the forces of evil in the day which He determines (16:14), and uses His Son to tread the winepress of the fierceness of His wrath (19:15). The four living creatures sing of this complete sovereignty. "Who was, etc.," indicates His eternity (see v. 9). These four praise Him for His infinite holiness, His absolute sovereign power and rule, and His eternal being.

vv. 9–10. *"And when the living creatures shall give glory and honor and thanks to him that sitteth on the throne, to him that liveth for ever and ever, the four and twenty elders shall fall down before him that sitteth on the throne, and shall worship him that liveth for ever and ever, and shall cast their crowns before the throne, saying."* The giving of glory, honor, and thanks to the Almighty by the living creatures becomes a signal for the twenty-four elders, the redeemed of God (see comments, v. 4), to fall down before Him in adoration and worship. In casting their crowns before Him the redeemed acknowledge that He is the source or cause of their salvation and victory.

Twice it is said that He lives "forever and ever," emphasizing God's eternity, which would stand in contrast to all heathen deities. These begin with their human creators and perish with the peoples that worshiped them. Jehovah's declaration, "I am the first, and I am the last; and besides me there is no God" (Isa. 44:6), stands verified. The living creatures' song praising the holiness, omnipotence, and eternity of God calls forth from the twenty-four elders the song of creation; for the eternal God who provides salvation is the Creator of all things and only He can provide such a benefit for the creature.

v. 11. *"Worthy art thou, our Lord and our God, to receive the glory and the honor and the power: for thou didst create all things, and because of thy will they were, and were created."* Because of His infinite and eternal quality of being and His excellent greatness, He merits this recognition as Lord and God. Anyone who would recognize the emperor or his statue as Lord or God is not worthy to offer such praise to God, and conversely, any one who recognizes the true God as Lord cannot pay homage to a man or idol. The foundation for definite decisions is being laid. The living creatures had given glory and honor (and thanks) to Him and to this praise the elders add "and the power," for it was by His divine power that all things exist: "For thou didst create all things, and because of thy will they were, and were created."

All creatures, animate and inanimate, that have been created are the product of God's will. Before they were brought into existence as realities, they were planned in the divine mind and were brought forth as expressions of His will; "For he commanded and they were created" (Ps. 148:5). As one studies any phase of the created universe he is thinking God's thoughts after Him. In writing of the glorious creation Isaiah asks, "Who hath directed the Spirit of Jehovah, or being his counselor hath taught him?" (Isa. 40:13). The self-evident answer is, No one. As the creation expresses God's will and is a product of His own plans, so redemption is according to the counsel of His will and of His plan formulated before the ages. Therefore any form of creature worship is idolatry.

CHAPTER 5
The Lamb and the Book

v. 1. *"And I saw in the right hand of him that sat on the throne a book written within and on the back, close sealed with seven seals."* Chapters four and five are closely related: chapter four sets forth the throne of the universe and Him who sits upon it; chapter five gives prominence to the Lamb, to whom is given equal praise with God, and the book which He takes out of God's right hand. "And I saw" introduces this new phase of the vision. The book seen by John lay in (Greek, "on") the open right hand of God. One is not to visualize the book as flat with leaves, such as those with which we are acquainted, but should think of it as a scroll of parchment or papyrus. Such a scroll was usually rolled over two cylindrical sticks, one on either end of the long sheet. As the sheet is wound over one stick, the material on the other is unwound, bringing fresh material to view. The vision refers to such a book or roll.

The book John saw was "written within and on the back," indicating fullness and completeness; nothing was to have been added. In a vision Ezekiel saw such a book which was also written "within and without," except that Ezekiel's book was open, revealing its content (Ezek. 2:10). The symbolic significance of the book on God's hand is discussed below (v. 8).

"Close sealed with seven seals," was to safeguard the material from being tampered with or exposed to view and to assure its reaching the proper destination intact. The seal was usually of wax or other soft substance on which the owner's or sender's name or emblem was impressed by his signet-seal. The "seven" symbolized perfection, completeness (see 1:4); thus the full roll was thoroughly sealed for its protection.

v. 2. *"And I saw a strong angel proclaiming with a great voice, Who is worthy to open the book and to loose the seals thereof?"* John's attention is directed next to a "strong" angel, a mighty or powerful one (mentioned also in 10:1; 18:21), whose great voice could be heard in every realm of rational beings. The proclamation was issued as a challenge, "Who is worthy?" literally, "of sufficient weight," i.e., of moral character and ability to open the book. "Worthy" (*axios*) occurs seven times in Revelation, six in a good sense, as here (3:4; 4:11; 5:2, 4, 9, 12), and once in a negative sense (16:6). To loose the seals would be to break them, thus allowing the book to be opened and its content made known.

v. 3. "*And no one in the heaven, or on the earth, or under the earth was able to open the book, or to look thereon.*" To open the book meant loosing the seals and exposing its content. To look upon it meant more than merely viewing it, for John had already seen it lying on God's right hand. To open and look thereon meant to comprehend, disclose, and execute its contents. Heaven, earth, and under the earth (cf. Phil. 2:10), include the living creatures, elders, and angels of heaven, all the great and mighty ones of earth and the spirits in Hades, the unseen world. From among this all-inclusive host no one responded, for no one was "able" (*dunamai*); i.e., no one possessed the power or ability by virtue of his own resources or through a state of mind to open the book. The book was not offered to John.

v. 4. "*And I wept much, because no one was found worthy to open the book or to look thereon.*" John was "weeping much," not from self-pity or because his curiosity regarding the book's content would not be gratified, but because it appeared that the purpose for which he had been caught up to heaven, "to see the things which must come to pass hereafter" (4:1), would not be realized. Therefore, he and the saints would be deprived of this knowledge and purpose of God by the want of one qualified to open the book; for as yet the Lamb had not been revealed to him in the vision.

v. 5. "*And one of the elders saith unto me, Weep not; behold, the Lion that is of the tribe of Judah, the Root of David, hath overcome to open the book and the seven seals thereof.*" One of the elders, who himself had been redeemed by the mighty power of Christ (see comment, 4:4), urged John to stop weeping; for though the created ones of heaven, earth, and under the earth had been contemplated for the task, there was yet another to be considered, one who is from everlasting (Mal. 5:2). Swete has well said, "Higher natures see that human grief is often needless, springing from insufficient knowledge" (p. 77).

"Behold" is an imperative which focuses attention on what is to be seen or heard: "The Lion that is of the tribe of Judah." This phrase looks back to the time when Jacob blessed his sons and said of Judah, "Judah is a lion's whelp. . . . The sceptre shall not depart from Judah, nor the ruler's staff from between his feet, until Shiloh come; and unto him shall the obedience of the peoples be" (Gen. 49:9-10).

This long-expected descendant of Judah, who would possess the strength of the lion, bear the sceptre of rule over the peoples, and speak peace or bring rest to men, had now come: "For it is evident that our Lord hath sprung out of Judah" (Heb. 7:14). Also, He is the "Root of David," which fulfills the promise God made to David (II Sam. 7:11-14), confirmed as a covenant by an oath (Ps. 89:3f.), and kept alive through the prophets (Isa. 11:1-10; cf. Rom. 15:12). As the Root of Jesse, the Seed of David, He has overcome, conquered, prevailed, and made Himself worthy to loose the seals, open the book, and make known and carry out its contents. In His conflict with Satan, the Lamb overcame him (see comments, 12:7-10), and in the conflict and through the cross He wrested from him the keys of death and Hades (1:17f.), and has sat down on the right hand of God, "having become by so much better than the angels as he hath inherited a more excellent name than they" (Heb. 1:3f.); "henceforth expecting till his enemies be made the footstool of his feet" (Heb. 10:13). In this victory he has secured redemption for the world. Therefore only he is worthy to open the book.

v. 6. "And I saw in the midst of the throne and of the four living creatures, and in the midst of the elders, a Lamb standing, as though it had been slain, having seven horns and seven eyes, which are the seven Spirits of God." "And I saw" indicates a new phase of the vision, as in 4:1. As new significance is given to what John sees, it seems that the sea of glass, the rainbow, and the thunders are not now seen or heard. John looks to see a Lion, the symbol of majesty and power; but instead, he sees a Lamb which, though it had been slain, was now standing and living. This introduces the sacrificial and redemptive aspect of the One whom John saw. He had overcome to open the book not by the power of kingly might, but by sacrifice through love. By this He had defeated His foes and had overcome the world (John 16:33), and by this His subjects must now conquer.

"In the midst" points to the position nearest the Eternal God. The Lamb is the center of creation and redemption; He has first place among living creatures, elders, and creation. God had summed up all things in Him, that is, He had brought together all things under one head in the Son (Eph. 1:9), "that in all things he might have the preeminence" (Col. 1:15-18).

Three words occur in the New Testament that are translated "lamb." *Arēn* is used once (Luke 10:3); *amnos*, four times (John 1:29, 36; Acts 8:32; I Peter 1:19); and *arnion*, once in John's Gospel (21:15), and twenty-nine times in Revelation; twenty-eight times it refers to Jesus and once to the earth-beast that "had two horns like a lamb" (13:11). *Amnos* points to the nature and character of His sacrifice (Vine). Delitzsch, commenting on Isa. 53:7 says, "All the references in the New Testament to the Lamb of God (with which the corresponding allusions to the passover are interwoven) spring from this passage in the book of Isaiah."[1] John the Baptist's reference to "the Lamb of God" (*amnos*) has either Isaiah or the sacrificial offerings of the law in mind (John 1:29, 36). Philip explained Isaiah's passage as pointing to Jesus' sacrifice for sins (Acts 8:32), and Peter wrote of Jesus' blood as that of a lamb (*amnos*) without blemish (I Peter 1:19), in which he seems clearly to have Isaiah's words in mind (cf. Isa. 52:3; 53).

Arnion (lamb), used by John in Revelation, presents Christ on the basis of His sacrifice and especially in His acquired majesty, dignity, honor, authority, and power (Vine). As to the difference between *amnos* and *arnion*, Lenski says "it is a merely linguistic matter in the Greek" (p. 198). In our thinking we are prone to magnify the true characteristics of a lamb seeing it as a docile, innocent, meek, submissive, and helpless creature. However John's use of "the Lamb of God" seems to emphasize the sacrifice of the Lamb—though it does recognize these other qualities. The one who rules as "the Lion of the tribe of Judah" gained that right through sacrifice, and those who rule with Him now must gain their right to rule with Him in the same manner.

A brief summary of "the Lamb" in Revelation indicates this principle. He stood in the midst of the throne through having been

---

[1] Franz Delitzsch, *Commentary on Isaiah* (Grand Rapids, William B. Eerdmans, reprint, 1950): II, 323.

slaughtered (5:6). As the Lamb He is worthy to receive praise (5:12) and to open the seals (6:1). He is capable of great wrath, before which His enemies cower in terror (6:16). The redeemed ascribe their salvation to Him (7:9–10), for they had washed their robes in His blood and made them white (7:14), had overcome by His blood (12:11), and now had their names in His book of life (13:8). These have the Lamb's name on their forehead (14:1), follow Him whithersoever He goes (14:4), sing His song (15:3), gain victory in warfare through His victory (17:14), and share in His marriage supper (19:7, 9).

In the final scene God and the Lamb are the temple (21:22), the Lamb is the lamp (21:23), and the Lord God and the Lamb share the throne together (22:1–3). "As though it had been slain" gives further credence to the idea of sacrifice, as does "standing" to the idea of victory. The vision gives emphasis to victory through sacrifice. The word *sphattō* (to slay "especially of victims for sacrifice," Vine), occurs eight times in Revelation, seven times with reference to Christ or of those slain for Him and His cause, and once of an apparent assassination (13:3). The use of the word confirms the definition above of its sacrificial meaning (see in addition to this passage v. 9, 12; 6:4, 9; 13:8; 18:24).

"Having seven horns." "Horn" was used metaphorically by the Hebrews for power; prophetically, "horn" described the strength of Joseph's sons among the tribes of Israel (Deut. 33:17), and that of Jehovah's king (I Sam. 2:10). Zedekiah, the false prophet, symbolized power by iron horns which he used as if to push the enemy (II Chron. 18:10), and the psalmists and prophets used the term repeatedly to express the idea of power. The seven horns of the Lamb symbolize the fullness and perfection of His power, for "All authority [power] hath been given unto me in heaven and on earth" (Matt. 28:18).

"And seven eyes," symbolizes full and perfect knowledge—omniscience—for "in him are all the treasures of wisdom and knowledge hidden" (Col. 2:3). This thought is expressed in the words of Hanani, the prophet who said, "For the eyes of Jehovah run to and fro throughout the whole earth, to show himself strong in behalf of them whose heart is perfect toward him" (II Chron. 16:9). Zechariah said of the stone set before Joshua, "Upon one stone are seven eyes" (Zech.

3:9), "which run to and fro through the whole earth" (Zech. 4:10. See my *Commentary on the Minor Prophets*, Baker, 1972) "which are the seven Spirits of God sent forth into all the earth." In 4:5 the seven Spirits are before the throne as burning torches; here they are sent forth into all the earth, bearing witness (John 15:26) and revealing truth (John 16:13). And so as the Lamb is omnipotent, having seven horns, and omniscient, having seven eyes, He is also omnipresent through His "seven" Spirits—the Holy Spirit—whom He sent forth to the apostles, through whom He revealed to the human family Himself, His truth, and His power which is everywhere at all times.

v. 7. *"And he came, and taketh it out of the right hand of him that sat on the throne."* Only through symbols in a vision could a lamb take a book out of anyone's hand. The Lamb, having overcome and thus proving Himself worthy in every possible way, now takes out of God's hand the book whose contents He will execute, revealing and carrying out the scheme of redemption. This was not something done while John watched, but rather it had taken place at His ascension, when the Savior sat down on the right hand of God and was given all authority in heaven and on earth (Matt. 28:18), "angels and authorities and powers being made subject unto him" (I Peter 3:21f.).

v. 8. *"And when he had taken the book, the four living creatures and the four and twenty elders fell down before the Lamb, having each one a harp, and golden bowls full of incense, which are the prayers of the saints."* Now is an appropriate time to identify the book, for clearly it is a symbol. What does it symbolize? John said that the book was written within and on the back, indicating fullness and completeness, and that it was "close sealed with seven seals," signifying that it was as originally purposed in the mind of God. Its contents had been neither made known nor altered. The Lamb who had conquered was the only one found worthy to open the seals and disclose the content of the book. The evidence indicates that the book symbolizes God's eternal purpose for man's salvation, the grand scheme of redemption. This plan was formulated in the mind of God and was a mystery—something unknown or hidden—until revealed. God purposed or planned that this salvation which existed as a mystery should be brought forth and made known in the fullness of time (Eph. 1:9–10). It was "foreordained according to the purpose of him who worketh all things after the counsel of his will" (Eph. 1:11), "according to the eternal purpose which he [God] purposed in Christ Jesus our Lord" (Eph. 3:11).

For ages this mystery had been hidden in God (Eph. 3:9), known only to Him. Principalities and powers (spiritual beings) did not understand what God was doing, but were now learning through the fulfilling and revealing of that purpose in Christ and the church (Eph. 3:10). Angels had desired to look into it (I Peter 1:12); prophets had been given glimpses of what it included, but they realized that the plan was not being revealed in their day, but would be fulfilled and made known later (I Peter 1:10f.). Christ had now provided the acceptable sacrifice, defeated Satan, conquered sin and death, and fulfilled the purpose of God. Now he was in a position to take the purpose or plan of God out of His hand, send forth the Holy Spirit to reveal this truth, and Himself carry out the purpose to its ultimate consummation. This concept of "the book" is in harmony with the entire New Testament and is confirmed by the remainder of Revelation.

As the Lamb took the book out of God's right hand, the four living creatures and the elders fell down before Him in adoration and praise, "having each one a harp." The harp or lyre symbolized praise; it and the psaltery or viol were the chief instruments of the Old Covenant worship. Mechanical instruments were not used in the New Testament church worship; the "melody" was produced with the heart, which is the only instrument authorized by God (Eph. 5:19). Paul refers to the harp, pipe, and trumpet to illustrate a point but makes no reference to their being used in worship (I Cor. 14f.). John heard the redeemed who were with Christ, the hundred and forty and four thousand singing, whose voice was "as the voice of harpers harping with their harps" (14:2); and he saw those who came off victorious from the beast and his image, "having harps of God" (15:2). Whatever these harps were they were provided by God and were suitable for heavenly praise. In contrast, John points out that the voice of all instruments of praise or social festivities would be mute in fallen Babylon (18:22).

"And golden bowls full of incense," which are identified as "the prayers of the saints," symbolized literal prayers. Incense and prayer are associated in the Old Covenant: David prayed, "Let my prayer be set forth as incense before thee" (Ps. 141:2), and as incense was being burned within the sanctuary, prayers were being offered without (Luke 1:10). The same combination of incense and prayer is found in 8:3-4. Neither the literal harp nor the burning of incense were a part of New Testament worship, but in the vision they symbolize praise and prayer of the saints.

v. 9. *"And they sing a new song saying, Worthy art thou to take the book, and to open the seals thereof: for thou wast slain, and didst purchase unto God with thy blood men of every tribe, and tongue, and people, and nation."* The singers are the four living creatures and the twenty-four elders (v. 8) who sing the new song, the song of redemption or of the new spiritual creation. The song is new (*kainos*) in kind because of its content (cf. also 14:3). A "new song" is "one which, in consequence of some new mighty deeds [or deed] of God, comes from a new impulse of gratitude in the heart."[2] The term occurs frequently in the Psalms; and with the coming of salvation through Jehovah's servant, Isaiah wanted all to "sing unto Jehovah a new song, and his praise from the end of the earth" (42:10).

Song (*ōdē*) occurs in the New Testament only in the praise of God and Christ (Eph. 5:19; Col. 3:16; Rev. 5:9; 14:3 [twice]; and 15:3 [twice]), The new song praises the Lamb for His worthiness through sacrifice to take the book of God's eternal purpose, open the seals, thereby making it known and carrying it out. Through this perfect and all-sufficient sacrifice the Lamb had purchased men with His blood. Paul uses *agorazō*, to purchase or buy, when he says, "for ye were bought with a price" (I Cor. 6:20; 7:23), and Peter uses it when he writes of those denying "the Master that bought them" (II Peter 2:1).

Being purchased by His blood is equivalent to His loosing us "from our sins by his blood" (1:5). These purchased unto God were representative of all peoples, being from "every tribe," clan or company united by kinship, "and tongue," that is of a common language (cf. Acts 2:4, 6 with verses 8, 11), "and people," of the same race or stock, "and nation," associated or living together, of the same nature or genus. This combination appears numerous times in Revelation, fulfilling the prophecy of Daniel (7:13f.). It is used to express the universality of

---

[2]Franz Delitzsch, *Commentary on the Psalms* (Grand Rapids: William B. Eerdmans, reprint, 1950): I, 402.

Christ's provision for redemption through His blood and of His kingdom.

v. 10. "And madest them to be unto our God a kingdom and priests; and they reign upon the earth." Since those bought with Christ's blood were purchased "unto God," that is, for Him, they therefore belong to Him now. Because those belonging to Him by this purchase price were "made unto our God a kingdom and priest," it follows that these are now the kingdom of God. Earlier John had said that those loosed from their sins by His blood were made a kingdom, to be priests unto God (1:5f.), and he had identified himself with the suffering saints "in the kingdom" (1:9). This is the kingdom that God would establish in the days of the fourth world empire (Dan. 2:44), and which was given to Christ when He ascended triumphantly to God. It was a kingdom in which "all the peoples, nations and languages should serve him" (Dan. 7:13f.). Daniel's prophecies find their fulfillment in this kingdom of people redeemed by Christ. If the people are priests now, they are a kingdom now, "a kingdom and priests" (1:6; 5:10). Peter says of those redeemed by the blood of the Lamb that they are "a holy priesthood" set apart unto Him, "a royal priesthood" related to the king, and "a holy nation," a people for God's own possession (I Peter 1:19; 2:5, 9). The mission of this new priesthood of redeemed people is to "offer spiritual sacrifices" and to "show forth the excellencies" of God who called them (cf. Heb. 13:15-16).

"And they reign upon the earth," for as Christ reigns now, so are the redeemed endued with kingly power to rule with Him upon the earth at this present time. These who are saved by grace were raised up to sit with Him in this spiritual realm (Eph. 2:5f.), and through this abundance of grace and the gift of righteousness they "reign in life" through Him (Rom. 5:17). A parallel is seen between the redeemed Israel whom God brought to Sinai and told, "Ye shall be unto me a kingdom and priests, and a holy nation" (Exod. 19:6), and these redeemed in Christ who are made "a kingdom and priests," "a holy nation." In summary, these purchased by Christ's blood are made a kingdom and priests, and they reign upon the earth, exercising kingly power with Him.

v. 11. "And I saw, and I heard a voice of many angels round about the throne and the living creatures and the elders; and the number of them was ten thousand times ten thousand, and thousands of thousands." It is difficult for us earth-bound creatures to think without concepts of space, hence we are prone to place the creatures or beings of our thoughts and imagination into spacial relationships. Although in the heavenly realm this spacial relation may or may not be true, the Lamb is usually pictured as being nearest the throne-occupant, the living creatures next, and the redeemed about these. Beyond this group and surrounding the throne is the great group of "many angels" who attend upon Him who rules over all. The expression "ten thousand times ten thousand, and thousands of thousands" is from the Greek "myriads of myriads, and thousands of thousands" (Westcott-Hort, *Greek New Testament*), an indefinitely great number, standing for a quantity expressed by the writer of Hebrews as "innumerable" (Heb. 12:22; cf. Ps. 68:17; Dan. 7:10).

v. 12. *"Saying with a great voice, Worthy is the Lamb that hath been slain to receive the power, and riches, and wisdom, and might, and honor, and glory, and blessing."* Christ's sacrifice made no provision for fallen angels (Heb. 2:16), and the holy angels need none; yet as ministering spirits doing service for the sake of the redeemed (Heb. 1:14), they desire to look into the grand scheme of redemption (Eph. 3:10; I Peter 1:12). As fellow-servants with men such as John and his brethren (Rev. 19:10; 22:9), they join in praising the Lamb who is worthy by virtue of His victory in conflict and sacrifice.

In 4:11, where God as Creator receives a threefold ascription of praise, and in 7:11 where it is sevenfold, the definite article appears before each specific attribute. But in this instance where the angels praise the Lamb there is only one article which begins the list of seven. In explaining this, Alford suggests, "We must regard them all as if they formed but one word."

In this sevenfold ascription to the Lamb there is no repetition; each expresses a quality peculiar to itself. He is worthy to receive (1) "the power" (*dunamis*), infinite or divine power, power to rule equal to that of God; (2) "riches" (*ploutos*), "wealth or abundance," riches in the fullness of His creation and Godhood (Col. 1:16–17; 2:9), "unsearchable" (Eph. 3:8) riches out of which He can provide fully for the abundant life (John 10:10); (3) "wisdom" (*sophia*), insight into the true nature of things by virtue of insight into their underlying causes and consequences. All the treasures of true wisdom are summed up in Christ (Col. 2:3); (4) "might" (*ischus*), expresses the idea of strength or might, "the attribute by which that power (*dunamis*) is put into action" (*Pulpit Commentary*); (5) "honor" (*timē*), high respect out of the value placed upon one, merit, preciousness; (6) "glory" (*doxa*), "brightness, splendor, radiance" (A. & G.)—the splendor of that light unapproachable in which God dwells (I Tim. 6:16) is now His (see comments, 1:6); (7) "blessing" (*eulogia*) signifies praise; the word is often used as a benediction, to wish happiness, honor, obedience to and respect for someone. The sevenfold ascription is complete as a unit, as one.

v. 13. "*And every created thing which is in the heaven, and on the earth, and under the earth, and on the sea, and all things that are in them, heard I saying, Unto him that sitteth on the throne, and unto the Lamb, be the blessing, and the honor, and the glory, and the dominion, for ever and ever.*" Beyond the innumerable host of angels a wider circle is now revealed which includes the whole of creation, animate and inanimate—all created things in every realm. These join in one thunderous acclamation of praise to the Creator and Redeemer. It is not said that John *saw* the whole creation, but that he *heard* the praise of the creation as it blended with that of the creatures of heaven and earth, the spirits under the earth (cf. v. 3), and all things on the sea. In this instance "the sea" is to be taken literally, as in heaven, earth, and Hades; it is introduced here for the first time. Its creatures are included in the total praise; "on the sea" probably means near the surface, though "all things therein" includes everything beneath.

The passage is reminiscent of Psalm 148 in which the whole creation is invoked to praise its Lord. The praise now being offered is to God the Creator and to the Lamb, the Redeemer, "unto him that sitteth on the throne, and unto the Lamb, be the blessing, and the honor, and the glory, and the dominion, for ever and ever." The whole creation begins where the angelic host had left off, with "the blessing." The creation expresses a fourfold attribute of praise, each preceded by a definite article indicating that the totality of the four perfections belong to God *and* the Lamb, for the creation and redemption were a joint work. "Dominion" (*kratos*, see comment, 1:6) is added to blessing, honor, and glory and belongs to both, for the Lamb now sits on the Father's throne and through Him the Father now rules.

Dominion is used to express active power in the rule of the universe. All creation recognizes these total *attributes* of its Creator and Redeemer, and joyously gives praise to the throne as exercising sovereign rule in the universe. This praise and dominion are to be eternal in the Godhead.

v. 14. "*And the four living creatures said, Amen. And the elders fell down and worshipped.*" The only word to be added to what has been seen and said is Amen—be it so! The redeemed fall down and worship, paying homage due to God and His Lamb. Total and complete praise has now been offered to the supreme Godhead: the throne rules.

In offering praise and paying homage befitting infinite Deity to God on His throne, the quartet of living creatures sing the song of His absolute perfection: Holy, Almighty, Eternal. The chorus of elders praise Him in the song of creation, for by His will "they were and were created." An ensemble consisting of the quartet and chorus of elders join in a song of praise to the Lamb as the Redeemer who purchased men unto God by His blood, proving Himself worthy to take and open the book. The myriad host of angels join the heavenly worshipers with their sevenfold song of priase to the Lamb. All creation then closes the series of songs with a stirring anthem of praise to God and the Lamb. The sound dies away with the quartet's hearty *amen* as a grand finale to the majestic scene.

CHAPTER 6
The Opening of the First Six Seals

The opening of the seals in chapter 6 marks the beginning of the Lamb's execution of the grand theme of the sealed book; this theme continues into chapter twenty-one. Several points must be emphasized as we enter this phase of John's revelation:

(1) If our interpretation of the symbolic sealed book is correct, that it is God's eternal purpose for man's redemption, i.e., His scheme of redemption, then as the Lamb begins to open the seals, we are introduced to His carrying out of that purpose. The long-anticipated Messiah has come, and the words of the prophets and the hope of Israel have been fulfilled in Him. He has been completely victorious over all foes; and now the *work* of world redemption, the *rule* over the whole creation, and the final *destruction* of all enemies who withstand Him and spiritual truth are in His hand. Whatever we see in the coming visions will pertain to that eternal purpose and the Lamb's place in it.

(2) As the seals are broken and the scroll unrolled, its contents are not disclosed in words but in symbols. God reveals His purpose in vivid and moving symbolism: horses and riders suddenly appear, cross the stage without saying a word, and vanish in the distance; voices cry from beneath an altar; and a great upheaval in the world and society is flashed before our view.

(3) No person in the vision is identified as a living character; no specific historical event is defined; and no definite point in time is recorded which would enable the reader to build his interpretation around any of these. One must rely on John's assurance, received from a divine source, that he writes of "the things which must shortly come to pass" (1:1), the general period of the church's beginning.

(4) Confronted with symbols and symbolic pictures, the reader faces the task of learning and interpreting their meaning and significance. In a work of this nature there are many interpretations; therefore a commentator must present conclusions without dogmatism but with confi-

dence that his presentation is the most accurate view that fallible human wisdom can determine.

(5) One must ever be conscious that he is interpreting visions. As an illustration of this principle, consider a vision of Ezekiel. In it Ezekiel saw a chariot throne where each of the wheels is described as a "wheel within a wheel," enabling the chariot to move in any of four directions without turning (Ezek. 1:16f.). In the physical world this is impossible, for no vehicle can exist without an axle extending from one set of wheels to the other—and an axle would be impossible with a wheel within a wheel. In a vision, however, this is clearly possible. Similarly, the student need not try to determine how one could open a seal and reveal the contents of a book, then open another seal and repeat the process through the seven seals. In the physical realm such may not be possible, but in a vision it is. As each seal is broken, an aspect of the book's content is flashed before us in action.

THE FIRST SEAL
vv. 1-2

v. 1. *"And I saw when the Lamb opened one of the seven seals, and I heard one of the four living creatures saying as with a voice of thunder, Come."* Which living creature John heard first is not identified; but since the next three are specified as "the second," "the third" and "the fourth," it may be inferred that John heard them in the order of their presentation in 4:7. The creature's voice "as of thunder" may signify the introduction of a revelation from God (cf. Exod. 19:16, 19), or it may indicate that some form of divine judgment is about to go forth (cf. 8:5). Most likely, however, it simply indicates a mighty voice capable of being heard in every realm (cf. 14:2). His cry is "Come"; the added "and see" (KJV) is rejected by nearly all biblical scholars.

But whom does the creature address? Is he speaking to John, telling him to move nearer? If the "and see" does not belong to the text, he is not calling to John; for John was already in a position to see and hear all that would be revealed to him (4:1). Neither is the cry to Christ that He might come forth and carry out His work, for He is already executing His mission as Lamb and Son of David by opening the seals. The thunderous call is to the horseman and horse to come forth on their symbolic mission, thereby revealing one part of the whole panoramic drama. This is true of each horse and rider to follow.

v. 2. *"And I saw, and behold a white horse, and he that sat thereon had a bow; and there was given unto him a crown: and he came forth conquering and to conquer."* Many expositors interpret the rider of the white horse to represent victorious militarism—either militarism in general, or Parthian or Roman in particular. But such a view seems out of harmony with the character and purpose of Revelation. It is evident that the vision indicates conquest of some kind, for the rider went forth carrying a bow, "conquering and to conquer." But what is the nature of his conquest?

Throughout the Old Covenant the horse, often associated with the war chariot, was a symbol of battle, strength, and speed. Job's eulogy to the horse describes his majesty and fearlessness in battle (Job 39:19-25); Jeremiah describes the horse in the siege as being "swifter than eagles" (Jer. 4:13), and Habakkuk says horses are "swifter than leopards, and are more fierce than the evening wolves" (Hab. 1:8). Zechariah describes horses of various colors: red, sorrel (speckled), and white, whose riders patrol the earth (Zech. 1:8, 10). Later he sees red, black, white, and grizzled (speckled) horses pulling chariots with riders, symbolizing those that go forth on missions for Jehovah that quiet His Spirit (Zech. 6:1-8). Prophetically speaking, the Lord said He would use Judah as His "goodly horse in the battle" (Zech. 10:3). Since white is the heavenly color and indicates holiness (see comments, 2:17), the rider of the white horse symbolizes a heavenly mission of conquest.

The rider carries a bow, a weapon of antiquity, used during biblical times for hunting (Gen. 27:3) and also in conquest and war (Gen. 48:22; I Chron. 5:18). David uses this idea metaphorically, saying that God has "bent his bow, and made it ready" against His enemies (Ps. 7:12). In Habakkuk's psalm, Jehovah is described as riding upon His horses, upon His "chariots of salvation" as He comes to rescue His people and thresh the nations. In the conflict His "bow was made quite bare," that is, it was taken out of its sheath or covering and made ready for use in war (Hab. 3:8-13). In a Messianic psalm it is said of the

King, "Thine arrows are sharp; the peoples fall under thee; they are in the heart of the king's enemies" (Ps. 45:5).

The crown given to the rider was the *stephanos*, the victory crown, indicating victory in the conflict as He went forth "conquering and to conquer." From these symbolic uses of horses, bows, and arrows, it is evident that this is a picture of the victorious Christ carrying out the content of the hitherto sealed book. Though He may lead the armies of earth in accomplishing God's purpose, He goes forth here not in military strength or war, but in the gospel to conquer the souls of men according to God's plan. Paul said of Christ, "And he came and preached peace to you that were far off, and peace to them that were nigh" (Eph. 2:17). He came and preached to Gentiles and Jews, not only in person, but in the gospel revealed by the Holy Spirit and preached by the apostles.

THE SECOND SEAL
vv. 3-4

vv. 3-4. "And when he opened the second seal, I heard the second living creature saying, Come. And another horse came forth, a red horse: and to him that sat thereon it was given to take peace from the earth, and that they should slay one another: and there was given unto him a great sword." It is generally agreed by biblical commentators that red, the blood color, indicates war and bloodshed. Again, however, the nature of the warfare here symbolized must be determined. Those who hold the view that the rider of the white horse indicates victorious or triumphant militarism see in the rider of the red horse carnage and slaughter, the result of military power and warfare. If it is true that the first horseman represents militarism, this would follow. But it would not be a correct interpretation if the rider of the first horse symbolizes the going forth of Christ in the gospel, or the going forth of the Word of God and the conquest by His kingdom, according to His divine purpose.

Jesus plainly told His disciples that they would be persecuted, delivered up, and put to death for His sake, and that members of their own families would lead in such opposition (Matt. 10:21). He continued, saying, "Think not that I came to send peace on the earth: I came not to send peace, but a sword" (Matt. 10:34). He continued by showing that the gospel would turn members of a household against one another, but that each individual must shoulder his own cross and lose his life for the Master's sake if need be (Matt. 10:35-39). Thus the persecution that would follow the preaching of the gospel seems best to fit the symbolic rider of the red horse. Here is the historical record: the Jews had opposed Christ and the gospel and persecuted the saints; Nero had bathed Rome in their blood; Domitian was beginning a persecution that had the whole empire steeped in their suffering before Constantine issued his edict of toleration more than two hundred years later. Persecution in some form has always been the lot of faithful children of God.

"That they should slay one another" indicates the slaughtering of men by their fellowmen. The word "slay" (*sphattō*), used here and also in reference to the Lamb slain in sacrifice (see comments, 5:6) and to the souls underneath the altar that had been slain for the Word of God and the testimony they held (6:9), confirms the position taken above. The sword (*machaira*) was the short sword of the Roman infantry, such as the one Peter used to cut off the ear of the high priest's servant (John 18:10f.). *Machaira* was the word used by Jesus to indicate the sword He would send forth (Matt. 10:34). In the Septuagint it is the word translated "knife" at the offering of Isaac by Abraham (Gen. 22:6, 10). Hence, the "great sword" given to the rider was a butchering sword or knife with which he would slaughter men in sacrifice; it was "great" (or "long," *megas*) because of the extent to which it would be used.

THE THIRD SEAL
vv. 5-6

v. 5. "And when he opened the third seal, I heard the third living creature saying, Come. And I saw, and behold, a black horse; and he that sat thereon had a balance in his hand." Black portrays grief and mourning; in it is no light. Blackness describes the cheerless sky clothed in sackcloth when Jehovah stretches forth His hand in rebuke

(Isa. 50:3). When the land is a desolation, the earth mourns and the heavens are made black (Jer. 4:28). In the midst of drought the depressed people express their grief by sitting in black (Jer. 14:2). In the judgment described at the opening of the fifth seal, the sun became black as sackcloth of hair (6:12). The rider of the black horse therefore symbolizes grief, woe, and mourning, the lot of persecuted saints who followed the preaching of the gospel. The grief would result from scarcity of food, symbolized by the balance in the rider's hand and the eating by weight (explained below, v. 6). It was said of old that when Jehovah "should break the staff of bread in Jerusalem," the people would eat bread by weight and drink water by measure "and in dismay" (Ezek. 4:16). Ezekiel was instructed to symbolize this in his own eating of food by weight and drinking water by measure (v. 10). As the balances in the rider's hand indicates a period of scarcity, black indicates the grief and woe accompanying such a time.

v. 6. *"And I heard as it were a voice in the midst of the four living creatures saying, A measure of wheat for a shilling, and three measures of barley for a shilling; and the oil and the wine hurt thou not."* The source of the voice is not identified, but the fact that it comes from the midst of the four living creatures implies that it expresses the sentiment of the four. The "measure" (*choinix*) is a dry measure of less than a quart and represents "about as much as would support a person of moderate appetite for a day" (Vine). The "shilling" (*dēnarian*) referred to only in this verse and in the Gospels, was the most important Roman coin circulated throughout the empire (Hastings, II. 199). It was worth between seventeen and twenty cents, which was apparently a day's wage of a common laborer during Christ's ministry (Matt. 20:2). Since barley was of less value than wheat, it sold for one-third as much, and this poorer fare enabled more persons to survive. If the shilling was a day's wage and could buy only enough for the laborer, there was scarcity and suffering for the family. However, oil and wine were not to be "hurt," that is, there was no common dearth on account of drought or similar calamity.

Wheat, barley, oil, and wine were the staple foods of the period, wine and oil being the more luxurious fare. On such a meager salary one could provide only a bare living and would find it impossible to afford any of these luxuries. The Christian who refused to compromise his conscience by sustaining membership in a pagan guild, as at Thyatira (2:18ff.), or bow to the emperor's image in worship, as at Pergamum (2:12ff.), or be injured in his occupation by Jewish influence, as at Smyrna (2:8ff.), would be hard-pressed to find work whereby he could earn a living. As the luxury items were not hurt, it appears that the rider of the black horse symbolizes hardship and suffering through prejudice against Christians. The price of discipleship might mean discrimination by the world, loss of earnings because of conviction, or difficulty with the world in competing where corruption so often reigns.

THE FOURTH SEAL
vv. 7–8.

vv. 7–8. "*And when he opened the fourth seal, I heard the voice of the fourth living creature saying, Come. And I saw, and behold, a pale horse: and he that sat upon him, his name was Death; and Hades followed with him. And there was given unto them authority over the fourth part of the earth, to kill with sword, and with famine, and with death, and by the wild beasts of the earth.*" The pale color (*chlōros*) was of an indefinite hue. The word occurs four times in the New Testament. Three times it is translated "green," twice as "green grass" (Mark 6:39; Rev. 8:7), once as "any green thing" (9:4), and in this instance it is translated "pale." The word might be used to describe a dull bluish or leaden color, or an ashen hue as the color of a person in sickness or death.

The rider of this horse personified death, while Hades, the unseen realm of spirits, followed with him. We are not told how Hades was traveling, whether likewise riding a horse or trotting along on foot. He was and is always present with death to gather his share of the booty. Each time Hades is mentioned in Revelation it is associated with death. Christ has the keys of death and Hades (1:18)—here, as horseman and attendant, the two are working together (6:8)—but at the end death and Hades give up the dead that are in them (20:13), and both are cast into the lake of fire (20:14).

"And there was given unto them authority over the fourth part of the earth, to kill with sword, and with famine, and with death, and by the wild beasts of the earth." The "given authority" indicates that Christ, who rules with all authority in all realms, allowed this rider to function, but not beyond the limit of His permission. In some way the Lord uses the service of the rider to carry out and accomplish the divine purpose which is bound up in the sealed book.

"The fourth part of the earth" includes a larger sphere of operation than that of the rider of the black horse, but a minor portion of the total. The rider's means of killing are fourfold: (1) He kills "with the sword" (*rhomphaia*), the great Thracian sword, distinguished from the butchering or sacrificial sword of verse 4 (see comments, also 1:16). In each instance that this sword (*rhomphaia*) is named throughout the remainder of Revelation it identifies the two-edged sword which proceeds out of the mouth of the Lamb, and with which He makes war (1:16; 2:12, 16; 19:15, 21). I believe that the sword with which Death the rider kills, symbolizes carnal or military warfare, introduced here for the first time. The Lord permits, even uses the sword of nations to execute judgment upon the earth. (2) He kills "with famine," which often swept countries in those days, taking its toll. Famine is a companion of warfare, and usually follows the ravages of war. (3) He kills "with death," which probably signifies "pestilence," since here it is closely related to famine. Jesus associated the two when telling of calamities to come against Jerusalem (Luke 21:11). This interpretation best fits the picture, since death is personified as killing by means of instruments. Pestilence goes hand in hand with famine as both follow the destruction of war. (4) He kills "by wild beasts of the earth," making the four correspond to God's four sore judgments in Ezekiel (5:16–17; 14:21). The judgment symbolized by this rider is against the world of unregenerate people, but in such judgments Christians must necessarily suffer with the rest.

In summing up the visions of these four seals and their significance, we conclude that they represent (1) the going forth of Christ in the gospel, or the word of redemption's scheme as it had been symbolized by the sealed book; (2) the persecution of saints which followed the preaching of the truth, which brought saints and the world into conflict; (3) discrimination in labor and business which added to the suffering of Christians; and (4) the judgments that fell upon society as a result of pagan rejection of the divine message.

THE FIFTH SEAL
vv. 9-11

v. 9. "And when he opened the fifth seal, I saw underneath the altar the souls of them that had been slain for the word of God, and for the testimony which they held." The Hebrew term for "altar" in the Old Covenant was from a word that meant "place for blood-sacrifice," which was derived from a word that meant "to slaughter or slay a victim" (*Baker's Dict. of the Bible*, p. 38); the New Testament term for altar (*thusiastērion*) "is derived from *thusiazō*, to sacrifice" (Vine). Except in this instance and in 16:7, where the altar refers to that on which sacrifices were offered, the word applies to the altar of incense before God (8:3, 5; 9:13; 11:1; 14:18). In the law it was said that the life "is in the blood" (Lev. 17:11, 14; Deut. 12:23) and that the blood of the sacrifices was to be poured out at "the base" of the altar (Lev. 4:7, 18, 30, et al.). Therefore, when the blood was poured out, it was the life that was being offered.

The "souls" (*psuchas*) which John saw beneath the altar were the lives of those who had been sacrificed for Christ. Jesus gave "his life [*psuchēn*] a ransom for many" (Matt. 20:28); and the saints "loved not their life [*psuchēn*] even unto death" (Rev. 12:11). These underneath the altar were those who had given up their own lives in sacrifice for the Word of God and the testimony which they held. They were being sacrificed for the same reason that John was on Patmos (cf. 1:9). The sacrificial concept is further confirmed by the word "slain," used of those in verse 4 and of Jesus (5:6, 9), who were slaughtered in sacrifice. They were slain "for," (*dia*), because of or by reason of the Word of God which they had accepted and believed, and which was the basis of their faith and hope; and "for" (*dia*) the testimony which they held, that is, the testimony to that faith confessed in word and in life. Later, John points out that one reason for their overcoming was "because [*dia*] of the word of their testimony" and that they loved not their life even unto death (12:11, see comments). In holding to the Word of God and the testimony of their faith in it and in Him, they had been offered on the altar of sacrifice to His cause. Paul used similar language to speak of his readiness to be offered in sacrifice for the saints and for the cause of Christ (Phil. 2:17; II Tim. 4:6).

v. 10. "And they cried with a great voice, saying, How long, O

Master, the holy and true, dost thou not judge and avenge our blood on them that dwell on the earth?" The cry from the souls underneath the altar is "great" because of the number represented and the importance of their cause and plea. "How long," suggests that this was not the beginning of the struggle but that it had been continuing for some time—from the Jewish persecution in Jerusalem, through that of Nero, and now the persecution in the days of Domitian. However, throughout the first section of the book the apostle is concerned with general principles and conditions for all time. The beasts that opposed the saints and put them to death are not introduced until chapter 13, although this struggle is definitely before him. When would it end? The question is not answered.

This cry had been on the lips of suffering or persecuted saints through the centuries; usually it was left unanswered, the answer being for Jehovah to decide (Ps. 6:3; 13:1f.; 35:17; 74:9f.; 79:5; 80:4; 89:46; 90:13; 94:3; Isa. 6:11 [which God answered]; Jer. 47:6; Hab. 1:2; Zech. 1:12). The word "Master" (*despotēs*) occurs only this one time in Revelation. As servants (*doulois*, bondservants) of Jesus (1:1), the saints would recognize Him as the Master of life and destiny. (For "the holy and true" see comments, 3:7.) The cry is not for revenge, but for a vindication of their death and the cause for which they had died.

The question is, How long will it be before He judges (*krinō*), determines, and pronounces a judgment in their favor, on their behalf, as opposed to those that had slain them? How long before He avenges (*ekdikeō*) their death, sees that they get justice against their opponents? They are crying for the just judgment which is due them. "Them that dwell on the earth" are the unregenerated earthlings or earth-dwellers (see comments, 3:10) who were responsible for the saints' death. Unavenged blood cries from the ground (Gen. 4:10), for expiation must be made and covering provided by the blood of the murderers (Num. 35:33; see also Job 16:18; Isa. 26:21; Ezek. 24:7). The saints cry for justice because when God called to the heathen nations He promised His own people saying, "Praise his people, ye nations [marginal reading]: for he will avenge the blood of his servants, and will render vengeance to his adversaries, and will make expiation for his land, for his people" (Deut. 32:43). The sacrificed souls are crying to God to fulfill His promise.

v. 11. *"And there was given to them to each one a white robe; and it* was said unto them, that they should rest yet for a little time, until their fellow-servants also and their brethren, who should be killed even as they were, should have fulfilled their course." The white robe (*stolē*) given to each was a long flowing garment of the victorious heavenly color. The saints had won the battle and were now at rest, but were not in the final state of glory; this would not be theirs until after the judgment. They first had to rest "a little time," during the period of persecution and tribulation through which the church was then passing. The speaker has in mind the present struggle rather than the total of time until the end and coming of the Lord. Their fellow-servants who were yet in the struggle must likewise fulfill their warfare, even as these had.

The words "for a little time" (*chronon mikron*) are the same as those used by Jesus when He said, "Yet a little while am I with you" (John 7:33), and "Yet a little while is the light among you" (John 12:35). But how long is a "little" time? Little compared to what? It is one period of time compared with another period of time; not time compared to eternity, for there can be no such comparison made. The little time of their waiting seems to be parallel to the time of Satan in great wrath, "knowing that he hath but a short time" (12:12). The "short time" of Satan terminates when he is defeated and bound (20:1-3, see comments), at which time the saints' "little time" ends and they are raised victoriously to sit on thrones and reign for a thousand years (see comments, 20:4-7).

"Their fellow-servants and their brethren who should be killed" include both those who were willing to be killed but escaped, and those who were killed. Both have fulfilled their course of faithfulness. John further distinguished these when he writes of those (1) "that had been beheaded for the testimony of Jesus," and (2) "such as worshipped not the beast, neither his image" (20:4). The faithful who were willing to die but were not put to death receive the same reward as those who suffered martyrdom.

THE SIXTH SEAL
vv. 12-17

v. 12. "*And I saw when he opened the sixth seal, and there was a great earthquake; and the sun became black as sackcloth of hair, and the whole moon became as blood.*" It is evident that the opening of this seal brings a judgment into view. Many expositors are certain that this is the final judgment which will take place at the Lord's return. But the following evidence shows that the judgment here described is not the great and final one, but a judgment against whatever ungodly world power was persecuting the saints. The saints underneath the altar had cried out for an avenging of their cause and had been told to wait a little time. And now in the opening of this seal God gives assurance that He will avenge their cause by a judgment upon those that inflicted the saints' death.

The Lord pictures a crashing world, earth-shaking events with no light to guide, and darkness engulfing wicked people. The Spirit in the seer draws heavily from Old Testament pictures and descriptions of final judgments brought upon heathen nations that had sought the destruction of God's people. Isaiah had used these same symbols concerning ancient Babylon: "For the stars of heaven and the constellations thereof shall not give their light; the sun shall be darkened in its going forth, and the moon shall not cause its light to shine.... I will make the heavens to tremble, and the earth shall be shaken out of its place" (Isa. 13:10, 13; cf. also 29:6). "I clothe the heavens with blackness, and I make sackcloth their covering" (Isa. 50:3; cf. Jer. 4:23f., 28). Joel also described a future judgment against Jerusalem: "The sun shall be turned into darkness, and the moon into blood" (Joel 2:31). Jesus used these same figures from nature's calamities to describe the coming destruction of Jerusalem by the Romans (Matt. 24:29f.).

Viewed in the light of descriptions of former judgments, the picture before us describes bloodshed and total blackness and the end of the world under consideration. However, this is not the ultimate end toward which we look; the goal is the destruction of the power responsible for the saints' death. The power responsible was the Roman Empire, but this is not revealed until chapter 13.

v. 13. "*And the stars of the heaven fell unto the earth, as a fig tree casteth her unripe figs when she is shaken of a great wind.*" In the writings of older prophets, rulers had been represented by stars (Num. 24:17; Isa. 14:12; Dan. 8:10); however, the falling of the stars in this instance only continues the picture of utter destruction and desolation described in verse 12. The metaphor is probably drawn from meteor showers which often invade our terrestrial atmosphere. The figs (*olun-*

thos) described are a kind of unripe fig "which grows during the winter, yet does not come to maturity, but falls off in the spring" (Thayer). In this instance the figs fall in a shower, as if by a mighty wind.

v. 14. "*And the heaven was removed as a scroll when it is rolled up; and every mountain and island were moved out of their places.*" As a scroll is read it is rolled up; so when a nation comes to an end, its heaven is rolled up, no longer visible. Isaiah had said of heathen nations as the end of their time had come, "And all the host of heaven shall be dissolved, and the heavens shall be rolled together as a scroll; and all their host shall fade away, as the leaf falleth from the vine, and as the fading leaf from the fig tree" (Isa. 34:4). Their heaven should pass away, for the nations and their world would be no more.

The mountains, symbols of permanence and strength and the very foundations of the earth, were removed. The isles were symbols to the ancient people of the most remote lands and far-flung portions of the earth, or of a nation's possessions. At the fall of Tyre, the great commercial power of its period, the isles would shake (Ezek. 26:15, 18; 27:35). These all indicate and illustrate the fall and passing of a great national power when judged by Jehovah.

v. 15. "*And the kings of the earth, and the princes, and the chief captains, and the rich, and the strong, and every bondman and freeman, hid themselves in the caves and in the rocks of the mountains.*" All classes, men of every degree and social standing, are brought into view. First in line of greatness are the kings of the earth, the rulers of the kingdoms or provinces of unregenerate mankind. These are followed by "the princes" (*megistan*), chief men or nobles (translated "lords" of Herod's nobles [Mark 6:21] but "princes" here and in Rev. 18:23). The "chief captains" were the military tribunes or leaders (*chiliarchos*), commanders of a thousand men. The "rich," the wealthy of earth; the "strong," men of strength or power in various positions of life; and every "bondman," a slave, one owned by another; and every "freeman," will all be filled with terror as the judgment strikes. Drawn together by a common calamity, they seek refuge and hide in the caves and rocks of the mountains.

v. 16. "*And they say to the mountains and to the rocks, Fall on us, and hide us from the face of him that sitteth on the throne, and from the wrath of the Lamb.*" Here is further evidence that this is not the final judgment, but the judgment of a kingdom in time; for when the Lord comes, it will be "in a moment, in the twinkling of an eye" (I Cor. 15:52), "as a thief; in the which [day] the heaven shall pass away... the earth and the works that are therein shall be burned up" (II Peter 3:10); at the Lord's coming there will be no time to seek a hiding place. Furthermore, this description of men seeking refuge in the caves and rocks and calling for mountains to fall on them, occurs three times in previous history; in each instance it refers to national calamity. Hosea used this language to describe the destruction of Samaria by the Assyrians (Hos. 10:8); Isaiah used it in prophesying of Jerusalem's fall at the hands of Babylon (Isa. 2:19); and Jesus said this same thing would occur when the Romans came upon Jerusalem (Luke 23:30). It is clear that the use of such symbols at the opening of the sixth seal points to the judgment of a persecuting world power. Later in Revelation it will be revealed that the Roman Empire suffered such a calamity. By divine judgment God will vindicate the cause of His saints.

v. 17. *"For the great day of their wrath is come; and who is able to stand?"* Isaiah had described the "day of Jehovah" as "cruel, with wrath and fierce anger; to make the land a desolation, and to destroy the sinners thereof out of it" (Isa. 13:9; see also Joel 2:11, 31; Zeph. 1:14, 15, et al.). Now that the Lamb has taken the book—the purpose of God—out of the Father's hand and has been delegated to carry out the plan, it is "the great day of their wrath"—God's and the Lamb's. "And who is able to stand?" Nahum asked this same question as Jehovah's impending judgment was about to fall on Nineveh, "Who can stand before his indignation?" (Nah. 1:6). No one was able to stand in either instance. Let it be remembered that the day of judgment against the enemies of God and tormentors of earth is also a day of deliverance for the people of God.

CHAPTER 7

An Interlude

As the seals were opened horsemen went forth on their missions; from beneath an altar souls were heard to cry out for an avenging of the sacrifice which they had made; in response to their cry came judgment. As their world ended crashing about them, the earth-dwellers were seen cowering before the Lamb, seeking a hiding place from His wrath. The reader waits breathlessly for the seventh seal to be broken that he may see the final outcome of this drama of God's divine purpose. With the judgment of earth described and the question asked, "Who is able to stand?" the reader wishes to know whether the saints on earth are able to stand and what happens to those underneath the altar.

However, there is an interlude between the opening of the sixth and seventh seals. During this interlude John sees a vision of two parts which answers our questions about the saints on earth and those underneath the altar. The saints on earth are sealed unto God and those who had died for Him are before His throne praising Him in glory. In these two scenes God assures His saints that He watches after each one, keeping an accurate account. In ancient times He had assured His people by pointing to the host of heaven and declaring that He brings them out by number, calling each by name, and that for all their number not one was lacking (Isa. 40:26). In the same way He assures His suffering saints that He is mindful of each one, whether living on earth or having died in the faith. Not one is lacking now.

SEALING THE 144,000
vv. 1-8

v. 1. "*After this I saw four angels standing at the four corners of the earth, holding the four winds of the earth, that no wind should blow on the earth, or on the sea, or upon any tree.*" There seems to be no

AN INTERLUDE 7:1

question but that here is a restraining of those destructive forces which bring judgment upon mankind. "After this" indicates that the revelation of the sixth seal is complete. Each phase of the new vision, the sealing of the elect and the heavenly scene which follows, is introduced by this phrase. The judgment is restrained for a reason known only to God. The four angels are not wicked angels who control evil forces, but they are servants of God fulfilling their appointed duties (see v. 2).

"The four corners of the earth" is an accommodative term used in Scripture to designate the four directions, the whole surface of the earth. Isaiah used the phrase to refer to Jehovah's gathering of the dispersed of Israel and Judah "from the four corners of the earth" (11:12), simply meaning "the uttermost part of the earth" (24:16). Jesus speaks of the same gathering as being "from the four winds, from one end of heaven to the other" (Matt. 24:31), from all areas whence they had been scattered. Also, at the end of the thousand years Gog and Magog are gathered from the four corners of the earth (20:8).

God speaks of evil going forth from nation to nation as "a great tempest" (Jer. 25:32). The tempest or winds of God are described as scattering winds, destroying winds, and winds of upheaval. The four scattering winds are indicated as He says, "I will bring the four winds from the four quarters of heaven, and will scatter them [the people of Elam] toward all those winds" (Jer. 49:36). God said He would bring against Babylon "a destroying wind" (Jer. 51:1); while upon the great sea would break the four winds of social upheaval out of which would come four great world empires (Dan. 7:2ff.). These four winds go forth from standing before the Lord of all the earth (Zech. 6:5). Winds may be strong or gentle, a curse or a blessing; but whichever they may be, they are held in restraint until God chooses to release them. Judgments are under His control.

"The earth," "the sea" and "the trees" may be interpreted symbolically: the earth signifies the world of the unregenerate as in other passages, the sea symbolizes society in turmoil and instability, and the trees stand for the great men of earth. Or, these may symbolize God's complete control over and use of His creation. Nothing can deter the carrying out of His purpose. Either view is possible, but the latter is probably more befitting the context. All winds, whether tempests or zephyrs, are controlled by God's majestic power, and nothing stirs within the realm of His creation without His permission or direction. The trees are probably mentioned because of their usefulness to man and their susceptibility to destruction by storms.

v. 2. *"And I saw another angel ascend from the sunrising, having the seal of the living God: and he cried with a great voice to the four angels to whom it was given to hurt the earth and the sea."* "Another [*allos*] expresses a numerical difference and denotes another of the same sort" (Vine); thus this angel is identified with the four (v. 1) as being angels of the same character. From "the sunrising" points to the directions of morning light, suggesting that this angel brings a message of cheer and encouragement. When Jehovah left Jerusalem, before 586 B.C. giving the city up to destruction, He departed to the east of the city (Ezek. 11:23); and when His glory returned, it "came from the way of the east" (Ezek. 43:2). God's glory is now appearing from that same direction as He sends His angel to preserve and give assurance to His saints.

The "living God" and His seal (on "living God" see 4:9f. and on "seal" see 5:1) is in contrast to the beast and his mark to whom life had to be given (13:16). Oriental monarchs had their special seals with which to mark and safeguard their possessions and to validate legal documents. Pharaoh gave his signet ring to Joseph (Gen. 41:42), and Ahasuerus, the king of Persia, gave his ring to Haman (Esther 3:10), but later retrieved it and gave it to Mordecai (Esther 8:2). To guarantee security Darius used his and his lords' signet to seal the stone placed at the mouth of the lion's den into which Daniel was cast (Dan. 6:17). In a strikingly similar manner the guards sealed the tomb in which Jesus' body was laid (Matt. 27:66). The Shulamite girl said to her beloved, "Set me as a seal upon thy heart, as a seal upon thine arm," for she belonged to him only and he to her (Song of Sol. 8:6). Paul writes of the sealing of the apostles as they were given "the earnest of the Spirit" (II Cor. 1:22), and of Christians being sealed with the Holy Spirit of promise (Eph. 1:13; 4:30). Jesus uses this expression in speaking of Himself and His work, "for him the Father, even God, hath sealed" (John 6:27). By the supernatural powers which He possesses, God had placed His seal of certification upon Him as His Christ. Paul says, "Howbeit, the firm foundation of God standeth, having this seal, the

Lord knoweth them that are his: and, Let every one that nameth the name of the Lord depart from unrighteousness" (II Tim. 2:19).

This angel in John's vision was coming with God's seal in his hand to act on His behalf in sealing those that are His. The angel cried to the four angels whose power was "to hurt the earth and the sea," that they restrain themselves from exercising that power.

v. 3. *"Saying, Hurt not the earth, neither the sea, nor the trees, till we shall have sealed the servants of our God on their foreheads."* In his cry to the four angels holding the four winds, the angel stated that the function of the winds was to "hurt." But whatever the hurt was, whether the judgment of the sixth seal or some other, it was not to fall until the servants (bondservants or slaves) of God were sealed. Nothing can happen to thwart God's purpose; without His control, no breeze can make the leaves of the trees to tremble; no sparrow "shall fall on the ground without your Father"; and "the very hairs of your head are numbered" (Matt. 10:29f.). God sees, knows, and controls all the forces of the universe and will allow nothing to hinder the sealing of His elect unto Himself. This sealing of His servants brings us to the heart of this first phase of the vision.

The scene is reminiscent of Ezekiel's vision before destruction was turned loose on Jerusalem (586 B.C.). The ancient prophet saw six men approaching the altar, each carrying a slaughter weapon in his hand. In the midst of the six was a man clothed in linen and having an inkhorn by his side. This seventh man was to go through Jerusalem, "and set a mark upon the foreheads of the men that sigh and that cry over all the abominations that are done in the midst thereof"; in other words, those concerned for the things of God. The six were to go through the city slaying without pity or mercy all the wicked people of the city; "but come not near any man upon whom is the mark: and begin at my sanctuary" (Ezek. 9:1-8).

There is this difference: in Ezekiel's vision the faithful received "a mark" upon their forehead, while in John's vision the servants received "a seal." In either case, those who belonged to Jehovah received a visible sign which distinguished them from all others. Sealed "on their foreheads" suggests a most conspicuous place, visible to all. Everyone who beholds the servant will recognize him as belonging to God (cf. II

Tim. 2:19). It should be observed that those to be sealed are *on earth,* and although sealed unto God and therefore preserved against destruction, these are not spared from persecution, for this would continue to plague God's people until victory should be completely won in the eternal home.

v. 4. "*And I heard the number of them that were sealed, a hundred and forty and four thousand, sealed out of every tribe of the children of Israel.*" John did not witness the sealing, but he heard the number. The sum, a hundred forty and four thousand, does not designate a literal numerical quantity, but is a symbolic figure. The most reasonable view is that twelve, the religious number (see Introduction, "Numbers") multiplied by itself and then by one thousand, indicating fullness or completeness, represents the total number of saints on earth at any given time. These are distinguished from the members of the victorious church in heaven before the throne.

Some Bible students think that the hundred and forty-four thousand symbolize the redeemed Jews, while the "great multitude" (v. 9) represents redeemed Gentiles. Based on this supposition that the one hundred forty-four thousand were Jews from the twelve tribes, an argument is made for the early date of Revelation, that it must have been written before the destruction of Jerusalem, A.D. 70. The argument holds that these Jews "by nature" are from the historical tribes, hence tribal identity was yet possible, implying that the Jewish nation still existed and occupied its own land. Therefore the sealing must have taken place before the destruction of Jerusalem. The argument further contends that the four winds against which these were sealed were to overtake the whole land of Judea (McDonald, p. 157).

However, as the number was symbolic, so were the tribes; thus they represented the total number of the redeemed on earth, spiritual Israel. Also the winds were "of the earth" (v. 1), and it was "the earth" that was to be hurt, not Judea. The vision is more inclusive and far-reaching than the early date theory allows. For several reasons the view that these sealed are physical Jews is incorrect: (1) In Revelation there is no distinction made between Jews and Gentiles in Christ—all are His servants, purchased with His blood and made unto Him a kingdom and priests. (2) These who are sealed are upon earth; the "great multitude" are those who are victorious and are before the heavenly throne

(9ff.). (3) The winds are restrained until "the servants of our God have been sealed." John is not speaking of a particular segment, for there were to have been no segments (II Cor. 5:17; Gal. 3:28; Eph. 2:14-17), but all are servants of God. (4) Satan puts a mark upon the foreheads of his subjects (13:16f.; 14:9; 16:2; 19:20; 20:4), and it seems reasonable to suppose that God would seal *all* His subjects unto Himself, not just some of them. (5) "It is the custom of the Seer to heighten and spiritualize all Jewish names. The temple, the Tabernacle, the Altar, Mount Zion, and Jerusalem are to him the embodiments of ideas deeper than those literally conveyed by them" (Milligan, p. 118. For a fuller presentation of this view see Milligan, pp. 117-121).

From this principle of usage it follows that John uses "every tribe of the children of Israel" in a sense beyond that of literal or fleshly Israel. Such is compatible with Scripture. Paul says, "For they are not all Israel, that are of Israel" (Rom. 9:6); "For neither is circumcision anything, nor uncircumcision, but a new creature. And as many as shall walk by this rule, peace be upon them, and mercy, and upon the Israel of God" (Gal. 6:15f.). Thus, the new creature or creation of verse 15 is the Israel of God of verse 16. The true circumcision is that of the heart, not of the flesh (Rom. 2:28f.), which characterizes those "who worship by the Spirit of God, and glory in Christ Jesus, and have no confidence in the flesh" (Phil. 3:3). Since there is no distinction between Jew and Gentile, it is clear that John is writing of all Christians, and not of Jews only.

vv. 5-8. "*Of the tribe of Judah were sealed twelve thousand... Reuben... Gad... Asher... Naphtali... Manasseh... Simeon... Levi... Issachar... Zebulun... Joseph... Benjamin....*" No discernable reason is disclosed for the arrangement of names as they appear in this list. Judah, through whom the Messiah came, is listed first; and Benjamin, the youngest of the twelve, is listed last. It is interesting to note that Ephraim and Dan are not listed, though Manasseh and Joseph are. Levi, who received no land inheritance, appears among the twelve, although his name does not appear in some of the Old Testament lists, e.g., the three lists in Numbers 1 and 2. Why Ephraim and Dan are omitted is not made known, and we can only speculate. A possible explanation is that through Jeroboam I, a descendant (I Kings 11:26), Ephraim led Israel into idolatry (I Kings

12:25-33) and Dan left his inheritance and moved north to Laish (later called Dan) where he settled and practiced idolatry (Judges 18).

The hundred and forty-four thousand who are sealed to God probably represent the active faithful church on earth at any time, called by some expositors "the militant church on earth." Under an entirely different circumstance and setting, the same group is presented again in chapter 14.

THE VICTORIOUS MULTITUDE
vv. 9-17

v. 9. "After these things I saw, and behold, a great multitude, which no man could number, out of every nation and of all tribes and peoples and tongues, standing before the throne and before the Lamb, arrayed in white robes, and palms in their hands." John introduces this second phase of the vision as he introduced the first (v. 1). This was not a new vision, but the counterpart of verses 1-8. To this point the heavenly scenes have revealed the throne and Him that sits upon it, the Lamb, the seven Spirits, the living creatures, the elders, and a great host of angels. Now for the first time there appears a multitude from among the family on earth. This group is described as "a great multitude, which no man could number," but which God can number. Only He knows those who are His and those who continue faithful until death.

The thought of such a number finds its parallel in Jehovah's promise to Abraham, "I will make thy seed as the dust of the earth: so that if a man can number the dust of the earth, then may thy seed also be numbered" (Gen. 13:16). God later repeated this promise, using the stars of heaven to illustrate the multitude's countless number (Gen. 15:5). And to Jacob He said that his seed would be "as the sand of the sea, which cannot be numbered for multitude" (Gen. 32:12). Today, "they that are of faith, the same are sons of Abraham" (Gal. 3:7); and "if ye are Christ's, then are ye Abraham's seed, heirs according to promise" (Gal. 3:29).

Those on earth who are sealed to God are symbolically numbered as a hundred and forty-four thousand, and the ones who are finally victorious are symbolically unnumbered as a great multitude which no man can number. The number of both groups is known only to God. The victorious multitude represents every race and tribe of people; people in the multitude come from the four quarters of the earth (see comments, 5:9; cf. also 11:9; 13:7; 14:6; 17:15). These are "before the throne and before the Lamb," in a position nearer than any hitherto occupied.

The robes of white, the heavenly color, indicate purity, for these saints have been purified and made holy, enabling them to stand before the throne in such proximity to God and the Lamb. The "palms in their hands" add to the festive spirit of the occasion reminiscent of the Feast of the Tabernacles, the most joyous of all Jewish festivals. This feast occurred in the fall of the year, after the harvest had been gathered and the fruit of the trees and vines was in. It followed the annual atonement when sacrifice had been made for sins (Lev. 23:26–32, 39–44). On the first day of this festive week the people were to take the branches of palm trees and boughs of other trees, and "rejoice before Jehovah your God seven days" (Lev. 23:40). When Jesus entered Jerusalem in what is referred to as His "triumphal entry," in a joyous and festive mood the people took "branches of the palm trees and went forth to meet him, and cried out, Hosanna: Blessed is he that cometh in the name of the Lord, even the king of Israel" (John 12:13). These uses of the palm branches indicate festive occasions. The explanation which follows (vv. 13–17) indicates that this heavenly scene is a joyous one to which all such occasions of the past had pointed.

v. 10. "*And they cried with a great voice saying, Salvation unto our God who sitteth on the throne, and unto the Lamb.*" The "great voice" of such an innumerable throng would make insignificant the shouts of all multitudes in the past. The shout of salvation is a shout of praise and gratitude to God and the Lamb for the salvation provided; the multitude acknowledges both to be the source of salvation. The phrase "our God" shows that all the saved have a common basis. God made provision in Christ for a common salvation (Jude 3), and Christ procured it through His blood (5:9–10).

Instead of translating *sōtēria* "salvation," Caird translates it "victory," saying that the multitude is celebrating its triumphant passage through persecution, for the saints had long since been released from their sins. Although victory indeed enters into their joy, it is best to let the word convey its usual meaning of salvation. They are praising God and the Lamb for their total salvation, which began with redemption through His blood, and continued by the divine help through the persecutions and trials to the present moment of triumph. Peter had meant complete redemption when he said that saints were redeemed by Christ's blood (I Peter 1:19), and were to receive "the end [objective] of your faith, even the salvation of your souls" (I Peter 1:9). It was because they had received the total redemption of their souls that the saints in the multitude were now praising God and the Lamb.

v. 11. *"And all the angels were standing round about the throne, and about the elders and the four living creatures; and they fell before the throne on their faces, and worshipped God."* These angels continue to maintain the position round about the throne, along with the elders and the living creatures, which they occupied when introduced in 5:11. The angels, through their intense interest in the scheme of redemption, desired to look into these things (I Peter 1:12); from Eden, the angels had served as ministering servants for the sake of these who should "inherit salvation" (Heb. 1:14), and had learned the true significance of the divine plan as they had seen it fulfilled in Christ and the church (Eph. 3:10f.). Now they fell before the throne in praise and adoration for what had been achieved.

v. 12. *"Saying, Amen: Blessing, and glory, and wisdom, and thanksgiving, and honor, and power, and might, be unto our God for ever and ever. Amen."* Their "Amen" voiced their approval and endorsement of the praise offered by the great multitude (v. 10). As in the throne scene (5:12) where the angels had offered their sevenfold ascription of praise to the Lamb, so here they offer a sevenfold attribution of worship and praise to God. In speaking of Him as "our God," the angels are identifying themselves with the redeemed as belonging to Him.

Of the seven words of praise used here and in 5:12, six are the same, though they do not appear in the identical order. In this song of praise "thanksgiving" appears instead of "riches," probably denoting thanksgiving for riches provided in Him. (For the meaning of each of the seven words, see comments, 5:12). In the praise offered by the angelic host in 5:12, only one definite article appears at the beginning of the list. Here, however, the article appears before each of the attributions, making each distinct, as in 4:11. The angels' praise to God does not exclude the Lamb, for He was included in their Amen to the praise offered to Him by the multitude. (On the phrase "for ever and ever" see 1:6.)

v. 13. "And one of the elders answered, saying unto me, These that are arrayed in the white robes, who are they, and whence came they?" Ever since the multitude was introduced (v. 9), this question asked by one of the elders has no doubt been on the reader's mind and on John's as well, "Who are they, and whence came they?" This focuses attention on their identity and whether they are in heaven or on earth. It seems appropriate that an elder, one who represents the redeemed, would ask and answer the question; it was also an elder who had come to John's aid earlier (5:5). The white robes in which the saints in the multitude are arrayed (v. 9) may have led to the suspicion that somehow these are related to those underneath the altar at the opening of the fifth seal (6:9-11). This question was not a rhetorical one; it was asked that it might be answered.

v. 14. "And I say unto him, My lord, thou knowest. And he said to me, These are they that come out of the great tribulation, and they washed their robes, and made them white in the blood of the Lamb." John's response was with the utmost respect; "my lord" (*kurios*, different from *despotēs*, 6:10), is equivalent to "sir" or "master." Elsewhere throughout Revelation *kurios* is used of God and Christ (except 17:14 and 19:16, where Christ is Lord of human "lords,"). "Thou knowest" is both a confession of John's ignorance and a request for information. The elder's reply identifies the multitude as "they that come out of the great tribulation." The verb tense here indicates a continuous coming, not a past or completed coming as implied by the King James translation, "they which *came*" out of the tribulation.

But what is this great tribulation out of which they were coming? Several answers may be considered:

(1) Jesus had told His disciples of "great tribulation" which would befall the people of Jerusalem in its destruction (Matt. 24:21, 29). However, that tribulation had already occurred some twenty or thirty years before John wrote, and these saints are said to "come" out of the tribulation as though it was continuing at the time.

(2) Some religious groups teach that "the great tribulation" spoken of here is to take place at the end of the present age between what they call "the rapture" and "the revelation" of Jesus. At this time, according to the theory, the saints are caught up to the marriage supper of the Lamb. This idea or assumption has no foundation in Scripture.

(3) Speaking of afflictions that would come upon His disciples, Jesus had forewarned them that in the world they would have tribulation (John 16:33). Paul foretold "that through many [note: not one only] tribulations we must enter into the kingdom of God" (Acts 14:22), and "all that would live godly in Christ Jesus shall suffer persecution" (II Tim. 3:12). The saints were passing through tribulation at the time John wrote and they have continued to pass through tribulations since. This position makes "the great tribulation" the sum of all tribulations from Pentecost to the coming of the Lord.

(4) A fourth view is that "the great tribulation" took place in the Roman period through which the saints contemporary with John were passing, beginning with Nero's persecution (A.D. 64) and continuing until the edict of Constantine (A.D. 313). Those saints are now beyond this life, before the throne of God, having gained the victory. Word of such victory offered tremendous assurance and encouragement to men and women facing trials and death, and likewise encourages all since who face similar tests of faith. The great persecution of this passage was thus confined to the Roman period covering 249 years of Roman-Christian conflict. This view is preferred, since it is in harmony with the theme of the book.

"And they washed their robes and made them white in the blood of the Lamb" raises another question: Are these martyrs who by their death washed their robes in His blood? Probably this is not the thought, for their robes were washed not in their own blood shed in martyrdom, but in the Lamb's blood. The white garments symbolize purity of soul, "holy array" (Ps. 110:3), or "beauty of holiness" (marginal reading, ASV). They had put on "the new man, that after God hath [had] been created in righteousness and holiness of truth" (Eph. 4:24; cf. Col. 3:10).

The Christian's redemption begins and ends "in the blood of the Lamb." By His blood the saint is "loosed from his sins" (1:5), purchased (5:9-10; I Peter 1:18f.), forgiven of sins (Matt. 26:28), kept clean as he walks in the light of divine truth (I John 1:7), and is able to overcome (12:11). If the saint must make a choice between life in Christ and death for the faith, he must love not his life "even unto death" (12:11). "They washed" is active; the saints were not passive. They had confessed their faith in Christ (Rom. 10:8–10), repented of their sins (Acts 17:30f.), and been baptized into His death (Rom. 6:3f.) for the remission of their sins (Acts 2:38). Their sins had been washed away in His blood (Acts 22:16); they had made the redemption in His blood their own.

In the first phase of the vision (vv. 1–8) the saints were being sealed for protection; in this second phase they are coming out of the conflict victorious. This great multitude includes those under the altar, the martyrs for Christ (6:9–11), and all who are victors through Christ. It also includes all who held fast from the beginning, those who were "firm unto the end" (Heb. 3:14).

v. 15. *"Therefore are they before the throne of God; and they serve him day and night in his temple: and he that sitteth on the throne shall spread his tabernacle over them."* Therefore, "because of this" (i.e., because they have washed their robes and made them white in the blood of the Lamb), these saints are before the throne, where they rejoice and serve God by offering praise (see v. 10). It is clear from Scripture that at death the faithful saint goes directly into the presence of God to be with Christ. However, he is not in his final state of glory, for this occurs beyond the ultimate judgment (chap. 21).

Paul indicates that the state or place of the Christian after death is with Christ when he says, "Whilst we are at home in the body, we are absent from the Lord.... We are of good courage, I say, and are willing rather to be absent from the body and to be at home with the Lord" (II Cor. 5:6, 8). Discussing the advantages of life and death, Paul also wrote, "I am in a strait betwixt the two, having the desire to depart and be with Christ; for it is very far better" (Phil. 1:23). And writing of the return of the Lord and the resurrection of the saints, he said, "For if we believe that Jesus died and rose again, even so them that are fallen asleep in Jesus will God bring with him" (I Thess. 4:14). We must note that Christ cannot bring these with Him if they are not with Him before He comes. Furthermore, as Stephen was being stoned to death, he cried, "Lord Jesus, receive my spirit" (Acts 7:59). It follows that they who fall asleep in Jesus are now with Him before His throne, and that when He comes, they will be brought with Him to be united with the resurrected body and will then enter into the final glory of the eternal home.

These now serve Him "day and night," suggesting continuous service. The temple in which they serve Him is the sanctuary or holy place (*naos*), as distinguished from the temple (*hieron*) with its various divisions for Hebrews, Gentiles, and women. And He, God who sits upon the throne, "shall spread his tabernacle over them," that is, shelter them that they may dwell securely under His protection.

v. 16. "*They shall hunger no more, neither thirst any more; neither shall the sun strike upon them, nor any heat.*" The blessings spoken of here are approached negatively, but positive blessings follow in verse 17. The saints who have passed through the great tribulation in which they suffered persecution, discrimination, and the various trials of the fourth seal are now beyond all these. Hunger and thirst, those fierce pangs from want of food and drink, are theirs no more. The sun, whose light is so essential to life but whose deeply penetrating rays can blister and burn, will no longer "strike upon them." And the heat, probably the fierce, burning hot wind (cf. Matt. 20:12; James 1:11), will affect them no more. These torments are all forgotten in the joy of victory.

v. 17. "*For the Lamb that is in the midst of [or before] the throne shall be their shepherd, and shall guide them unto fountains of waters of life: and God shall wipe away every tear from their eyes.*" Two metaphors are here combined: the Lamb who purchased and redeemed the saints by the blood of His sacrifice is also the Shepherd who leads them. Among the ancient Hebrews, Jehovah was the Shepherd who fed, gathered, and led His flock (Isa. 40:11). He gathered and kept them (Jer. 31:10), and He gathered those who had been scattered in the cloudy day of judgment (Ezek. 34:12). When Jesus came, He fulfilled the prophecy of a Davidic shepherd (Ezek. 37:24), for He was the Good Shepherd who laid down His life for the sheep (John 10:11).

Even when His sheep have fulfilled their mission on earth, the Shepherd who led them here shall continue to lead and guide them. "Life" is the key word in the phrase, He "shall guide them unto fountains of waters of life," "to life's watersprings" (Swete). As Jesus has provided the water of life here (John 4:10), so there He provides water for eternal life. As a mother tenderly wipes away the tears of a child who has been deeply hurt, so the heavenly Father wipes away every tear from the eyes of His faithful and devoted children. The psalmist said long ago, "They that sow in tears shall reap in joy" (Ps. 126:5). So it had been with these. Their joy is now complete.

There are excellent scholars who believe this last section (vv. 9–17) describes the sealed saints' (vv. 1–8) victorious life here on earth. These scholars see in this great multitude the church throughout all time victoriously praising God, washing their robes in the Lamb's blood, and serving Him in His temple, the church, with uninterrupted service. They see God's protecting care and the Lamb's leading and guiding counsel, as God comforts the saints in all their afflictions and the Lamb provides for all their spiritual needs. Although these principles are true and are taught in Scripture, the interpretation set forth above has stronger support and is in harmony with the theme of the book.

CHAPTER 8

The Seventh Seal and the First Four Trumpets

THE SEVENTH SEAL: PRAYER AND RESPONSE
vv. 1-5

v. 1. *"And when he opened the seventh seal, there followed a silence in heaven about the space of half an hour."* Now resumed is the opening of the seals which had been interrupted by the interlude of chapter 7. This interlude revealed by imagery the sealing unto God of those on earth and assured the saints on earth of the welfare of the martyrs who had died in the faith. Thus far have been heard the voices and thunders which proceeded from the throne of God (4:5), the songs of the living creatures (4:8) the elders (4:11) angels (5:12) and all created things (5:13), the cry of those under the altar (6:10), the shout of the multitude before the throne (7:10), and the response of the angels (7:12). In contrast to the constant singing of songs and shouts of praise which have filled heaven's court, there is now a solemn and awe-inspiring silence bringing in an air of expectation shared with heavenly beings. The tension is the kind that grips one while he waits for some singular event, whether honor or calamity. The opening of the seals now reaches a climax; but is this climax to be the glorious sabbath rest of promise and of hope (Heb. 4:9), or is it the prelude to judgment?

Let the reader keep in mind that the book is a revelation of the fortunes of the church in the world and the destiny of the world as it opposes the church. The climax is judgment and a revealing of the invincible power of the Christian's secret weapon: the divine response to the prayer of faith. The Father watches over His own; He hears their petitions and responds with action. As in ancient times when His people were threatened with invasion and destruction by the great pagan power of that day, Babylon, the Lord's response was, "Jehovah is in his holy temple: let all the earth keep silence before him" (Hab. 2:20). From that temple He then assured His people of His coming in power

215 THE SEVENTH SEAL AND THE FIRST FOUR TRUMPETS 8:3

to bring salvation to them and judge the enemy (Hab. 3). And now, from heaven's viewpoint it is revealed what is about to happen, and all heaven is quiet with a deathlike silence. "About the space of half an hour" indicates dramatic suspense. A half hour is ordinarily a short period of time, but it seems long when one is waiting. The impressive pause focuses attention on heaven's interest as all wait in breathless suspense and expectation for what is to follow.

v. 2. "And I saw the seven angels that stand before God; and there were given unto them seven trumpets." The seven is not to be taken literally, rather it represents completeness. There were seven Spirits, yet there is one Spirit; seven churches, but one church; seven horns, perfection of power; seven eyes, perfection and fullness of insight; seven seals, completeness and perfection of God's plan set forth in one book. Here are seven angels and seven trumpets, signifying unity, perfection, fullness, and completeness of whatever the angels were to do and the trumpets were to signify. The definite article, "*the* seven angels" by which they are introduced, indicates that these stand in some special relation to God, but they are not necessarily of a higher order than other angels who have been and will be presented.

v. 3. "And another angel came and stood over [or, before] the altar, having a golden censer; and there was given unto him much incense, that he should add it unto the prayers of all the saints upon the golden altar which was before the throne." The angel introduced here is not the Christ, since He is never represented anywhere in Revelation as an angel. The word "another" (*allos*, another of the same kind) identifies this angel and the seven as being of a common order or rank before God (see comments, 7:2). The altar in this scene is not the same as the one of 6:9 under which the souls of the martyrs rested, of which the altar of burnt offerings was the prototype. This altar upon which the incense was offered was foreshadowed by the golden altar before the veil of the tabernacle and nearest to the mercy seat (Exod. 30:6; Heb. 9:3-6).

The altar of the present vision is before the heavenly throne, the seat of God's divine power, dominion, and rule. The angel is before it or leaning over it. The censer was a golden dish or pan on which coals of fire from the altar were placed, and on these coals grains of incense were burned before God (cf. Lev. 10:1; 16:12). The angel does not act as a mediator between man and God through whom the saints pray, but in the vision he assumes the place of the priest of the Old Covenant who burned the incense; he simply appears as a servant. In the Hebrew order of worship, incense had come to be associated with prayer (see comments, 5:8). To the prayers of "all the saints," not prayers of the martyrs only (6:9ff.), was added "much incense," which appears to be the intercessory petitions or endorsement of the Lord Jesus, who makes intercession for the saints (see Luke 22:31-34; Rom. 8:34; Heb. 7:25), and who taught the disciples to ask in His name (John 16:23, 24, 26).

v. 4. *"And the smoke of the incense, with the prayers of the saints, went up before God out of the angel's hand."* The prayers of the saints are now before God as clouds of sweet aromatic incense, symbolic of prayer, sanctioned and commended by the mediator of the redeemed, the Lord Christ.

v. 5. *"And the angel taketh the censer, and he filled it with the fire of the altar, and cast it upon the earth: and there followed thunders, and voices, and lightnings, and an earthquake."* The angel is the same one to whom the "much incense" had been given and who had offered it upon the coals placed on the censer. After offering the incense, the angel next takes the censer and fills it with coals from the same altar and casts the coals upon the earth. This symbolic action reveals the heavenly response to the prayers ascending from the saints upon earth. This is the apocalyptic counterpart to Jesus' parable of the importunate widow, spoken "to the end that they ought always to pray, and not to faint." Jesus told of a judge who granted a widow's request that he avenge her of her adversaries, not because he cared, but because he wanted her to stop bothering him. Jesus explained that the Father also grants requests, although He does not share the judge's attitude: "And shall not God avenge his elect, that cry to him day and night, and yet he is longsuffering over them? I say unto you, that he will avenge them speedily" (Luke 18:1-8).

In the vision, the prayers of the saints on earth, crying that they be avenged, now come before the Father. He responds to their cry by casting the fire of His righteous judgment upon the world of the ungodly. As in so many instances in Revelation, "the earth" signifies the realm of the unregenerate in contrast with the kingdom of God's blood-bought people. Thunders, voices, and lightnings were introduced earlier as proceeding out of the throne (4:5, see comments). To these (which express the divine power, majesty, and glory of God) is added, "and an earthquake." The earthquake as an expression of judgment was introduced at the opening of the sixth seal in response to the cry of the souls beneath the altar; God would bring the world's persecuting powers to an end (see comments, 6:12).

The earthquake was a familiar Old Testament figure used to describe Jehovah's judgment against heathen powers and the enemies of His people. Against those who would bring Judah low the Lord says, "She shall be visited of Jehovah of hosts with thunder, and with earthquake, and great noise, with whirlwind and tempest, and the flame of a devouring fire" (Isa. 29:6). Joel says that when Jehovah shall roar from Zion, and utter his voice from Jerusalem in judgment against the heathen, "the heaven and earth shall shake" (Joel 3:16). So now, as the prayers of Jehovah's servants come before His throne, He responds with the fire of judgment upon the world of the wicked.

The fire from the altar sums up the judgments of the trumpets which follow. Since the prayers "of all the saints" (v. 3) were before the throne, it follows that these judgments cannot be localized or made to fit into any specific time and event; they are God's judgments against the wicked in answer to the prayers of His people at any point in time. It is true that this also includes judgments against the Roman Empire. Earthshaking events follow as the trumpets sound.

THE FIRST FOUR TRUMPETS
vv. 6-12

v. 6. "And the seven angels that had the seven trumpets prepared themselves to sound." At this point the narrative resumes. The seven trumpets are not a continuation of the seals; that is, the seventh seal does not extend to include the seven trumpets. The seals are complete, and the altar scene serves as a prelude or introduction to the trumpets. An understanding of the purpose and service of the trumpets may be gained from a study of their place in the Old Testament. Moses was instructed to make two silver trumpets of "beaten work" to be used for special occasions: a call to assembly, a pilgrimage, a festival, and war

(Num. 10:1–10). In later years trumpets were used to sound an alarm to warn of approaching danger (Amos 3:6; Hos. 5:8), impending judgment (Joel 2:1), or to call the people to a holy convocation (Joel 2:15). By the mouth of Ezekiel Jehovah said of the duties of the watchman, "If, when he seeth the sword come upon the land, he blow the trumpet, and warn the people; then whosoever heareth the sound of the trumpet, and taketh not warning, if the sword come, and take him away, his blood shall be upon his own head" (Ezek. 33:3f.).

The seven trumpets in the vision before us symbolize partial judgments upon the wicked, serving as warnings of greater judgments to come. If these warnings are not heeded, the sword of destruction shall come and destroy the wicked. The trumpets of warning to the world also serve to call God's people to a holy convocation as they draw closer and closer to Him. The trumpet is used in other parts of the New Testament as a symbol of ushering in the resurrection and great judgment day (I Cor. 15:52; I Thess. 4:16). The angels have the trumpets at their lips and are ready to sound when the order is given.

v. 7. "*And the first sounded, and there followed hail and fire, mingled with blood, and they were cast upon the earth: and the third part of the earth was burnt up, and the third part of the trees was burnt up, and all green grass was burnt up.*" As with the seven seals, the trumpets fall into two divisions of four and three. When the first four are blown, various aspects of the physical or natural world are affected; and at the sounding of the last three the physical and spiritual lives of men are involved. The first four trumpets are closely related; the last three are more independent of each other. In the judgments which follow the sounding of the trumpets, many features similar to the Egyptian plagues are discernible, but with increased intensity.

Any explanation of these phenomena which follow the trumpet sounds is generally unsatisfactory, even to the one who interprets. To interpret them literally and apply them to certain places and definite periods in history is impossible; to allegorize them leads into severe difficulties, although it is clearly evident that there was symbolical significance to the consequences which followed the trumpets. To view these evils as physical calamities which occurred throughout the Roman Empire is likewise not satisfactory. It can, however, be concluded with certainty that these trumpets represent warnings of a supernatural judgment from the Almighty.

Hail and fire are spoken of in the Old Testament as God's arsenal of weapons for use in the day of battle (Job 38:22f.), in the destruction of His enemies (Isa. 30:30f.), as instruments of judgment against the rebellious (Exod. 9; Isa. 28:2), and against the falsehood of idolaters, "the hail shall sweep away the refuge of lies" (Isa. 28:17). The hail and fire in John's vision were "mingled with blood," and were "cast upon the earth." The blood could represent blood shed amid the hail and fire; but since these were "*cast* upon the earth," it seems more reasonable to conclude that in this judgment the blood of the wicked people was returned upon their own heads. From the time immediately following the flood God has demanded blood for blood (Gen. 9:6); that blood can be expiated only by the blood of the one who shed it (Num. 35:33). When Jehovah would "punish the inhabitants of the earth for their iniquity: the earth shall disclose her blood, and shall no more cover her slain" (Isa. 26:21); nations such as Egypt would be made a desolate wilderness "because they have shed innocent blood in their land" (Joel 3:19). Furthermore, the avenging of the blood of God's servants, which has been shed ruthlessly, should be known among the nations (Ps. 79:10). All this seems to point to judgment upon the heathen as their blood is brought upon their heads.

The burning of a third part of the earth and the trees and all the grass seems to indicate suffering and destruction among the earth-dwellers, the world of the unregenerate in which the seat of world powers operate. "A third part" suggests a large portion, but not total destruction; life is still possible. God created the good earth for man's benefit and use, and out of it his life is sustained. But man has misused the earth, and it is now affected by sin; it has become a partial waste and his enemy. This principle is expressed over and over by the prophets of the Old Testament (e.g., Jer. 7:20; Zeph. 1:2f. Nah. 1:6, et al.). The judgment is against the wicked and upon the realm in which the unregenerate find their life and objects of worship. Living only for the material and physical, theirs is a life spent in rebellion against God and the spiritual. With the destruction of that for which man lives, his pride is humbled.

vv. 8, 9. *"And the second angel sounded, and as it were a great mountain burning with fire was cast into the sea: and the third part of the sea became blood; and there died the third part of the creatures which were in the sea, even they that had life; and the third part of the ships was destroyed."* Mountains and sea are often used in the imagery of the Old Testament prophets and writers. Mount Zion, the holy mountain, symbolizes the city of God's habitation among His people (Ps. 48:1f.). The prophets said that God's dwelling place among His people in the new spiritual kingdom, likewise, would be a holy mountain (Isa. 2:2-4; 11:9; Mic. 4:2; Heb. 12:22). The prophets occasionally spoke of great heathen powers as mountains (Isa. 41:15; 64:1; Amos 4:1). The fall of Babylon, the capital of a mighty world kingdom, was described by Jehovah through Jeremiah, "Behold, I am against thee, O destroying mountain, saith Jehovah, which destroyeth all the earth; and I will stretch out my hand upon thee, and roll thee down from the rocks, and will make thee a burnt mountain" (Jer. 51:25). The prophet continued, saying, "The sea is come upon Babylon; she is covered with the multitude of the waves thereof" (51:42).

From such usage we must seek our interpretation of John's vision. He beholds a spectacular scene, "as it were a great mountain burning with fire cast into the sea." This symbolizes the fall of an eminent unidentified power cast down as Babylon of old; it could be any such city at any period in time. The sea, which signifies the mass of humanity or society (see comments, 13:1), is greatly affected.

The judgment is much more far-reaching than the plague in Egypt in which the waters were turned into blood (Exod. 7:14-21); and the addition of the sea to the scene makes this plague more severe than that which followed the sounding of the first trumpet. In the first, blood was mingled with the fire and hail; in this, a third of the sea becomes blood. Further, a third of the sea creatures die, and a third of the ships are destroyed. Men are not specifically mentioned, but they are probably included in the suffering. The vision indicates judgment upon a worldly society when its center of power is cast down and its economy falls with it. To go beyond this broad application by designating a particular city is unwise, although this pattern fits both Rome and the entire empire when they fell. The description reveals a general corrupt condition and its consequences, which could involve any society.

221 THE SEVENTH SEAL AND THE FIRST FOUR TRUMPETS 8:11

vv. 10, 11. "*And the third angel sounded, and there fell from heaven a great star, burning as a torch, and it fell upon the third part of the rivers, and upon the fountains of the waters; and the name of the star is called Wormwood: and the third part of the waters became wormwood; and many men died of the waters, because they were made bitter.*" In the overall vision of the trumpets, the first affects vegetation, the second the sea with its marine life and ships, and this, the third, involves the inland waters and springs. All these trumpets appear to have a broader significance than describing simple natural calamities within the Roman Empire; in fact, the Roman Empire has not been specifically introduced.

At the sounding of the third angel "a great star, burning as a torch" falls upon a third of the inland waters. Solitary meteors of great size often invade the atmosphere with unusual brilliance, seen even in the daytime. Fragments or portions of these "visitors from outer space" sometimes reach the earth and are not burnt up in the atmosphere. An interpretation of what John saw is helped by looking at Isaiah's description of the king of Babylon's fall, "How art thou fallen from heaven, O day-star [*Lucifer,* KJV], son of the morning! how art thou cut down to the ground, that didst lay low the nations" (Isa. 14:12). The prophet further described this boastful one as seeking to ascend into heaven, exalt his throne above the stars of God, and make himself like the Most High, "the man that made the earth to tremble" (Isa. 14:13–17). Anyone seeking such an exalted height is bound to fall, and as a fiercely burning torch he will work havoc among men. He shall, however, be extinguished. In contrast to the seven torches before the throne which illuminate and comfort (4:5), this blazing torch brings bitterness and woe to society. "And the name of the star is called Wormwood," a bitter wood mentioned a number of times in the Old Testament, usually in connection with the consequences of idolatry. God warned the people of Israel that their turning to idols would bear the fruit of wormwood (Deut. 29:18); for as a divine chastisement He would feed the idolaters of His people with wormwood and give them water of gall to drink (Jer. 9:15); the prophets who would lead them into idolatry would share the same fate (Jer. 23:15). In their unfaithfulness to God, the idolatrous judges in Israel turned away from Him and served idols, perverted principles of right judgment, turned "justice to wormwood, and cast down righteousness to the earth" (Amos 5:7; 6:12). Wormwood and gall aptly symbolize calamity and sorrow and bitterness of life. The fall of this star, Wormwood, caused a third of the inland waters to become wormwood, that is, charged with trouble, sorrow, and death.

Wormwood, the star of any Babylon, "has poisoned by its idolatry the springs of its own life" (Caird, p. 115), and therefore brings bitterness and death to men. Pride and arrogance, which are part of idolatry and rebellion against God, are destined to fall, carrying misery and sorrow with them. When men prefer the bitter waters of idolatry to the fountain of the living water, they will receive these bitter waters with the fatal consequences which follow.

v. 12. "*And the fourth angel sounded, and a third part of the sun was smitten, and the third part of the moon, and the third part of the stars; that the third part of them should be darkened, and the day should not shine for the third part of it, and the night in like manner.*" The heavenly bodies testify to God's majesty and greatness and to the comparative insignificance of man (Ps. 8:3-4). These were created and set in the heavens to give light, the sun to rule the day and the moon to rule the night; and "he made the stars also" (Gen. 1:16-18). The psalmist writes, "Praise ye him, sun and moon: praise him, all ye stars of light" (Ps. 148:3).

Throughout the Old Testament, light from the sun, moon, and stars signifies salvation, well-being, happiness, truth, wisdom, and joy. The fading of light in the removal of these heavenly bodies symbolizes judgment from God (Isa. 13:10; Joel 3:15; Amos 8:9). In describing the moral decay and physical destruction of Jerusalem the prophet cried, "I beheld the earth, and, lo, it was waste and void; and the heavens, and they had no light" (Jer. 4:23). And in lamenting the fall of Pharaoh and Egypt, Ezekiel says, "And when I [Jehovah] shall extinguish thee, I will cover the heavens, and make the stars thereof dark; I will cover the sun with a cloud, and the moon shall not give its light. And all the bright lights of heaven will I make dark over thee, and set darkness upon thy land, saith the Lord Jehovah" (32:7f.).

These symbols of joy and wisdom are ashamed at earth's wickedness, and in the vision a third of them are smitten, indicating a partial judgment meant to serve as a warning to the ungodly. God's word is a lamp (Ps. 119:105), giving light and understanding (Ps. 119:130) which is the basis of all true wisdom (I Cor. 2:6-13) now summed up in Christ (Col. 2:3). It seems, therefore that the darkness in John's vision indicates a lack of understanding and insight on the part of those who direct human affairs. In ancient times God took away the wisdom of Judah's wise men (Isa. 29:14) and destroyed the wise men and their understanding out of Edom (Obad. 8; Jer. 49:7). No specific people or time is indicated in this vision, making general its application as were the first three. Before total darkness engulfs any society, God sounds a trumpet warning to that society. He sends minor judgments which mark the beginning of the society's destruction unless repentance turns the course of its destiny. These four trumpets call for the reformation, not the destruction of mankind.

THE EAGLE: HERALD OF WOES
v. 13

v. 13. *"And I saw, and I heard an eagle, flying in mid heaven, saying with a great voice, Woe, woe, woe, for them that dwell on the earth, by reason of the other voices of the trumpet of the three angels, who are yet to sound."* The next three trumpet blasts are introduced as three woes which will befall the non-Christian dwellers of earth. John sees and hears an eagle as it flies in mid heaven where it is visible to all, for the message is for all the earth. The KJV uses the word "angel," but according to most authorites "eagle," as in the ASV, is correct. Some think the object of John's vision is a vulture, which is probably the correct idea in Matthew 24:28 and Luke 17:37, where the same Greek word (*aetos*) appears. In describing Jerusalem's destruction, Jesus speaks of the eagles or vultures gathering about a carcass. However, since the eagle flies alone and not in a flock as do vultures, it seems that in Revelation 8:13, as in 12:14, it is more probable that an eagle is in the seer's vision, warning the world of the wicked, and ready to swoop down upon its prey.

The eagle was noted for its strong wings (Exod. 19:4; Rev. 12:14), but Scripture also emphasizes the keenness of sight with which the eagle "spieth out the prey" (Job 39:29), and the swiftness with which it swoops down upon it (Job 9:26). In warning against impending judgment, Hosea cried, "Set the trumpet to thy mouth. As an eagle he [the enemy] cometh against the house of Jehovah" (Hos. 8:1). Habakkuk described the horsemen of the invading Babylonians by saying, "They fly as an eagle that hasteth to devour" (Hab. 1:8). The disasters now to come upon the earth are heralded by the voice of this eagle as it cries, "Woe, woe, woe." This takes the form of an ominous warning set forth in the trumpets which follow.

CHAPTER 9

The Beginning of the Woes

THE FIRST WOE
vv. 1-12

The student of Revelation must be ever conscious that he shares with John signs and symbols of a vision which God showed to him. He has not been dealing with literal trumpets, hail, fire, a burning mountain, a sea of blood, etc., or now with real locusts, scorpions, or horsemen, but with symbols which convey ideas and reveal messages from God to man. Therefore, in the following vision of the three woes we need not look for some specific time in history when terrible locust hoardes invade a land, bringing a scourge upon it. Rather, we need to see spiritual forces at work in the world of unregenerated, wicked men—forces which are symbolized by these monsters of the infernal realm.

v. 1. *"And the fifth angel sounded, and I saw a star from heaven fallen unto the earth; and there was given to him the key of the pit of the abyss."* John saw the star where it had fallen, not "saw it fall" as in the KJV. In 8:10 John beheld a star as it fell from heaven, but now he sees a star "fallen." A star usually symbolizes a great person of high position (see comments, 8:10); here, however, it seems not to represent a particular human individual, but Satan. This view is supported by Jesus' statement, "I beheld Satan fallen as lightning from heaven" (Luke 10:18), and serves as a prelude or introduction to the scene in 12:7-12, where the great dragon is cast down to earth. This star appears as the antithesis to "the bright, the morning star" (22:16), and of Him who has the keys of death and Hades (1:18). The terrible woe which this star turns loose upon the earth could be the work of none other than the devil, and this confirms the opinion that the star represents Satan. Lenski dissents from this view, contending that the star is simply a personification of the judgment which is from God (p. 288).

Since the key, a symbol of power (see comments, 1:18), "was given"

225

to him, it is implied that Satan was permitted to open the pit of the abyss, exercising only that degree of power which God allowed; beyond that he cannot operate (cf. Job. 1:12; 2:6). "The pit of the abyss" ("bottomless pit," KJV), points to the infernal region to which demons were consigned (Luke 8:31); from there also issued the smoke from whence came the locusts. The abyss, from which the spirit of persecution arose (11:7; 17:8), was ruled over by "the Destroyer" (v. 11), and into it Satan was cast when finally bound (20:1, 3). The abyss is not to be confused with Gehenna (hell), which is to be the final abode of the devil, his angels, and the wicked of earth who have served him (Matt. 25:41; Rev. 20:10, 14–15). The abyss signifies the present abode of the devil and his demons.

v. 2. *"And he [the star, Satan] opened the pit of the abyss; and there went up a smoke out of the pit, as the smoke of a great furnace; and the sun and the air were darkened by reason of the smoke of the pit."* From the opening of the abyss there billowed forth a noxious smoke that obscured the sun and polluted the air. The use of the word *as* (the smoke was *as* the smoke of a great furnace) indicates the symbolic quality of the vision. It was the smoke and not the locusts that filled the air. The light of truth which directs men's lives and guides them in the right way, giving peace to the soul, is darkend by the deceptions and delusions set loose by Satan. This darkness is the veil by which "the god of this world hath blinded the minds of the unbelieving, that the light of the gospel of the glory of Christ . . . should not dawn upon them" (II Cor. 4:3f.). The "god of this world" is Satan, "the prince of the powers of the air," who rules over "this world" and perverts the spirit which works "in the sons of disobedience" (Eph. 2:2), who "walk according to the course of this world" in an atmosphere completely polluted by the smoke out of the pit.

v. 3. *"And out of the smoke came forth locusts upon the earth; and power was given them, as the scorpions of earth have power."* Out of this noxious smoke there emerge hellish locusts to whom are given power, whose nature is described in verses 4–6. Dreaded by men, these invaders are voracious destroyers of earth's vegetation, and are used by God as His instrument in an effort to bring men to repentance.

Locusts are first mentioned in Exodus when God said He would bring them in judgment upon Pharoah's land because of his rebellion against God (Exod. 10:4-20; Ps. 105:34f.). To His own people He said that if they would turn away from Him and commit sin, He would bring the dreaded scourge upon their land to destroy it (Deut. 28:38; I Kings 8:35, 37; II Chron. 7:13f.). A large locust invasion occurred in the days of Joel when Jehovah brought upon the land His "great army" as a means of bringing the people back to Himself (Joel 1, 2). The very atmosphere of deception and delusion turned loose upon the earth brings its locusts of destruction. Sin spawns its own means of ravage, ruin, and perdition.

These were no ordinary locusts, for "power was given them, as the scorpions of earth have power." Scorpions are mentioned in the Old Testament as dwelling especially in the wilderness of Sinai (Deut. 8:15), and as symbolizing the people among whom Ezekiel dwelt in Chaldea (Ezek. 2:6). Rehoboam spoke figuratively when he said to the people, "I will chastise you with scorpions" (I Kings 12:11), indicating a more severe treatment than that employed by Solomon his father.

The scorpion, a member of the spider family, has an elongated body with two pincer-like claws in front, four pairs of legs and a tail which curves above its body. A stinger at the tip of its tail injects a venemous poison into its victim. The sting is rarely fatal, but is very painful. The scorpion is mentioned in the New Testament only here (vv. 3, 5, 10), and in Luke (Luke 10:19; 11:12). Jesus assured His disciples, saying, "I have given you authority to tread upon serpents and scorpions, and over all the power of the enemy: and nothing shall in any wise hurt you" (Luke 10:19). These serpents, scorpions, and enemies symbolize the forces of spiritual evil in the world which the disciples would overcome and tread under foot.

v. 4. "And it was said unto them that they should not hurt the grass of the earth, neither any green thing, neither any tree, but only such men as have not the seal of God on their foreheads." Again the writer makes clear the difference between locusts in nature and those in a vision; the latter do not harm vegetation or feed on the herbage of earth, but affect only human beings. When the locusts came upon Egypt they left no green thing, either grass, herb, or fruit of the trees (Exod. 10:15). When God brought the locusts upon His land and people, it was said, "The land is as the garden of Eden before them, and behind them a desolate wilderness" (Joel 2:3); everything was stripped bare. Not so with the locusts of John's vision: they hurt only men, those who do not have the seal of God on their foreheads.

Before turning loose the winds of persecution and destruction upon the earth, God had sealed His own unto Himself, a hundred and forty and four thousand (see comments, 7:4). The distinction made here between the sealed and those not sealed is further proof that the number one hundred and forty-four thousand represents the saints on earth at any point in time, and not a special group of saved persons in the final day. As the people of God escaped certain (if not all) of the plagues of Egypt (Exod. 8:22; 9:4, 6, 26; 10:23), so now the sealed of God escape the deception and delusion that torture those who reject the truth; for "the Lord knoweth them that are his" (II Tim. 2:19), and He knows "how to deliver the godly out of temptation" (II Peter 2:9).

v. 5. *"And it was given them that they should not kill them, but that they should be tormented five months: and their torment was as the torment of a scorpion, when it stingeth a man."* The devil and his agents do not have unlimited power even over evil men, but are restrained within the limits circumscribed by God. These scorpion-like locusts cannot kill even those who have not the seal of God on their foreheads, though they are given the power to torment. The final destruction of wicked men is retained in the hand and will of God; only He determines the final judgment of nations, societies, and individuals. As mentioned above, the scorpion sting is seldom fatal, but results in acute pain.

"Torment" is from a noun (*basanismos*) which occurs only in Revelation: twice in this passage of the earth-dwellers, once of those that worship the beast (14:11), and three times of the great harlot (18:7, 10, 15). In each instance the word refers to mental and spiritual torment. The verb (*basinizō*) was used by the demon that urged Jesus not to torment him before his time (Mark 5:7; Luke 8:28), by Lot whose righteous soul was "vexed" ("tormented," marginal reading, ASV, II Peter 2:8), and in Revelation of these who were tormented five months (v. 10), of those who received the mark of the beast (14:9f.) and of Satan, the beast, and the false prophet who "are tormented day and night for ever and ever" (20:10). In two additional instances the verb is used to refer to the two prophets who tormented the dwellers of earth by their message (11:10) and to the woman who was in pain (tormented) to be delivered of her child (12:2).

The specific meaning of "five months" is uncertain. A number of explanations by various writers is listed by Plummer. Hendriksen thinks the five months indicates a definite time determined and decreed by God (p. 290); Swete thinks it is used to give definiteness to the picture and points to the incompleteness of the visitation (p. 117). Others think the five months indicates the life span of the locusts; however, there is little evidence for this. The torment was for five months, and no locust scourge is known to have lasted for that period of time. Probably the number gave definiteness, as in the story of the five wise and five foolish virgins (Matt. 25:2) and the parable of the five talents (Matt. 25:15). It probably also indicated the incompleteness of the woe, as the first four trumpets indicated incomplete judgments. The torment inflicted was spiritual and mental; it did not kill, although the pain was intense and the outlook seemed hopeless.

v. 6. "And in those days men shall seek death, and shall in no wise find it; and they shall desire to die, and death fleeth from them." This vividly portrays the torment of those stung by the locust-scorpions: death is actually preferred to such torment. These are men who have left God out of their lives and have been polluted by sin. This condition reflects the words of Job who asked, Why is life "given unto the bitter in soul; who long for death and it cometh not?" (Job 3:20–22), and of Jeremiah describing the condition to come upon Jerusalem when he said, "And death shall be chosen rather than life by all the residue that remain of this evil family, that remain in all the places whether I [Jehovah] have driven them" (Jer. 8:3). The words echo the condition described by Koheleth who "praised the dead that have been long dead more than the living that are yet alive," esteeming even more than either, "him that hath not yet been" (Eccles. 4:2f.). Physical death is no gain to the wicked, for the anguish of soul cannot be assuaged by death (cf. the rich man in Hades, Luke 16:23). This is why they do not commit suicide.

v. 7. "And the shapes of the locusts were like unto horses prepared for war; and upon their heads as it were crowns like unto gold, and their faces were as men's faces." Next, a description of the locusts is set forth, while up to this point the emphasis has been on their function and infliction of pain. This description is reminiscent of Joel's portrayal of the invading locusts of his day, "The appearance of them is as the appearance of horses; and as horses [war-horses] do they run... as a strong people set in battle array" (Joel 2:4f.; cf. Joel 1, 2). These locusts of John's vision are as horsemen prepared for war in the camp of the unregenerated as they represent sin's own destructive force. Sin inflicts pain and culminates in the self-destruction of those involved. The sinner is actually at war against himself.

Upon their heads rested "as it were crowns like unto gold." This is the only place in the Book of Revelation where the victory crown (*stephanos*) is used of any other than Christ and the saints; and even in this instance these are not crowns of permanent victory or of genuine gold, but "as it were crowns like unto gold." The victory of wickedness is only an imitation of the genuine; it is never lasting or true. The locusts' terrifying appearance and their crushing conquest will not last for ever. Their human faces indicate intelligence and show that these terrible inflictions were brought about by deluded and deceived mankind whose intelligent wills are in rebellion against God. Their spiritual faculties have been befogged by the cloud of spiritual falsehood, guile, and deceit turned loose on earth by the evil one.

v. 8. "And they had hair as the hair of women, and their teeth were as teeth of lions." The hair "as the hair of women" adds to the demoniacal appearance of the locusts. And it is possible that relating the hair of women with the faces of men identifies the origin of the woe with both sexes; however, this is purely conjectural. In defining the word hair (*thrix*), Vine suggests that in this instance the long hair "is perhaps indicative of their subjection to their Satanic master (cf. I Cor. 11:10, RV)." This explanation is more satisfactory than the explanations given by most writers. It is probably safer to consider this point as a detail of the general picture of terror and torment rather than to attempt a specific explanation. The locusts' "teeth of lions" follows Joel's description of the locust army that God brought upon the land: "His teeth are the teeth of a lion, and he hath the jawbone of a lioness" (Joel 1:6). By these he devours and destroys.

v. 9. "And they had breastplates, as it were breastplates of iron; and the sound of their wings was as the sound of chariots, of many horses rushing to war." The thorny substance encrusting the locust gives the appearance of military armor worn by horses in battle. But the breastplates worn by locusts in the vision were "as it were breastplates of iron." They sought to give the impression of invincibility; but this also was a deception.

As we listen to the whirring sound of these agents from the pit we are reminded again of Joel's description of the locust hoard of his day as he says, "Like the noise of chariots on the tops of the mountains do they leap, like the noise of a flame of fire that devoureth the stubble, as a strong people set in battle array" (Joel 2:5). If you can imagine the sound of thousands, or even hundreds, of chariots rumbling over mountains, you have the scene described by the seer. The sound should have struck terror to the hearts of the wicked, but they of the earth refused to give heed (cf. v. 21). Spiritual warfare and destruction were in their midst, and they did not know it. In contrast to the tormented earth-dwellers, those who had the seal of God on their foreheads were secure and had neither fear nor terror.

v. 10. "*And they have tails like unto scorpions, and stings; and in their tails is their power to hurt men five months.*" In the general description of the locusts, this is a good place to pause and take note of some things said of them between verses seven and ten. The use of *like unto* with which John begins and concludes the description, saying, "the shapes of the locusts were like unto horses" (v. 7), and, "they have tails like unto scorpions" (v. 10), emphasizes the *symbolic* significance of what he is seeing. In further describing the locusts he uses *as (hos)* six times, "*as* it were crowns of gold," "*as* men's faces," "*as* the hair of women," "*as* the teeth of lions," "*as* it were breastplates of iron" and "*as* the sound of chariots." All this adds to the symbolic significance of the vision. The character and likeness of the locusts, introduced in verse 3 and enlarged upon in verse 5 where the thrice-repeated "torment" is brought into view, are now further expounded. The body of the locust ended in an elongated tail as the tail of a scorpion, containing its stinger with power to hurt but not to kill men. The "five months" (see comments, v. 5) seems to be repeated for emphasis, indicating the time of torment and not the life span of the locusts or scorpions.

v. 11. "*They have over them as king the angel of the abyss: his name in Hebrew is Abaddon, and in the Greek tongue he hath the name Apollyon."* Is this "angel" Satan himself, who rules over and leads this hellish army of locusts? Or does this angel-king exist only in the vision as the essence of deception that leads the locust-scorpions as they torment? Is he a principal of Satan's bad angels, or is there another meaning which lies hidden from our view? Scholars are divided on the subject.

As we review the book we find that each church had its angel, the altar had its angel that cast fire upon the earth, there was the angel of the waters, and so on throughout, with here a parallel in the angel over the abyss. But it probably matters little whether we think of the angel as representing a spirit or as Satan himself. Satan, symbolized as a great red dragon having seven diadems (crowns of royalty) on his seven heads (12:3), is thus portrayed as ruling over the realm which is at war with God and His purpose. As the embodiment and source of all that is evil and as the one who brings torment and destruction to wicked men and God's beautiful world, Satan rules over the forces represented by the locusts. (For "abyss" see comments, vv. 1-2.)

This king has two names, the Hebrew, "Abaddon," and the Greek, "Apollyon." The Hebrew word translated "Destruction" or transliterated "Abaddon," is used in the Old Testament of Destruction personified (Job 31:12), of Destruction in connection with Sheol (Job 26:6; Prov. 15:11; 27:20), of Destruction and Death (Job 28:22), and in association with the grave (Ps. 88:11). The Greek name Apollyon means Destroyer; this is the only place where either of the two names are found in the New Testament. Both names are appropriate for this one who rules over destruction. He was a murderer from the beginning, and the great liar and deceiver (John 8:44) who rules through deception and falsehood. No more appropriate appellation could be given such a one than Destruction and Destroyer, for that is what he is in any language.

v. 12. "The first Woe is past: behold, there come yet two Woes hereafter." Although the eagle flying in mid heaven first announced the three woes to come (8:13), these words concerning the two woes to come are John's.

We may ask what is signified by this first woe, with its smoke as a great furnace and the emergence of terrible locusts and their king.

Numerous answers and explanations have been given to this question. It seems that we have before us a vivid picture of moral and spiritual decay which brings torment to the souls of men. The torment does not kill, but it abides for a definite period. Sin is responsible for bringing this decay into the world, behind which is Satan with his diabolical purpose to destroy.

Sin is disobedience to God's rule and is accompanied by deception and mental or spiritual torment from which man cannot escape by his own will or power. Sin carries with it the poisonous venom of moral decay and ultimate perdition, and Satan is the father and king of it all. This condition should serve as a trumpet warning to the world of unregenerate men to turn from Satan and sin to God—but how seldom do men heed the warning!

THE SECOND WOE
vv. 13-21

Many commentators believe that the following woe, the invasion of a great destroying army, points to the Parthian threat against Rome. These writers see in this vision an assurance given to the saints that Rome would not destroy or overcome them. This conclusion rests on what seems to be a mistaken view of the rider of the white horse at the opening of the first seal (6:2), that the rider represents victorious militarism, especially against Rome (see comments, 6:1f.). However, up to this point in Revelation, Rome and the empire have not been specifically introduced. The visions have been general, dealing with principles that set forth God's care for His chosen saints throughout history and His assurance of judgment against the rebellious and sinful world. God has been revealing that wickedness is self-destructive.

At the sounding of the first four trumpets God sent forth partial judgments which were to have warned the unregenerated inhabitants of earth. These first four pointed to (1) the collapse of the sinner's world in which he trusted (8:7); (2) the fall of any great world power which would drastically affect the society involved (8:8–9); (3) the fall of earth's eminent men and the folly of idolatry which brings its own waters of wormwood (8:10–11); and (4) the partial darkening of human wisdom and understanding (8:12). These symbols are all drawn from calamities in nature. The sounding of the fifth trumpet revealed the torment of men which accompanies the internal decay and rottenness of society without God; this torment does not kill, but it contributes to the final destruction of any community of men. The sounding of the sixth trumpet introduced the external forces which threaten and finally bring destruction to the ungodly world. Sin and rebellion against God bring terrible judgments, the consequence of darkened human wisdom and its folly.

v. 13. *"And the sixth angel sounded, and I heard a voice from the horns of the golden altar which is before God."* These trumpet sounds and judgments are in response to the prayers of the saints sent up before God (8:3-5). The saints were looking to God and praying not only for an avenging of their cause but also for the subjugation of the world to God that men might be saved (I Tim. 2:1-4). Even God's judgments were meant to contribute to this end by revealing the folly and vanity of all things earthly.

The voice (Greek, "one voice") comes from the horns of the altar; the "four" (KJV) is of doubtful authenticity, though indicated in Exodus 30:2. The altar is the golden altar before the throne, upon which the saints' prayers were offered (8:3) and from which the judgments were let loose. It is not the altar from under which the souls of the martyrs cried (6:9). The source of the voice is not revealed; it may be the voice of the saints' prayers, the voice of the angel who stood over the altar (8:3), or the personification of the altar itself.

v. 14. *"One saying to the sixth angel that had the trumpet, Loose the four angels that are bound at the great river Euphrates."* These angels, presented neither as good nor evil, are messengers or ministering servants of God, carrying out orders received from the throne and executing the judgment of God's wrath. These four are not to be identified with the four angels of 7:1; there the angels were restraining the four winds of earth, whereas here the angels themselves are bound or restrained, waiting to be loosed.

The Euphrates river had played an important role in the history of ancient Israel. God promised Abraham that the land of his possession would extend "from the river of Egypt [probably the brook of Egypt; Num. 34:5, known as the Wady el Arish] unto the great river, the river

Euphrates" (Gen. 15:18). This promise was realized during the reign of Solomon who ruled over the land that extended to those boundaries (I Kings 4:21). In later years, after much of Israel's territory had been lost, the Euphrates formed the boundary between the West and Assyria, Babylonia, and Persia, the great world powers of the East. Prophetically, Isaiah identified the river with the Assyrians themselves as he spoke of Jehovah's judgment upon Judah: "The waters of the River [Euphrates], strong and many," would come as a mighty flood to Jerusalem (Isa. 8:5-8). It was at the Euphrates that Pharaoh would be defeated and crushed by the armies of Babylon, thus opening the way for the Babylonian army to push westward to Egypt (Jer. 46:6-10).

John's use of the Euphrates is not geographic but symbolic: God's forces of vengeance were held in restraint at their border until a time determined by Himself when, under His judgment, the flood would once again overflow the land. The view held by some that this trumpet blast looked to the overflowing Mohammedans' scourge and conquest is farfetched, with even less foundation than the Parthian theory.

v. 15. "*And the four angels were loosed, that had been prepared for the hour and day and month and year, that they should kill the third part of men.*" Since four is the world or creation number, "the four angels" may signify a judgment of worldwide proportions, or a judgment against the realm or world of the unbelieving. These four angels of judgment had been prepared for a time fixed in the mind of God, for He determines when the appropriate moment has come for judgment according to His purpose: "It is not for you to know times or seasons, which the Father hath set within his own authority" (Acts 1:7). With each sounding of a trumpet or group of trumpets the judgments become progressively intense. At the sound of the first four trumpets a third of each realm is affected; with the fifth trumpet men are tormented but do not die; now in this sixth judgment a third of mankind is killed.

v. 16. "*And the number of the armies of the horsemen was twice ten thousand times ten thousand: I heard the number of them.*" There is now a sudden transition from angels (v. 15) to armies of horsemen (v. 16). Since the angels of the seven churches most likely represent the spirit or inner life of the churches, the one church in its completeness (see comments, 1:20), so these angels represent the very mind and spirit of this great world army. Since the churches are one church, so the armies are one army and not four, each being led by an angel. John could not number them, but he heard the number announced. "Twice ten thousand times ten thousand" equals two hundred million—the number defies the imagination. Summers estimates that in regular formation this number of men would make a column one mile wide and eighty-five miles long (p. 159). But we are not to think of this number as a literal quantity, but as a symbol of a mighty host, full and complete—literally, two myriads of myriads (cf. Ps. 68:17; Dan. 7:10). It is a grand total, sufficient to accomplish God's purpose in any judgment at any time.

v. 17. *"And thus I saw the horses in the vision, and them that sat on them, having breastplates as of fire and of hyacinth and of brimstone: and the heads of the horses are as the heads of lions; and out of their mouths proceedeth fire and smoke and brimstone."* In John's vision the horsemen and the horses are as one, making it difficult to determine whether the armor belongs to both or only to the riders. However, since the equipment of the horses is described later, this probably refers to the riders only. The breastplates were "as of fire" or "fiery, the color of fire" (A. & G.), probably a glowing reddish color, "and of hyacinth," having the color of hyacinth, "doubtless meant to describe the blue smoke of a sulphurous flame" (Swete); "and of brimstone," from *theion*, sulphur, translated "brimstone," which was a pale yellowish color. In both the Old and New Testaments, brimstone signifies the wrath of God and is used always with reference to judgment and punishment upon the wicked. Its use here is no exception.

The terrible nature of this awesome and formidable cavalry is emphasized by the description of the horses as having heads of lions, strong, fierce, and frightful, from whose mouths issues forth fire and smoke and brimstone, by which men are slain in wrath and judgment. These three proceeding out of the horses mouths relate the horses to the horsemen whose breastplates were of fire and hyacinth and brimstone.

v. 18. *"By these three plagues was the third part of men killed, by the fire and the smoke and the brimstone which proceeded out of their mouths."* The disastrous calamities caused by the horses and horsemen by which men were killed are here called "plagues." In the Old

Testament, plagues were generally sudden outbreaks of disease or adversity, a divine visitation in the general sense of a punitive disaster. These were in the nature of "a public calamity, heavy affliction" (Thayer), tormenting or destroying the bodies, directly or indirectly. The word (*plēgē*) is translated "wound" (Luke 10:30), "stripes" (Acts 16:33), and in Revelation some twelve times as a "plague" or "plagues." In this plague, the death-dealing agents to one-third of mankind proceeded out of the lion-like heads of the horses' mouths. The use of the definite article before fire, smoke, and brimstone indicates the threefold instrumentalities by which the judgment was executed.

v. 19. "*For the power of the horses is in their mouth, and in their tails: for their tails are like unto serpents, and have heads; and with them they hurt.*" These horses thus possess a twofold power: their lion-like heads from which issue fire, smoke, and brimstone which kill; and their serpent-like tails with heads that inflict great hurt. There have been many explanations of these heads and tails, but it seems wise to say simply that this great destroying cavalry-plague killed as it marched and left a terrible hurt in its aftermath. Seldom is the serpent-poison of war's aftermath completely eradicated; it continues to bear its evil influence.

v. 20. "*And the rest of mankind, who were not killed with these plagues, repented not of the works of their hands, that they should not worship demons, and the idols of gold, and of silver, and of brass, and of stone, and of wood; which can neither see, nor hear, nor walk.*" It is clear from this description of those affected that only the wicked, worldly, and rebellious against God are included in the one-third who were killed and the two-thirds who were not killed. In these trumpet judgments the saints have not been considered; they are not directly involved.

In any event, these judgments which God sent upon the world of the ungodly as warnings failed to impress them, for they repented not of the evil works of their hands. In essence, the judgment was against idolatry, the root of their sinful condition. Paul pointed this out to the Romans when he said, "For the wrath of God is revealed from heaven against all ungodliness and unrighteousness of men, who hinder the truth in unrighteousness; because that which is known of God is manifest in them; for God manifested it unto them" (Rom. 1:18-19). He then added, "Professing themselves to be wise, they became fools, and changed the glory of the incorruptible God for the likeness of an image of corruptible man, and of birds, and four-footed beasts and creeping things" (Rom. 1:22-23); "Wherefore God gave them up in the lusts of their hearts unto uncleanness. . . . For this cause God gave them up to vile passions" (Rom. 1:24, 26); "And even as they refused to have God in their knowledge, God gave them up to a reprobate mind, to do those things which are not fitting" (Rom. 1:28).

In his vision John sees the terrible wrath of God against the rebellion and wickedness of man described by Paul. Idols, the works of sinners' hands, are presented in order of value from gold to wood. To worship (*proskuneō*), meaning to "kiss the hand toward," indicates "an act of reverence whether paid to a creature or to the Creator" (marginal note, Matt. 2:2, ASV). In the Old Testament demons are related to the idol gods to whom the people sacrificed (Deut. 32:17; Ps. 106:37), for the word *demon* "seems originally to have had two closely related meanings: a deity, and a spirit, superhuman, but not supernatural" (*I.S.B.E.*). Apparently they were the unclean spirits associated with idols and idolatry. A similar relationship is indicated in the New Testament when Paul parallels idols and demons; he says that an idol to which the Gentiles sacrifice is nothing, for they "sacrifice to demons and not to God" (I Cor. 10:19f.).

The folly of sacrificing to idols is set forth in Revelation as John scathingly says, "which can neither see, nor hear, nor walk." This, too, is reminiscent of the Old Testament Scriptures where God repeatedly warned His people against idolatry, spelling out the lifeless impotence of idols and testifying to the people that all who worship such objects will become like them (Deut. 4:28; Ps. 115:4-8; 135:15-18; Isa. 44:12-20; cf. also Dan. 5:23).

v. 21. *"And they repented not of their murders, nor of their sorceries, nor of their fornication, nor of their thefts."* The first section of the two categories of sins which brought judgment was idolatry, a violation of all regard and respect for the God of heaven, the creator and ruler of all (v. 20). The second section (v. 21) involves man's relationship to man. Moral depravity grows out of idolatry, which expresses a condition of the heart (Mark 7:21). The order of the process which leads to this condition is (1) exchanging the truth of God for a lie; (2) worshiping the creature, whether the human intellect or the works of human hands; and (3) decay and depravity which sinks into the basest forms of conduct toward self and contempt for the life and rights of others. John emphasizes the result of this sinful condition by repeating the charge, "They repented not... they repented not."

Murder reveals a disdain for life, a contempt for the creature made in the image of God, and is a crime for which God said man should pay with his own blood (Gen. 9:6). And God also said, "for blood, it polluteth the land; and no expiation can be made for the land for the blood that is shed therein, but by the blood of him that shed it" (Num. 35:33); judgment must eventually fall upon a society that allows the murderers to go free.

"Nor of their sorceries"; the word (*pharmakeia*) occurs only here, 18:23, and in Galatians 5:20, where it is translated "witchcraft" in the KJV. The word indicates the use of drugs, simple or potent, generally accompanied by incantations and appeals to occult powers (Vine). This sorcery also seeks to bring the victim under the power of the sorcerer. All forms of sorcery and witchcraft are satanic in nature and are condemned by God as worthy of His wrath and judgment.

Their "fornication" probably included all forms of sexual perversion and moral uncleanness which grew out of unbridled lust, the fruit of idolatry. "Thefts" manifest a disregard for the property rights of others, and together with false swearing are under the curse of God (Zech. 5:3f.).

As the first woe fell upon mankind, clouds of smoke from the abyss contaminated the moral and spiritual atmosphere of earth, corrupting and debasing the minds of men. Out of this moral atmosphere came locusts to torment (but not kill) as decay and corruption set in upon mankind. In the second woe, at the sounding of the sixth trumpet, destruction comes from without as the armies of the earth, symbolically portrayed as one huge army, march across the pages of history. Though inspired by the very spirit of Satan and of hell, these armies are used by God to accomplish His purpose. We are not to think of one physical army at a given point in history, but of God's death-dealing judgments as He uses the armies of time to execute His wrath; here one-third of mankind is killed as a result of God's judgment against idolatry and its fruit.

This interpretation is supported by God's repeated use of the armies of wicked men in ancient times. In the eighth century B.C. the Assyrian was the rod of His anger as He sent him against Israel and Judah, the people of His wrath, to "take the prey, and to tread them down like the mire of the streets. Howbeit he meaneth not so, neither doth his heart think so; but it is in his heart to destroy and to cut off nations not a few" (Isa. 10:6f.). Although it was used by Jehovah as the executor of His judgment, the proud and cruel nation did not know this. When His purpose was accomplished, God set His hand to destroy the Assyrians (vv. 25-26). About a century later the Chaldean power under Nebuchadnezzar was raised up as God's instrument of judgment to destroy Assyria and also to execute His wrath against wicked Judah. This is graphically described by the prophet Habakkuk as through him God says, "For, lo, I raise up the Chaldeans, that bitter and hasty nation, that march through the breadth of the earth.... They are terrible and dreadful.... Their horses are swifter than leopards and more fierce than the evening wolves...they fly as an eagle that hasteth to devour.... Then shall he sweep by as a wind, and shall pass over and be guilty, even he whose might is his god." (Hab. 1:6-11; cf. the entire book, at least chapters 1 and 2). Later God raised up Cyrus of the Medes and Persians as His servant to conquer Babylon and to let His people return to their land (Isa. 44:27—45:7; Jer. 51:11, 28). God uses the wickedness and brutality of men to destroy the wicked and to achieve His purposes. His use of these forces affords an excellent basis on which to understand Revelation 9:13-21.

The words of Albertus Pieters eloquently express my own feeling:

> As for the great happening of the trumpet series, I do not take much interest in locating them here or there in history, for it seems to me I know them. Have we not ourselves twice, in 1914-1918 and again in 1939-1945 seen the bottomless pit opened, and the heavens darkened by swarms of evil things that issued from it? Has not the thunder of the two hundred million hellish horsemen shaken the earth in our own day, so that we can never forget it? So it seems to me, as I see the pageant unroll act after act; and finally I turn away with profound confidence in the plans of Him that sitteth on the throne, written in the unsealed orders that are in the hands of the Lamb (p. 129-130).

CHAPTER 10
The Angel and the Little Book

Between the opening of the sixth and seventh seals (see chapter 7), the Spirit paused to reveal two significant visions which would give assurance to the oppressed saints. First of all, before the winds of earth were let loose upon it, the servants of God were sealed unto Him. This was followed by a vision of a multitude of victorious saints who had come out of the tribulation and were now before the throne, praising God and rejoicing in their redemption. By these two visions the faithful still living are assured that in the midst of trials and persecutions the church is not forgotten. The opening of the seventh seal reveals the prayers of the saints being presented before the throne, which causes the release of the trumpet judgments upon the world of the ungodly.

Now at the conclusion of the second woe—between the sounding of the sixth and seventh trumpets—there is an interlude which serves as a transition from the second to the third woe. God's saints have not been directly in view since their prayers were presented before God (8:3–5). This section (10:1—11:13) gives assurance that the witnessing of truth is not silenced during the trumpet soundings, but continues victoriously. This passage also introduces and prefaces John's future prophecy of nations that would persecute the saints and of their ultimate defeat by the victorious Christ (chaps. 12—20). Then follows the sounding of the seventh trumpet which reveals the total victory of God's cause over the world.

v. 1. *"And I saw another strong angel coming down out of heaven, arrayed with a cloud; and the rainbow was upon his head, and his face was as the sun, and his feet as pillars of fire."* This angel is distinguished from the seven angels of the trumpets and the four who were bound at the Euphrates (9:14). The similarity of the description of this angel to the description of Jesus in chapter one has led some to conclude that this angel is Jesus. It was there said of the Lord, "his countenance was as the sun" (1:16), and "his feet like unto burnished brass" (1:15), and that "he cometh with the clouds" (1:7). Those who justify this conclusion appeal to the likeness of the rainbow round about the throne (4:3), and the rainbow upon the angel's head.

However, similarity does not prove identity, for as "another strong angel" he is identified as an angel of the same rank or class as the "strong angel" of 5:2 and 18:21. The entire description indicates that he was sent on a very special mission and that his work was of unusual importance. This is indicated by his being "arrayed with a cloud." Of the twenty-five times that the word "cloud" (*nephelē*) appears in the New Testament, in all but three (Luke 12:54; II Peter 2:17; Jude 12), it is used in some relation to deity or of a divine appearance, often in judgment. This indicates that the angel before us comes clothed with a divine mission relating to judgment.

Only here and in 4:3 does the word "rainbow" (*iris*) occur in the Bible The word "bow" occurs four times in the Old Covenant, three times in reference to God setting His bow in the cloud as a token of the covenant between Himself and the earth (Gen. 9:13-16), and once in Ezekiel's vision when the prophet saw about the throne and its occupant the brightness of a bow which enhanced the appearance of the glory of Jehovah (Ezek. 1:28). The appearance of the angel with the rainbow as a halo upon his head, his face as the sun, and his feet as pillars of fire indicates the angel's close relation to God and Christ and the importance of his mission. As an angel he is a minister of Christ, serving as His messenger—he is not the Christ Himself.

v. 2. *"And he had in his hand a little book open: and he set his right foot upon the sea, and his left upon the earth."* The "little book," which is one word in the Greek (*biblaridion*, a diminutive of *biblion*) and could be translated "booklet," occurs only in this vision (vv. 2, 8, 9, 10), and is not to be confused with the book in Revelation chapter five. The sealed book, apparently much larger than this "little book," sets forth the destiny of God's eternal purpose, and its contents could be made known only by the Lamb who had overcome. This small book sets forth only one aspect of God's purpose, and was already open, indicating that John could assimilate and understand it. The significance of the little book is made known later (vv. 9-11). The angel's setting his feet upon the sea and upon the earth indicates the far-reaching inclusiveness of his mission; it pertained to the entire unregenerated world, the great mass of society. It included both proclaiming the gospel and sending judgment.

v. 3. "And he cried with a great voice, as a lion roareth: and when he cried, the seven thunders uttered their voices." "As a lion roars" gives emphasis to his mighty voice and great cry; it was heard throughout the whole creation. In ancient times when Jehovah warned the wicked He did so with a great roar (Jer. 25:30), and when He called His children it was with the roar of a lion (Hos. 11:10). Likewise when He warned of judgment and called His own to take refuge in Him, it was with a roar that shook the heavens (Joel 3:16). The words of His prophets caused men to fear as when a lion roars (Amos 3:8). So now, what this angel says should be heard and heeded by all, both the wicked and God's own. The seven thunders responded to the angel's cry with voices of their own.

v. 4. "And when the seven thunders uttered their voices, I was about to write: and I heard a voice from heaven saying, Seal up the things which the seven thunders uttered, and write them not." There is something awesome and terrifying about lightning flashes and the rolling, rumbling thunder which follows. Thunder accompanied the plague of hail in Egypt (Exod. 9:23) and the appearing of the Lord on Horeb, causing the people to tremble (Exod. 19:16; 20:18). By His great thunder Jehovah discomfited the Philistines (I Sam. 7:10), and with the arrows of His lightnings and His thunders from heaven He scattered the enemies of His servant David (II Sam. 22:14f.). Job asks, "But the thunder of his power [mighty deeds, margin] who can understand?" (Job 26:14); and David heard the seven voices expressing God's awesome power in the thunder of the storm at sea as it came in upon the land (Ps. 29). These majestic voices of thunder should help us understand that these seven thunders carried some foreboding of power and judgment.

As John was about to carry out the charge to write the things which he saw (1:11, 19), his hand was stayed, for he had not been told to write all that he heard. "Seal up the things which the seven thunders uttered, and write them not." We shall never know what the message or words were. The purpose of inserting this in the revelation is most likely to assure His saints that God has many unrevealed weapons in His arsenal of judgments to be used at His discretion; man cannot know all of God's ways. To "seal up" is not to "cancel the doom of which they were the symbol" (Caird, p. 126). Neither does it signify that the end is near; therefore there is no need to write. To seal up is to declare that the case is closed and that, apart from a new revelation, the message cannot be known to man (cf. Dan. 12:4, 9).

v. 5. "And the angel that I saw standing upon the sea and upon the earth lifted up his right hand to heaven." This gesture always accompanies a solemn oath or swearing, indicating an appeal to God as witness to the oath. Abraham had lifted up his hand in such an affirmation (Gen. 14:22), as Jehovah lifted up His, swearing by Himself (Deut. 32:40; Ezek. 20:5ff.). The angel whom Daniel saw above the river, lifted up both hands toward heaven as he "swore by him that liveth for ever" (Dan. 12:7). To swear "as Jehovah liveth" or "by the living God" was a characteristic practice in ancient Israel (Judg. 8:19; II Sam. 2:27; Jer. 38:16). Mention is made a second time that the angel's feet are upon the sea and upon the earth, for the word of the oath is going to involve both ocean and land.

v. 6. "And sware by him that liveth for ever and ever, who created the heaven and the things that are therein, and the earth and the things that are therein, and the sea and the things that are therein, that there shall be delay [time, margin] no longer." A more solemn oath could not be imagined as the angel swears by the eternity and omnipotence of God, which guarantees the certain fulfillment of the prophecy. The difficulty of interpreting the angel's words which he affirmed by the oath is obvious in light of the various interpretations of the phrase by commentators. *Chronos* may be translated "time" or "delay," and the interpretation of 11:15-19 will be determined largely by which of these words are used. Does the sounding of the seventh trumpet "usher in the completion when the clock of time shall finally stand still" as Lenski and others view it? Or does it usher in the completeness of the gospel plan and the church according to that plan? Vine says, "Speaking broadly *chronos* expresses the duration of a period," and continues by stating that in Revelation 10:6 it "has the meaning of delay." Arndt and Gingrich and Vincent hold this same view. In the light of the overall context, i.e., the prayers of the saints (8:3-5), the trumpets of judgments which followed (8:7—9:21), and the remainder of the vision and the sounding of the seventh trumpet (10:8—11:19), it seems best to interpret the angel as saying that there shall be no more delay before the fulfillment of the divine purpose regarding the fortunes of the church on earth.

v. 7. "*But in the days of the voice of the seventh angel, when he is about to sound, then is finished the mystery of God, according to the good tidings which he declared to his servants the prophets.*" In the interpretation of this verse there is a continuation of the problem introduced above (v. 6): Is this verse speaking of the end of time and the point of entrance into eternity, or is it dealing with the end of delay for the fulfillment of the divine purpose respecting the church? These words of the angel fall into three sections: (1) the days of the voice of the seventh angel; (2) the finishing of the mystery; and (3) the good tidings which He declared by His servants the prophets.

The view that this passage is not speaking of the final end of time is supported by the angel's introduction of the seventh angel's sounding, which would bring to pass the third woe. Following the vision of the measured temple and the victorious mission of the two witnesses (11:1-13) it is said, "The second Woe is past: behold the third Woe cometh quickly" (11:14). The word "quickly" (*tachu*) is defined by the lexicons to mean "quickly, speedily, without delay, at once" (A. & G.; Thayer). The third woe was to come quickly, but the end of time did not come speedily, at once, or without delay; in fact, after nineteen hundred years it has not yet come. Therefore, what was to be without delay was something other than the end of time; thus, it must have been the completion of the mystery.

"Then is finished the mystery of God." This mystery was God's plan for human redemption, conceived in His mind, after the counsel of His will, and summed up in Christ (Eph. 1:9-11; 3:8-11). It was revealed by the Holy Spirit (Eph. 3:1-5; I Cor. 2:6-13; I Peter 1:12), made known to the Gentiles (Col. 1:26f.; 2:2), and preached by the apostles to all men (Eph. 6:19; Col. 4:3; I Peter 1:12). This mystery was something that man could not know until it was revealed. In the gospel Christ was being preached, "according to the revelation of the mystery which hath been kept in silence through times eternal, but now is manifested, and by the scriptures of the prophets, according to the commandment of the eternal God, is made known unto all the nations unto obedience of faith" (Rom. 16:25-26). This complete fulfilling of God's mystery and its revelation was about to be finished. To finish (from *teleō*) means "to bring to an end, complete something...to carry out, accomplish, perform, fulfill" (A. & G.; so Thayer.

and Vine); hence, that purpose which the prophets looked forward to and the apostles preached was about to reach the completion of its fullness—it would not terminate, but be carried out in its entirety.

"According to the good tidings which he declared to his servants the prophets." What prophets are before the angel's mind? Of the 143 times the word "prophet" (including *prophētikos*, Rom. 16:26) occurs in the Gospels, Acts, and the Epistles, New Testament prophets are definitely spoken of fourteen times; but these never have the prominence ascribed to the apostles. John speaks of prophets eight times in Revelation, but it is difficult in some instances to determine whether he has in mind those of the Old Testament or of the New. Twice he speaks of "his servants the prophets" (10:7; 11:18), an expression used by Jeremiah six times, Ezekiel once, Daniel twice, Amos once, and Zechariah once. This special identification of prophets as "his servants" occurs only here in the New Testament, which leads to the conclusion that in these two instances the angel refers to the Old Testament prophets.

If this conclusion is correct, then this statement points to the completion of God's plan and not the end of time and entrance into eternity. The good news which was declared to those servants the prophets was the news of salvation provided by God's grace in the suffering Servant. The prophets sought and searched diligently for this, but it was reserved to be announced by the apostles through the Holy Spirit (I Peter 1:10–12). The end to which they looked was now being finished or completed. The Old Testament prophets never dealt with specific events beyond the coming redemption, the permanent establishment of the spiritual kingdom, the termination of the Jewish theocracy, the persecution of the saints, and the destruction of the fourth world empire (the Roman Empire—see Dan. 2, 7). This point considered further in the light of 11:15–19 seems clearly to establish the fact that this angel's message looked not to the end of time but to the completion of God's mystery, the gospel, the firm establishment of His kingdom and power, and the destruction of world powers.

v. 8. *"And the voice which I heard from heaven, I heard it again speaking with me, and saying, Go, take the book which is open in the hand of the angel that standeth upon the sea and upon the earth."* Once more John hears from heaven the voice which had told him to seal up and not write the things uttered by the seven thunders (v. 4). In neither instance is the speaker revealed, but the voice which had formerly told John what not to do now tells him what he must do. For the third time John emphasizes the angel's stance, one foot on the sea and one on the earth (vv. 2, 5), thereby stressing the far-reaching inclusiveness of His message. As yet the contents of this small roll that lay open in the angel's hand are undisclosed; this is reserved for verses 9-11.

v. 9. "*And I went unto the angel, saying unto him that he should give me the little book. And he saith unto me, Take it, and eat it up; and it shall make thy belly bitter, but in thy mouth it shall be sweet as honey.*" Whether John is now in heaven or on earth makes little difference, for in a vision he can be in either place without being physically transported from one to the other. However, he may have left his place in heaven (4:1) and come to where the angel stood. This scene from John's vision is similar to Ezekiel's vision of an open roll of a book being handed to him with instruction to take it and eat it. He was to fill his belly and bowels with it, thus mastering its content thoroughly; his whole being was to be saturated with the message from God (Ezek. 2:8—3:3). In his mouth it was "as honey for sweetness," but when he went on his mission carrying out the charge from God, he went "in bitterness, in the heat" of his spirit (3:14). Jeremiah had a similar experience when he found Jehovah's words and ate them: they were unto him as joy and rejoicing, but the loneliness of his position which followed left his heart filled with the deepest grief (Jer. 15:16f.). So it would be with John.

v. 10. "*And I took the little book out of the angel's hand, and ate it up; and it was in my mouth sweet as honey: and when I had eaten it, my belly was made bitter.*" John responded immediately to the instruction given him, with the results which had been predicted by the angel. What preacher or teacher cannot testify to a similar experience? The reception and comprehension of God's Word is sweet, but fraught with bitterness of spirit in the condemnation of sinners and the proclamation of Scripture's judgments against men and nations, declaring the consequences of disobedience, the wickedness of sin, and the terror and finality of judgment.

v. 11. "*And they say unto me, Thou must prophesy again over many peoples and nations and tongues and kings.*" It is not revealed who spoke to the seer; the "they," plural, may refer to the voice from heaven and the angel's voice combined, or it may indicate an indefinite source, as we would say, "it was said to me." But the instruction is clear; John must prophesy "again," indicating additional prophecies to those already written in this first section of the book. This additional prophecy is to include "many peoples and nations and tongues and kings." Except for "kings" instead of "tribes," these are the same as those from whom the saints were purchased, that is, the world (see comments, 5:9).

We are now ready to raise the question of the significance of this little book. Some have concluded that it is the open Word of the gospel and that within it there is the sweet and the bitter of its message—both salvation and judgment. However, the sealed book of chapter five contained God's purpose of salvation, set forth in the gospel, and consequences and judgment that would follow. Also, the similarity between Ezekiel's "roll of a book" in which were written "lamentations, and mourning, and woe" (Ezek. 2:10), and that which John was to eat, shows that it is unlikely that this little book was the gospel.

John's previous prophecies (chaps. 1—10) had been of hope and assurance to the saints and of judgment upon the world of the wicked. To this point specific forces of evil have not been identified. Probably the fresh charge to prophesy concerning "peoples and nations and tongues and kings" refers to the prophecies of chapters 11—22, the second section of the book. In it we shall find that judgments of strong secular powers, religious forces, and worldly seductive influences, together with the victory of God's people over all these antagonists, occupy the attention of the seer with more specific application. We believe this to be the significance of the seer's eating the little book, and of its sweetness and bitterness. It was sweet to learn that God's cause would be victorious in His saints, but it was bitter to prophesy of their suffering and of the destructive judgments which would befall the wicked world.

CHAPTER 11
The Vision Continues

THE MEASURED TEMPLE AND THE TWO WITNESSES
vv. 1-13

This chapter is a continuation of the vision in which John was told to eat the little book (chap. 10), which was interpreted to be the prophecies of judgment to be spoken against the world of the ungodly (chaps. 11—20). According to those prophecies, what is to be the lot of God's faithful servants during the great trials, calamities, and judgments? The 144,000 who had been numbered and sealed unto God (7:1-4) are now represented as a "measured temple" of worshipers, separated from the world and under divine protection. There is also the assurance that the preaching of truth would not cease regardless of what should transpire in carrying out the future judgments.

The difficulty of this chapter, as in chapter 10, is indicated by the space devoted to it and the profusion of interpretations by various commentators. The futurists, historicists, and extreme preterists wrest from this section views that are often unreasonable. These shall be passed over in favor of an interpretation most consistent with the positions taken on related previous passages and visions.

v. 1. *"And there was given me a reed like unto a rod: and one said, Rise, and measure the temple of God, and the altar and them that worship therein."* Until John was given the little book and told to eat it, his active participation in the revelation had been confined to writing what he saw and heard. Now he is given a reed like a rod, and told to measure the temple, altar, and worshipers. It is not said who gave John the reed, but it was probably the angel who had given him the little book and instructed him to eat it (10:9). The description "like a rod" indicates that the reed was stiff and strong; but whether there was any relation between this rod and the "rod of iron" by which Christ and saints rule (2:27; 12:5; 19:15) is uncertain.

Because John is told to rise and measure the temple, some writers conclude that the Jewish temple was yet standing, indicating that John wrote before its destruction, in A.D. 70. However, it must be kept in mind that this is a vision, and that in a vision an object can be seen, whether or not it actually exists. The Greek word here for temple is the sanctuary (*naos*) and not the temple (*hieron*) with its buildings, courts, and porches (cf. John 2:14). Since so much of the imagery in John's visions reflect the early period of Hebrew national history, it is possible that the sanctuary of the Old Testament tabernacle is before him. That sanctuary had only one court, with the altar and ark of the covenant within it; as reflected in the Book of Hebrews, the tabernacle was a type of the church.

The church is referred to in the Epistles as "the temple [sanctuary] of God," God's place of habitation among men (I Cor. 3:16–17; II Cor. 6:16; Eph. 2:21), made of living stones (I Peter 2:5), redeemed with the blood of Christ (I Peter 1:18f.), a holy priesthood offering spiritual sacrifices to God. In John's vision the temple is this sanctuary of God, the church, in which are all the true worshipers, "who worship by the Spirit of God, and glory in Christ Jesus" (Phil. 3:3), worshiping in spirit and truth (John 4:23f.). The altar is the golden altar upon which the incense of prayer and devotion are offered (8:3). These worshipers are the true circumcision, the Israel of God (Phil. 3:3; Gal. 6:15f.), who had been numbered (7:4), and now are measured.

This instruction to measure the temple brings to mind Ezekiel's vision in which he saw the frame of a city on a high mountain and watched an angel as he measured the temple, court, and walls. Ezekiel's vision emphasizes the principle that every detail of the ideal temple should be according to divine measurement and completely separate from the profane or common (Ezek. 42:20; cf. also 22:26 and 44:23). In Zechariah's vision of the measured Jerusalem, the city would be without walls, for Jehovah would "be unto her a wall of fire round about" (Zech. 2:5). All that pertained to this archetypal temple of John's vision and Ezekiel's vision is measured by the divine will and standard, and is to be holy and kept separate from the common (cf. II Cor. 6:14—7:1). Only as one comes under the measuring rod of God, that is, His standard of truth and protection, does he find safety. The scene is figurative and symbolic, not literal.

v. 2. "And the court which is without the temple [sanctuary] leave without, and measure it not; for it hath been given unto the nations: and the holy city shall they tread under foot forty and two months." Before attempting an explanation of the court it might be well to note that the ancient tabernacle with its sanctuary had one court (Exod. 27:9), whereas Solomon's temple (*hieron*) had an "inner" court (I Kings 6:36), an outer or "greater" court (I Kings 7:12), a "court for the priests" (II Chron. 4:9), and an "upper court" (Jer. 36:10). Herod's temple also contained several courts—the great outer court was eventually known as "the court of the Gentiles" because it was open to everyone. Beyond a certain point, however, the Gentile dared not venture, for the penalty was death. The sanctuary in John's vision had only one court, which was not measured, i.e., protected or separated from the common. It was left out, or literally "cast out" (from *ekballō*). The word *ekballō* meant cast out by force and was so used by Jesus (Matt. 22:13; 25:30), by Paul (Gal. 4:30), and by John (III John 10); it can also mean to leave out of consideration or to remove from favor, as it is used here. This court, left out of or cast out from God's protecting care, had been given to the nations—the Gentiles or heathen.

"*And the holy city shall they tread under foot forty and two months.*" This presents three questions: Who or what is symbolized by (1) the court without, (2) the holy city, and (3) the forty and two months? To the first of these, two answers commend themselves: (a) The measured temple symbolizes the inner or spiritual life of the true worshipers which neither Satan nor his instruments of persecution can reach; this is measured and protected by God. But He has not promised to protect the physical life of the body of Christians from being sacrificed and trampled under foot: "In the world ye have tribulation" (John 16:33). This view is supported by the fact that the holy city should be trodden under foot forty-two months. In the measured temple the spirit and worship shall remain inviolable though the outward church shall pass through the terrors of tribulation and death. (b) A second view is that the measured temple and its worshipers represent those faithful to God, those untouched by the world, and the court without symbolizes the worldly or unfaithful of the church. This latter group would include those in the church who succumb to the doctrine of Balaam, Jezebel, and the Nicolaitans in courting the favor of the world. It would also include those who had left their first love, those who were lukewarm and indifferent, and the apostates who had left the Lord for paganism (chaps. 2, 3). Both views are consistent with Scripture, so it is difficult to determine which was in the mind of the seer.

The second subject of inquiry raises the question of what is the "holy city." Some conclude that it is the old Palestinian Jerusalem (so called because of its former glory as God's holy city) which should be "trodden down of the Gentiles" (Luke 21:24). But it seems out of place in a book of images and symbols to have the writer switch in the same breath from a symbolic temple to a literal city. Either both temple and city must be taken literally or both must be taken symbolically.

Although Jerusalem is spoken of twice in the New Testament as "the holy city" (Matt. 4:5; 27:53), it is not the old city which is before John in the vision. When the "holy city" is spoken of elsewhere in Revelation it is as "the New Jerusalem coming down out of heaven from God" (21:2, 10), and as the city in which the saints have a part (22:19). Once John calls it the "beloved city," the camp of the saints (20:9). When Jerusalem is named in Revelation, it is "the city of my God" (3:12), or the holy city (21:2, 10). Paul writes of the Jerusalem which is above as "our mother" (Gal. 4:26), and the writer of Hebrews says to those addressed, "Ye are come unto Mount Zion, and unto the city of the living God, the heavenly Jerusalem" (Heb. 12:22). Therefore, we can conclude that the holy city is our spiritual Jerusalem. The vision indicates that although the faithful are numbered and measured, thus protected by the Lord, nevertheless the church shall be despised and rejected of the Gentiles and trodden under foot forty-two months.

To tread under foot is to trample upon (*pateō*). This word was used by Jesus of physical Jerusalem (Luke 21:24); it is used here by John to describe the holy city being trampled upon, and later in the book to describe the treading the winepress of divine judgment and wrath (14:20; 19:15). Unlike the literal city which would be trodden down by the Gentiles till the end (Luke 21:24), the holy city in John's vision shall not be trampled under foot forever, but for a limited time only.

The forty-two months of the third question indicates a broken period of time, a period of trial, persecution, and oppression (see introduction, pp. 47f.). It represents the same period covered by the twelve hundred sixty days (11:3; 12:6); the time, times and half a time (12:14);

and the forty-two months (13:5). The period is also related to Daniel's "time and times and half a time" (Dan. 7:25; 12:7). For a fuller discussion of this period and its significance, see comments under 13:5.

v. 3. *"And I will give unto my two witnesses, and they shall prophesy a thousand two hundred and threescore days, clothed in sackcloth."* Having assured His church that it is under divine protection while being trodden under foot by the Gentiles for forty-two months, the Lord proceeds further to assure His saints that prophesying and witnessing should not fail during that period. Time is now reckoned by days and not months as above (v. 2). Perhaps this indicates a day-by-day testifying during this time.

The speaker is the same one who gave John the reed and told him to measure the temple; it is unclear whether Christ or an angel is speaking. Immediately two questions are raised: Who are the two witnesses, and what is meant by "prophesy"? Expositors have given many answers as to the identity of the two. Some consider the two witnesses to be Moses and Elijah or Enoch and Elijah, who are yet to come. Others believe that the two are the true church and its preachers, who never cease to declare the faith. A popular view with some is that the Old and New Testaments are the witnesses; while others hold that the witnesses are prophets and apostles. This is only a partial list of answers to the question, none of which are completely satisfactory.

In the Old Testament two witnesses were needed for the competent legal testimony necessary to secure a conviction (Deut. 17:6; 19:15; Num. 35:30; Heb. 10:28). Jesus made the number two essential to confirm a point of discipline (Matt. 18:16), and for confirmation of truth (John 8:17). In view of this need for more than one to testify, He sent out the seventy in pairs, two by two (Luke 10:1). Paul likewise appealed to the same need for two or three witnesses to validate a judgment (II Cor. 13:1; I Tim. 5:19).

But is the number of witnesses to be considered literally, or is it to be viewed collectively, representing the number needed to convince the world that Jesus is the Christ? If we assume that God uses the number literally, it seems clear that the Holy Spirit and the apostles are in view here. Jesus said of the Holy Spirit whom He would send from the Father, "He shall bear witness of me: and ye [apostles] also shall bear witness of me" (John 15:26f.). The apostles had been specially selected as witnesses to the ministry, death, and resurrection of Jesus; thus they were able to testify to His deity. They were also to be "clothed with power from on high" (Luke 24:49), which they received when the Holy Spirit came upon them (Acts 1:8, 21f.; 2:1-4). The Spirit would guide them into all truth (John 16:13f.), and confirm their message by signs and wonders (Mark 16:19f.; Heb. 2:4). Peter appealed to these two witnesses for evidence to the exaltation of Christ (Acts 5:32); John appealed to the same two for testimony to the eternal life which is in Christ (I John 1:1-3; 5:7).

However, if "two witnesses" is used figuratively to describe the total testimony to be borne during the troubled period, not only would the phrase refer to the apostles and the Holy Spirit who bore the original testimony as eyewitnesses, but also it would include the testimony of the saints. The witness of the saints would be their testimony to the Word of God which they received from the apostles by the Spirit and held to its power in their own lives. They could not bear testimony as eyewitnesses, but by their confession and death they testified to the confidence of their faith (see 6:9; 12:11, 17; 19:10; 20:4).

The prophecy was to speak and teach by inspiration of the Spirit (Acts 2:17f.). God would put the words to be spoken in the mouth of the prophet (Deut. 18:18f.). In the apostolic period the ability of certain people to prophesy was a gift from God by the Holy Spirit (I Cor. 12:7, 10). This special gift was to end when revelation of the Word was complete (I Cor. 13:8-10). The two witnesses that prophesied included the apostles and prophets of the apostolic era, for by the Spirit they spoke the word of prophecy. This testimony would continue in the Word held and proclaimed by the saints (Eph. 2:20; 3:5; 4:11, 12).

The witnesses are clothed in sackcloth, a coarse fabric woven from goat or camel hair. Such garments were worn by ancient people in time of mourning, lamentation, and penitence, and in time of deep humiliation and supplication to God as they sought His special favor. The sackcloth garment seems to have been the characteristic garb of prophets. Such clothing now being worn by the witnesses indicated mourning; they lamented the treading under foot of the holy city and their own oppression from enemies of truth. The sackcloth expressed their dependence upon God and an earnest supplication to Him for divine support.

v. 4. "These are the two olive trees and the two candlesticks [lampstands], standing before the Lord of the earth." This explanation of the two witnesses is drawn from the vision in Zechariah 4, in which Jehovah gave much-needed encouragement to Zerubbabel the governor, assuring him that the temple would be built, "not by might [an army, margin], nor by power, but by my Spirit, saith Jehovah" (Zech. 4:6). By that same power God would now achieve His purpose in the church. The lampstands support the light, and the olive trees provide the oil for the lamps. God's witnesses would support and hold forth the light of truth "in the midst of a crooked and perverse generation," being seen "as lights in the world, holding forth the word of life" (Phil. 2:15f.), which would be provided by the Spirit of God. As "the Lord of the earth" God would amply support His witnesses as they encouraged the saints and testified to the inhabitants of earth concerning the grace and truth of God. "For the Lord hath power to make him [his servant] stand" (Rom. 14:4).

v. 5. "And if any man desireth to hurt them, fire proceedeth out of their mouth and devoureth their enemies; and if any man shall desire to hurt them, in this manner must he be killed." In this and the following verse the vision draws from acts of various prophets—from Elijah and his power over drought and rain, and from Moses who had power to turn water into blood. The figures symbolize power, both for protection of the witnesses and conquest of their enemies. Elijah had called down fire to devour two groups of fifty soldiers who were sent against him by King Ahaziah (II Kings 1:10–14); the fire of the furnace into which Daniel's three friends were thrown slew those who cast them into it (Dan. 3:22). Through Jeremiah Jehovah said, "Because ye [the faithless people] speak this word, behold, I will make my words in thy [Jeremiah's] mouth fire, and this people [the faithless] wood, and it shall devour them" (Jer. 5:14). Later the prophet complained that when he would refrain from speaking, "then there is in my heart as it were a burning fire shut up in my bones, and I am weary with forbearing, and I cannot contain" (Jer. 20:9). In the same way, His witnesses had this assurance that in the midst of all opposition their witnessing should not be stayed: they would have power to prevail until the testimony should be finished.

v. 6. "These have the power to shut the heaven, that it rain not during the days of their prophecy: and they have power over the waters to turn them into blood, and to smite the earth with every plague, as often as they shall desire." Again allusion is made to Elijah and his power to shut the heavens so it would not rain for a certain period, according to his word (I Kings 17:1; 18:1-45; for the time of the drought, three and a half years, see Luke 4:25; James 5:17). As the fire killed, so the lack of rain brought suffering and death. These witnesses also had the power of Moses to turn water into blood (cf. Exod. 7:20f.). As the enemies of God's people refused the truth and sought the blood of the witnesses, so these were able to give them blood to drink (cf. 16:4-7). Not only were they able to cause the waters to become blood, but they were also able to smite the earth with plagues.

It is evident that these plagues or judgments were not literal, for no such visitations were ever sent upon men by the witnesses. Nevertheless, their power was very real, even as it had been with their Lord who could not be killed until His hour was come (Luke 13:31-33; John 7:30; 8:20). Even so, no power could destroy these nor prevent their completing the work God sent them to accomplish. The powers exerted by Moses, Elijah, and Jeremiah were vested in the witnesses, to the end that God's cause should achieve its goal.

v. 7. "*And when they shall have finished their testimony, the beast that cometh up out of the abyss shall make war with them, and overcome them, and kill them.*" (This wild beast [*thērion*] is not to be confused with the "living creatures" [*zōon*] of chaps. 4 and 5, translated *beasts* in the KJV.) Although this is the first mention of the beast, John's use of the definite article indicates that the beast was known already to his readers. The introduction at this point is anticipatory, for the beast will not assume a leading role until chapter 13 and 17:3, 7. There he is identified as a great, imperial world power standing in opposition to the kingdom of God. The beast comes from the abyss, from where the smoke and locusts came, confusing and tormenting men (see comments, 9:1). The beast makes war with the witnesses, overcoming and killing them; but this is not done until they have finished their testimony. Although the witnesses were opposed, beaten and driven from place to place, the gospel was preached "in all creation under heaven" in the apostolic age (Col. 1:23), confirmed by God through the Holy Spirit (Mark 16:19f.) and written for posterity (I Peter

5:12). The beast could not thwart the advance of God's purpose to reveal the truth; for though he killed the witnesses and sought to destroy their work, by then it was too late.

v. 8. *"And their dead bodies [carcase, margin] lie in the street of the great city, which spiritually is called Sodom and Egypt, where also their Lord was crucified."* The singular, "corpse," is used as we would say "their heart" or "their head" (Lenski). In verse 9 "corpse" is used in both the singular and plural. The "great city" is not the "holy city" or the "new Jerusalem," for neither of these is ever called "great," but holy (see comment, 21:10). The "great city" is always Babylon, the world city, referred to ten times as "great" (14:8; 16:19; 17:5, 18; 18:2, 10, 16, 18, 19, 21). Neither does it represent literal Jerusalem, as some hold; it is parallel with Isaiah's world-city.

In chapters 24—27 of Isaiah, the prophet looks beyond or outside of Judah and sees the earth as a world of sin calling for judgment. This world is represented as a "waste city" (24:10), a city of desolation (24:12). As the earth is shaken violently (24:19), this world-city is left "a heap," "a ruin" (25:2); "the lofty city" is brought low, even to the dust (26:5). Out of this upheaval and desolation of the world-city there would emerge a strong people, "a city of terrible nations" that would fear Jehovah (25:3). In the midst of this world of sin, wickedness, judgment, and waste, Jehovah reigns "in mount Zion, and in Jerusalem" (24:23); and in His "mountain shall Jehovah provide abundantly for all peoples who will hearken and come" (25:6). In contrast to the world-city and its desolation and doom, Jehovah's people would have "a strong city" with impregnable walls and bulwarks (26:1).

It is through such a revelation as Isaiah's that we are to understand John's vision. The "great city" of verse 8 is the lofty city, the world-city, a waste city, for it is devoid of all spiritual life. It was doomed to fall, and in its fall men were frightened and gave glory to God. But was this conversion? There seems to have been no real repentance, only men's recognition of their own downfall and Jehovah's enduring power (v. 13). John sees the world as a city of evil, as Hosea had seen Gilead, "a city of them that work iniquity; it is stained with blood" (Hos. 6:8). John sees this great city as a spiritual Sodom in its moral depravity, as an Egypt holding all people in bondage to lust and sin, and as a Jerusalem that rejected truth and put to death the author of truth; it was in such an ungodly world that Jesus was crucified. Literal Jerusalem does not fit the picture, nor does literal Rome, except as each might represent the world of its day. It was in the street (*plateia*), a broad way or main avenue of the city of this world, that their bodies were left.

v. 9. "*And from among the peoples and tribes and tongues and nations do men look upon their dead bodies [singular] three days and a half, and suffer not their dead bodies [plural] to be laid in a tomb.*" Again their dead bodies are spoken of in the singular ("their corpse," as in v. 8), but then the writer speaks of them in the plural, "their dead bodies." They witness both as one, for truth is a unit, and as individuals. The accuracy of the above interpretation of the great city is further sustained by the character of those who look upon the corpses; they are from all nations of the world's unregenerated peoples who dwell upon the earth (v. 10, also see comments on "peoples," "tribes" etc., 5:9). The contempt held for the witnesses and their testimony is demonstrated by the world's treatment of their corpses; they are left unburied, exposed to the gaze of all. Those who look upon the corpses refuse to allow them the courtesy and respect of burial in a tomb. The beast would publicly declare its efforts to destroy the testimony of these witnesses or martyrs. The three and a half days again represent a half seven, a broken and troublous time. The number is analogous to the forty-two months and the twelve hundred sixty days (vv. 2, 3), except that in comparison this period of time is much shorter.

v. 10. "*And they that dwell on the earth rejoice over them, and make merry; and they shall send gifts one to another; because these two prophets tormented them that dwell on the earth.*" It is evident that the word "earth" (*gē*), repeated so often throughout the book, refers to the world of unregenerated people. These earthlings, who rejoice over the dead bodies of the witnesses, do not appear to be members of the apostate church who call the world to share a feast with them; rather, they seem to be citizens of the great world-city who rejoice over the suffering of the saints. They declare a great holiday for the death of the witnesses, making merry and sending gifts. It is a festive spirit over death such as had characterized the father's household upon the return of the lost son from death (Luke 15:23–32). As the Lord had said that the world would rejoice over His death (John 16:20), so now it rejoices over the death of the two witnesses. The messages and lives of these two prophets had condemned the world that refused to hear and change.

v. 11. *"And after the three days and a half the breath of life from God entered into them, and they stood upon their feet; and great fear fell upon them that beheld them."* The rejoicing of the ungodly merrymakers was short-lived; the rejoicing of wickedness is always but for a moment. The breath of life from God which had been taken from the witnesses is now renewed. As the deceased man whose body touched the bones of Elijah was restored to life and stood upon his feet (II Kings 13:21), and as the dry bones of the house of Israel had life infused into them and they rose to their feet (Ezek. 37:10), so God revives His witnesses and they stand upon their feet. Like Belshazzar whose merrymaking was turned into fear by the finger of God as it wrote upon the wall, so those who look upon the dead bodies of the witnesses no longer rejoice, but fear as they behold the power of God before them.

v. 12. *"And they heard a great voice from heaven saying unto them, Come up hither. And they went up into heaven in the cloud; and their enemies beheld them."* Their Lord's witness to truth had brought Him death, but he had been gloriously crowned with a victorious and triumphant resurrection and ascension into heaven; so it is with His witnesses. The Lord who had commissioned them raises their dead bodies and calls them to heaven, indicating a total and complete victory for His word of truth. As the Lord had ascended in a cloud of glory (Acts 1:9), so do these. No man had witnessed the actual resurrection of the Lord, and only a few saw Him ascend into heaven; but here the enemies behold both the resurrection and ascension of the witnesses. All the enemies of the faith can testify to its victory.

v. 13. *"And in that hour there was a great earthquake, and the tenth part of the city fell; and there were killed in the earthquake seven thousand persons: and the rest were affrighted, and gave glory to the God of Heaven."* The people of Asia were thoroughly familiar with earthquakes and the destruction and terror which they wrought, for there was scarcely a city in the entire area that had not at some time experienced an earthquake. Such natural calamities had furnished the prophets with challenging illustrations of destructive judgments. Isaiah announced that the multitude of Jehovah's foes would be visited with an earthquake (Isa. 29:5f.), and Jeremiah said that at His wrath the earth trembled (Jer. 10:10). Job saw in Jehovah's shaking the earth an expression of His mighty power (Job 9:4–6), and the psalmist saw the earth tremble as the fire of God's judgment consumed His adversaries (Ps. 97:3f.). In announcing Jehovah's judgment upon the ungodly earth, the scene of his world-city (see above, v. 8), Isaiah painted a vivid picture of the forthcoming judgment. "The foundations of the earth tremble. The earth is utterly broken, the earth is rent asunder, the earth is shaken violently. The earth shall stagger like a drunken man" (Isa. 24:18f.).

And now in indignation at the treatment of His witnesses, God's judgment is manifested in the great earthquake that destroyed a tenth part of the city and left seven thousand dead. The city is the great world-city (v. 8) which experiences partial judgment. Possibly the earthquake and fall of part of the city indicates a gradual breaking up of the old pagan world. Although many explanations have been offered concerning the tenth part of the city and the seven thousand, this tenth likely indicates a partial or restrained judgment, and the seven thousand a full, complete number, commensurate with the wisdom and demands of God. The rest who were terrified gave glory to the God of heaven; but to conclude that these were converted to the faith is an unwarranted conclusion. To recognize Jehovah as God out of fear, the consequence of personal failure, or the weakness of a system alien to God does not of itself denote repentance; and without repentance there is no conversion. The reaction may indicate that with the collapse of the world-city and its entrenched paganism there was a moving toward God; but there appears to be no more than this in their fright and recognition of the God of heaven.

Verses 1–13 of the chapter may be summarized as follows: The sanctuary with its worshipers is under the protection of God; Satan cannot touch these. However, the holy city, the personnel of the church, would be trodden under foot by her enemies for a troubled period of tyrannical opposition. In spite of the tribulation during that time, God's witnesses would continue to bear testimony as they passed through trials, oppressions, and death. Ultimately, they would be victorious.

The time of witnessing falls into three periods. The first is the apostolic age, during which the witnesses could not be destroyed (vv. 3-6). When the apostolic testimony was complete, the church definitely established, and when truth had been preached and written, witnessing entered a second period. It was during this period that the beast out of the abyss attempted to destroy the witnesses, causing them to endure great trials, in which they were killed (vv. 7-10). The third period is one of victory for the faith and its martyrs, symbolized by their resurrection and ascension to heaven (vv. 11-13). Since that time the witnessing has been carried on by those who hold fast the blood of the Lamb, the word of their testimony to the faith, and who love not their lives even unto death (12:11). In the trial of this victory the corruption of the world-city and old paganism begin to break up as men come to recognize the power of God and truth. There is no wholesale conversion of the world, but there is a weakening of paganism's former control over men.

THE THIRD WOE—THE SEVENTH TRUMPET
vv. 14-19

v. 14. "The second Woe is past: behold, the third Woe cometh quickly." This statement serves as a transition between the second and third woes. It should be remembered that when the woes were introduced by the cry of an eagle that it was said, "Woe, woe, woe, for them that dwell on the earth" (8:13). In response to the prayers of the saints, fire was poured out upon the earth (8:3-5), and the trumpets sounded, bringing judgments upon the earth. The judgments against the earth give assurance to the saints that evil will be defeated and truth will be victorious. If the interpretation of 10:7 and 11:1-13 is correct, the third woe does not usher in the final judgment, but signals the completion of God's mystery which was looked for and sought by the prophets. This conclusion is further supported by the word "quickly" (*tachu*), which means "without delay, quickly, speedily" (see comments on 10:7).

v. 15. "And the seventh angel sounded; and there followed great voices in heaven, and they said, The kingdom of the world is become the kingdom of our Lord, and of his Christ: and he shall reign for ever and ever." A great silence had followed the opening of the seventh seal

(8:1), but great voices follow the sounding of the seventh trumpet. It is not revealed whether the voices are those of angels or of the four living creatures. However, because of the relation between the living creatures and the elders in past scenes and because of the response of the elders in the song which follows (vv. 16-18), it may be inferred that the voices belong to the living creatures. Their song is one of victory for the Lord and His Christ. The battle had been hard fought, but victory was won. The usurper of power over God's creation was now cast down, and the power of rule is in God's hand where it rightfully belongs. The victory of Christ and His witnesses accomplished the defeat of the world and its powers. This conflict will be the major theme of the next section of the prophecy. The sounding of the seventh trumpet serves as a prelude to what follows, as the opening of the seventh seal served as a prelude to the sounding of the trumpets. This victory and complete rule of God was effected through the victory of His cause (vv. 1-13).

v. 16. *"And the four and twenty elders, who sit before God on their thrones, fell upon their faces and worshipped God."* The twenty-four elders, identified as God's redeemed of both covenants (see comments, 4:4), are prompt to offer worship and praise to God because of their place in His plan of redemption. From their position before the throne they fall upon their faces in adoration of God and His Christ whose reign shall not again be interrupted.

v. 17. *"Saying, We give thee thanks, O Lord God, the Almighty, who art and who wast; because thou hast taken thy great power, and didst reign."* Thanks are given to God, the Almighty (see comments, 4:8), who is now addressed as "who art and who wast" (the "and art to come" of the KJV is omitted in the ASV, cf. 1:8; 4:8), for He has now come in the assertion of His power and the assumption of His rightful rule. Jesus had assured the church at Philadelphia that in time of need He would "come quickly" (3:11); He told the church at Pergamum that unless the faithless would repent, He would "come quickly" to make war against them (2:16). Among His closing words in the book was the promise that either in time of need or of judgment He would "come quickly" (21:7, 12, 20). From these promises it may be concluded that His now having come is not the final coming when judgment would take place and eternal punishment and rewards be meted. The earth had been made to tremble; the things earthly had been shaken that the things which were unshakeable might remain (Heb. 12:27f.). The kingdom of prophecy was now a definite realization among men (Dan. 2:44; 7:13f.), for at the defeat of His enemies God had taken His power and rule over the world.

v. 18. *"And the nations were wroth, and thy wrath came, and the time of the dead to be judged, and the time to give their reward to thy servants the prophets, and to the saints, and to them that fear thy name, the small and the great; and to destroy them that destroy the earth."* Interpretation of this song draws from two Old Testament passages, the second Psalm and Daniel 7. Both of these seem to be in the mind of the seer here, and are definitely before him in chapters 12 and 13. The nations in their wrath tried to break asunder the bond between Jehovah and His anointed by putting the Son to death. But in disdain for the nations and in derision of their efforts, the Lord set His son upon His holy hill of Zion by raising Him from the dead and exalting Him to His right hand (Ps. 2:3-6; Acts 4:25f.; 13:33). Heathen forces continued to set at naught God's counsel by setting their hand against His church and His truth, but again they were defeated. In Daniel's vision of the beast that made war against the saints and prevailed against them, the time came for judgment to be given on behalf of His saints, that they should possess the kingdom (Dan. 7:22). The sounding of this trumpet seems to reveal the fulfillment of both the psalm and the passage in Daniel.

On behalf of the saints, the dead in sin (cf. Eph. 2:1, 5; 5:14; Col. 2:13) are judged. The prophets who had looked for and foretold the coming of the King and His kingdom of promise now have their reward in seeing their prophecies fulfilled. These have had a part in God's great plan, which was a mystery until the kingdom was come and its nature and king were revealed (see comments, 10:7).

From among both Jews and Gentiles, small and great, the saints see their cause triumphant. With the prophets and saints rewarded, the time has come to destroy the destroyer of earth. To destroy (*diaphtheriō*) does not mean to extinguish or bring to extinction, but "to change for the worse, to corrupt" (Thayer), as moths corrupt garments (Luke 12:33), as evil dispositions corrupt minds (I Tim. 6:5), or as time causes the outer man to perish (same word, II Cor. 4:16).

"Destroy" is used here to refer to men led by Apollyon the destroyer (see comments, 9:11), who inhabit and destroy the earth.

v. 19. *"And there was opened the temple [sanctuary] of God that is in heaven; and there was seen in his temple the ark of his covenant; and there followed lightnings, and voices, and thunders, and an earthquake, and great hail."* As this section began with the door opened in heaven to reveal the throne that rules the universe (4:1), so now it ends with the temple in heaven opened that all might behold the ark of God's covenant which rested there. In the tabernacle and in Solomon's temple the Holy of Holies contained the ark of the covenant, wherein were the tables of the covenant that God had made with His people. The *shekinah*, or glory of His presence, dwelt above the ark, between or above the cherubim (Exod. 25:22; II Kings 19:15). The presence of God and the ark of His covenant assured His people that He would remember and keep His covenant with them.

But the veil had been rent, and the way into the holy of holies laid open for us by the Lord Jesus (Heb. 10:20). The door into His holy temple was now open that the ark of God's covenant might be seen. God was giving assurance to His people that whatever might come, He would keep His covenant with them, for it is ever before Him. Great activity follows the sounding of this trumpet; God's heavenly artillery is already active. All this anticipates the things to come in the next section (chapters 12—22) as the prophecies of the little book which had been given to John are unfolded and carried out.

PART TWO
Chapters 12—22

WAR AND VICTORY!

CHAPTER 12
The Woman and the Dragon

Part one (chaps. 1–11) sets forth general principles of the moral and spiritual conflict between the forces of God and right and the forces of Satan and evil. God assures His faithful people that in the midst of strong opposition He will provide the necessary help for their victory, and will defeat their enemies by judgments upon the world. Though the Roman Empire and its emperor worship were not specifically brought into view, the beast out of the abyss was introduced (11:7). Clear identification of the beast, however, is reserved for the visions of section two.

In this section the content of the little book which John received from the angel and ate (10:9–11) is revealed and developed. The Roman Empire, paganism which was backed by the imperial power, and worldliness, are brought into focus. These three—force, false religion, and the lusts of the world—are revealed as Satan's allies. In opposition to these, the victorious Lamb, the faithful saints who hold the truth even in the face of death, and God's righteous judgments are set forth as His allies. God depends on these three for the victory of His cause. The conflict is to be bitter and bloody, but it will be decisive in its victory for righteousness and truth and in its defeat for Satan and wickedness. There is little doubt that the scene and theme of these chapters are rooted in God's promise to Satan and the woman when He said, "And I will put enmity between thee and the woman, and between thy seed and her seed: he shall bruise thy head, and thou shalt bruise his heel" (Gen. 3:15). The conflict between God's purpose and Satan continued until Satan's defeat by Christ.

THE WOMAN, THE DRAGON, AND THE MAN CHILD
vv. 1–6

v. 1. "*And a great sign was seen in heaven: a woman arrayed with the sun, and the moon under her feet, and upon her head a crown of twelve stars."* The Lord introduces this section of His revelation by "a great sign" seen in heaven (i.e., seen from heaven's viewpoint) which portends something from God. In his Gospel, John used the word "sign" (*sēmeion*) instead of "miracle" (*dunamis*, also translated "power" or "mighty works") which was used by the three synoptic writers; he uses "wonder" (*teras*) only once (John 4:48). As John viewed it, any miracle was a work common to deity, a sign of divine power. *Sēmeion* is defined as "a sign, prodigy, portent, i.e., an unusual event, transcending the common course of nature" (Thayer). The word occurs seven times in Revelation, three times referring to special revelations from God (12:1, 3; 15:1), and four times of deceptions imposed by Satan's helpers (13:13, 14; 16:14; 19:20).

The sign now shown to the seer is that of a woman arrayed or clothed (from *periballō*, to throw around, as a wrap or garment) with the sun, with the moon under her feet and a crown of twelve stars upon her head. She is thus arrayed with the total of divinely-revealed light of the three dispensations—the Patriarchal, Mosaic, and Christian. In the time from Adam to Moses, which is sometimes referred to as the starlit age, God was revealing Himself and His will "in divers manners" (Heb. 1:1). Through Moses and the prophets, the moonlit age, God was revealing the development of His will and purpose, but this was not clearly understood (Eph. 3:4f.). Now under Christ, through the apostles by the Holy Spirit, God revealed truth in its entirety. As the redeemed of the ages, the woman of John's vision is thus clothed with the totality of the revealed will and truth of God.

The woman seems not to be the Jewish nation, a view held by some; neither is she the church in its general New Testament sense, as suggested by others; nor could she be the virgin Mary, as contended by a third group. The Jewish nation rejected the Christ; the church in its limited or New Testament concept is the product of His redemptive work; and to make her the virgin Mary is entirely too limited in scope. The woman can best be thought of as the spiritual remnant of God's people who, in faithfulness, had kept covenant with Him. This position is sustained by Micah who said, "Be in pain and labor to bring forth, O daughter of Zion, like a woman in travail; for now shalt thou go forth out of the city, and shalt dwell in the field, and shalt come even unto Babylon: there shalt thou be rescued; there will Jehovah redeem thee from the hand of thine enemies" (Mic. 4:10). So, according to Micah, the nation would be given up until the time that "she who travaileth [the remnant, the daughter of Zion] hath brought forth." The one brought forth by the travailing daughter of Zion should be the ruler in Israel, the Messiah-King, for whom the people looked (Mic. 5:2f). Likewise, Isaiah identifies the bearer of the man child as the spiritual remnant of Zion, emphasizing the birth of both the man child and the new nation that would come through Him (Isa. 66:7f.). It was through this faithful remnant that the man child was born and the new spiritual nation brought forth.

However, the woman arrayed in light symbolizes more than just the Old Covenant remnant; after bearing the man child she came to represent all of God's people, for her children are those "that keep the commandments of God, and hold the testimony of Jesus" (v. 17). Further verification that she signifies the sum of God's people is the fact that those called under the first covenant obtain the eternal inheritance through Christ (Heb. 9:15), and "that apart from us they [the faithful under the Old Covenant] should not be made perfect" (Heb. 11:40). Apart from us they are not made perfect; we are made perfect in Christ; therefore, they are made perfect together with us in Christ. Since we are all one perfected group in Christ, it follows that they and we are the collective spiritual body of God's people, symbolized by the radiant woman of this passage.

v. 2. "And she was with child; and she crieth out, travailing in birth, and in pain to be delivered." The promise of God and the hope of a messiah, a redeemer, had been in the womb of the faithful remnant since Genesis 3. Symbolized as a woman arrayed in light, the faithful had cried out, longing to be delivered of Him (the Messiah) whom she should bear. Though experiencing birth pains for a long time, she gave birth quickly (Isa. 66:7); He came suddenly to His temple (Mal. 3:1).

v. 3. "And there was seen another sign in heaven: and behold, a great red dragon, having seven heads and ten horns, and upon his heads seven diadems." As in verse 1, the sign is beheld from heaven's viewpoint; the vision is seen in heaven. The dragon, the central figure in the sign, is not in heaven, but in the vision. The dragon is clearly identified as the devil and Satan, the old serpent (v. 9). The dragon symbol describes Satan's ferocious nature, "great" denotes his power and influence, while his blood-red color emphasizes his murderous character, for "he was a murderer from the beginning" (John 8:44), ever working for the death of God's people. His seven heads indicate fullness of intelligence and infernal wisdom, the master mind of craftiness and cunning which operates through lying and deceit (II Cor. 11:3). His ten horns symbolize fullness of power within his realm of operation. The picture is one of complete diabolical power, wisdom, and cunning against which the church must fight for its survival.

Upon his heads are seven *diadems*, symbolic of royalty in the realm of evil. The word "diadem" (*diadēma*), which occurs only three times in Revelation and nowhere else in the New Testament (12:3; 13:1; 19:12), is here introduced for the first time. It should not be confused with *stephanos*, the victory crown found elsewhere throughout the New Testament (see comments, 2:10). The diadem, which originated with the Persians, signifies the headdress of royalty. Monarchs of ancient Persia wore a blue band interwoven or marked with white, with which they bound on the turban or tiara (Thayer). In time, "diadem" came to designate the royal headdress of monarchs, ornamented with gold and jewels. In the three instances where it occurs, the word diadem is used metaphorically of royal power or rule. It is used of Satan, who rules in the realm of opposition to God (12:1); of the beast out of the sea, whose reign is in the political or imperial realm (13:1); and of Christ, who wears "many diadems," exercising royal rule in the many realms over which He reigns as "King of Kings and Lord of Lords" (19:12-16). Satan never wears the victory crown (*stephanos*); he wears only the diadem, for he wins no permanent victories.

v. 4. "*And his tail draweth the third part of the stars of heaven, and did cast them to the earth: and the dragon standeth before the woman that is about to be delivered, that when she is delivered he may devour her child.*" The dragon's greatness is pictured as he is seen dragging (*surō*, "to drag, pull, draw, drag away," A. & G.) a third part of the stars, casting them to the earth. Probably indicated here is the stronger idea of the dragon slashing his tail furiously, sweeping away the stars and casting them down. The "third part" is reminiscent of the first four trumpet sounds when a third of each realm was affected. Three explanations are offered for the casting down of the stars: (1) The verse emphasizes the power and might of the dragon; in his fury his slashing tail sweeps away a third part of the stars. (2) The scene points to Satan's rebellion against God when he led many angels, who are now cast down and doomed to eternal judgment (II Peter 2:4; Jude 6). (3) There is a parallel between a vision of Daniel and this one of John: Daniel envisioned the coming of Antiochus Epiphanes who is described as waxing exceeding great, "even to the host of heaven: and some of the host and of the stars it [he] cast down to the ground, and trampled upon them" (Dan. 8:10); "And he shall destroy the mighty ones of the holy people" (v. 24). Parallel to Daniel's vision, John sees the slashing tail of the dragon casting down a part of God's host.

All three explanations lead to this conclusion: certainly the great power of Satan is stressed. His ability to lead angels to their destruction should be a warning of his subtle cunning by which he can cast down God's saints; in Daniel's vision, an implacable enemy of God's people was able to lead some of His mighty ones to turn away from Him. Let God's people beware!

However, at this point the dragon is more concerned with the one about to be born than with the woman and her seed who might yet come. If he can devour her child, he will have struck the master blow. From the scene in Eden to this point in the conflict, the dragon has stood ready to destroy the seed when He would come.

v. 5. *"And she was delivered of a son, a man child, who is to rule all the nations with a rod of iron: and her child was caught up unto God and unto his throne."* As one reads this he is not to think of Mary and Bethlehem, but of the entire period from the child's birth until He ascended to heaven, where He sat down on the right hand of God, sharing the throne of the universe with His Father (3:21; 5:6f.). The whole experience from birth to coronation is contemplated in the few words of this verse. His being caught up was not for his protection but to establish his rule. The double expression, "a son, a man child" or male, indicates that He was no weakling, but a virile man who would wage war vigorously against His enemies and exercise His rule with firmness. In the expression, "who is to rule all the nations with a rod of iron," He is identified as the Son whom Jehovah would raise to sit as King on His holy hill of Zion, and to whom He would give the nations for an inheritance. These He would "break with a rod of iron," dashing "them in pieces like a potter's vessel" (Ps. 2:6–9). He rules in His spiritual kingdom with the scepter of uprightness (Ps. 45:6; Heb. 1:8), but in the kingdoms of the world with a rod of iron, smashing to pieces and bringing them to an end as He deems fit (Ps. 110:5f.; Rev. 19:15). The destiny of all nations of the world is in the hands of the Lord Jesus.

v. 6. "And the woman fled into the wilderness, where she hath a place prepared of God, that there they may nourish her a thousand two hundred and threescore days." The woman is now revealed in the fuller role of God's spiritual Israel, the church. As we have stated, the woman (v. 1) is Zion, the faithful remnant that gave birth to the man child (Mic. 4:10; 5:3; Isa. 66:7f.), now one in Christ with us. Since the redeemed have come unto Zion, the heavenly Jerusalem (Gal. 4:26; Heb. 12:22), the woman who now goes into the wilderness as the church, the new spiritual Zion, symbolizes all of God's redeemed people. Now that her child is caught up unto God, the woman flees into the wilderness, a place of safety provided for her.

Many similar instances out of biblical history might flash before the reader's mind. Moses fled from Pharaoh into the wilderness, and Israel escaped from a later Pharaoh into the same great wilderness where God nurtured and disciplined His people for future service. Elijah fled from the wrath of Ahab and Jezebel, coming to Sinai where he found protection and received instruction from God. Mary and Joseph eluded the wrath of Herod by fleeing into Egypt where the young child Jesus might be safe. Paul went away into Arabia, apparently to be taught and prepared by the Lord for his future work. The wilderness is the place of withdrawal where God's people are protected and disciplined. "There they"—the child (v. 5) and God—"nourish her" for twelve hundred sixty days, the same period during which the holy city was to be trodden under foot and the witnesses would testify in sackcloth (11:2, 3; see comments, 13:5). As Israel was nurtured in the wilderness with manna from God, so now the new spiritual Israel is nurtured by the true bread which came down from heaven (John 6:50f.). The woman reappears in verses 13-17.

THE GREAT SPIRITUAL WAR
vv. 7-12

vv. 7-8. "And there was war in heaven: Michael and his angels going forth to war with the dragon; and the dragon warred and his angels; and they prevailed not, neither was their place found any more in heaven." Before continuing with the fortunes of the radiant woman, the seer is shown a vision of a great spiritual conflict in which Satan and his forces are cast down to the earth. The dragon is no longer great or ferocious or apparently invincible; he is actually a defeated foe. Then suddenly, Satan as a great red dragon is no longer slashing and sweeping the stars to the ground; he becomes a warrior, leading an army in battle. Michael, whose name means, "Who is like God?" stands as the dragon's opponent. He is named three times in the Book of Daniel as "one of the chief princes" (10:13), "the prince of Israel" (10:21), and the "great prince" (12:1), who stood for the people against their enemies, Persia and Greece. He is called "the archangel" who contended with the devil over the body of Moses (Jude 9), and possibly is the archangel of I Thessalonians 4:16.

The words of Albertus Pieters serve as a cautious reminder in interpreting this vision of the war in heaven (vv. 7–9):

> Let us settle firmly in our hearts, and stick to it consistently, that the Apocalypse is a book of spiritual cartoons, the pictures not in any case to be mistaken for the reality, no matter how vividly drawn. As already pointed out, the rest of this chapter, concerning the Radiant Woman, the Red Dragon, and their adventures, is clearly seen by all interpreters to be symbolic, although they do not agree on what is symbolized. Is it not, then, to introduce confusion into the interpretation to suppose that the apostle suddenly shifts from symbolism to reality when he tells of the war in heaven? (pp. 172–73).

Let us not think of an actual war in heaven, but of such a war seen in the vision, intended to teach some great spiritual truth. In the conflict Satan is defeated and cast down from his high-handed control over men. Some have thought that the scene looks back to a primeval war in which Satan and his angels were cast out of heaven and imprisoned in dungeons of darkness, but this does not agree with the context or consequence of verses 10–12.

v. 9. "And the great dragon was cast down, the old serpent, he that is called the Devil and Satan, the deceiver of the whole world [*inhabited earth*]; *he was cast down to the earth, and his angels were cast down with him."* The great dragon is called "the serpent," identifying him with the serpent in Eden (Gen. 3), through whom sin was introduced into the world, and who has been the active enemy of God and man through the ages since. His name, the Devil (*Diabolos*), means accuser, slanderer, one who maligns; it should be used only of Satan and not of demons (as with KJV), for there is only one devil. His second name, Satan (*satanas*), identifies him as an adversary, one who stands as an opponent or an antagonist, an enemy (cf. Job 1:6ff.; 2:1ff.; Zech. 3:1f.). He is further described as the deceiver of the whole inhabited earth, for it was by deception that the world of mankind was plunged into sin (I Tim. 2:14), and by which he has continued since to control men (12:9; 20:3, 8, 10). It is by deception that false religion, symbolized by the beast out of the earth, also gains adherents (13:14; 19:20); and it is by deception that worldliness, signified by the harlot, the great city, seduces her victims (18:23). Expose and remove the deception of sin, and its power is nullified. The war resulted in Satan and his angels being cast down to the earth where he operates in the world of the unregenerate.

Of the numerous views held concerning the vision of this war in heaven, the three major views are: (1) The vision portrays the primeval war between Satan and God, indicated above; (2) there was an actual war in which Satan attempted to invade heaven that he might defeat the man child, but Satan was repulsed and cast down to earth; and (3) the vision symbolizes a spiritual warfare which had been going on from the beginning, but reaches its climax in Christ's victory over Satan. The third position is more defensible by Scripture.

In foretelling the vicarious suffering of Jehovah's servant, Isaiah revealed him as an "offering for sin." Many would be justified by the knowledge of Him, and by His victory through sacrifice He would "divide the spoil with the strong" (Isa. 53:10-12). When casting out demons in fulfilling His mission as Jehovah's servant, Jesus said, "When the strong man fully armed guardeth his own court, his goods are in peace: but when a stronger than he shall come upon him, and overcome him, he taketh from him his whole armor wherein he trusted, and divideth his spoils" (Luke 11:21f.; cf. Matt. 12:29). Satan is the strong man, but Jesus is stronger than he, and He binds the strong man and divides his spoils. Isaiah's prophecy is thus fulfilled. As

Jesus drew near the end of His earthly conflict He said of His foe, the devil, "Now is the judgment of this world: now shall the prince of this world be cast out" (John 12:31); "For the prince of this world cometh: and he hath nothing in me" (John 14:30), that is, Satan had nothing on Christ by which to defeat Him or to hold him in death. And as Christ anticipated His death, resurrection, and return to the Father, He added, "because the prince of this world hath been judged" (John 16:11). This meaning of the vision is further confirmed by the great voice which follows.

v. 10. *"And I heard a great voice in heaven, saying, Now is come the salvation, and the power, and the kingdom of our God, and the authority of his Christ: for the accuser of our brethren is cast down, who accuseth them before our God day and night."* With Satan's defeat and downfall, God's purpose of providing salvation, of demonstrating His great power, and the establishing of His spiritual kingdom, all promised through the prophets, "is now come," that is, His Word is fulfilled. The position taken on verse 9 and this affirmation are both established by the announcement, "Now is come... the authority of his Christ." Following His victory over Satan, which was climaxed by His death and resurrection, Jesus claimed this authority, saying, "All authority hath been given unto me in heaven and on earth" (Matt. 28:18). His authority was preached by Paul who said that Christ was at the right hand of God with all things "in subjection under his feet" (Eph. 1:20–23), and by Peter who also said that He "is on the right hand of God, having gone into heaven; angels and authorities and powers being made subject to him" (I Peter 3:21f.). He now has the name which is above every name and must be confessed by all, and before whose feet every knee must bow (Phil. 2:9–11).

In the conflict which culminated in the cross, He "despoiled the principalities and the powers," making "a show of them openly, triumphing over them in it [the cross, v. 14]" (Col. 2:15). He partook of flesh and blood "that through death he might bring to nought him that had the power of death, that is, the devil" (Heb. 2:14). "The sting of death is sin" (I Cor. 15:56), but since Christ was not stung by sin, "it was not possible that he should be holden of it [death]" (Acts 2:24). Wherefore when He came forth from the grave He could say, "I am the first and the last, and the living one; and I was dead, and behold I am alive for evermore, and I have the keys of death and of Hades" (1:17f.). The salvation long hoped for was now provided; the power of God over Satan, sin, and death had now been demonstrated; and the kingdom of promise was now a reality.

Christ's authority is complete and absolute; and the accuser and maligner of the brethren, who constantly accused them day and night, is cast down. Victory for weak and fallen men is now assured through God and Christ. This is the war seen by John in the vision; it is a conflict that had continued from Eden, which was won by the seed of the woman, as Satan's head was bruised beneath His heel.

v. 11. *"And they overcame him because of the blood of the Lamb, and because of the word of their testimony; and they loved not their life even unto death."* The Holy Spirit in the seer now points to the three means of the brethren's victory: (1) They, "the brethren" (v. 10), which would include the martyrs (6:9–11) and all others, conquered because of the blood of the Lamb. This says in a word all that was said under verses 9–10. The cross of Christ, where His blood was poured out, was a victory through which God's power was demonstrated. The brethren were now enabled to attain the same victory. The blood of the Lamb, which is the divine provision for deliverance and triumph, was the primary cause for the brethren's victory. (2) Another cause for their overcoming was the saint's response, which was one of faith; they held fast the word of their testimony. Not only did they hold fast the Word of Christ, but also the word of their testimony to the faith, which they had manifested when they confessed Him to be the Christ, the Son of God (John 20:30–31; Acts 8:37 [KJV]; Rom. 10:9f.; Phil. 2:11; Heb. 3:1). This testimony must be held unwaveringly by all saints in spite of all obstacles (Heb. 3:14; 10:23). Peter summed this up when he said of the saints under trial, "who by the power of God are guarded through faith unto a salvation ready to be revealed in the last time" (I Peter 1:5). (3) Together with these two essentials to their overcoming, the victors had the martyr spirit. Although they may never be called upon to die for the Name, they nevertheless must "love not their life even unto death." As in 2:10, the faithfulness is not "until death," though this is required, but "unto death." The saints must be willing to die for Christ if called upon.

v. 12. *"Therefore rejoice, O heavens, and ye that dwell in them. Woe for the earth and for the sea: Because the devil is gone down unto you, having great wrath, knowing that he hath but a short time."* Although the heavens, plural, occurs many times in the synoptic Gospels and the Epistles, this is the only time the word occurs in John's writings. It is possible to account for the plural, heavens, by including those who are made alive in Christ, raised up, and made "to sit with him in the heavenly places [Greek: the heavenlies], in Christ Jesus" (Eph. 2:5f.). This would include those in heaven and those on earth who dwell with Him in a heavenly realm and relationship. The rejoicing of the heavens and those that dwell in them is contrasted to the woe for the earth and the sea. The heavens rejoice because of the Lamb's triumph over the dragon, thus providing for the victory of the saints.

Those who dwell (from *skenoō*, to tabernacle) in the heavens are probably, in part, those who come out of the great tribulation, for God is said to have spread His tabernacle over them (7:15). These rejoice in the victory which they share. In 13:6 it is said that the beast blasphemed "them that dwell [tabernacle] in the heaven"; and God is described in chapter 21 as tabernacling with His victorious ones (21:3).

In contrast to the rejoicing of the heavens, it is "Woe for the earth and for the sea," because these become the field of Satan's activity. If "the earth" signifies the world of unregenerate people, and "the sea" signifies the mass of society (see comments, 13:1), then the woe is upon these two symbolic representations of the world which must bear the effects of Satan's diabolical wrath. Swete, however, does not agree to an allegorical sense of the two words, but accepts them literally as the scene of Satan's future operations.

The dragon is enraged at his defeat, for he knows that he has "but a short time." Does this "short time" refer to the period until he shall be cast into the lake of fire, his final end (20:10), or is it until the time when he should be bound and cast into the abyss (20:1–3)? Though contrary to the view of many expositors, the "short time" of Satan seems to be equivalent to the "little time" of the martyrs (see comments, 6:11). For when Satan would be bound and cast into the abyss, the martyrs would be raised to sit on thrones and reign with Christ a thousand years (see comments, 20:1–3), at which point Satan's short time would be over and the martyrs' little time ended. Thus the two are parallel.

PERSECUTION OF THE WOMAN
vv. 13-17

v. 13. "And when the dragon saw that he was cast down to the earth, he persecuted the woman that brought forth the man child." After an interruption to reveal the war and Satan's defeat (vv. 6-9), the coming of God's power and Christ's authority (v. 10), and the ground of the Christians' overcoming (v. 11), the description of the plight of the woman is now resumed. Since the man child is beyond Satan's power to attack, the dragon seeks to hurt the child by persecuting the woman who gave Him birth. This further confirms the view that the woman is spiritual Zion, the sum of God's people. Satan did not carry his war to the Jewish nation, nor to the Jewish remnant that had kept faith with God under the Old Covenant, but to the new spiritual Zion, the church. To persecute (*diokō*, used only here in Revelation), means "to run after... to pursue (in a hostile manner)... hence, to persecute" (Thayer). Jesus had forewarned His disciples of such hostile pursuit when He said, "If they [of the world] persecuted me, they will also persecute you" (John 15:20).

v. 14. "And there were given to the woman the two wings of the great eagle, that she might fly into the wilderness unto her place, where she is nourished for a time, and times, and half a time, from the face of the serpent." The serpent is no match for the Lord, whose power has been demonstrated in the conflict revealed above; and now by that same power the Lord comes to the rescue of the woman. Interpretation of this part of the vision must be drawn from the account of ancient Israel's deliverance from Egypt. When Jehovah delivered His people from Pharaoh's threats of destruction, He said, "I bare you on eagles' wings, and brought you unto myself" (Exod. 19:4; cf. Deut. 32:11); the psalmist asserted, "and the children of men take refuge under the shadow of thy wings" (Ps. 36:7). By His provision He brought them into the place which He prepared (Exod. 23:20). Years later, in anticipation of their deliverance from the power of their captor, the prophet said, "They that wait for Jehovah shall renew their strength; they shall mount up with wings as eagles" (Isa. 40:31). The Lord delivers, protects, and provides for His own; there is no point of weakness or failure on His part. The time, times, and half a time is equivalent to the twelve hundred sixty days of verse 6 (for a discussion of the period see comments, 13:5). Though the wilderness is that place of withdrawal where God's people are protected and nurtured for a particular period (v. 6), there is a sense in which they are ever in the wilderness, withdrawn from the world, protected and disciplined by the Lord; for we sit with Him in heavenly places (Eph. 2:6), and our life "is hid with Christ in God" (Col. 3:3).

v. 15. "And the serpent cast out of his mouth after the woman water as a river, that he might cause her to be carried away by the stream." The idea of floods threatening to engulf God's people was not new; it is found repeatedly in the prophets and psalms. Isaiah had pictured the coming up of Assyrian hosts to absorb Judah as the mighty Euphrates overflowing its banks, and sweeping onward toward Judah, reaching even to the neck but not able to reach the head, Jerusalem (Isa. 8:5–8). Jehovah assured those whom He redeemed, saying, "When thou passest through the waters, I will be with thee; and through the rivers, they shall not overflow thee" (Isa. 43:2). In need of help, the psalmist cried unto Jehovah to stretch forth His hand and deliver him "out of great waters, out of the hand of aliens" (Ps. 144:7) and called upon the godly to pray in a time when God could be found, that "when the great waters overflow they shall not reach unto him" (Ps. 32:6).

Now the serpent tried to sweep the woman away by the river that issued out of his mouth: delusions in the form of lies, false impressions of invincible power, false religious teachings, false philosophies, false charges, and malicious reports intended to destroy the church. To these he would add the seductive temptations of lust. Let the saint remember that everything the devil says and does is a lie, for "he standeth not in the truth, because there is no truth in him. When he speaketh a lie, he speaketh of his own: for he is a liar, and the father thereof" (John 8:44). But the church has withstood the assault of the serpent because a way has been provided for her deliverance.

v. 16. "And the earth helped the woman, and the earth opened her mouth and swallowed up the river which the dragon cast out of his mouth." The concept of water being absorbed by the sands of an arid country would be familiar to John's readers. The rivers flowing eastward from the Lebanon mountains about Damascus disappear beneath the sands of the eastern desert. Job accused his friends of being like deceitful brooks that vanish away. When the weary traveler comes to them for water, there is none; they have vanished beneath the sands (Job 6:15-20). In the same way the earth, that is, the unregenerated earthlings, helped the woman by opening its mouth and swallowing up the lies of the dragon. In doing this the earth established a clear distinction between the world, satiated with its false religions and philosophical teachings, on the one hand, and the church, clothed with truth and righteousness, on the other. From the viewpoint of Satan and the world, the earth's help was incidental and unintentional; but from the viewpoint of the church, it was providential. As long as the world absorbs the river of Satan's lies, and the church drinks from the fountain of divine truth, the separation between the two will remain clear and distinct. But when the woman begins to compromise with Satan and his lies, becoming submerged in his river of falsehood, tragedy follows.

v. 17. *"And the dragon waxed wroth with the woman, and went away to make war with the rest of her seed, that keep the commandments of God, and hold the testimony of Jesus."* The dragon was now furious. He had been defeated in his effort to devour the man child, who was caught up to God and His throne; and he had failed to sweep away the woman when the earth swallowed up his river of lies and she escaped into the wilderness. Incensed by these two defeats, he turned on the woman's seed to do battle with them. "The rest of her seed" are the saints. Jesus is "the firstborn among many brethren" (Rom. 8:29), and "is not ashamed to call them brethren" (Heb. 2:11). The rest "that keep the commandments of God" are not Jews or followers of the Jewish law, but the faithful servants under Christ, the saints (14:12) who keep the commandments of the gospel. The word "commandment" (*entolē*) occurs ten times in the Gospel of John; it is used once of the Pharisees' commandments, and nine times to refer to the commandments of the Father and Jesus. It occurs fourteen times in First John, in which not once does it refer to the Old Law, but each time to the commandments of the New. John here speaks of those who keep these commandments. These are also to "hold the testimony of Jesus," both the truth to which Jesus bare witness (John 18:37), and their own testimony of faith in that truth, being willing to die for it if need be (20:4). These are they who now come under the destructive wrath of the dragon, but are assured of victory in Christ.

CHAPTER 13
The Two Wild Beasts

Failing in his effort to destroy the man child and the woman, the dragon was cast down to the earth where he rallies two allies through which he seeks to defeat and destroy God's purpose, people, and rule. These two helpers of Satan are revealed in this chapter: a wild beast (*thērion*) from the sea, and another out of the earth. Chapters twelve and thirteen provide the key to an understanding of part two (chapters 12—22), and a careful interpretation here is of utmost importance to an overall understanding of the book.

THE BEAST OUT OF THE SEA
vv. 1-10

v. 1. "*And he [the dragon] stood upon the sand of the sea. And I saw a beast coming up out of the sea, having ten horns and seven heads, and on his horns ten diadems, and upon his heads names of blasphemy.*" This translation rests upon textual evidence superior to that of the KJV, "And I stood"; for where John stood is immaterial, but where the dragon stood in gathering his helpers is significant. Two important details of the vision to be interpreted are now before us, namely, the sea and the beast out of the sea.

The ancient Hebrews were not seafarers, but a pastoral and agricultural people. From their point of view the sea was an awesome and fearful part of creation from whence came storms and destructive forces which filled them with awe. David saw a storm coming inland from the sea, breaking the cedars of Lebanon and shaking the wilderness of Kadesh; but in it was the voice of Jehovah, revealing strength and power (Ps. 29). In another psalm the singer of Israel compared "the roaring of the seas" with "the tumult of the peoples [nations]" (65:7). In a series of prophecies concerning the heathen nations, Isaiah cried, "Ah, the uproar of many peoples, that roar like the roaring of the seas;

and the rushing of nations, that rush like the rushing of mighty waters!" (Isa. 17:12). And again he says, "But the wicked are like the troubled sea; for it cannot rest, and its waters cast up mire and dirt. There is no peace, saith my God, to the wicked" (Isa. 57:20f.; cf. Jer. 49:23).

In addition to comparing the sea to the turbulence of the nations, the prophet compares "the abundance of the sea" with "the wealth of the nations" (Isa. 60:5). Jeremiah describes the many peoples over which Babylon ruled and upon which she dwelt "as many waters" (Jer. 51:13). He described her destruction as the nations came upon her, "The sea is come up over Babylon; she is covered with the multitude of the waves thereof" (Jer. 51:42). The cry of her destruction was heard, "For Jehovah layeth Babylon waste, and destroyest out of her the great voice"; and the destroyer is described as the prophet continues, "And their waves roar like many waters... for the destroyer is come upon her, even upon Babylon" (Jer. 51:55f.). Likewise, Ezekiel compares many nations to the sea and its waves as they came up against Tyre (Ezek. 26:3).

Daniel 7 is probably the most helpful passage in interpreting John's use of "the sea," and the one upon which his vision rests; it shall be appealed to repeatedly in the interpretation of the sea and the beast of chapter 13. In his vision, Daniel saw the four winds of heaven as they broke forth "upon the great sea. And four great beasts came up from the sea, diverse one from another" (7:2f.). From the prophet's use of the word, it seems clear that the sea symbolizes the human societies or nations with their stormy upheavals, out of which the empires of earth arise. These four beasts were four great kingdoms which emerged from such upheavals. In Revelation, John refers to the sea: (1) literally, as a part of creation (5:13; 10:6; 14:7); (2) to describe the limits of the angel's voice (7:1-3); (3) symbolically, indicating God's transcendence (4:6; 15:2), and (4) to signify the whole of society known at that time (8:8f.; 10:2, 8; 12:12; 13:1; 20:13; 21:1).

The wild beast of John's vision (see comments, 11:7) which arises out of the turmoils, wars, and violence of society becomes the central figure of this vision. The beast is described as having "ten horns," symbolizing fullness of power, and "seven heads," indicating completeness of intelligence and wisdom. "And on his horns ten diadems" (for a discussion of "diadems" see comments, 12:3), indicating rule in the realm which he represents. The dragon was also described as having seven heads and ten horns, but the diadems are upon his heads and here they are upon the beast's horns. The similarity of the two indicates that this beast is thoroughly satanic—he possesses the characteristics and qualities of the devil.

"And upon his heads names of blasphemy," indicates a totally irreverent attitude toward God and all that is sacred. His intelligence, wisdom, and will are directed against God. The Roman emperors' arrogation of titles pertaining to deity would apply here; their accepting worship would be most obnoxious to all who hold God and Christ in the reverence belonging to the divine Godhead.

v. 2. *"And the beast which I saw was like unto a leopard, and his feet were as the feet of a bear, and his mouth as the mouth of a lion: and the dragon gave him his power, and his throne, and great authority."* From the description of the beast in these two verses it seems beyond question that this beast out of the sea is the fourth beast of Daniel's vision (Dan. 7). Daniel saw four great beasts come up out of the sea: the first was like a lion with a man's heart, therefore human in character (v. 4); the second was like a bear, strong and crushing in its power (v. 5); the third was like a leopard, having four wings and four heads, swift and powerful (v. 6); while the fourth is not compared to any animal known to man, but is pictured as being "terrible and powerful and strong exceedingly; and it had great iron teeth; it devoured and broke in pieces, and stamped the residue with its feet: and it was diverse from all the beasts that were before it; and it had ten horns" (v. 7).

It is revealed to Daniel that these beasts are "four kings, that shall arise out of the earth" (v. 17). These are more fully identified as four kingdoms: "The fourth beast shall be a fourth kingdom upon earth, which shall be diverse from all the kingdoms, and shall devour the whole earth, and shall tread it down, and break it in pieces" (v. 23). This vision of Daniel is parallel to the dream of Nebuchadnezzar in which there are four kingdoms, the Babylonian being the first (Dan. 2). These four kingdoms, symbolized by the four beasts out of the sea, are the Babylonian of Daniel's day; the Medo-Persian kingdom, which also came into power in Daniel's lifetime (Dan. 10:1); the Macedonian, represented by the leopard, which fell into four parts after Alexander's death; and the Roman, signified by the terrible fourth beast.

The beast of John's vision is a synthesis, or an embodiment of Daniel's first three, for as their dominion was taken away, "their lives were prolonged for a season and a time" (Dan. 7:12); that is, each lived in spirit in the next until the climax was reached in the fourth beast. The belief that John's beast is this fourth of Daniel's vision, therefore the Roman Empire, is further confirmed by Daniel's description, that "it had ten horns," as does the beast in John's vision. Here is a plain introduction of the Roman Empire as an instrument of Satan's diabolical and blasphemous power, cruelty, and opposition to God's kingdom. In the mighty, worldwide Roman Empire was combined the tearing power of Chaldea (the lion), the crushing force of Medo-Persia (the bear), and the swift and ferocious character of Macedonia under Alexander (the leopard). This beast symbolized all the anti-God opposition by force that could ever be brought against the people of God, but to John and the saints to whom he wrote it definitely personified the empire of their day.

"And the dragon gave him his power, and his throne, and great authority." Though defeated and cast down, Satan continues to rule in the kingdom of evil. As God had given the Lamb His power, throne, and authority by which to carry out His purpose, so Satan gives the beast his power, throne, and authority by which to wage his war. The divine rule has its diabolical counterpart in the dragon and misdirected political power which serves as the dragon's vicegerent. This is not to say that civil government is of the devil in its origin, for it is ordained of God (Rom. 13:1); however, it can depart from the role for which it was intended. Although times had changed greatly since Paul wrote Romans 13:1 and Peter had urged the same in I Peter 2:13ff., there is no hint in Revelation that the saints should resist the cruel power of the monster, but rather that they should submit to it even unto death (13:10).

v. 3. "And I saw one of his heads as though it had been smitten unto death; and his death-stroke was healed: and the whole earth wondered after the beast." The widely divergent and differing interpretations of "the head that had been smitten [Greek, *slain*]; and his death-stroke was healed" indicate that here is another difficult point in understanding and interpreting the book. A fuller discussion of the problem is reserved for comments on 17:7-11. Pieters lists ten interpretations compiled from many writers (pp. 219-224), then accepts Swete's conclusion that the head receiving the deathstroke was Nero. Only three views seem worthy of serious consideration: (1) The deathstroke administered to one of the heads was the resurrection, ascension, and coronation of Christ, which stunned the beast until the church had gained a sound foothold in the world; (2) the seven heads are seven heathen or anti-God powers which had arose and would arise in opposition to God and His people; (3) the deathstroke is the death of Nero, the first emperor to persecute the church, whose policy of persecution was revived by Domitian, in whom "the death-stroke was healed."

Recognizing that any view taken presents difficulties, the third is preferable. The death of Nero dealt a severe blow to the empire, which was immediately thrown into a two-year state of anarchy and confusion. Order was restored by Vespasian of the Flavian family. But to the church, which is John's interest, the healing of the death-stroke came with the revival of persecution under Domitian. Tacitus points out that after Nero's death there were various rumors that the return of the tyrant was at hand, whereupon pretenders arose claiming to be the deceased emperor (*Hist.* II. 8). Seutonius, another early Roman historian, writes that after Nero's death friends circulated his edicts, "pretending he was still alive and would soon return to confound his enemies"; he tells of one in particular who came forward claiming to be Nero (*Nero*, 57).

John would not have been influenced by these rumors, but saw in the renewal of persecution under Domitian a healing of the death-stroke inflicted by the death of Nero. Tertullian wrote of "Domitian—a man of Nero's type" (A-N-F. III, p. 22). Victorinus (d. A.D. 304), the earliest author to write a commentary on Revelation (only a fragment of which has survived) in commenting on 17:10, lists the five emperors whom he considered had fallen, then says, "One remains, under whom the Apocalypse was written—Domitian, to wit." He adds on verse 16, "Now that one of the heads was, as it were, slain to death...he speaks of Nero" (A-N-F. VII. p. 358).

"And the whole earth wondered after the beast," that is, the world of unregenerated people followed the beast, being filled with awe and amazement at it. The Christians were not impressed, but held to their faith in Him who in His death had triumphed over all powers and ever lives.

v. 4. "And they worshipped the dragon, because he gave his authority unto the beast; and they worshipped the beast, saying, Who is like unto the beast? and who is able to war with him?" Alienated from God and awed by the power of the beast, against whom none dared to war, the world followed him, rendering homage to the dragon who had given his power, throne, and authority to the beast; for to the world this power seemed absolute and invincible. In rendering homage to the emperor the world was worshiping him who had given his authority to the Roman power. This worship is the counterpart to the worship of God, for in worshiping Christ to whom God gave His authority, the Christians worship God who sent the Christ and provided all blessings through Him. Caird suggests that men had prayed to the old gods to no avail, for the gods had not supplied their needs. Rome was now displaying unbelievable power and was giving the people what the gods had failed to give—worldly wealth, glory, and influence. Thus it was an easy transition from worship of the gods to worship of emperor and state. Not knowing the true God, the heathen world was ignorant of His ability to war with the beast and to give victory to His own who refused to yield to satanic pressure.

v. 5. "And there was given to him a mouth speaking great things and blasphemies; and there was given to him authority to continue forty and two months." When John speaks of the beast, it is sometimes difficult to determine whether he has in mind the emperor or the empire. However, it may not make a great difference, since the emperor personified the empire. In verses five and seven John says that four things were given to the beast: (1) "a mouth speaking great things and blasphemies," (2) "authority to continue forty and two months" (v. 5), (3) authority "to make war with the saints, and to overcome them," and (4) "authority over every tribe and people and tongue and nation" (v. 7). Though the dragon had given his power, throne, and authority to the beast, it was not he who had given these four (vv. 5, 7) to the beast; for "the powers that be are ordained of God." Each power serves as God's minister (Rom. 13:1, 4), who would have no power except it be given him from above (John 19:11). Therefore whatever the beast does is by God's permission; God allows him to act. As stated above, there were upon the heads of the beast "names of blasphemy" (v. 1), titles which belonged to God but which the emperors now arrogated to themselves. Not content with these divine claims, through his mouth the beast pours forth blasphemies against God and His saints. The blasphemies fulfill the prophecy of Daniel that a horn would arise among the ten horns with "a mouth speaking great things," "whose look was more stout than its fellows" (Dan. 7:8, 20).

"And there was given to him authority to continue forty and two months." "To continue" is translated in the marginal reading (ASV), "to do his works during" forty-two months; thus his period of operation was determined by God. This length of time has been previously introduced four times. All five instances refer to the same period and are not to be taken literally. The holy city should be trodden under foot forty-two months (11:2); the witnesses should prophesy twelve hundred sixty days (the same period of time) under trying and oppressive conditions, clothed in sackcloth (11:3); the woman would spend twelve hundred sixty days in the wilderness where she would be protected by God and the Lamb (12:6) and where she would be "nourished for a time, and times, and half a time, from the face of the serpent" (12:14). The latter, time, times, and half a time, is equivalent to the twelve hundred sixty days or three and a half years: time, one year; times, two years; half a time, half a year. The duration of these four parallel periods is the same as that of the beast's authority and blasphemies. This is related to the explanation given concerning Daniel's dream when he was told that the little horn who spoke great things "made war with the saints, and prevailed against them" (Dan. 7:21); "and they [the saints] shall be given into his hand until a time and times and half a time" (v. 25), which is identical with John's vision of forty-two months. These six equivalent periods point to the period of Roman persecution, a period of oppression and trials for the saints.

v. 6. *"And he opened his mouth for blasphemies against God, to blaspheme his name, and his tabernacle, even them that dwell in the heaven."* This reveals the true character of the beast. Not only does he wear names of blasphemy on his seven heads, but he opens his mouth to revile, slander, and profane the holy name of God. God's name stands for all that He is, so to blaspheme His name is to rail against all that pertains to the Divine One. His tabernacle, "even them that dwell [tabernacle] in the heaven," refers to the church, made up of those whose citizenship is in heaven (Phil. 3:20), and who sit with Him in heavenly places in Christ (Eph. 2:6; see comments, 12:12). All these are the objects of the beast's blasphemous revilings.

v. 7. *"And it was given unto him to make war with the saints, and to overcome them: and there was given to him authority over every tribe and people and tongue and nation."* Daniel 7 continues to be the best source of help in interpreting this section. The beast was allowed to overcome the saints only for the time that God permitted. In the eyes of the world the beast was being victorious, but it was a momentary victory allowed by the Lord. The beast had made war against the witnesses and had overcome them, but only for a moment (11:7, 12). Of the little horn Daniel says, "I beheld, and the same horn made war with the saints, and prevailed against them; until the ancient of days came, and judgment was given to [on behalf of] the saints of the Most High, and the time came that the saints possessed the kingdom" (Dan. 7:21f.). The "little horn" in Daniel's vision seems to represent the persecuting element of the Roman emperors, for not all persecuted the church. These would make war with the saints and prevail over them for forty-two months, the total period of Roman persecution, which would end with a judgment from God. All opposition to God's saints ends with a divine judgment from Him. This judgment was beheld by Daniel in the second part of his dream in which the fourth beast was brought to an end (Dan. 7:9–12).

The beast of John's vision, which, as pointed out above, is the fourth of Daniel's dream, was brought to an end through the judgment executed by the Lamb, in which the beast was cast into the lake of fire (19:19f.). The authority of the beast extended over all the earth-dwellers—"over every tribe and people and tongue and nation" of "them that dwell on the earth" (14:6). These were they from among whom the redeemed had been purchased (5:9), and out of which had come the great multitude standing before the throne (7:9). It was these of the world who had looked upon the corpses of the witnesses, suffering them not to be buried (11:9), and to whom the everlasting gospel was being preached, calling upon them to fear God and give Him glory (14:6f.).

v. 8. *"And all that dwell on the earth shall worship him, every one whose name hath not been written from the foundation of the world in the book of life of the Lamb that hath been slain.*" Those of the earth, every tribe, people, tongue, and nation over whom the beast executes authority, not only obey the emperor, but also pay homage to him by acknowledging him as god. However, there are exceptions, for a clear distinction is made between those who worship him, whose names have not been written in the Lamb's book of life, and those whose names have been written in the book of life. (On "the book of life" see comments, 3:5). Scholars are divided between acceptance of the text and the marginal reading: the text (ASV) says, "hath been written from the foundation of the world in the book of life of the Lamb that hath been slain"; the marginal reading says, "written in the book of life of the Lamb slain from the foundation of the world." Either translation is possible and both points are true, but it is difficult to determine which may have been in the apostle's mind. In 17:8 John omits the phrase, "of the Lamb," saying, "whose name hath not been written in the book of life from the foundation of the world"; this clearly points to the names written or not written from the foundation of the world. But in this passage (v. 8) the writer seems to be writing of the Lamb having been slain from before the foundation of the world. This point is made by Peter when he said of Christ, by whose "precious blood" saints are redeemed, who "was foreknown indeed before the foundation of the world, but was manifested at the end of the times for your sake" (I Peter 1:20). This death was "by the determinate counsel and foreknowledge of God" (Acts 2:23), which His hand and counsel "foreordained to come to pass" (Acts 4:24). Jesus' word, "for thou lovedst me before the foundation of the world" (John 17:24), makes it evident that the phrase "the foundation [casting down] of the world" refers to the beginning of the age and that which pertains to time, and not to the beginning of the Hebrew economy; for God's love for the Son is eternal.

But what is the significance of either idea, "the Lamb slain before the foundation of the world," and the saints' name being written in the "book of life from the foundation of the world"? The answer is found in the Ephesian letter where the apostle says, "Even as he chose us in him before the foundation of the world . . . having foreordained us unto adoption as sons through Jesus Christ . . . in whom we have our redemption through his blood . . . according to his good pleasure which he purposed in him unto a dispensation of the fulness of the times... having been foreordained according to the purpose of him who worketh all things after the counsel of his will" (Eph. 1:4–11). The death of Christ and the writing of the names of the saints in the book of life before or from the foundation of the world was in the purpose and after the counsel of God. It was not that Christ actually died before the foundation of the world or that as individuals we were selected then, but it was in the purpose—a "setting before Him"—or plan, that Christ died and the saints were chosen. From before the foundation of the world God had determined that through Christ's death those in Him should be His.

v. 9. *"If any man hath an ear, let him hear."* As in the letters to the churches where each who has an ear is to hear (chaps. 2, 3), so here also the ear is the spiritual faculty through which one is to hear, understand, and comply with what is said. The exhortation embraces what had been taught about the Lamb being slain and the names written in His book from the foundation of the world; it also points to what is about to be said in verse 10.

v. 10. *"If any man is for captivity, into captivity he goeth: if any man shall kill with the sword, with the sword must he be killed. Here is the patience and the faith of the saints."* There are two possible interpretations of the verse: (1) The people of the world who would lead the saints into captivity shall themselves be held in the captivity and damnation of sin; and those who kill saints with the sword shall themselves be killed with the sword. This had been the lot of those whom Jehovah had cast out of His sight (Isa. 33:1; Jer. 15:2; 43:11). (2) The saints who are destined for captivity or death shall yield. They shall not retaliate in kind, for their master had said, "All they that take the sword shall perish with the sword." This would apply to either group, those destined for captivity or the sword.

In revealing the beast and his great power, John had shown the beast's ability to overcome the death-stroke (v. 3), his power to make war against the saints and to overcome them (v. 7), and the worship that would be given to him by the world (v. 8). How shall the saints react to this power and opposition? They were not to resist the civil powers (Rom. 13:2; I Peter 2:13), but were to fight against the powers of evil with spiritual weapons (II Cor. 10:3–5; Eph. 6:10–18). Nor were they to fear them that could destroy the body, but who had no power beyond that; they were to fear Him whose power extended beyond the body to include the soul (Luke 12:4f.); for their victory would be in their faith (I John 5:4). This leads to the conclusion that John was writing of the saints: if they follow the world's method of warfare by resisting with the sword, they will suffer the world's consequence of such methods. Therefore, they are to accept captivity or the sword; in doing so they clearly demonstrate the patience (steadfastness) of the saints and their faith in God to give the victory in His own way.

THE BEAST OUT OF THE EARTH
vv. 11-18

v. 11 "*And I saw another beast coming up out of the earth; and he had two horns like unto a lamb, and he spake as a dragon.*" A second beast of the same genus as the first arises to serve the purpose of the dragon; both are called "a wild beast" (*thērion*), but they are not of the same origin. As the dragon "stood upon the sand of the sea" (13:1), in the same proximity to each, the first beast came up out of the sea and the second out of the earth. It could be said the one was to serve as his right hand and the other as his left.

This second beast has the outward appearance of a docile, probably inoffensive creature, having two horns like a lamb. But his voice exposes his true character, for he speaks as a dragon. No doubt this voice of a dragon suggests a great roar, designed to strike terror in the hearts of those who hear. But there is probably more intended than simply to terrify; for since he serves the cause of the great dragon, the devil, he would also speak as the devil, whose word is a lie (John 8:44).

The fact that the beast is coming up out of the earth indicates that he has fully imbibed the spirit of the river—lies, false charges, deceits, and so forth—which had been emitted from the dragon's mouth and swallowed up by the earth (12:16). Later references to him as "the false prophet" (16:13; 19:20; 20:10) indicate that this beast represents some aspect of false religion, one of the devil's means of deceiving and seducing people. Jesus had warned His disciples, saying, "Beware of false prophets, who come to you in sheep's clothing, but inwardly they are ravening wolves" (Matt. 7:15); and Paul had warned of Satan's ministers who "fashion themselves as ministers of righteousness" (II Cor. 11:15).

To the people of John's day, this beast represented paganism, or the sacerdotal system of paganism, in one of its most repulsive forms—emperor worship. The Caesar cult is indicated by his relation to the sea-beast in the verses that follow. However, a representation of this form of paganism probably does not exhaust its significance, for its spirit is reflected in all forms of false worship which followed, including the papacy and many other systems of false religion.

v. 12. *"And he exerciseth all the authority of the first beast in his sight. And he maketh the earth and them that dwell therein to worship the first beast, whose death-stroke was healed."* The inferiority of this beast to the first is manifested by his acting under the authority of the first beast; for whatever he does is supported by the beast out of the sea, to whom the dragon had given his power. Emperor worship was enforced by the imperial power of the sea-beast, supported or regulated in Asia by a delegated commune. According to Ramsay, "a 'Province' to the Roman mind meant literally 'a sphere of duty,' and was an administrative, not a geographical, fact" (p. 95), though today the word refers to a geographical realm. "In the first place, the Province of Asia was the entire circle of administrative duties connected with that division of the Empire.... In the second place, the Province was the whole circle of religious duties and rites, which constituted the ideal bond of unity holding the people of Asia together as a part of the Imperial realm; and this ritual was expressed to the Asian mind by representative priests, constituting the Commune of Asia," which spoke for Asia (p. 96). Ramsay then adds, "The Province of Asia in its double aspect of civil and religious administration, the Proconsul and the Commune, is symbolized by the monster described in 13:11" (p. 97); the two horns thus correspond to this double feature. Both proconsul and commune acted by the authority of Rome and spoke with the voice of the dragon.

This beast, symbolizing the proconsul, the political power, and the commune, the religious parliament of the geographical province, backed by the power of the empire, would insist that the earth-dwellers worship the state symbolized in the emperor. This worship was emphasized under Domitian, in whom the death-stroke was healed.

Some defenders of the Neronean date for the writing of Revelation see in this beast the combining of the power exercised against Christians in Judea by the proconsul and Jewish leaders. This is untenable as the book was written to the churches in Asia and includes a much broader scope than only the affairs of Judea.

v. 13. *"And he doeth great signs, that he should even make fire to come down out of heaven upon the earth in the sight of men."* On the word "sign," see comments, 12:1. A question of special importance is whether these were actual miracles, or deceptions. Throughout the book when the genuine or true has been introduced, its false, imitation counterpart has likewise appeared; so it is here. The true witnesses were to have power over fire by which to devour their enemies (11:5); so the false prophet would imitate this power with pseudo-miracles and signs by which to deceive the world. Jesus had forewarned His disciples of such efforts to deceive when He said, "For there shall arise false Christs, and false prophets, and shall show great signs and wonders; so as to lead astray, if possible, even the elect" (Matt. 24:24). Paul echoed the warning, describing the man of sin, "whose coming is according to the working of Satan with all power and signs and lying wonders, with all deceit of unrighteousness for them that perish; because they received not the love of the truth, that they might be saved" (II Thess. 2:9f.). Again the apostle wrote, "Evil men and impostors shall wax worse and worse, deceiving and being deceived" (II Tim. 3:13).

Miracles were signs from God affirming that the word of His messenger, whether apostle or prophet, was from Him; they confirmed the divine source of the message (Mark 16:20; II Cor. 12:12; Heb. 2:3f.). In contrast to this, the false prophet (16:13; 19:20; 20:10) must sustain his word and demands by the deception of false, imitation signs; deception is the very power of evil and sin. The next scene establishes that these signs were deceptions.

v. 14. *"And he deceiveth them that dwell on the earth by reason of the signs which it was given him to do in the sight of the beast; saying to them that dwell on the earth, that they should make an image to the beast who hath the stroke of the sword and lived."* The deception imposed upon the worldly-minded was by the false, imitation signs of the earth-beast. The phrase "which it was given him to do," simply means that which God allowed him to do (see comments, v. 5). If God allowed Satan to deceive by genuine miracles He would thereby nullify His own witness to truth. The difference between the deceptions of Satan and the true miracles of God is clearly set forth in the contrast between the sorceries of Simon and the signs of Philip (Acts 8:5-13). Signs of deception were meant to impress the heathen populace when the Roman dignitaries and the provincial governor with the religious hierarchy, the commune, met for religious purposes to dedicate a new image of a Caesar in the temple, or to establish the decrees of religious ritual. This spirit of delusion and deception continues to live in the false religions throughout the world; deception is their breath and life.

The people of the province were to make an image of the beast who had received the stroke of the sword and lived; in this instance the image was probably of Domitian. (See Historical Background, pp. 70f.). The importance of this one who had received the death-stroke and lived is indicated by the fact that he is mentioned for the third time (see vv. 3, 12).

v. 15. *"And it was given unto him to give breath to it, even to the image of the beast, that the image of the beast should both speak, and cause that as many as should not worship the image of the beast should be killed."* It was given to him, that is, it was the responsibility of the earth-beast to give breath (spirit, hence life) to the image of the emperor. But how was this to be done? Was it through ventriloquism and other magical arts? Or was it the function and obligation of the commune to make the Caesar-worship live and speak the mind of the empire? This latter seems to be more plausible. The power of death for those who refused to pay homage to "Augustus and Rome" rested in the magistrate and religious hierarchy. This put the Christian in the position where he must confess either Christ or Caesar as Lord, thus choosing between immediate death and a few added years of life before eternal death. This same spirit continued to live and find expression in the apostate churches of later years.

v. 16. *"And he causeth all, the small and the great, and the rich and the poor, and the free and the bond, that there be given them a mark on their right hand, or upon their forehead."* Here is another counterpart to divine action: as God had sealed His people unto Himself by impressing His own name and the name of the Lamb upon their foreheads (7:3, 9:4; 14:1), and has promised to write His name upon the foreheads of the victors (3:12; 22:4), so the beast imitates this by requiring all to indicate their allegiance to him by a mark upon their right hand or upon their forehead. This "mark" (*charagma*) was a stamp, etching, engraving, or impress; it could be an engraved stone or a brand on a horse or a slave. In "causing" this to be done, the beast established a policy which required that they all be marked. There would be no exception; "the small and the great, and the rich and the poor, and the free and the bond," would include all from the highest official to the lowest slave.

It is difficult to determine what the mark was. Was it a literal stamp or brand impressed upon the hand or forehead? Or is the language a figurative expression of a physical object which individuals carried with them, corresponding to modern identification cards? It is also possible that the language is used metaphorically of the devotion to the emperor in mind or deed and service. As Ramsay says, "We know too little to explain it with certainty" (*Seven Churches*, p. 106). However, as the seal which God caused to be placed on the foreheads of His subjects was not physical but a spiritual recognition of devotion to Him, it is best to think of the mark of the beast as the stamp of paganism impressed upon the character and conduct of idolaters. The boycott of Christians and the idolatry of pagans could indeed be maintained without a literal visible sign, for the Christian's character and life caused the world to boycott him.

The word *charagma* occurs once in Acts, and eight times in Revelation. It is possible that as gold, silver, and stone could be "graven (*charagmati*) by art and device of man" (Acts 17:29), so the minds and service of men could be completely marked or graven by the wiles of the commune and by the attractiveness of the world with its power, glory, and pride symbolized in the empire and the image of the emperor.

v. 17. "*And that no man should be able to buy or to sell, save he that hath the mark, even the name of the beast or the number of his name.*" Whatever the mark was (here it is identified with his "name," as the "seal" of God was identified with His name), no one could enter the field of trade or earn a living without it. The view advanced in interpreting the opening of the third seal (see comments, 6:6), that the rider of the black horse signified scarcity through discrimination, seems to be confirmed here. The saints who refused the mark even at the risk of death, were boycotted by the world, being discriminated against even to the point of hunger or possible starvation. On "the number of his name" see comments below.

v. 18. *"Here is wisdom. He that hath understanding, let him count the number of the beast; for it is the number of a man: and his number is Six hundred and sixty and six."* Although this passage is fraught with difficulties, one should not conclude as did some ancient writers that God does not intend for us to understand it. John begins by saying, "Here is wisdom," and "He that hath understanding, let him count the number." This indicates that the message is an expression of divine wisdom and that it is possible to understand what the seer is saying by the application of the Christian's wisdom (cf. James 1:5). This depends on a Christian's spiritual insight into underlying causes and consequences of matters, and his understanding of the purpose and message of Revelation. However, to say that one can understand is not to say that the interpretation offered below is positively the correct one; it only affirms that one with wisdom and understanding may grasp its meaning. The reader is to "count the number of the beast," which focuses attention on the number and its significance, not on a particular individual.

A peculiar application of numbers in vogue among later Jews and early Christians, *Gematria,* "is the use of the letters of a word so as by means of their combined numerical value to express a name, or a witty association of ideas" (I.S.B.E., Vol. IV. p. 2162). One of the early (perhaps the earliest) church writers to apply this method of interpretation was Irenaeus (A.D. 120–202), who offered three suggested names for the number: Euranthas, which seems to have no significance; Lateinos, from an early king of Latium, but not of Rome, for the "Latium at the present bear rule"; and Teitan or Titan, a name which would be given to the Antichrist who was to come. But Irenaeus urged caution in accepting any of these (*Against Heresies*, V. 30.3. A-N-F., I. p. 559). Alford tentatively accepted Irenaeus' conclusion that the 666 signifies Lateinos, for they were under Latin rule and were threatened by Latin paganism, which culminated in the Latin church and Latin Christianity. Though he favored this view, he wrote in the Prolegomena, "Even while I print my note in favor of the *Lateinos* of

Irenaeus, I feel almost disposed to withdraw it" (Vol. IV. p. 252). Philip Schaff also thought this name suggested by Irenaeus was the most plausible of any suggested.[1]

Of the many efforts to reduce the 666 to the name of a man, the most popular choice has been Nero Caesar, which in the Greek is Neron Kaisar. Translated into the Hebrew script and applying the Hebrew system of gematria, the name can be translated into the desired number, 666; however, in Greek it would be 1005 (Pieters). It is doubtful that John would have referred to Hebrew numbers when writing in the Greek language to a Greek audience; and it is questionable whether these Asian Christians would have been able to translate the Hebrew numbers. In other instances (9:11; 16:16) John took pains to designate the Hebrew words he used; here he does not. By this method of assigning numbers to letters men have come up with many names; all are beset with difficulties, and it cannot be said positively that any of them are correct (see Caird, Moffatt, Schaff, Summers, Swete, et al.). Caird has well said, "Though it is easy enough to turn a name into a number, it is not so simple to proceed in the opposite direction" (p. 174).

I believe, however, that the number does not represent an individual such as Nero, Domitian, or others *per se*, but the sum of that which is human.[2] The number is "the number of the beast," apparently the first or sea-beast, for it was his image that was to be worshiped; it was not the number of an individual. When John adds, "It is the number of a man," he omits the definite article before "man," thereby indicating that he has no particular individual in mind. He is saying that the number represents that which is human; it is therefore a human number. He followed the same pattern later when he said of the measured wall, it was "according to the measure of a man, that is, of an angel" (21:17). An angel measured it, but he used a human standard or measurement. Neither the man nor the angel were specific individuals, and it seems that the same interpretation would apply

---

[1] For an instructive discussion of the various views and names that have been suggested, and of the numerical values of letters in the Hebrew and Greek, see Philip Schaff, *History of the Christian Church*, vol. I, pp. 841–853.

[2] For a discussion of this view see Caird, Hendriksen, Milligan, Summers, Swete, and especially Lenski, to whom I am particularly indebted.

here. Paul said of the gospel which he preached, "it is not after man" (Gal. 1:11), that is, it was not human in origin or substance.

Since the Apocalypse abounds in the symbolic use of numbers which express ideas rather than persons or literal quantities, the same principle should be followed in the interpretation of this number. Throughout the book, seven expresses the idea of perfection or completeness: the seven churches, seven horns, seven eyes, seven spirits, and so forth. So six, which falls below the sacred seven, can never be seven or reach perfection; therefore, it symbolizes the imperfect, that which is human and destined to fail. It is said that to the Jews the number six was an omen or symbol of dread and doom, so when it was tripled, 666, it represented the completeness of doom and failure.

In these comments it has been concluded that the first beast represented the Roman Empire in its power and opposition to the kingdom of God. It epitomized the sum of all the world's political opposition to God and righteousness for all time. It was further concluded that the second beast symbolized the pagan priesthood or commune of the emperor cult, backed by the political power of the empire; this also in turn generally represented all false religion since the fall of the Roman pagan system. It is now concluded that the number of the beast, six-six-six, stands for the complete and total failure of all human systems and efforts antagonistic to God and His Christ—all are doomed to ultimate and complete defeat and failure. This explanation is in harmony with the theme and purpose of Revelation.

CHAPTER 14
Righteous Judgment

From the vision of cruel oppression by the two wild beasts backed by the dragon (chap. 13), the scene shifts to one of triumphant victory and righteous judgment. The transition is from earth and the unstable sands of the seashore to Mount Zion and the permanence of the stone on which the church had been built. As is characteristic of the entire book, these visions shift from oppression and persecution to victory and judgment and back again. The helpers on whom Satan relies are the two beasts which symbolize force and false religion, which oppress and blaspheme. In contrast, the two allies on which God depends for victory are the triumphant Lamb and His followers, and His righteous judgments.

Chapter 14 is divided into three sections, each one beginning with the phrase, "And I saw" (vv. 1, 6, 14). The first scene presents the Lamb and His victorious saints on Mount Zion. The second section makes known the messages of three angels and a voice from heaven who call to action, warn and comfort. The third part reveals the divine ingathering of the righteous and a judgment of the world: harvest and vintage.

THE LAMB AND THE 144,000 ON MOUNT ZION
vv. 1-5

v. 1. "And I saw, and behold, the Lamb standing on the mount Zion, and with him a hundred and forty and four thousand, having his name, and the name of his Father, written on their foreheads." Two questions immediately arise: What is the significance of "the mount Zion"? Who are the hundred and forty four thousand standing with the Lamb on Mount Zion? A number of scholars contend that this scene pictures the end of time with the redeemed in heaven; others hold that it is a symbolic vision of the redeemed who are secure with the Lamb on Mount Zion to which they have come. A study of the place of "Mount Zion" in the Old and New Testaments will help us reach a solution to the question.

Zion was initially introduced as the stronghold and city of David (II Sam. 5:7; I Chron. 11:5). In time it came to represent Jehovah's dwelling place among His people (Ps. 9:11; 135:21; Isa. 8:18; Joel 3:17), "the city of the great king" (Ps. 48:2), a refuge and stronghold of the people because God was there (Ps. 48:3, 13). The people's help and strength in time of need would go forth out of Zion (Ps. 20:2); this became to those who trust in Jehovah a symbol of security which could not be moved (Ps. 125:1)—in Zion the afflicted of His people would take refuge (Isa. 14:32). Further, praise waited for Jehovah in Zion (Ps. 65:1), for the people could not sing Jehovah's song in a foreign land (i.e., in Babylon, Ps. 137:1, 4); but "the children of Zion" could "be joyful in their king" only in Zion (Ps. 149:1-2).

Zion played an important role in the messianic prophecies of the Old Testament. In the midst of worldwide rebellion God would set His anointed one, the messianic King upon His holy hill of Zion (Ps. 2:6), from where Jehovah would reign through the restored dominion of David, that is, the Messiah (Mic. 4:7f.). The rod of the Messiah's strength would go forth out of Zion as He ruled in the midst of His enemies, judging among the nations and filling the places with corpses (Ps. 110:2, 6). Though the storm of judgment would rage without, those in Zion would escape (Joel 2:32); for many people would come to this mountain of Jehovah to learn of His ways, being drawn by the law going forth from out of Zion (Isa. 2:2f.). With singing and rejoicing, these ransomed ones would come to the spiritual Zion, where everlasting joy and gladness would be upon their heads, and sorrow and sighing would flee away (Isa. 35:10). To these in this glorified Zion there would be given "a garland for ashes, the oil of joy for mourning, the garment of praise for the spirit of heaviness," and their permanence would be as trees planted by Jehovah (Isa. 61:3). All these prophecies look to the Zion of the Messiah under the present covenant and rule, and find their consummation in this scene of John's vision.

In addition to our present text, the phrase "Mount Zion" occurs six times in the remainder of the New Testament. Matthew and John quote Zechariah 9:9, where Zion is called upon to rejoice at the coming of her king, pointing to Jesus' entrance into the city as fulfilling the prophecy (Matt. 21:5; John 12:15; cf. also Isa. 62:11). Paul and Peter quote Isaiah 28:16, where God said through the prophet, "Behold, I lay in Zion for a foundation a stone, a tried stone, a precious corner-stone of sure foundation: he that believeth shall not be in haste [be put to shame]" (Rom. 9:33; I Peter 2:6). It was upon this stone in Zion that the saints found their permanent security. Paul quotes Isaiah 59:20 when he says, "There shall come out of Zion the Deliverer; he shall turn away ungodliness from Jacob" (Rom. 11:26), and he applies the prophecy to the present redemption of Israel through Jesus Christ.

The writer of Hebrews sums up the prophecies of Isaiah 2:2-4 and Micah 4:1-8 when he says, "But ye are come unto mount Zion, and unto the city of the living God, the heavenly Jerusalem, and to innumerable hosts of angels, to the general assembly and church of the firstborn [ones] who are enrolled in heaven, and to God the judge of all, and to the spirits of just men made perfect, and to Jesus the mediator of a new covenant, and to the blood of sprinkling that speaketh better than that of Abel" (Heb. 12:22-24). These are standing in a heavenly presence, before God, Christ, and the perfected spirits of the redeemed. As Westcott observes in commenting on Hebrews 12:22, "In a sense the heavenly Jerusalem is already reached: in another sense it is still sought for (13:14)" (Westcott, p. 413). Here in John's vision, the redeemed have, in one sense, reached Zion, the heavenly Jerusalem pointed to by the prophets. In another sense Zion still lies ahead (21:2). From the relationship of Zion to God in the Old Testament and the prophecies of the Messiah and Zion found there, and from the application of Old Testament prophecies quoted in the New Testament as being fulfilled in Jesus, we conclude that John is not describing a final scene in heaven, but the Zion of the Messiah to which the saints of this dispensation have come. John's use of the definite article, *the* Mount Zion, further confirms this view. The scene symbolizes security, permanence, and a victorious spirit of rejoicing enjoyed by the church on earth at any time, because the Lamb is in their midst.

There is no valid reason not to accept the 144,000 as the same group that was sealed in chapter 7 (vv. 1-8), even though the definite article is absent. In the former vision the 144,000 received the seal of their God upon their foreheads; in this scene they have the name of the Lamb and of His Father written on their foreheads—indicating that the seal in chapter 7 was the name of these two. There they were sealed unto God in anticipation of the storm to be let loose upon the earth; here the same group is pictured as safe with the Lamb in His stronghold. The woman who went into the wilderness (12:6, 14) finds security in the stronghold of God, on the rock which was laid in Zion: for, "The firm foundation of God standeth, having this seal, The Lord knoweth them that are his: and, Let everyone that nameth the name of the Lord depart from unrighteousness" (II Tim. 2:19). As these on earth who receive the mark of the beast belong to him, so those on Mount Zion who have the seal of God belong to Him. The 144,000 are not a group of special saints or of martyrs, but they are God's redeemed on earth who have the martyr spirit (12:11); they surround the Lamb at all times.

v. 2. *"And I heard a voice from heaven, as the voice of many waters, and as the voice of a great thunder: and the voice which I heard was as the voice of harpers harping with their harps."* The voice which John hears is from heaven, the source of an earlier voice (10:4), and from where another voice will be heard later (18:4). Each description of the voice is a comparison—*as* the voice of many waters, *as* the voice of a great thunder, *as* the voice of harpers. This combination of descriptive phrases occurs only here. The voice as of many waters characterizes the voice of Him who walks among the lampstands (see comments, 1:15), and shall describe the voice of the great multitude shouting the hallelujahs of heaven (19:6). The voice as a great thunder (6:1; 19:6, see comments), indicates the voice's volume as it resounds through the universe. The voice as of harpers symbolizes melody (for "harps" see comments, 5:8; 15:2). The qualities of the voice which John heard indicate majesty, volume, and the melody of praise.

v. 3. *"And they sing as it were a new song before the throne, and before the four living creatures and the elders: and no man could learn the song save the hundred and forty and four thousand, even they that had been purchased out of the earth."* Who are these that sing this new song before the throne, the living creatures, and the elders? Earlier the living creatures and the elders sang "a new song" in praise of redemption (5:9f.); now the song is sung before them and before the throne. It does not appear to be the 144,000 who sing, for they, and only they, learn the song—they appear to be continuing to learn it. Nor does the voice appear to be that of angels, though they rejoice in the salvation of sinners (Luke 15:9f.) and desire to look into these matters (I Peter 1:12); for they learn of redemption through God's plan as it is fulfilled in Christ and the church (Eph. 3:10f.). Angels did not share in the saving help provided in Christ (Heb. 2:16); therefore, they could not sing this new song. The voice from heaven therefore is probably that of the multitude who came out of the great tribulation, who cry before the throne with a great voice ascribing their salvation to God and the Lamb (7:9–17). The one hundred forty-four thousand are those on earth who have come unto Mount Zion and the Lamb (cf. Heb. 12:22ff.), and are learning the song of full and complete redemption. They are identified not as any special group of saints, but as all the saints on earth at any time. Five characteristics identify them in verses 3–5:

(1) They have been purchased out of the earth, purchased from among the earth-dwellers, purchased by the blood of the Lamb (cf. 5:9f.); they are the redeemed.

v. 4. "These are they that were not defiled with women; for they are virgins. These are they that follow the Lamb withersoever he goeth. These were purchased from among men, to be the firstfruits unto God and unto the Lamb."

(2) The 144,000 are further described as not having been defiled with women, but as being virgins. This quality refers not to physical celibacy, but to spiritual virginity, for the spiritually chaste belong to Christ (II Cor. 11:2). Throughout the Old Testament idolatry was looked upon as spiritual adultery or fornication; therefore, John had warned the Christians, saying, "My little children, guard yourselves from idols" (I John 5:21), that is, from any fictional concept of God, whether emperor worship or other forms of false religion. For one to prostitute himself before an idol or image is to commit spiritual fornication or adultery, and to become bound to such is spiritual whoredom.

(3) "These are they that follow the Lamb whithersoever he goeth."

They had been purchased and now they follow Him wherever the road may lead. Jesus had said to Peter, "Whither I go, thou canst not follow me now; but thou shalt follow afterwards" (John 13:36); later He instructed Peter to "follow thou me" (John 21:22). Each disciple is called to follow the steps of Him who did no sin (I Peter 2:21), and "to deny himself, and take up his cross, and follow" Him (Matt. 16:24). These on Mount Zion are faithful disciples who continue to abide in and walk with the Lord.

(4) The fourth characteristic is that they "were purchased from among men, to be the firstfruits unto God and unto the Lamb." Under the law the firstfruits of the harvest were offered to God in acknowledgment that all the land and its increase belonged to Him. Paul applies the word figuratively to the first converts in Asia and Achaia (Rom. 16:5; I Cor. 16:15), indicating that others followed. He speaks further of Christ's resurrection as the firstfruits from the dead, to be followed by all (I Cor. 15:20, 23). James writes of those brought "forth by the word of God" as "a kind of firstfruits of his creatures" (James 1:18); he probably refers to the Jewish converts, since he was writing to "the twelve tribes which are of the Dispersion" (James 1:1), and looks toward others who would likewise be brought forth. Jeremiah once said, "Israel was holiness unto Jehovah, the first-fruits of his increase" (Jer. 2:3). Consequently this number (144,000) indicated by the seer as firstfruits is probably the new Israel, those on earth at that time who had been purchased and were holiness unto the Lord; it also points to others to come who would likewise be devoted to Him.

v. 5. *"And in their mouth was found no lie: they are without blemish."*

(5) This sets forth the fifth quality that identifies the 144,000: there was no religious falsehood in their mouth; they had neither subscribed to nor taught anything untrue. They had refused to confess Caesar as Lord, or to deny the Lord Christ; they were without spiritual or moral blemish. As had been said of the Lamb who was offered without blemish and without spot (I Peter 1:19), nor "was any deceit in his mouth" (Isa. 53:9), so also it could be said of these. They fulfilled the divine standard for the church, "that it should be holy and without blemish" (Eph. 5:27).

ANGELS' MESSAGES AND A VOICE OF WARNING FROM HEAVEN
vv. 6-13

v. 6. "And I saw another angel flying in mid heaven, having eternal good tidings to proclaim unto them that dwell on the earth, and unto every nation and tribe and tongue and people." "And I saw" introduces the second section of the chapter, which contains the messages of three angels and a voice from heaven. "Another angel" (cf. 7:2; 8:3; 10:1) may indicate an angel of the same order as the last angel mentioned (11:15), or more probably, it may simply identify this angel with the two who follow (vv. 8, 9). "In mid heaven" (*mesouranēma*, 8:13; 14:6; 19:17) indicates that point where the sun has reached the meridian, "the highest point in the heavens," which it occupies at noon (Thayer). At this point the angel can be seen and heard throughout the earth, for the message is "unto them that dwell on the earth ... every nation and tribe and tongue and people." These are the earth-dwellers from among whom the redeemed had been purchased (5:9), who looked upon the dead bodies of the witnesses (11:9), over whom the beast exercises authority (13:7), and the waters upon which the harlot sits (17:1, 15, except that here "multitudes" is substituted for "tribes"). The message is therefore to be proclaimed to the entire world of the unregenerate.

This is the only occurrence of the word "gospel" in any of John's writings. It raises the question whether this is the gospel revealed throughout the New Testament which was to be preached to all the world, or a special message to be announced just before the end of time. However, it is evident that it could not be the latter for the faith has been once for all delivered to the saints (Jude 3), to be preached to all nations, the whole creation (Matt. 28:19; Mark 16:15f.). The treasure was deposited in earthen vessels (II Cor. 4:7), and if an angel from heaven preaches any other gospel, he stands *anathema*, devoted to destruction (Gal. 1:8). Therefore, it is not a special gospel or announcement of the gospel by an angel "in the latter times," but it is the everlasting gospel, the gospel formulated in the mind of God before the beginning of time, pointed unto by the prophets and summed up in Christ (Rom. 16:25-27). The things in the book are written to the churches, to be read and observed by them (1:3, 11). Its warnings and consolations are given to the church to be announced and heeded. The vision of an angel proclaiming the message is symbolic of God's messengers, His saints, preaching the gospel to the whole world (Matt. 24:14; Col. 1:23).

v. 7. "*And he saith with a great voice, Fear God, and give him glory; for the hour of his judgment is come: and worship him that made the heaven and the earth and sea and fountains of waters.*" As the angel was in mid-heaven where he could be seen by all, so he cried with a great voice that he might be heard by all. The message of the gospel announced by the angel is summed up in three phrases, "fear God," "give him glory," and "worship him," the creator, and not the creatures; because "the hour of his judgment is come." The word *fear* (*phobēo*) as it occurs throughout the four Gospels can mean "to be afraid, to become frightened," or, as it is used often in Acts and the Epistles, to "have reverence, respect, as for God" (A. & G.). Cornelius "was one that feared God" (Acts 10:2, 22), possessing a quality of character open to the gospel when it was preached to him. Men of such disposition in every nation are acceptable to God (Acts 10:35); wherefore Paul called upon the Jews to "be not high-minded, but fear" (Rom. 11:20). The gospel thus calls upon all nations to respect and reverence God that they may give Him glory in their acceptance of and obedience to the faith of the gospel: "that in all things God may be glorified through Jesus Christ, whose is the glory and the dominion for ever and ever. Amen" (I Peter 4:11). Reverence for God and glory to Him through accepting and obeying His truth leads to faithful devotion to Him in worship (I Thess. 1:9).

Judgment should motivate and bring men to repentance (Acts 17:30f.). But what judgment is in the divine mind here—the final judgment, or an immediate one? In the light of this exhortation to fear God, give Him glory, and worship Him, it is impossible to make "the hour of his judgment" refer to the final judgment (cf. comments, 11:18); but rather, it refers to the hour in which God is to judge Babylon (cf. v. 8 below). However, His hour of judging cannot be restricted even to Babylon, for His hour to judge occurs over and over in history.

v. 8. "*And another, a second angel, followed saying, Fallen, fallen is

Babylon the great, that hath made all the nations to drink of the wine of the wrath of her fornication." Here Babylon is introduced for the first time, and the angel, the second, announces the good news that as an act of divine judgment Babylon is fallen. She had been warned by the message of the first angel who called upon all to fear God and give Him glory, for the hour of His judgment had come. The angel speaks of Babylon as already fallen, for when God decrees a matter it is as if already accomplished: "I am God, and there is none like me, declaring the end from the beginning, and from ancient times things that are not yet done" (Isa. 46:10); and, "I have declared the former things from of old; yea, they went forth out of my mouth and I showed them: suddenly I did them, and they came to pass" (Isa. 48:3). At least fifty years before ancient Babylon fell to the Medes, God said through His prophet, "Babylon is suddenly fallen and destroyed: wail for her" (Jer. 51:8).

Each time Babylon is named in the Apoclypse it is identified as "great" (14:8; 16:19; 17:5; 18:2, 10, 21), or as "the great city" (see comments, 11:8). Later, Babylon is identified as Rome, symbolic, not of the world power which was represented by the beast out of the sea, but of the world of lust and seduction, of which more will be said in discussing chapters 17 and 18.

Scholars find difficulty with "the wine of the wrath of her fornication." The picture is probably drawn from Jeremiah, "Babylon hath been a golden cup in Jehovah's hand, that made all the earth drunken: the nations have drunk of her wine; therefore the nations are mad" (Jer. 51:7). Alford suggests, "Two things are mingled: (1) the wine of her fornication, of which all the nations have drunk (17:2); and (2) the wine of the wrath of God which He shall give her to drink, verse 10 and 16:19. The latter is the retribution for the former: the former turns into the latter: They are treated as one and the same" (Alford, p. 688). Lenski translates the phrase, "the wine of her whoring passing" (Lenski, p. 438). A. & G. give one definition of *thumos* (wrath) as "passion," then translate the phrase, "she has caused the nations to drink the wine of her passionate immorality" (A. & G., p. 336). Swete's comment is, "The wine of Rome, as of Babylon, was the intoxicating influence of her vices and her wealth; but viewed from another point it was the wine of wrath, the wrath which overtakes sin; cf. Ps. 75:8" (Swete, p. 184). The logical conclusion is the phrase looks to the passionate lusts of the world, represented by Rome, by which Rome intoxicated the nations, bringing upon that world God's wrath; for sin always brings wrath. In verses 6–7 God is calling to repentance, warning of the impending judgment. In verse 8 He declares the fall of Babylon, the world-city of lust which does not heed the warning; it is doomed, for God's wrath is about to be poured out upon it.

v. 9. *"And another angel, a third, followed them, saying with a great voice, If any man worshippeth the beast and his image, and receiveth a mark on his forehead, or upon his hand."* These three angels are in mid-heaven where they can be seen and heard. Like the first angel, this third one cries with a loud voice that may be heard throughout all lands. His message declares the consequence of worshiping the beast and his statue; it is a voice from heaven crying against the idolatry of emperor worship supported by the Roman system (13:14f.). The mark on one's forehead or hand is that of 13:17f. (see comments). The message is announced to deter all men from false worship, but to those of John's day it laid special emphasis on the cult of emperor worship.

v. 10. *"He also shall drink of the wine of the wrath of God, which is prepared unmixed in the cup of his anger; and he shall be tormented with fire and brimstone in the presence of the holy angels, and in the presence of the Lamb."* He who "shall drink" is the same one who worshiped the beast (v. 9); as he has worshiped, so also shall he bear the consequence. The wrath of God is His righteous indignation, which is warned against many times in the Epistles (Rom. 1:18; 3:5; Eph. 5:6; Col. 3:6), and which the worshiper of the beast and his image must now drink. The illustration of drinking such a cup is found in Jehovah's message to Jeremiah where He said, "Take this cup of the wine of wrath at my hand, and cause the nations, to whom I send thee, to drink it" (Jer. 25:15, 27–29; 51:7). The wine drunk by the ancients was mixed with spices and water (I.S.B.E., vol. V. p. 3087), but the wine of God's wrath is here prepared unmixed in the cup of His anger. It is undiluted with mercy, for the day of mercy and longsuffering is now past; these had been offered in the gospel which had been proclaimed and should have been accepted (v. 6), but the offer of salvation had gone unheeded. Now these shall be tormented with fire and brimstone instead of the sword as in the message of Jeremiah (Jer. 25:27–29).

The idea of destruction by fire and brimstone was not new. Both had been literally rained upon Sodom and Gomorrah (Gen. 19:24); and figuratively the destruction of Assyria had been as a pile of wood, which "the breath of Jehovah, like a stream of brimstone, doth kindle" (Isa. 30:33; cf. also vv. 27-32). In His recompense for Zion and indignation against Edom, God warned that "the streams of Edom shall be turned into pitch, and the dust thereof into brimstone and the land thereof shall become burning pitch. It shall not be quenched night or day; the smoke thereof shall go up for ever" (Isa. 34:9f.). This would also be the lot of Gog (Ezek. 38:22). Having been made a gazing stock by reproaches and afflictions before their tormentors (Heb. 10:32ff.), the saints had endured a great conflict of suffering; but now the tables are turned. Those who reject the truth and persecute the faithful suffer the torment of fire and brimstone in the presence of the Lamb and angels. Angels who through the ages had watched the unfolding and revealing of God's eternal purpose and the conflict between good and evil, now see the consummation of that purpose and final consequence of evil.

v. 11. *"And the smoke of their torment goeth up for ever and ever; and they have no rest day and night, they that worship the beast and his image, and whoso receiveth the mark of his name."* The smoke of the tormented (cf. v. 10) shall be like the punishment of Sodom and Gomorrah, who "are set forth as an example, suffering the punishment of eternal fire" (Jude 7), "an example unto those that live ungodly" (II Peter 2:6), and the smoke of Edom's destruction that "shall go up for ever" (Isa. 34:10). Such a destiny likewise awaits the devil who deceived the ungodly and who is responsible for all rebellion and opposition to God (20:10). This description of the future of the wicked is in harmony with Jesus' teaching concerning their destiny after death (Luke 16:23, 28), and beyond the judgment (Matt. 18:8f.; 25:41, 46). In contrast to the victorious saints before the throne who "serve him day and night" (7:15), these who worship the beast have "no rest day and night." As the day of the righteous is a glorious, eternal day, the night of the wicked is a dreadful, eternal night; the two abide side by side, continuing simultaneously. What a terrible price to pay for rejecting the Christ and bowing to Caesar as Lord! (For comments on "the mark," see 13:16.)

v. 12. *"Here is the patience of the saints, they that keep the com-*

mandments of God, and the faith of Jesus." Jesus promised His disciples, "In your patience ye shall win your souls" (Luke 21:19), and said to the faithful in Philadelphia, "Because thou didst keep the word of my patience, I also will keep thee from the hour of trial" (3:10, see comments). The dragon had gone away to make war with those "that keep the commandments of God, and hold the testimony of Jesus" (12:17). The patience (steadfastness) of the saints was in accepting death or captivity for their faith (13:10). Steadfastness is developed by meeting faithfully the trials which come because of one's relationship to Christ and the gospel (James 1:2-4; Rom. 5:3). The opposition of the beast in demanding worship of the emperor image supplied the trial of faith that worked patience, as the saints kept the commandments of God and the faith which has Jesus as its object. These words of encouragement and assurance to the saints are from the Lord, not from John. The message is: In the light of ultimate ends, be steadfast.

v. 13. *"And I heard a voice from heaven saying, Write, Blessed are the dead who die in the Lord from henceforth: yea, saith the Spirit, that they may rest from their labors; for their works follow with them."* The three former messages were delivered by angels; the voice now heard is of unrevealed heavenly origin. In the message of the first angel the earth was called upon to heed the gospel and the warning of judgment. In the second, the fall of Babylon was decreed as if already accomplished; it would be folly, therefore, to trust in the world-city. The third angel set forth the consequence befalling those who would prolong their life on earth by worshiping the beast and his image. This life might be extended for a few years, but a second death awaited it in the divine judgment. There is next revealed by the voice from heaven the destiny of those who refuse to burn the incense demanded by the empire: their earthly life may be terminated by force, but the real life continues in glory beyond.

The voice charges John to write. The message from heaven is in the form of a beatitude, one of seven occurring in the book (cf. note, 1:3). Happy are the dead "who die in the Lord," that is, in a proper relationship to the Lord. These would be exalted in a heavenly joy; blissfully complete even in death. These are the ones who keep the commandments of God and the faith of Jesus (v. 12). Paul assured the saints of Corinth that those who had fallen asleep "in Jesus" had not perished, but would be raised in Christ (I Cor. 15:20-23); and likewise he assured the brethren at Thessalonica that the saints sleeping in Christ should be raised at His coming (I Thess. 4:13-18). It had been revealed to John that the martyrs underneath the altar were at rest (6:9-11), and that those coming out of the great tribulation were before the throne serving God day and night (7:9-17). Now the Lord adds an additional word of hope and assurance for future sufferers—"from henceforth." Immediately, the message was directed to martyrs in contrast to those who would not confess faith in Jesus. But the assurance is not limited to John's contemporaries, but includes all faithful saints in every age who need comfort and consolation, who have seen their loyal brothers and sisters in Christ laid to rest.

The phrase, "Yea, saith the Spirit," identifies the message as being from the Holy Spirit, not John's spirit. Whether the voice heard from heaven is that of the Spirit, or whether it is the voice of one announcing what the Spirit says, is not clear. The rest promised to the saints is from their present and past labors which they are leaving behind. But it is not so with their works in the Lord; these go with them as testimony of their faith. These continue to live in the lives and memories of those left behind, as well as to commend the faithful at the judgment (Matt. 25:34-40). In the light of this hope, Paul urged the saints to abound always "in the work of the Lord, forasmuch as ye know that your labor is not vain in the Lord" (I Cor. 15:58).

TWOFOLD VISION OF HARVEST AND VINTAGE OF THE EARTH
vv. 14-20

Commentators generally agree that this vision pictures a judgment of God upon the earth in some measure and manner. But what is its nature? Is it the final judgment, or one in time? And further, does the passage describe the ingathering of the Lord's harvest now and the judgment of the wicked at the end of time, or is it a twofold picture of one judgment? Scholars differ in their views on this point.

v. 14. "And I saw, and behold, a white cloud; and on the cloud I saw one sitting like unto a son of man, having on his head a golden crown, and in his hand a sharp sickle." This section is introduced by the same phrase as were the first two, "And I saw" (vv. 1, 6), indicating a fresh aspect of the vision. John beheld a white cloud with one sitting enthroned upon it, "like unto a son of man." The Scriptures speak of bright clouds, thick clouds, a dark cloud, a swift cloud, and a great cloud, but this is the only reference to a white cloud, and thus it must carry special significance. White is the symbol of purity and holiness (see comments, 1:14); therefore, whatever the cloud symbolizes is associated with these two attributes. Clouds often symbolize judgment or the appearing of judgment. Jehovah came in judgment against Egypt, riding "upon a swift cloud" (Isa. 19:1), and He would "come up as clouds" against wicked Jerusalem (Jer. 4:13). Jesus would come against Jerusalem "on the clouds of heaven with power and great glory" (Matt. 24:30; 26:64; so Mark and Luke), and John describes His comings in judgment as coming "with the clouds" (see comments, 1:7). Therefore some aspect of judgment is symbolized in the white cloud. Its nature will be pointed out below.

"One like unto a son of man, having on his head a golden crown," is none other than the victorious Christ (cf. 1:13), enthroned upon the white cloud. The one "like unto a son of man" who came to the Ancient of Days that He might receive the kingdom and dominion and glory (Dan. 7:13f.), now carries out His work in that kingdom, exercising judgment commensurate with the dominion and glory which He received. Upon His head is the *stephanos*, the victory crown, which was given Him as He went forth riding upon a white horse, conquering and to conquer (6:1f.). But now, instead of a bow, He has in his hand a sickle, an instrument of harvest. Except for its occurrence in Mark 4:29, the sickle is mentioned only in this chapter, where it occurs seven times.

v. 15. "*And another angel came out from the temple, crying with a great voice to him that sat on the cloud, Send forth thy sickle, and reap: for the hour to reap is come; for the harvest of the earth is ripe.*" In introducing the angel as "another angel," the seer does not indicate that the Son of man is an angel, nor does he identify Him as such; but he classifies this angel with the three mentioned above and those that follow. The fact that the angel comes "out from the temple, crying with a great voice," reveals that he acts as "the messenger of the will of

God" (Alford), possibly indicating that this is one of the times and seasons "which the Father hath set within his own authority" (Acts 1:7). The one on the cloud is told to send forth His sickle and reap— "for the hour to reap is come," which hour is determined by the condition of the plants. "For the harvest of the earth is ripe." The word "ripe," from *xērainō*, is translated "withered away" (eleven times), "dried up" (three times), "pined away" (once), and "ripe" (in this instance). The word thus indicates a dried condition as when the season for growth has ended, a time determined by the Lord.

v. 16. "*And he that sat on the cloud cast his sickle upon the earth; and the earth was reaped.*" The one who controls or directs the reaping is described in Scripture as "Lord of the harvest," who sends forth laborers into the fields (Matt. 9:38; Luke 10:2). These laborers may be human agents (Matt. 9:38; Luke 10:2), or angels (Matt. 13:39, 41). The picture clearly indicates that it is the Christ who puts in the sickle; but a conclusion concerning the nature of this reaping is reserved for the end of the chapter.

v. 17. "*And another angel came out from the temple which is in heaven, he also having a sharp sickle.*" "Another angel," a fifth, identifies this one as equal in rank with the one above, who had come out from the temple (v. 15), the inner sanctuary of heaven. And though this angel bears a sharp sickle, as did the Son of man, again Christ should not be identified as an angel. Angels are ministers of God, messengers of the divine will, whereas the Christ is King and Judge.

v. 18. "*And another angel came out from the altar, he that hath power over fire; and he called with a great voice to him that had the sharp sickle, saying, Send forth thy sharp sickle, and gather the clusters of the vine of the earth; for her grapes are fully ripe.*" This sixth angel in the vision comes out from the altar and has power over fire. Two altars have been introduced thus far in the visions: (1) the altar of burnt-offerings, under which the souls of the martyrs rested (6:9-11), and (2) the altar of incense before God, upon which the prayers of the saints are offered. From this second altar an angel had taken fire and cast it upon the earth, indicating a judgment from God upon the ungodly world in response to the prayers of the saints (8:3-5). The expression the "angel that hath power over fire" refers to the second altar from which the angel had cast fire upon the earth. He is thus identified with judgment. It is he who brings word to the angel bearing the sharp sickle to send forth the sickle "and gather the clusters of the vine of the earth; for her grapes are fully ripe."

Three words attract attention, two being peculiar to this passage and a third occurring only one other time: "Gather" (*trugaō*), to gather in ripe fruit, of the fruit gathered (Luke 6:44 is the only passage other than vv. 18, 19 in which this word occurs). "Clusters of the vine" (*botrus*), occurs only here; "fully ripe" (*akmazō*), also found only here, means "to flourish, to come to maturity" (Thayer), "to be at the prime, fully ripe" (Vine). Indeed, the earth is fully ripe for judgment.

v. 19. "*And the angel cast his sickle into the earth, and gathered the vintage of the earth, and cast it into the winepress, the great winepress, of the wrath of God.*" Since the clusters of the vine were to be gathered (v. 18), we conclude that "vintage" (*ampelon*, "vine") refers to the plant from which the clusters were gathered, that is, the vine or vineyard of the earth. The fruit, not the vine itself, was cast into the winepress. Two Old Testament passages immediately come to mind: (1) God's call to the nations to come up to the valley of Jehoshaphat for judgment, saying, "Put ye in the sickle; for the harvest [*vintage*, margin] is ripe: come, tread ye; for the winepress is full, the vats overflow; for their wickedness is great" (Joel 3:13); and (2) Jehovah's answer to the prophet's question, "Who is this that cometh from Edom, with dyed garments from Bozrah?" to which He replies that He had trodden the winepress alone as He Himself trampled the peoples, staining His garments with their blood (Isa. 63:1–6; see also comments, 19:11ff.). The winepress of Jehovah's wrath must eventually be experienced by those that leave God out of their lives and thinking. All fruit of man's rebellion and sin against Him must be trodden under foot. The vine of earth and its fruit stand in contrast to the true vine and its fruit, which is borne to the glory of God (John 15:1–8).

v. 20. "*And the winepress was trodden without the city, and there came out blood from the winepress, even unto the bridles of the horses, as far as a thousand and six hundred furlongs.*" The city is probably the holy city, spiritual Jerusalem (see comments, 11:2). As the bodies of the sin-offerings were burned outside of the camp, and as a sin-offering Jesus "suffered without the gate" (Heb. 13:11f.); so it is appropriate that the world that rejected Him and His salvation should be trodden without the city. The blood which came out of the winepress to a depth reaching the horses bridles, and extending as far as sixteen hundred furlongs, about two hundred miles, is quite difficult to explain. Literalism is ruled out by the whole picture. If old physical Jerusalem is the city in the vision and the area of Palestine is the lake, one cannot interpret the picture literally because that territory is not two hundred miles long or wide; also, the low depth of twelve hundred ninety feet below sea level at the Dead Sea makes any literal interpretation impossible. Probably the picture intends only to indicate the magnitude and completeness of the judgment. Some have sought to explain the sixteen hundred as four, the world number, multiplied by itself, then multiplied by ten times ten, giving the idea of earthly completeness. I have no better suggestion. The picture indicates the gory completeness of God's judgment upon the wicked, as the horsemen wade through the sea of blood that reaches to the bridles.

This is the twofold picture; now comes the question, What is God revealing? The symbol of harvest is used of the wicked, "For thus saith Jehovah of hosts, the God of Israel: The daughter of Babylon is like a threshing-floor at the time when it is trodden; yet a little while and the time of harvest shall come for her" (Jer. 51:33). The symbol has also been used of the saints, "Then saith he unto his disciples, the harvest indeed is plenteous, but the laborers are few. Pray ye therefore the Lord of the harvest, that he send forth laborers into his harvest" (Matt. 9:37f.). Similarly, the word *harvest* has been used to include both the saints and the wicked in one gathering, "Let both [wheat and tares] grow until the harvest: and in time of harvest I will say to the reapers, Gather up first the tares, and bind them in bundles to burn them; but gather the wheat into my barn" (Matt. 13:30, cf. also v. 39). In the light of these various usages one cannot be positive in interpretation, or assert that any one of the three applications is absolutely correct. However, it seems logical that verses 14–16 symbolize the ingathering of His harvest by the Lord as He gathers "his wheat into the garner" (Matt. 3:12); for "when the fruit is ripe, straightway he putteth forth the sickle, because the harvest is come" (Mark 4:29). He has been doing this work and will continue it in spite of opposition by the dragon and his aides.

But what then, is the judgment, if any, indicated in the harvesting of wheat by the Lord? The gospel message preached to the world would be a savor of life to some and death to others (II Cor. 2:16). Jesus did not come to judge the world, yet through the preaching of His Word those who love darkness and reject His teaching are judged by that Word and their attitude toward it (John 3:17ff.). Jesus confirmed this principle when He said, "For judgment came I into the world, that they that see not may see; and that they that see may become blind" (John 9:39). He did not come to judge, yet He came for judgment: He was "set for the falling and rising of many in Israel" (Luke 2:34; see also Matt. 21:44; Rom. 9:32f.; I Peter 2:6-8). In thrusting away the offer of the gospel, men judge themselves unworthy of eternal life (Acts 13:46), and therefore remain under the judgment of damnation. We conclude that as the Lord reaps His harvest through preaching the gospel, judgment falls on all who reject it (vv. 6-7, 14-16).

While He will be gathering His own harvest, the judgment of the wicked in time will continue. The metaphor of the winepress indicates this idea rather than the final judgment at His second coming. Jehovah's treading the winepress of His wrath symbolized judgment against the heathen nations of earth at that time (Isa. 63:1-6; Joel 3:12f.). Also, the judgment against the nations, which would include the beast and the kings of the earth, is likewise described as treading the winepress of His wrath (19:11-16, see comments). The final judgment against the hosts of wickedness is described as destruction by fire (Matt. 13:40-42, 50; 25:41; Rev. 14:10; 20:10, 14f.; 21:8). Treading the winepress of God's wrath in time brought the Roman Empire, its provincial kings, and Roman paganism to an end. Similar judgments may be repeated in the history of nations, but the finality of judgment against the beast and false prophet is described as their being "cast alive into the lake of fire that burneth with brimstone" (19:20). It is more consistent with Scripture usage to consider this vision of judgment (vv. 17-20) as one in which the Lord uses His agents to destroy the wicked in time, while the final judgment to be executed by Himself will be one of fire.

CHAPTER 15
The Seven Bowls of Wrath

The accounts of the trumpets sounding (chaps. 8, 9) and the bowls of wrath being poured out upon the ungodly world have underlying similarities, but there are marked differences as well. The trumpets affect only a third of society; but the bowls of wrath indicate completeness or totality of judgment. Trumpets warn the earth-dwellers, while at the same time they draw God's people into a holy nearness to Himself. On the other hand, bowls of wrath bring final judgment. If proclaiming the good news of redemption does not cause men to fear before God, and if partial judgments do not turn them from humanism and materialism to repentance, then such an unregenerated society forfeits its right to continue. A destruction by judgment is inevitable and just.

In previous visions the condition and judgment of the wicked was contrasted to the victory and joy of the saints. For example, the sealing of the saints and their prayers before God (chap. 7; 8:3-5) precedes the sounding of the trumpets; the vision of the redeemed host on Mount Zion (14:1-5) is seen before the voices of the angels are heard. So now, before the bowls of wrath are poured out, the victorious saints are manifested, standing on the sea of glass singing God's praise. This indicates a characteristic of apocalyptic writings, showing various scenes and conditions from different points of view.

THE SEVEN ANGELS INTRODUCED
vv. 1-8

v. 1. "And I saw another sign in heaven, great and marvelous, seven angels having seven plagues, which are the last, for in them is finished the wrath of God." This is the third time the seer has seen a great sign in heaven; each sign introduces a special revelation from God (12:1, 3; see comments); as "another sign," this vision is connected with the former two. The phrase once again relates to a beginning, introducing something that is to follow in action and consequence, as in the sign of the radiant woman (12:1) and the dragon (12:3). So now a finished judgment is introduced to be traced to its consummation. In each instance the sign is seen from heaven's point of view. This one is "great and marvelous," producing wonder because of its terrible nature and significance.

In this verse the seven angels are introduced, but they do not actually appear on the scene until later (v. 6). As in other instances, seven need not be taken as a literal number, but as a symbol of completeness, fullness, and finality of the judgment. The seven angels possess seven plagues, which are public calamities or heavy afflictions sent by God as judgments or punishments upon men. Other plagues had come as judgments before (9:20; 11:6); but these are spoken of as the last, "for in them is finished the wrath of God." "To finish" is from *teleō*, which means to "find its consummation, or reach perfection," and also, "to carry out, accomplish, perform, fulfill" (A. & G.); in these judgments God's wrath reaches its goal.

v. 2 *"And I saw as it were a sea of glass mingled with fire; and them that come off victorious from the beast, and from his image, and from the number of his name, standing by [upon, margin] the sea of glass having harps of God."* The sea which John saw was "as" (*ōs*) of glass, clear, calm, and firm, with victorious saints standing upon [margin] it. Although the definite article does not appear before "sea of glass," nor is the location of the sea specified, it seems certain that the sea is the one introduced in the throne scene (4:6, see comments). There is now a difference, however; the sea is mingled or reddened with fire. What is the significance of the fire? Is it the fire of judgment about to fall, the fire of judgment which had fallen upon the world and affected the saints, or does the fire symbolize the fiery trials through which the victors had emerged?

It could be any or all of these; for both impending and executed judgments could be reflected in the sea, and the saints had indeed passed through terrible trials. But inasmuch as these who stand upon the sea of glass mingled with fire are victors who have overcome in the conflict with the beast, his image, and the enforcers of emperor worship, the fire probably symbolizes the trials endured. Jehovah had said that His people under the promised Messiah would be brought into "the fire" where He would "refine them as silver is refined, and try them as gold is tried" (Zech. 13:9; cf. Mal. 3:2f.). Paul wrote that a man's work should be proved; and though the work be lost, in his own faithfulness "he himself shall be saved; yet so as through fire" (I Cor. 3:12-15). Peter encouraged the saints who were enduring fiery trials that in these trials, "the proof of your faith, being more precious than gold that perisheth though it is proved by fire, may be found unto praise and glory and honor at the revelation of Jesus Christ" (I Peter 1:7). The faith of these now standing on the glassy sea mingled with fire had been tested by the blazing trials through which they had passed, and through which all of God's victorious saints must eventually be tested. In their victory they are given "harps of God" with which to praise Him for His greatness and power by which they had overcome (on harps, see 5:8; 14:2).

v. 3. *"And they sing the song of Moses the servant of God, and the song of the Lamb, saying, Great and marvelous are thy works, O Lord God, the Almighty; righteous and true are thy ways, thou King of the ages [nations, margin]."* The song of Moses is sung by victorious warriors who had overcome in the conflict set forth in verse 2. The song is one of victory and praise to Jehovah and the Lamb who gives victory. "The song of Moses" is the song sung by Moses and the children of Israel after crossing the Red Sea (Exod. 15), praising God for their deliverance from the Egyptians. Pharaoh's army lay dead in the sea; Jehovah had redeemed His people and would bring them in "and plant them in the mountain of [his] inheritance." And now, under the same mighty hand of God, the Lamb had given deliverance and victory to these who had overcome the forces of the dragon. The phrase, "singing the song of Moses... and the song of the Lamb" adds support to the position taken in 12:1, that the woman represents the faithful ones of the Old and New Testaments who become one in Christ. This is not to confuse the two groups, for they are clearly distinguished, but to unite them as one redeemed people. As God's servant Moses delivered His people from an oppressive nation, so God's son, the Lamb, redeemed a people from spiritual bondage (cf. Heb. 3:5f.). One conquered and delivered from the foe of physical bondage and tyranny; the other conquered the world and death, delivering from Satan's power.

The song which follows, though not quoted verbatim, is a combination of praises compiled from the Psalms, the Prophets, and the writings of Moses. The song praises and glorifies God as it magnifies His eternal greatness. The singers ascribe no glory to themselves for their victory or achievement in the conflict; all praise belongs to God, for it is He who "gives us the victory through our Lord Jesus Christ" (I Cor. 15:57). As Swete suggests, the singers seem lost in the joy of being before God, and in their praise they completely forget what they have been through to attain this position. "Great and marvelous are thy works" (cf. Ps. 40:5; 92:5). His works of greatness, physical or redemptive, had long excited the admiration and evoked the praise of men (cf. Ps. 8), causing them to acknowledge Him as "Lord God, the Almighty." "Righteous and true are thy ways" (cf. Ps. 145:17). Even if we do not fully understand our redemption through the blood sacrifice, our own purifying and perfecting for heaven through the fires of life's trials, or the judgments that fall upon the world of the ungodly, we as believers bow in praise to Him whose ways are always right and true (on "true," see comments, 13:7). "How unsearchable are his judgments, and his ways past tracing out!" (Rom. 11:33).

Out of this recognition comes further acknowledgment of His supremacy, "Thou King of the ages [nations]." The phrase "of the saints" (KJV) is rejected by all modern scholars since it has little textual support, but whether it is King "of the ages" (*aiōnōn*) or "of the nations" (*ethnōn*), is not easy to determine. Ancient manuscripts are about evenly divided between the two. However, in the light of the context "all the nations shall come and worship before thee" (v. 4), and Jeremiah's statement, "Who should not fear thee, O King of the nations" (Jer. 10:7), "of the nations" seems preferable. As King of the nations, Jehovah rules and governs their destiny according to righteousness and truth, whether that nation be Egypt, Babylon, Rome, or the United States.

v. 4. "Who shall not fear, O Lord, and glorify thy name? for thou only art holy; for all the nations shall come and worship before thee; for thy righteous acts have been made manifest." "Who shall not fear" is likewise from Jeremiah 10:7 (cf. also Ps. 86:9). Because of the greatness of the Lord's works and the righteousness and genuineness of His ways as King of the nations, all should be impelled to fear and glorify His name. "Fear," as in 14:7, means to reverence, treat with deference, and from this disposition render obedience (Thayer). The Lord's name stands for all that He is; reverence for Him as Lord and glory to His great name are both due to Jehovah.

The word translated "holy" is from *hosios*, not *hagios*, which Lenski translates "sacred." Vine says, "It signifies religiously right, holy, as opposed to unrighteous or polluted" (II. p. 227). All nations shall come and worship before God (cf. Ps. 86:9) after recognizing the failure of the beast and the religion he defends and beholding the triumph of God's cause, "For thy righteous acts have been made manifest," that is, made evident in the sight of all (cf. Ps. 98:2). God's righteous ways which are set forth in the law and in Christ, His verdicts which are announced, and judgments which are executed, will be vindicated in history.

v. 5. "And after these things I saw, and the temple of the tabernacle of the testimony in heaven was opened." "After these things" occurs seven times in the book, and each time it introduces a new and emphatic point (see 4:1). The temple John saw was the *naos*, the Holy of Holies in heaven, which was symbolized by the inner sanctuary of the tabernacle. His vision was not of the ancient temple of Solomon nor of the temple constructed by Herod, which stood in Jerusalem prior to A.D. 70. "The tabernacle [tent] of the testimony" erected by Moses (Num. 1:50; 9:15; 10:11; 17:7; 18:2) was so called because within the Holy of Holies rested the ark of the covenant containing the tables of the law, called "the testimony," which God gave Israel (Exod. 25:21). Previously John had seen the sanctuary opened to reveal the ark of the covenant, the seat of God's righteous laws (11:19); now it was opened that the angels of judgment against those who rejected Him and His law might come forth.

v. 6. "And there came out from the temple the seven angels that had the seven plagues, arrayed with precious stone [linen, margin], pure and bright, and girt about their breasts with golden girdles." The seven angels introduced in verse 1 now appear bearing the seven plagues to be poured out upon the earth. These plagues of judgment come from the very holiness of God, for "righteousness and justice are the foundation of his throne" (Ps. 97:2). The seven are clad alike, but there is a question as to whether the attire should be "pure and white linen"

(KJV), or "with precious stone, pure and bright" (ASV); there is weighty textual evidence for each. *The Greek New Testament* (United Bible Societies, 2d ed.) presents an impressive array of ancient texts where each, linen (*linon*) and stone (*lithos*), is found (p. 874). The word *linon* (linen) occurs only twice in the New Testament, here (if it indeed is linen and not stone), and in Matthew 12:20, where it is translated "flax." The word generally used for "fine linen," occurring only in Revelation, is *bussinos* (18:16; 19:8, 14); and a second, *bussos*, occurs only in Luke 16:19 and Rev. 18:12. Because the words *bussinos* and *bussos* and not *linon* (unless this is an exception) are generally used for linen, some have decided in favor of "stone" (*lithos*). But after all has been said, it seems that linen is preferable. Linen, pure and bright, describes the attire of the Lamb's bride (19:8), while that of the heavenly horsemen is similarly described as linen, white and pure (19:14). It may be noted also that the apparel or robes of angels who appeared on various occasions after Jesus' resurrection was white, even "white as snow" (Matt. 28:3; Mark 16:5; John 20:12; Acts 1:10). These who came out bearing the seven bowls had around their breasts a golden girdle such as that worn by the glorified Christ (1:13 see comments). These golden girdles seem not to identify their work as priestly, but to signify that they were angels of high rank, entrusted with a solemn obligation.

v. 7. "*And one of the four living creatures gave unto the seven angels seven golden bowls full of the wrath of God, who liveth for ever and ever.*" It is not revealed which (and why only one) of the four living creatures was commissioned to give the bowls of wrath to the seven angels. How they came out from the sanctuary having the seven plagues (vv. 1, 5), and then had the seven plagues given to them, is likewise not indicated. (For comments on the living creatures, see 4:8). The Greek word for bowl (*phialē*), that is, a broad shallow vessel or deep saucer, occurs only in Revelation (twelve times), and is to be distinguished from the cup (14:10), which is exclusively a drinking vessel. The bowl is similar to some of the vessels used in Old Testament sacrifices and ritual. The four living creatures and the twenty-four elders had "golden bowls full of incense, which are the prayers of the saints" (5:8) offered unto God. Next these seven angels come forth from the divine presence with bowls of wrath and await the instruction from God to empty them. Lenski has well observed that the seven seals *reveal*, the seven trumpets *announce* and *warn*, and the seven bowls *execute* (p. 461).

v. 8. *"And the temple was filled with smoke from the glory of God, and from his power; and none was able to enter into the temple, till the seven plagues of the seven angels should be finished."* The smoke which filled the temple may be (1) a sign of God's glory in action, as when He descended upon Mount Sinai in fire—the whole of it smoked (Exod. 19:18) as the glory of Jehovah covered the heavens (Hab. 3:3). (2) It may be indicative of His anger in judgment and calamity, as the fire out of His mouth devours and His anger and jealousy smoke against the wicked (Deut. 29:20; Ps. 18:8; 74:1). (3) It may be a token of His favorable protective presence (Isa. 4:5), but this would apply only to the saints, and it is doubtful if this is its meaning here. When the tabernacle was erected, the glory of Jehovah filled it, and Moses was not able to enter it (Exod. 40:34f.). Likewise, when Solomon had completed the temple, the glory of Jehovah filled the house, "so that the priests could not stand to minister" (I Kings 8:10f.). And so now, until the seven plagues would be finished, no one could enter the temple. The smoke from His glory was being vindicated by the smoke of His anger, demonstrated in expressions of His great power. Swete has well summed up the significance of this verse as he says, "The Divine judgments are impenetrable until they are past; when the last plague has fulfilled its course, the smoke will vanish, and the Vision of God be seen" (p. 200). No intercessions can change the determinate counsel of God; but when it is fulfilled, we can then see clearly that which is now obscured.

CHAPTER 16
The Bowls of Wrath Poured Out

Before the contents of the bowls were poured out upon the earth, John was permitted to see the victorious saints standing upon the sea of glass and to hear them singing the song of triumph. This would assure the saints to whom John was writing of their own victory. With this assurance and consolation for the saints on earth, the time had now come for the judgments to fall. God's judgment upon the wicked of earth was set forth in the closing verses of chapter 14, where it was symbolized as a vintage—so why is judgment pictured again here? There seems to be little doubt that before us is a repetition of that judgment in which God reveals its intensity. The present vision also reveals the finality of judgment upon the forces of evil and God's complete use of all His weapons in the administration of justice. There can be no more complete judgment until the final judgment, which is not introduced until chapter 20. Rather than pertaining either to the end of time or to events just prior to the end, the scene in this chapter deals with God's judgment against the dragon, the beast, the earth beast, and their associates. Such judgments may be repeated at intervals throughout history.

Certain similarities between the trumpet blasts and the bowls of wrath, comparable to some of the plagues upon Egypt, will be pointed out in the discussion of the outpouring of the individual bowls. It is evident that here are final judgments upon certain spiritual, political, and moral forces; but it is very difficult to assign definite meaning to the specific bowls. One cannot afford to be dogmatic; he can present only what he interprets to be the message from God. Albertus Pieters candidly admits, "On the whole, it seems clear that the true interpretation has not yet been found, and probably cannot be found." Pieters further points out that what we see is a "vivid dramatization of the fight God puts up from heaven in behalf of His church" (p. 244f.). In his excellent commentary Lenski critically examines the meaning of each bowl and its consequent action, only to admit, "We do not claim that

325

we have succeeded in understanding all the symbols and have fully discovered the realities beneath them" (p. 464). Milligan makes a similar admission, saying, "No attempt to determine the special meaning of the objects thus visited by the wrath of God—the land, the sea, the rivers and fountains of the waters, and the sun—has yet been, or is ever perhaps likely to be, successful; and the general effect alone appears to be important" (p. 265). Others make similar confessions, and I hasten to add my own name to the list, suggesting with timidity and reservation what seem to be reasonable interpretations as each passage is considered in its context.

BOWLS INVOLVING NATURE
vv. 1-9

v. 1. "And I heard a great voice out of the temple [sanctuary], saying to the seven angels, Go ye, and pour out the seven bowls of the wrath of God into the earth." John does not identify the source of the great voice; it may have been that of an angel, of the Lord Jesus, or of God the Father. Some have concluded that because none could enter the temple at this time (15:8), the voice was God's, but this is not revealed. A great or loud voice has been heard many times before; however, this time the command comes from within the sanctuary, so it is from a divine source. The instruction is to all seven angels, and is not repeated; each angel carries out his order as directed. Being poured out "into the earth," all bowls affect the world of unregenerate men. (For comments on "bowl," see 15:7).

v. 2. "And the first went, and poured out his bowl into the earth; and it became a noisome and grievous sore upon the men that had the mark of the beast, and that worshipped his image." The first three angels poured out their bowls "into" (*eis*) the earth, the sea, and the rivers (as in 8:5; 14:19); but the next four poured out their bowls "upon" (*epi*) the sun, the throne of the beast, the Euphrates, and the air. If there is any special significance in the two different prepositions used, "into" and "upon," it is not clear. As the seven were told to pour out their bowls "into the earth" (v. 1), apparently there is no special point to be made in the transition from one to the other.

"It became," or preferably, "there came" (margin, ASV), or "there occurred" (Lenski), "a noisome and grievious sore upon the men who had the mark of the beast, and that had worshipped his image." It was not until the sixth Egyptian plague (Exod. 9:9ff.) and the fifth trumpet (9:4ff.), that men were affected directly, although the first five plagues upon Egypt and the third trumpet affected men indirectly. But in the series of bowl-plagues, man is grievously smitten from the very first. Noisome (from *kakos*) is most often translated "evil"; Thayer defines it as "troublesome, injurious, pernicious, destructive, baneful," therefore bad or distressing, whether to mind or body (p. 320). Grievous (from *ponēros*) indicates that which is "painful, virulent, serious" (A. & G.). The sore (*helkos*) was an abscess or ulcer, a foul and angry sore (A. & G.); the word occurs only in Luke 16:21, here, and in verse 11 below. As in the human body where sores break out from an accumulation of impurities that permeate the whole body, so also in this case it is the corruption of the world breaking out. Only those are afflicted who participated in the false worship of the beast and his image and became corrupted by the immorality of pagan standards. This would include the heathen priests as the sixth plague in Egypt included the Egyptian magicians. A like judgment may be repeated in history from time to time, but to those John addressed, the judgment concerned the Roman system of emperor worship: this is a reaping of the corruption which had been sown (cf. Gal. 6:7f.).

v. 3. *"And the second poured out his bowl into the sea; and it became blood as of a dead man and every living soul died, even the things that were in the sea."* In the best manuscripts "angel" is omitted, although understood, and so also in the remainder of the chapter. Each bearer of a bowl goes forth until all have carried out their appointed tasks. At the sounding of the second trumpet a third part of the sea becomes blood, which results in the death of a third part of the creatures which were in it; however, when the second bowl is poured out into the sea, the whole of it and its creatures are affected.

Is the sea here a part of the whole creation which suffers from the consequences of sin, or does it represent the society of earthlings who are spiritually dead? In 13:1, the sea out of which the first beast emerged was the whole of society that produced such monsters in its upheavals. As in 8:8f. the "sea" here symbolizes the whole society of worldly mankind (see comments, 13:1 and also 8:8f.). The bowl of wrath thus brings into focus the utter putrefaction of a dead society. Lenski contends that instead of "it became," the phrase "there occurred" is the preferable translation for *egeneto* (vv. 2, 3, 4). If this is correct, the passage would read, "there occurred blood as of a dead man." Society was dead in sins and trespasses, and now there occurs the blood as of a dead man, putrid and rotting—a revealing illustration of the true nature of the spiritually dead. The result is death to all who come into such a society—not inherited, but consequential death.

Moses wrote that "the life of the flesh is in the blood" (Lev. 17:11). Consequently, when the life is gone, decay and rottenness set in until one returns to the dust from whence he came. This is the irrevocable judgment of God from the very beginning (Gen. 3:19). Likewise, when the spiritual quality of a society decays, like a sea of coagulated blood from dead men, it putrefies and rots, issuing a foul and obnoxious odor. Eventually it returns to the unseen (*Sheol*, Ps. 9:17); this, too, is by the judgment of God. Consider Sodom, the Canaanites, Israel, Judah, and all the rest of the ancient nations; when, due to spiritual decay, they were no longer fit to continue, God removed them. A society abandoned to idolatry and its consequent morals, as was the Roman Empire of John's day, is spiritually dead. In such a society, morals decline to the lowest level; the family collapses, schools breed anarchy and rebellion, business ethics are forgotten, entertainment becomes base and sordid, and printing presses exude smut and filth, until the whole is strangled in its own death blood and suffocated by its own stench. Our society too must listen to the trumpet warnings before God pours out the bowls of wrath.

v. 4. "*And the third poured out his bowl into the rivers and the fountains of the waters; and it became blood.*" As in the case of the third trumpet, so here, the rivers and springs of water are affected, though with far more drastic results. In the former, just one-third of the rivers and springs became wormwood so that many died from the bitter waters; now all drinkable water is turned to blood. This plague is reminiscent of the first that befell Egypt when the waters of the Nile were turned to blood, became foul, and killed the fish. At that time, however, the people could dig and find water to drink (Exod. 7:20ff.); under the plague of the third bowl, even the underground springs are turned to blood.

v. 5. "And I heard the angel of the waters saying, Righteous art thou, who art and who wast, thou Holy One, because thou didst thus judge." Two voices are next heard, one explaining the cause of this plague, and the other (v. 7) proclaiming the righteousness of God's judgment. The first to speak is "the angel of the waters," for each element has its angel, and each angel has his work to accomplish (see comments, 1:20; 14:18). This angel, who is over the rivers and fountains which are so essential to life, proclaims the righteousness of this judgment. It proceeds from the righteous character of God whose judgments and ways are always right, for they are expressions of His holy nature (cf. comments, 15:3). When men pollute, corrupt, and destroy, it is just that they receive a commensurate retribution for their wicked deeds. A servant had poured out the contents of the bowl, but the judgment was from God.

v. 6. "For they poured out the blood of saints and prophets, and blood hast thou given them to drink: they are worthy." The cause for such a judgment is now announced, "for they poured out the blood of saints and prophets." "They" are the Caesar worshipers of verse 2, who cried for the blood of God's saints and prophets—that is, the New Testament prophets, for those of the Old Testament are not under consideration. Because they had been so eager for blood, they shall be satiated with blood; it shall be given them to drink, which is more than they had looked for. All innocent blood shed willfully by murderous men must be expiated by the hand of man or God (Num. 35:33; Deut. 32:42). "They are worthy," means that those who have poured out the blood of the righteous and upon whom the judgment falls, fully deserve what they receive. Jehovah's words toward Edom, carried out in His final judgment against that wicked nation, are again appropriate: "As thou hast done, it shall be done unto thee; thy dealing [recompense, margin] shall return upon thine own head. For as ye have drunk upon my holy mountain, so shall all the nations drink continually; yea, they shall drink, and swallow down, and shall be as though they had not been" (Obad. 15, 16). The retribution of a righteous judgment must finally overtake the wicked would-be destroyers of God's people.

v. 7. "And I heard the altar saying, Yea, O Lord God, the Almighty, true and righteous are thy judgments." The angel of verse 5 had proclaimed the righteousness of God, from whom the judgment proceeded; this voice proclaims the righteousness of the judgment itself. It is indeterminable whether the altar, which adds its testimony to that of the angel of the waters (v. 5), is a personification of the altar itself (cf. 9:13), or the angel of fire from the altar (14:18). It is also uncertain whether the altar is the brazen altar from under which the martyrs had cried (6:9-11), or the golden altar on which the prayers of the saints were offered (8:3, 5; 9:13; 14:18); but the latter seems preferable. In each instance the saints cry for a vindication of their death on behalf of Christ and His cause; their plea is now being answered. This voice adds its testimony to that of the angel, praising the overall greatness of God and His judgments which are true (genuine), proceeding from an infinite source; His righteous actions are infallible. What, then, is the lot of God's people in a world where all fountains and rivers are turned to blood? God promised those who would make Him their strength and salvation, "Therefore, with joy shall ye draw water out of the wells of salvation" (Isa. 12:3). And to this promise Jesus added, "Whosoever drinketh of the water that I shall give him shall never thirst; but the water that I shall give him shall become in him a well of water springing up unto eternal life" (John 4:14). Believers have a life-sustaining water unknown to the pagans to whom God had given blood to drink.

v. 8. "And the fourth poured out his bowl upon the sun; and it was given unto it to scorch men with fire." From a waterless world filled with blood, the vision now focuses upon the blazing sun, which scorches men with fire. Unlike the fourth trumpet which caused the sun, moon, and stars not to shine for a third part of the day, and unlike the ninth plague in Egypt, which produced a three-day darkness that could be felt (Exod. 10:21ff.), this plague turned the sun into a source of blistering heat, burning and painful, by which men were scorched. The source of light, intended to guide, warm, and cheer, is turned into an instrument of pain, for God "maketh winds his messengers; flames of fire his ministers" (Ps. 104:4); all are at His service. The psalmist has also said, "A fire goeth before him, and burneth up his adversaries round about.... Let all them be put to shame that serve graven images, that boast themselves of idols" (Ps. 97:3, 7). This principle of divine action was now being carried out.

The men of John's vision were as the astrologers, stargazers, and monthly prognosticators of Isaiah's day, whom Jehovah challenged to stand up and save the people; but "the fire shall burn them; they shall not deliver themselves from the power of the flame: It shall not be a coal to warm at, nor a fire to sit before" (Isa. 47:13f.); it would be the scorching heat of God's wrath. And again Jehovah warned the rebellious, saying "Behold, all ye that kindle a fire, that girdeth yourselves about with firebrands; walk ye in the flame of your fire, and among the brands that ye have kindled. This shall ye have of my hand; ye shall lie down in sorrow" (Isa. 50:11). In John's visions God is simply carrying out what He had proposed and done all along. In their effort to lead people astray these masters of deceit had even made "fire to come down out of heaven upon the earth in the sight of men" (13:13); and now God responds with a scorching fiery judgment. In contrast to the condition of these, God's people who had suffered martyrdom at the hands of the heathen were where the sun should not "strike upon them, nor any heat" (7:16).

v. 9. "And men were scorched with great heat: and they blasphemed the name of God who hath the power over these plagues; and they repented not to give him glory." Instead of recognizing their sin and repenting toward God, men added two additional crimes to their already sin-cursed lives: they blasphemed the name of God who had power over these plagues, and withheld from Him the glory that is rightfully His due—"they glorified him not as God, neither gave thanks" (Rom. 1:21). The beast from the sea, with names of blasphemy upon his heads, had reviled the name of God and them that dwell in the heaven (13:1, 6). The beast's subjects had so imbibed his spirit and absorbed his characteristics that they, too, blasphemed God's name. As Pharaoh had hardened his heart against God, so these also rebelled against His efforts to soften them. Even the scorching heat of God's wrath could not mellow their obstinate hearts; rather it hardened them. "Behold then the goodness and severity of God" (Rom. 11:22), for both characteristics are intended to bring men to repentance (Rom. 2:4–11). Their failure to repent indicates that in these plagues the final judgment has not been reached, for then is no opportunity for repentance. The final judgment is not intended to bring men to repentance, but this bowl should have. This completes the first section of the plagues involving earth, sea, inland waters, and sun.

BOWLS INVOLVING THE MORAL AND POLITICAL
vv. 10-21

vv. 10-11. *"And the fifth poured out his bowl upon the throne of the beast; and his kingdom was darkened; and they gnawed their tongues for pain, and they blasphemed the God of heaven because of their pains and their sores; and they repented not of their works."* The realm affected by the plagues moves from the natural to the moral and spiritual. When the beast emerged from the sea it was said that "the dragon gave him his power, and his throne, and great authority" (13:2). This throne was the seat of world power, which would have been thought of by the saints of John's day as the world rule from Rome. But this throne should not be restricted to Rome only; for wherever world power is worshiped, there the beast has his throne.

"And his kingdom was darkened" probably indicates, as in the plague of the fifth trumpet, the loss of wisdom and understanding by which to guide the empire. Here, however, it is pictured in a more advanced and complete stage, for the entire kingdom was darkened. In time of distress David prayed against the wicked, saying, "Let their eyes be darkened, so that they cannot see" (Ps. 69:23); and Isaiah said, "Through the wrath of Jehovah of hosts is the land darkened" (Isa. 9:19, margin). Beginning at the beast's throne, such darkness was now falling upon his kingdom.

The pain of the sores from the first plague (v. 2) and the scorching heat of the fourth plague are now further intensified by the darkened and hopeless condition of the political outlook. Men gave vent to their feelings of pain and despair by gnawing their tongues. To gnaw (from *massaomai*) occurs only here in the New Testament, and means to chew or bite, to eat, consume (Thayer). Instead of recognizing and acknowledging their own pride, stubbornness of heart, and rebellion against God as the cause of their condition, these men blasphemed the God of heaven (cf. v. 9). This had been their reaction to the fourth bowl, where "they repented not to give him glory" (v. 9); again here "they repented not of their works." They neither recognized the glory due God on the one hand, nor their diabolical works as the cause of His wrath and jugment on the other.

In letters to the five churches which had sin in their midst (all except

Smyrna and Philadelphia), God had called upon church members to repent that they might escape judgment and receive the promised rewards (chaps. 2, 3). Also, God caused the everlasting gospel to be preached to men of earth (14:6f.) and sent His plagues upon them to bring them to repentance, that they, too, should escape inevitable judgment and condemnation. But all of this was to no avail; therefore, total judgment had to eventually come.

v. 12. *"And the sixth poured out his bowl upon the great river, the river Euphrates; and the water thereof was dried up, that the way might be made ready for the kings that come from the sunrising."* The Euphrates river was introduced at the sounding of the sixth trumpet, but with a different purpose and action than here (9:13ff.). In the first instance the four angels bound at the river had been loosed so that a hellish army might be released. But at the pouring out of the sixth bowl, the waters of the Euphrates are dried up to make way for the coming of kings and their armies from the east. (For comments on the Euphrates as the northernmost frontier of Israel's territory and the boundary between east and west, see comments, 9:14). This Euphrates here is not a physical or geographical location; it symbolizes a barrier or deterrent to invasion, which is now removed. Are these kings from the sunrising Christ and His saints, or are they antagonistic forces of destruction that war against Him? Plummer sees these kings as symbolic of God's judgments: "The kings of the east are certainly the forces ranged on the side of God" (p. 395). But this does not fit the picture; they are the forces gathered together as enemies of God's cause, mustered by the unclean spirits, "to the war of the great day of God, the Almighty" (v. 14).

v. 13. *"And I saw coming out of the mouth of the dragon, and out of the mouth of the beast, and out of the mouth of the false prophet, three unclean spirits, as it were frogs."* "And I saw" introduces a new phase of the vision (see comments, 4:1). The word "coming" is not in the original text. Though the unclean spirits issued from the mouths of the dragon, the beast, and the false prophet, John does not say he saw them coming out; but he saw them "out of the mouth" of each, that is, he saw them at work (v. 14). Out of the mouth of the dragon had been emitted a river of lies by which he sought to engulf the woman, but which the earth swallowed up (12:15f.); out of the mouth of the beast had been uttered great pretenses and blasphemies (13:5); and out of the mouth of the false prophet had come seductive propaganda, enticing the world to accept and practice the Caesar cult (13:14-17). The false prophet is the beast out of the earth who performed the signs to deceive (13:11ff.; cf. also, 19:20).

John sees unclean spirits or messages as frogs at work in the world. Frogs are mentioned only in the second Egyptian plague (Exod. 8:1-15), twice in the Psalms in association with the plagues (Ps. 78:45; 105:30), and here. In the plague they came in swarms; here, there are only three. The psalmist says that Jehovah sent among the Egyptians "frogs, which destroyed them" (Ps. 78:45), but in what way they destroyed them we are not told. Frogs are thought of as unclean, loathsome, a nuisance and an aggravation; their croaking probably symbolizes confusion. It is likely in this sense that these unclean spirits are called frogs. According to the law such creatures were to be held in abomination (Lev. 11:9ff.), and coming from such a source as these three came, there was no doubt that they were unclean.

v. 14. *"For they are spirits of demons, working signs; which go forth unto the kings of the whole world, to gather them together unto the war of the great day of God, the Almighty."* These frogs are further described and identified as "spirits of demons," not "devils" as in the KJV (see comments, 9:20; 12:9), which are "working signs" with intent to deceive. Their signs were fradulent impostures, for neither Satan nor his helpers can work a *bona fide* miracle (see comments, 12:1; 13:13f.). Satan, assisted by his two allies who are no less involved than he, is the prime instigator of this whole movement. Jesus had warned His disciples against false prophets and false signs (Matt. 24:24), and Paul likewise warned the saints against them (II Thess. 2:9; I Tim. 4:1). Since Christians are thus warned, only unbelievers would succumb to such delusions.

The objective of these unclean spirits was to gather "the kings of the whole world" (*oikoumenē*, "inhabited earth"), "unto the war of the great day of God, the Almighty." Neither the Parthian threat to Rome nor some great battle just before the end of time is in the seer's view. In the vision at this point the battle has not begun, and the campaign has not opened; what John sees is the mustering of forces. The battle is that of verse 16, discussed below. The day is determined by God, but the battle of that day is not described as being fought until the nineteenth chapter; even there the battle itself is not described, only the results are given (vv. 19–21). "The great day of God" is a day of judgment, but not the final or ultimate judgment, for there will be no battle fought at that time—all will be over.

v. 15. "(Behold, I come as a thief. Blessed is he that watcheth, and keepth his garments, lest he walk naked, and they see his shame.)" As John is receiving and recording the vision of the gathering forces for the war of the great day of God, a voice breaks in, whose words can be from none other than the Lord Jesus Himself. "I come as a thief" indicates that His coming will be unannounced (cf. 3:3). This idea of coming as a thief had been spoken by the Lord during His ministry to encourage constant watch and preparedness for His coming (Luke 12:39f.). The phrase was used by the apostles with reference to the day itself (I Thess. 5:2, 4; II Peter 3:10). It is therefore impossible to know the day of the Lord's coming, either for a judgment in time or for the final coming.

In view of this, the Lord announces a third "blessed" as a promise and a warning (cf. 1:3); a bliss that cannot be taken away will reward him who watches and who keeps his garments. The present tense, "watches" and "keeps," indicates a constant conflict necessitating a daily watchfulness; one must be continuously on guard. In the midst of the scene of the gathering army and decisive battle, there is a parenthetical warning and exhortation to the saints not to be deceived or led astray by what is taking place. At both the beginning and the conclusion of the revelation the Lord said that He was revealing things which "must shortly come to pass (1:1; 22:6), "for the time is at hand" (1:3; 22:10). Therefore His coming in this instance is not at the end of time.

To keep one's garments is to keep them undefiled, for they that do "not defile their garments... shall walk with me in white" (3:4). A Christian must not become or act as the Laodician church (3:17f.), whose warning seems to be reiterated here; for without garments of righteousness in Christ, "our disgraceful sin would be open to all eyes" (Lenski).

v. 16. "And they gathered them together into the place which is called in Hebrew, Har-Magedon." John resumes his narrative which had been interrupted by the parenthetic warning of verse 15. The demon spirits had gone to the kings of the whole world "to gather them together unto the war" (v. 14); "and they gathered them into the place called Har-Magedon." This leads to the conclusion that Har-Magedon, more familiarly known as Armageddon, after the KJV, is the locale where the war is to take place. The text only says they were gathered; it says nothing of the battle itself. The battle and its results are reserved for chapter 19.

Great mystery and obscurity surrounds the name Har-Magedon (Armageddon), which means "Mount of Megiddo." The Bible speaks geographically of "Megiddo and its three heights" (Josh. 17:11), "Megiddo and its towns" (Judg. 1:27), "the waters of Megiddo" (Judg. 5:19), and "the valley of Megiddo" (II Chron. 35:22; Zech. 12:11), but makes no mention of a Mount of Megiddo. Megiddo was a strategic point in the protection of Israel and Judah, since it guarded the northern entrance to Israel. It was in this area that several decisive battles had been fought, the most memorable being that of Deborah and Barak against Jabin and Sisera of the Canaanites; a decisive victory was given Israel by Jehovah (Judg. 4, 5). It was in this valley of Esdraelon (Jezreel), "west of the hill of Moreh," that Gideon's three hundred men defeated and drove out the Midianites, another decisive battle determined by Jehovah (Judg. 7:1). Saul and Jonathan were slain at the eastern extremity of the plain (I Sam. 31:1–6); and it was at Megiddo that Ahaziah, king of Judah, in league with Joram of Israel, died, having been slain at the command of Jehu (II Kings 9:27). King Josiah fought against Pharaoh Neco in the valley of Megiddo, where he was slain (II Kings 23:29f.; II Chron. 35:22). This proved to be a decisive battle of history in that Josiah slowed Neco in his effort to reach Haran and aid Assyria against Babylon. This delay of Neco allowed Babylon to defeat the Assyrian army, making Babylon the leading power of the east.

In view of these battles of historical significance we conclude that John used the word symbolically to describe a great decisive spiritual battle between the army of Satan and the forces of God, which would determine the fate of each. This battle was fought and won by the Lord in the complete defeat of the Roman Empire and paganism behind which Rome threw its total power (see 19:11–21). To look for a physical military battle between human armies to be fought in northern Palestine at some future date is completely without scriptural support and foreign to the spirit and purpose of Revelation.

v. 17. "And the seventh poured out his bowl upon the air; and there came forth a great voice out of the temple, from the throne, saying, It is done." The seventh bowl poured out upon the air symbolically completes the gamut of natural elements: earth, water, fire (sun), and air. The disturbances that follow the outpouring of this bowl appear more severe than those before, though all are fearful and awesome. There can be little or no doubt that "air" is used symbolically; but what is its symbolic significance? The key to an interpretation may be found in Paul's letter to the Ephesians when he said, "Wherein ye [Gentiles] once walked according to the course of this world, according to the prince of the powers [Greek, "power"] of the air, of the spirit that now worketh in the sons of disobedience" (Eph. 2:2). The prince can be none other than Satan, "the prince of this world" (John 12:31; 14:30; 16:11), "the god of this world" (II Cor. 4:4). As the fifth bowl had been poured out upon the throne of the beast, which was sorely affected, and the sixth opened the way for the gathering of Satan's forces to the great war, being called together by demon spirits, it is reasonable to conclude that the seventh bowl would affect the whole sphere of Satan's operation. Air would be an appropriate emblem of the prevailing influence or surroundings of the realm in which the wicked live, move, and breathe, being dominated by the devil. Thus the course of this world, which is itself evil, a life of trespasses and sin, ruled by the prince of its power, controlling his subjects by a spirit of rebellion and disobedience to God, is now brought under judgment.

The "great voice" which came "out of the temple, from the throne," as did the voice of verse 1, is not identified. But coming from the throne within the sanctuary indicates that it is from God or Christ. The message is, "It is done"; "it has come to pass" (Swete); "It has become" or "it has occurred" (Lenski). The series of plagues is now completed; God's wrath expressed in righteous judgments has now exploded as an atomic bomb upon the world of ungodly and wicked men.

v. 18. "And there were lightnings, and voices, and thunders; and there was a great earthquake, such as there was not since there were men upon the earth, so great an earthquake, so mighty." In the heavenly scene there had proceeded out of the throne flashes of lightning, voices, and peals of thunder (4:5). The opening of the seven seals closed with "thunders and voices, and lightning, and an earthquake" (8:5). The sounding of the seven trumpets was concluded with these same four, to which was added "and great hail" (11:19). And now the seven bowls of the seven plagues are brought to a conclusion with the same four elements, with an added intensity, for the earthquake is "a great earthquake," and the hail is "great hail" (v. 21). These indicate an increasing severity in God's actions. The earthquake is so great, so mighty, "such as was not since there were men upon the earth." This plague is earthshaking because of what is affected: Satan's own realm receives a devastating shock, together with the fall of Babylon and the empire over which she ruled. Since there had never been a greater realm than this present Babylon and the Roman Empire, there would never have been a greater earthquake when it fell.

v. 19. *"And the great city was divided into three parts, and the cities of the nations fell: and Babylon the great was remembered in the sight of God, to give unto her the cup of the wine of the fierceness of his wrath."* The "great city" has appeared several times. It was initially introduced in 11:8 (see comments), where it received a partial judgment in an earthquake in which one tenth of the inhabitants were killed (11:13). Its doom was proclaimed later by the voice of the second angel as though it had already fallen, for God had determined its destruction (14:8). It is uncertain what is meant by the division of the city into three parts. In prophesying of Jerusalem's destruction Ezekiel had said that a third part should be burned, a third part devoted to the sword, and a third part scattered to the wind (Ezek. 5:2f.). This indicated total destruction of the city and could suggest the threefold division of the Babylon of John's vision. Lenski thinks the picture before us indicates total collapse, as the walls fall outward to the right and left, and the roof to the floor. But it is possible that the three parts are those indicated in a later chapter where the fall of Babylon is enlarged upon (death, mourning, and famine—utter destruction [18:8]). Whatever may be concluded concerning the "three parts," a total destruction from the Lord is clearly indicated.

But Babylon does not fall alone, for the satellite cities whom she had made "to drink of the wine of the wrath of her fornication" (14:8), also go down. The scene pictures the collapse of the pagan world-city and its daughters, a description of which follows (chaps. 17, 18). The city is called to mind before the Lord, as Cornelius' alms "were had in remembrance before God" (Acts 10:31). God now gives to her "the cup of the wine of the fierceness of his wrath," that is, the hot burning anger of His wrath. The cup (*potērion*) was a drinking vessel, whereas the bowl (*phialē*, "vial," KJV) was a shallow dish or saucer (cf. 5:8; 15:7). As God had promised He would give this cup to the worshipers of the beast and his image (14:10, see comments), so now he also gives it to Babylon.

v. 20. "*And every island fled away, and the mountains were not found.*" A similar removal of islands was introduced at the opening of the sixth seal, where "every mountain and island were moved out of their places" (6:14). In this plague upon Babylon, the fleeing of the islands is parallel to the disappearance of the mountains. Both had vanished, for the great earthquake (v. 18) touched all realms where men dwell. Ezekiel similarly described the fall of Tyre when he said, "Now shall the isles tremble in the day of thy fall; yea, the isles that are in the sea shall be dismayed at thy departure" (Ezek. 26:18). Later John draws from Ezekiel's picture when he describes the fall of Babylon (chap. 18). In the fall of this great world power there would be no place for refuge, for all such places will have been removed.

v. 21. "*And great hail, every stone about the weight of a talent, cometh down out of heaven upon men: and men blasphemed God because of the plague of the hail; for the plague thereof is exceeding great.*" This was no ordinary hail, for each stone weighed about a talent, estimated by scholars to have been between sixty and a hundred pounds, though probably more precisely between ninety and niney-six pounds. Whatever the weight, it was sufficient to kill instantly. These "came down out of heaven," indicating their source, "upon men," the object of the divine judgment.

Hail had been a symbol of divine wrath and judgment since the plagues upon Egypt, for the seventh plague had been "a grievous hail" upon man and beast (Exod. 9:18–26; cf. also Ps. 78:47; 105:32). Jehovah had fought for Israel at Beth-horon by sending great stones from heaven upon the Canaanites (Josh. 10:11). And concerning those in Jerusalem who made lies their refuge and under falsehood hid themselves, the Lord said that the hail should sweep away their refuge of lies and the flood would overflow their hiding place (Isa. 28:15–18; cf. also Ezek. 38:22). But once again, God's judgment upon wickedness and idolatry, demonstrating that a final end must eventually come, failed to change the hardened hearts of wicked men. Instead of repentance, "they blasphemed God because of the plague." Because of man's wickedness, God's judgments do not necessarily bring repentance.

These plagues did not introduce the final judgment; for after hail had killed whom it killed, there were those left who blasphemed God. The severest of divine judgments had now been poured out upon wicked and ungodly men, touching all phases and realms of Roman society and power. Only the final judgment, which would bring all men, nations, and wickedness to a total end, could surpass in intensity and finality judgments such as these.

CHAPTER 17
The Infamy and Fall of Babylon

The character and lot of two women and two cities occupy a prominent place in the second section of the book. Chapter twelve opened with the introduction of a woman arrayed with the sun, having the moon under her feet and a crown of stars upon her brow. She gave birth to a man child, the Christ, and was then forced to flee into the wilderness, where she was nurtured and protected. She had other children, those who kept the commandments of God and held the testimony of His Son. Now a second woman is introduced—a harlot, the direct opposite of the first—who is arrayed in all the embellishments of earthly splendor. She has on her forehead a name which identifies her as the mother of the harlots of the earth. Each woman is further identified as a city, the latter as the great city, Babylon, which holds sway over the kings of the earth who make war against the saints. The fall of Babylon has been introduced and now the nature of the city and its complete fall are enlarged upon. The first woman, arrayed in light, is identified as "the beloved city" (20:9), the holy city, New Jerusalem, "made ready as a bride adorned for her husband" (21:2). These two women, and the cities they personify, stand in direct antithesis to each other in character, position, and destiny.

In the comments on chapter twelve the woman was identified as the faithful remnant of God's people; she represented all His redeemed ones—His church or people in the broadest and most inclusive sense. In identifying the harlot, several positions have been proposed: (1) One view is that she symbolizes apostate Palestinian Jerusalem, the head of hostile Judaism (Wallace). (2) Another opinion is that she represents the apostate church which developed in the centuries following Pentecost. Some scholars narrow their application to the Roman Catholic church that developed to its present state; others enlarge the symbol to include all apostate groups, all faithless so-called "Christians." To these who hold the latter position, the figure describes the degenerate part of the church of God, the world in the church (Alford, Milligan,

Plummer, et al.). (3) A third view held is that the harlot symbolizes pagan Rome, which in turn represents the world of lust, all that is seductive, enticing, and appealing to the desires of the flesh and the mind (e.g., Caird, Pieters). For an excellent summary of the arguments made for the second and third views, see Pieters (pp. 250–261), who accepts the third position. The third view is preferred above the others.

Satan has three approaches by which he seeks to destroy the work and people of God: (1) Political or brute force, symbolized by the beast out of the sea; (2) false religion, whether paganism or perverted revealed religion—apostates who hold and teach false doctrines—symbolized by the beast out of the earth; and (3) the world of lust, all that appeals to the flesh or mind (Eph. 2:3; I John 2:15-17), represented by the harlot. Against these three the early church waged relentless war; and against these the saint of today must stand immovable and uncompromising. There may be less political force used today, but it continues to operate through political, economic, or social pressures brought to bear on the Christian's actions to turn him from Christ, or cause him to deny the faith.

This section (17:1—19:10) falls into three parts: (1) the harlot and her seductive wiles (chap. 17); (2) the judgment and fall of the harlot (chap. 18); and (3) the hallelujahs of heaven over her fall, and the victory of the saints (19:1-10).

THE BABYLON HARLOT IDENTIFIED
vv. 1-6

v. 1. "And there came one of the seven angels that had the seven bowls, and spake with me, saying, Come hither, I will show thee the judgment of the great harlot that sitteth upon many waters." It is inconsequential which of the seven angels rendered this service; if it had been of any significance the Lord would have revealed it. The angel would show John the judgment (Greek, *krima*), that is, the judicial verdict, the condemnation and punishment of the harlot (A. & G.). This subject occupies the next two chapters.

The great harlot is described as sitting upon many waters, which are "peoples, and multitudes, and nations, and tongues" (v. 15; see comments, 5:9). This metaphor rests upon Jeremiah's description of ancient Babylon's position, as he said, "O thou that dwellest upon many waters" (Jer. 51:13). Probably the prophet referred to the Euphrates river, with its canals, trenches, dykes, and marshes surrounding the city, giving it added protection and wealth. The waters on which the harlot of John's vision sits are symbolic of the nations and such over which she ruled, which stood between her and invading nations and that added greatly to her wealth. She is further described as "Babylon the great, the mother of the harlots and of the abominations of the earth" (v. 5); and as "the great city which reigneth over the kings of the earth" (v. 18).

As introduced above, does the harlot symbolize old apostate Jerusalem, apostasy within the church, or worldliness in all its seductions through lust? There can be little or no doubt that the Babylon of this section is Rome; and Rome itself is a symbol of the great world city of lust and seduction. In the Old Testament three cities are designated as harlots and another as a voluptuous mistress given to pleasure. Nineveh, the bloody city full of lies and rapine, is described as a "well-favored harlot, the mistress of witchcrafts," noted for "the multitude of her whoredoms" (Nah. 3:1, 4). By force, intrigue, and seduction she had conquered the world; she was the harlot of conquest.

Tyre, the harlot that for seventy years had been forgotten, would once again "play the harlot with all the kingdoms of the world" (Isa. 23:15-17); she was the great harlot of commerce. Babylon, a mistress of nations, cruel, and voluptuously given to the enjoyment of wealth and prosperity, would be mistress for ever (Isa. 47:5-15); she was the mistress of pleasure. A fourth city designated a harlot was Jerusalem, of whom Isaiah said, "How is the faithful city become a harlot!" (Isa. 1:21; cf. Jer. 2:20); Jerusalem was the great religious harlot.

Over and over Jeremiah, Ezekiel, Hosea, and Micah charged Israel and Judah with playing the harlot and committing spiritual whoredom. Because of this repeated charge by the prophets that Jerusalem and the two nations (Israel and Judah) constantly played the harlot, some have concluded that the harlot of John's vision is false or apostate religion. But this does not necessarily follow, for Israel's and Judah's playing the harlot was motivated by lust for material things and physical pleasure, "For thou hast played the harlot, departing from thy God; thou hast loved hire upon every grain-floor" (Hos. 9:1; cf. also 2:5, 12). As the beast out of the sea was a synthesis of the three great beasts before it, Babylon, Medo-Persia, and Macedonia (see comments, 13:2), so this harlot is a combination of the characteristics of the harlots of old: the conquest, rapine, and cruelty of Nineveh; the commerce of Tyre; the pleasures of Babylon; and the religious whoredom of Jerusalem. Truly, Rome was an adequate symbol of all that had gone before her.

v. 2. "With whom the kings of the earth committed fornication, and they that dwell in the earth were made drunken with the wine of her fornication." The kings of the earth are the world's rulers or great ones who committed political, economic, and religious whoredom with the harlot for the pleasures and rewards gained from such intercourse. They purchased her favors by promoting Rome's objectives and by yielding to her whims and fawning over her with flatteries and exaggerated deference. All classes of society were involved, both kings "and they that dwell in the earth," the subordinate citizens of the world who were intoxicated with the lusts that seduced them. "The wine of her fornication" was introduced earlier (14:8, see comments). Like those of whom Isaiah wrote, saying, "Take your pleasure, and be blind: they are drunken, but not with wine; they stagger, but not with strong drink" (Isa. 29:9), so these that dwell in the earth were drunken. But they were intoxicated with the strong drink of lust and the treacherous wine of power and conquest (cf. Hab. 2:5, 15).

v. 3. "And he carried me away in the Spirit into a wilderness: and I saw a woman sitting upon a scarlet-colored beast, full of names of blasphemy, having seven heads and ten horns." John began his visions of Jesus among the churches, and his view of the throne in heaven and its wonders, "in the Spirit" (1:10; 4:1, see comments). And now "in the Spirit," or "in Spirit" (the definite article is omitted in the original), John is carried away into a wilderness where he beholds the harlot and her destiny. The seer uses the same word (*apopherō*, "carried away") here and in 21:10 that Jesus used of the beggar who died and "was carried away by the angels into Abraham's bosom" (Luke 16:22). So, in this vision, under the power of the Holy Spirit, he was transported into the wilderness. (For a comparable experience, see Ezek. 8:3).

Because the woman arrayed with the sun was last seen in the wilderness (12:6, 14), and now the immoral woman is seen in a wilderness, some find evidence in this that the harlot represents the apostate element of the church that succumbed to the spirit of the beast and the false prophet. They contend that the church that went into the wilderness a pure virgin came out a harlot, or at least that the faithless play the harlot. However, this does not necessarily follow, for a wilderness may be a place of protection and discipline where God leads and provides, for "He [God] led forth his own people like sheep, and guided them in the wilderness like a flock" (Ps. 78:52).

God turns rivers into a wilderness, or vice versa, and turns "a wilderness into a pool of water" (Ps. 107:33, 35). "At my rebuke I dry up the sea, I make the rivers a wilderness: their fish stink, because there is no water, and die for thirst" (Isa. 50:2); but on the other hand, "Jehovah hath comforted Zion; he hath comforted all her waste places, and hath made her wilderness like Eden, and her desert like the garden of Jehovah; joy and gladness shall be found therein, thanksgiving and the voice of melody" (Isa. 51:3). In the time when the Messiah would be the shepherd and prince of His people, Jehovah would make a covenant of peace with them and cause the evil beasts to pass out of the land, "and they shall dwell securely in the wilderness, and sleep in the woods" (Ezek. 34:25f.). In contrast to this security and protection of His people in the wilderness of His provision, Nineveh would be "a desolation, and dry like the wilderness" (Zeph. 2:13); Babylon would be "the wilderness of the sea," the many waters on which she sat, for, "Fallen, fallen, is Babylon" (Isa. 21:1, 9); and Edom's heritage would be given "to the jackals of the wilderness" (Mal. 1:3). Therefore a wilderness may be a place of peace and protection of life, or it may be a place of desolation, drought, and the rubble of the ruin of centuries. The church is in the one place and the harlot in the other.

John saw the harlot "sitting upon a scarlet-colored beast, full of names of blasphemy, having seven heads and ten horns." There can be little doubt that this beast is the same as that which emerged from the sea (13:1). There are some differences, but the similarities overshadow them. Each has seven heads and ten horns, though they are mentioned in reverse order in the two accounts. Each has "names of blasphemy"; the first had these names on his heads, the second is "full of names of blasphemy." The names of blasphemy originated in the beast's mind, then permeated the whole empire until it festered under the rotting influence and blasphemy of emperor worship. The beast represents the Roman world empire, described as scarlet-colored, which supports the harlot, who is attired in scarlet (v. 4; 18:16). Scarlet was the symbol of luxury and splendor, providing a mark of distinction. Likewise, it was a color of royalty: they arrayed Jesus with a scarlet robe as they mocked Him, saying, "Hail, King of the Jews!" (Matt. 27:28f.). The harlot is thus arrayed in the splendor and royalty of the empire that supported her. Isaiah identifies scarlet as the sin color: "Though your sins be as scarlet, they shall be as white as snow" (Isa. 1:18). The scarlet of sin is opposite to the white of righteousness and purity.

v. 4. *"And the woman was arrayed in purple and scarlet, and decked with gold and precious stone and pearls, having in her hand a golden cup full of abominations, even the unclean things of her fornication."* The harlot makes herself as attractive as possible, bedecking herself in all the dazzling splendor of earth's riches. The colors purple and scarlet are slightly different, but when blended they represent royalty, luxury, and splendor. The harlot is adorned or gilded with gold, precious stones (jewels) and pearls, all that attracts attention, allures, impresses with a sense of seductive grandeur. She strives to cover her true harlot's character with the outward splendor and glory of a queen.

In her hand is a golden cup, another symbol of luxury and wealth, from which one would expect a pure and delightful drink. But instead, it is "full of abominations, even the unclean things of her fornication." These summarize the detestable things of her idol worship, her vices and corruptions which the world offers and by which it would seduce mankind. The world may serve its drink in a golden cup, but what it offers is abominable in the sight of God, and leads to degradation and death (Prov. 9:13–18). It contains all that appeals to the lust of the flesh, lust of the eyes, and pride of life, but it results in base and filthy consequences. Although Babylon offers the cup to the world, in turn she becomes a golden cup in the hand of God to madden the nations (Jer. 51:7). She holds in her hand the cup of her own self-destruction as the consequences of her sins are turned back upon her (cf. v. 16).

v. 5. *"And upon her forehead a name written,* MYSTERY, BABYLON

THE GREAT, THE MOTHER OF THE HARLOTS AND OF THE ABOMINATIONS OF THE EARTH." The name written upon her forehead announces to all who the woman actually is: she is the mother-harlot of all harlots and abominations of the earth. Is the word "mystery" a part of the woman's name, or does it suggest a "mysterious name"? It is probably a part of the name itself, indicating not something hidden but something made known; for whatever mystery may have enshrouded this woman is now openly exposed. A mystery conceals the true meaning of a thing from those who look only at the literal sense, but it is a medium of revelation to all who can and do properly interpret (see Matt. 13:11; Mark 4:11; Luke 8:10). Most often the word is used in the New Testament of God's scheme of redemption, hidden until revealed by the Holy Spirit (see Paul's use). Therefore the true character and identity of the woman, which she may have sought to keep concealed, are now to be clearly revealed.

The harlot is Babylon the Great (14:8; 16:19), which to John's readers would have symbolized Rome. But, as pointed out earlier, Rome in turn symbolizes the world of lust and seduction. Satan constantly strives to conceal the true nature and consequence of sin through lust. He appealed to Eve through the lust of the flesh, the lust of the eye, and the pride of life, but tried to conceal the consequence by saying, "Ye shall not surely die ... ye shall be as God, knowing good and evil" (Gen. 3:1–5). He approached Jesus through the same three avenues of lust, again trying to keep the consequence hidden, but without success (Matt. 4:1–11). He would seduce us through the same three avenues (I John 2:15–17), but leave unrevealed the corruption through lust (II Peter 1:4) and the ultimate wage of sin, which is death (Rom. 6:23). That which the harlot would keep hidden is now unmasked; she is indeed the mother-harlot of all seduction and everything detestable in the sight of God. Just as the harlot, stripped of sham and external covering, allows her true nature to be seen, so lust, without its hidden consequence, loses its intoxicating luster and appeal. Whatever form the whorish appeals of her daughters may assume, they go back to the mother-harlot—worldly lust—the true source of them all.

v. 6. "And I saw the woman drunken with the blood of the saints, and with the blood of the martyrs of Jesus. And when I saw her, I wondered with a great wonder." As John beholds the harlot astride the beast in the midst of the great wilderness, he has occasion to see her in her true light, without obstruction or distraction. While the earth-dwellers were drunk with the wine of her fornication, intoxicated with the enticements of lust, she herself was drunk with the blood of saints and martyrs of Jesus. The idea of drunkenness on the blood of men was not new; an unknown satirist had written of the emperor Tiberius,

> He is not thirsty for neat wine
> As he was thirsty then,
> But warm him up a tastier cup—
> The blood of murdered men.[1]

And so it could be said of the harlot. Later John writes, "In her was found the blood of prophets and of saints, and of all that have been slain upon the earth" (18:24).

In the harlot's intoxicating drink is the blood of martyrs who had offered their lives for Christ on the sacrificial altar, whether in the arena, under the sword, or on the fiery pile. They had been slain for the entertainment of the depraved and to sate the bloodthirstiness of their enemies. It had been lust for power, honor, prestige, wealth, and pleasure, together with hate, ill-will, self-will and malice—all seated in the flesh—that had led to the slaughter of God's people. All of these qualities are symbolized in the harlot. But do not her victims include more than the martyrs? Many saints in God's kingdom had fallen slain at her feet, victims of her wiles and their own weakness. The wise man said of the strange woman who flatters and seduces with her lips, that "her house inclineth to death; and her paths unto the dead" (Prov. 2:18); and in warning against the wiles of the harlot, he says, "Let not thy heart decline to her ways; go not astray in her paths. For she hath cast down many wounded: yea, all her slain are a mighty host" (Prov. 7:25f.).

When John saw the woman he said, "I wondered with a great wonder." He stood astonished, amazed at what he saw: a drunken harlot, arrayed in splendor, in a wilderness of desolation. We know not

---
[1] Seutonius, *The Twelve Caesars* (p. 138).

what the seer expected to see when invited to behold the judgment of the great harlot, but apparently he was not prepared for this.

EXPLANATION OF THE MYSTERY OF THE WOMAN AND THE BEAST
vv. 7-14

v. 7. "And the angel said unto me, Wherefore didst thou wonder? I will tell thee the mystery of the woman, and of the beast that carrieth her, which hath the seven heads and the ten horns." Something in the expression on John's face, or an exclamation from his lips, led the angel to ask why he wondered at what he saw. There was no censure in the angel's words, for the vision was intended to strike an emotional chord in the seer's mind; also, a part of the angel's mission was to explain the mystery to John. The woman and the beast are indivisible, for lust rides upon, controls, and governs any ravenous, persecuting, and self-seeking political beast. At the same time the beast supports such a harlot.

v. 8. "The beast that thou sawest was, and is not; and is about to come up out of the abyss, and to go into perdition. And they that dwell on the earth shall wonder, they whose name hath not been written in the book of life from the foundation of the world, when they behold the beast, how that he was, and is not, and shall come." This and the following three verses are perhaps the most difficult passage in the entire book to interpret. John seems now to identify the beast with the emperor, for the empire is personified in its emperor. It is the beast who authorizes the persecution of the saints on whose blood the harlot was drunk. In the discussion on the head that received the deathstroke and was healed (13:3, see comments), it was concluded that Nero had received the deathstroke, and his life was revived in Domitian. This thought is now enlarged upon. The abyss is the realm out of which the smoke and locusts came that had darkened the sun and air (9:1-3) and over which Satan rules (9:11). Also from this source emerged the beast who made war with the witnesses and overcame them (11:7); and out of this satanic realm the woes and persecutions of the saints originated.

In the place of one persecutor "who was, and is not," another arises from Satan's domain to take his place. But whoever he might be, however long he might abide, and whatever evil he might do, he is to go into perdition. "Perdition," *apōleia*, occurring in Revelation only here and in verse 11, means destruction or utter ruin, loss of well-being. The earth-dwellers are amazed at the beast's vitality—how he can enter the abyss of destruction, revive, and come forth in another form to continue his nefarious work. But the saints, whose names are in the book of life (see comments, 3:5; 13:8), are not amazed, for they understand that the beast is doomed; God's cause will be victorious.

vv. 9–11. *"Here is the mind that hath wisdom. The seven heads are seven mountains, on which the woman sitteth: and they are seven kings; the five are fallen, the one is, the other is not yet come; and when he cometh, he must continue a little while. And the beast that was, and is not, is himself also an eighth, and is of the seven; and he goeth into perdition."* The mind is composed of faculties for perception and understanding which, when combined with wisdom (the ability to discover the underlying meaning of things) provides the insight to John's revelation. James insists that if anyone lacks wisdom, "let him ask of God, who giveth to all liberally and upbraideth not; and it shall be given him" (James 1:5). However, this wisdom must come from insight into the revealed Word of God (I Cor. 2:6–8). Through understanding of God's purpose and His actions set forth in Scripture, one may hope to understand what God is revealing through the angel to John and to us. The angel says he will tell John the mystery; understanding must come from insight into what the angel says.

The angel continues, saying, "The seven heads are seven mountains, on which the woman sitteth." The seven hills bordering the Tiber on which Rome was built had long been the theme of Roman poets and writers (for examples, see Alford, pp. 109, 110; and Caird, p. 216). Rome would immediately come to the mind of John's readers. But the mountains had a symbolic meaning: "and they are seven kings." Alford contends that in reference to the woman (Rome), they are hills on which she sits; but in their reference to the beast they are kings. They are not to be thought of as seven individual kings or seven forms of government, but as a symbol of secular anti-Christian power (p. 710).

"The five are fallen, the one is, the other is not yet come, and when he cometh, he must continue a little while." The difficulty of the angel's meaning here is indicated by the diverse positions taken by commentators. Here are three of the more popular, and we might say, possible interpretations:

(1) William Hendriksen believes these are pagan kingdoms which have opposed God's kingdom and objective, beginning with Old Babylonia (Nimrod, Gen. 10:8–11) and continuing through Assyria (Nineveh), Neo-Babylonia (Babylon), Medo-Persia, and Greece-Macedonia; all of these perished and are no more. The sixth, "the one [which] is," refers to Rome. The seventh head is the collective title for all anti-Christian governments between the fall of Rome and the final empire of the Antichrist, which is the eighth in the days preceding Christ's second coming; all, however, go into perdition (pp. 203–205). William Milligan's interpretation is similar, but he begins with Egypt instead of the Old Babylonian empire, making Rome the sixth head, as does Hendriksen. The seventh is the ten horns which will occupy the place of the seventh head. On the eighth Milligan is not so clear, but he indicates that in it the beast reaches his highest attainment before the end of time (pp. 284, 285). It seems that the spirit which worked in these ancient kingdoms reaches its climax in Rome. The difficulty with this line of interpretation is with the seventh and eighth heads, which are not sufficiently explained in this interpretation.

Alfred Plummer sees in these kings reference to anti-theistic world powers who have come, who existed, and who would come; but he thinks it unwise to identify these as particular powers (p. 417). Henry Alford argues from the words *epesan*, "have passed away" and *epensen*, "the cry over Babylon herself" (from *piptō*, which means to perish, disappear, to pass off the scene, A. & G.). Alford says *epesan* "is a word belonging to domination overthrown, to glory ruined, to empire superseded." He follows this by pointing out that these are forms of empire, secular powers, violently overthrown and destroyed. The eighth king will be the embodiment of the beast who will meet his destruction at the hand of the Lord Himself (pp. 710, 711).

(2) Probably the most popular view is that the angel had specific Roman emperors in mind, five of which were fallen, one was then on the throne, and another was yet to come. However, there is no uni-

formity among those who hold this view as to where one should begin numbering emperors. Foy Wallace begins with Julius Caesar, making Nero the sixth. Wallace says, "Omitting quite properly the subordinates, or mock rulers, Domitian was the seventh Caesar." But were Vespasian and Titus, Otho and Vitellius mock rulers? They are not so considered by historians, for with Vespasian began the Flavian family; Titus and Domitian were his sons. Wallace seems to depart from the literal interpretation of the six rulers and interpret that which follows as figurative or symbolic, for he continues, "The seventh king, or emperor, *must continue a short space*—that is, the persecutions would not end with Nero, but would continue to be prosecuted in reigns of short duration of the successive emperors" (pp. 371, 372, italics his).

Schaff, Summers, Swete, et al., begin counting with Augustus Caesar, which makes Nero the fifth. They omit Galba, Otho, and Vitellius, who were "usurpers," and calculate Vespasian as the sixth, Titus as the seventh, and Domitian as the eighth. This would make Domitian a reincarnation of Nero, a view held by many ancient thinkers. According to Schaff, this would put the writing of Revelation early in A.D. 70, under Vespasian. But nothing in Vespasian's reign could have led to John's banishment to Patmos or his apprehension of a worldwide persecution. Swete accepts this listing of emperors, and admits that the vision would then belong to the reign of Vespasian (A.D. 69–79), but defends the date of the Apocalypse in Domitian's reign. He offers the following solution to the problem: "It is possible that in the vision of the Woman and The Beast he [John] purposely transfers himself in thought to the time of Vespasian, interpreting past events under the form of prophecy after the manner of apocalyptic writers" (p. 22f.). This appears to be a forced explanation, for there is no valid reason for such a flashback, transferring John back to Vespasian's reign. If it were not for a preponderance of evidence for the Domitian date (see Introduction, pp. 26ff.), the Neronean or Vespasian date might be acceptable; but neither of these suits the internal or external evidence.

(3) Probably the best solution to the problem is to adhere to the symbolic character of the book. Repeatedly John has used seven as the symbol for completeness or perfection, and ten for the fullness of

power. The seven churches in chapter 1 were not literally seven congregations; they represented the church in its fullness (see comments, 1:4). The same could be said of the seven spirits, the seven lamps, and so forth. When the book was read to the churches the members would have thought of Rome as they were told of the harlot, and of the empire when they heard of the beast on whom the harlot sat; in this their understanding would be correct. But the symbolism extends beyond this. The beast represented the total of forceful anti-Christian or anti-theistic opposition, and the harlot represented that which is lustful, enticing, and seductive—all that appeals to the flesh. The seven kings, therefore, were a symbolic number, representing all kings or kingdoms, past, present, and future that would oppose the kingdom of God. Each who would come would still be part of the seven. Although kingdoms arise out of the upheavals in the sea of society, their anti-God rulers originate in the abyss, the satanic realm. Each continues for a little while, then goes into perdition, which is the end of all who oppose God. This third view is preferable.

v. 12. *"And the ten horns that thou sawest are ten kings, who have received no kingdom as yet; but they receive authority as kings, with the beast, for one hour."* Again here is a symbolic number, ten being the number for power. These ten "have received no kingdom as yet," therefore they look to the future for their reign. Since these receive their authority "with the beast," there are two possibilities. It is possible that these are the kings who were to be gathered together to the war, called by the demon spirits of the dragon, the beast, and the false prophet (16:14). Or it may be that they symbolize the total future powers aligned with the beast, the total number of kings and small kingdoms that ally themselves with the world opposition to Christ. From this point of view they could symbolize the total of future powers which would unite themselves with the world opposition to the kingdom of God. The time period of these is relatively short—"for one hour"—a period signifying brevity. This phrase also occurs three times in the following chapter (18:10, 17, 19).

v. 13. *"These have one mind, and they give their power and authority unto the beast."* As the saints are to be perfected together in one mind and one spirit, with one soul, striving for the faith of the gospel

(I Cor. 1:10; Phil. 1:27), which mind is the mind of Christ (Phil. 2:5), so the beast and his associates are of one mind—the mind of the dragon. These with one accord give their power and authority to the beast in opposition to the Lamb.

v. 14. *"These shall war against the Lamb, and the Lamb shall overcome them, for he is Lord of lords, and King of kings; and they also shall overcome that are with him, called and chosen and faithful."* These ten kings who have subordinated themselves to the beast, together with the beast, shall war against the Lamb and His forces. These kings have been called to the war (16:14), and when they shall receive their kingdom (v. 12), they shall war against the Lamb, but will be completely defeated (19:19ff.). The dragon has sought the destruction of the Lamb from the beginning (12:4). All opponents of the Lamb are doomed to defeat, however, for when the dragon was cast down (12:7-10) all authority and power were given to the Lamb (Matt. 28:18), and all things were put in subjection under His feet (Eph. 1:20-23; I Peter 3:22).

Jehovah led Israel as "God of gods, and Lord of lords" (Deut. 10:17); He received this acknowledgment by the pagan ruler, Nebuchadnezzar (Dan. 2:47), and was so revered in the New Testament (I Tim. 6:15). As the divine Son of God, the Lamb now assumes this title "Lord of lords, and King of kings," for Himself (cf. 19:16). These kings and lords are not the saints, as thought by some, though saints are identified with royalty (Heb. 2:12; I Peter 2:9). They are, rather, the lords and kings of the earth who war against Him, for He is "the ruler of the kings of the earth" (1:5); He is King of the earthly kings. Not only shall He be victorious in this war, but His followers, identified as "called and chosen and faithful," shall share in the triumph. These had been called by God through the invitation of the gospel (Matt. 22:1-13; II Thess. 2:14), "chosen" (from *eklektos*, "picked out, or chosen") as God's own (Eph. 1:4); they are "the few chosen" (Matt. 22:14). The victory of the chosen was to the "faithful," those who "follow the Lamb whithersoever he goeth . . . and in [whose] mouth was found no lie: they are without blemish" (14:4f.). Also, they overcome because of the blood of the Lamb and the word of their testimony. They love not their life even unto death (12:11). This is what it means to be with Him.

FURTHER IDENTIFICATION OF THE HARLOT
vv. 15-18

v. 15. "*And he saith unto me, The waters which thou sawest, where the harlot sitteth, are peoples, and multitudes, and nations, and tongues.*" Though she was introduced as "sitting upon many waters" (v. 1), when John saw the harlot she was sitting upon the scarlet-colored beast (v. 3). The angel next explains that the many waters represent the empire and the many ethnic groups and nationalities over which Rome held sway (cf. 5:9; 13:7). A major weakness of Rome was its inability to amalgamate the diverse peoples into one. Rome could conquer and control by force, but it had no cohesive power with which to cement the conquered into a homogeneous kingdom. This weakness had been revealed in a dream to Nebuchadnezzar, when he saw the fourth great empire to come, the Roman, as "part iron and part clay, so the kingdom shall be partly strong, and partly broken... and they shall not cleave one to another, even as iron doth not mingle with clay" (Dan. 2:42f.).

v. 16. "*And the ten horns which thou sawest, and the beast, these shall hate the harlot, and shall make her desolate and naked, and shall eat her flesh, and shall burn her utterly with fire.*" The ten horns—the future kings or kingdoms which would arise—that would join themselves to the world power (see comments, v. 12) would hate the harlot. Love among men or nations has often turned to hatred as intense as the affection it replaced. This change would result in the destruction of the harlot; she would be made desolate, stripped of her grandeur and wealth, her flesh eaten and consumed, and her remains destroyed by burning with fire. This is an example of evil's self-destruction. The principle of love being corrupted to lust and turning to hate, which in turn destroys, can be illustrated by nations today. As long as nations can get what they want from one another, they continue to commit economic and political fornication. But actually, nations and states hate all government, which is being destroyed by greed and lust. And so it is with individuals. First, allured by the world, they commit fornication with her. Then, realizing their delusion, they hate what they have done, but too late—they are irrevocably lost and destroyed.

Such metaphors of nakedness and cannibalism are not unknown in Scripture. Jehovah said of Nineveh, "I will uncover thy skirts upon thy face; and I will show the nations thy nakedness, and the kingdoms thy shame" (Nah. 3:5); Nineveh would be laid waste with none to mourn her fall. The figure of cannibalism is vividly expressed through Micah when Jehovah condemned the wicked destroyers of His remnant, calling them those "who pluck off their skin from off them, and their flesh from off their bones; who also eat the flesh...flay their skin...break their bones, and chop them to pieces, as for the pot, and as flesh within the caldron" (Mic. 3:2f.).

v. 17. *"For God did put in their hearts to do his mind, and to come to one mind, and to give their kingdom unto the beast, until the words of God should be accomplished."* To ask how God "put it in their hearts to do his mind" is futile; this is known only to Him. Scripture clearly reveals that throughout history God used men and nations to carry out His purpose. He could turn a nation to fighting within itself, as in the case of Midian during the time of Gideon (Judg. 7:22), and of the Philistines in the days of Saul (I Sam. 14:20). In the battle of Moab and Ammon against Mount Sier, God gave victory to King Jehoshaphat without Judah's army lifting a sword (II Chron. 20:23). God's objective in putting it in their (the kings') hearts to come to one mind was that His words of judgment against the harlot should be accomplished. Not a word failed—all came to pass.

v. 18. *"And the woman whom thou sawest is the great city, which reigneth over the kings of the earth."* If there remains any doubt concerning the identity of the woman, Babylon, the harlot (vv. 3, 7), that uncertainty should now be removed. She is not the apostate church, in spite of the influence and power the apostate church has exercised at different periods in history; she is Rome, the mistress of nations. However, Rome symbolizes the world-city, envisioned by Isaiah, set forth in a world of spiritual desolation, and revealed in her fullness to John (see comments, 11:8). She symbolizes the world of lust, seduction, and the allurements of all that appeals to the flesh.

The church has had two great enemies and one rival for the affection which is rightfully hers. The enemies who sought her destruction were the beast out of the sea (i.e., the world of power that would crush and trample under foot) and the beast out of the earth (i.e., false religion that demanded worship at her shrine). The rival, who was also an enemy, is the world which tries to entice and persuade her to commit spiritual fornication.

CHAPTER 18
The Fall of the Harlot

HEAVEN'S DECREE: "FALLEN IS BABYLON"
vv. 1-8

v. 1. "After these things I saw another angel coming down out of heaven, having great authority; and the earth was lightened with his glory." "After these things" does not indicate a period of hours, weeks, or years, but simply a sequence in the revelation. The harlot has been identified as Rome, the symbol of lust and seduction (chap. 17). Now God prepares to reveal the total collapse of the harlot, spiritual Babylon, the great world-city of pride, lust, and corruption. One of the seven angels had shown John the harlot in the wilderness; now another angel, apparently not one of the seven, came down from heaven with a special message of the harlot's judgment and destruction. The angel is described as having great authority, the right and power to act. He is to announce the sentence against Babylon and to disclose its divine execution. At the angel's descent the earth was "lightened with his glory," indicating his greatness and the greatness of his mission.

v. 2. "And he cried with a mighty voice, saying, Fallen, fallen is Babylon the great, and is become a habitation of demons, and a hold of every unclean spirit, and a hold of every unclean and hateful bird." In anticipation of what was destined to come, the fall of Babylon had been announced in earlier visions (14:8; 16:19). In a "mighty" or strong voice, corresponding to the solemnity, importance, and magnitude of his message and mission, the angel announces the future fall of the great world-city as if it were already accomplished. John does not see or describe the actual fall, but assures the saints of its certainty. Instead of being the glorious city that ruled as mistress of nations, clothed in worldly splendor, enticing and seducing kings of the earth, she would become a habitation for demons (see comments, 9:20; 16:14), and a prison for unclean spirits and hateful birds.

A century and a half before the fall of ancient Babylon, Jehovah had said to Isaiah as the prophet looked from his watchtower, "Fallen, fallen, is Babylon; and all the graven images of her gods are broken unto the ground" (Isa. 21:9). The overthrow would be like that of Sodom and Gomorrah; it would never be inhabited, but would become a dwelling place for wild beasts of the desert, and of doleful creatures, wild goats, wolves, and jackals, which were symbols of the spirit of her idol worship; it would be swept "with the broom of destruction" (Isa. 13:19–22; 14:3–23; cf. Jer. 50:2). Likewise Rome, symbol of the world-city of lust, would become desolate; a "hold," that is, a place of guarding, a prison for detention; foul and gruesome, where the demons, unclean spirits, and every hateful or detestable bird would dwell. These would haunt the temples of idolatry and the fallen glory of the world. Such a prison of unclean spirits stands in contrast to the holy city into which nothing unclean or abominable shall enter (21:27).

v. 3. *"For by the wine of the wrath of her fornication all the nations are fallen; and the kings of the earth committed fornication with her, and the merchants of the earth waxed rich by the power of her wantonness."* (For "the wine of the wrath of her fornication," see comments, 14:8; 17:2). The nations of earth which followed her lascivious ways and yielded to her seductive practices, committing political fornication with her to gain power and prestige, were destroyed by the passionate lust of her lewdness. The angel now explains the fornication more fully. It was an unholy, idolatrous political and economic alliance of kings for business and commercial advantage, through which their pleasures were purchased.

Such connections and associations are seen all over the world today as men seek to gain wealth by immoral, avaricious, and unscrupulous means. Great businesses built on such principles are involved in armaments and munitions deals, including unethical pacts among nations. Internal corruption of a nation is expressed in pornographic movies, magazines, and lewd entertainment, which prey on the depravity of human beings. Underworld establishments of prostitution, gambling, and narcotics make up only a portion of the world of corrupt, anti-God, destructive forces, which thrive on lust.

Introduced for the first time are merchants whose involvement is discussed later (vv. 11, 15). These with the earth's great were made wealthy by the seductive power and influence which belong to riches, "ministering to luxury" and unrestrained desire.

v. 4. *"And I heard another voice from heaven, saying, Come forth, my people, out of her, that ye have no fellowship with her sins, and that ye receive not of her plagues."* Although the source of the voice is not disclosed, it was either directly from the Lord or from an angel representing Him; the voice speaks for God and addresses the people as "my people." This call to "come forth" out of sinful fellowship had been heard many times in the past by God's people. Abraham had been called to get out of Haran and from among his kindred (Gen. 12:1-3); Lot was urged to flee from Sodom, a doomed city (Gen. 19:12, 17); Israel was called to leave Egypt (Exod. 3:10); over and over the captives in Chaldea were exhorted to "go ye forth from Babylon" (Isa. 48:20; 52:11), for "Babylon is suddenly fallen and destroyed" (Jer. 50:8; 51:6, 8); and "My people, go ye out of the midst of her, and save yourselves every man from the fierce anger of Jehovah" (Jer. 51:45). In writing to the saints in the midst of an idolatrous society, the apostle Paul charged the Corinthians, "Wherefore, Come ye out from among them, and be ye separate, saith the Lord, and touch no unclean thing; and I will receive you ... saith the Lord Almighty" (II Cor. 6:17). They were to cleanse themselves "from all defilement of flesh and spirit, perfecting holiness in the fear of God (7:1).

The call of the voice John heard was not instruction to leave the city of physical Rome, for wherever one goes he is amidst people of the world. To suggest literal, physical Rome is to miss the point. The exhortation is to come out from the influence of worldly lust so that there is no partaking of the sins of the world and the flesh. As Paul expressed it, "Have no fellowship with the unfruitful works of darkness, but rather even reprove them" (Eph. 5:11). A complete separation of the Christian from the sins of the world and the corruption in the world by lust is absolutely essential if he is to escape the plagues to be poured out into the earth and upon the harlot city, Babylon.

v. 5. *"For her sins have reached even unto heaven, and God hath remembered her iniquities."* In His longsuffering God allows man to continue in his own way until his sins have reached an intolerable point of saturation; then judgment falls. The phrase used by Amos,

"For three transgressions, yea for four" (Amos 2, 3), expresses the idea. The rage of Israel against Judah "reached up unto heaven" (II Chron. 28:9); the judgment of Babylon reached "unto heaven," and was "lifted up even to the skies" (Jer. 51:9); and the iniquities and guilt of the Jews had "grown up unto the heavens" (Ezra 9:6). Iniquity piles upon iniquity until it becomes a stench in the nostrils of God—it reaches unto heaven. When this point is reached, then "the cup of the wine of the fierceness of his wrath" (16:19) is given into the hand of the offender. One wonders, How long until America's sins shall reach unto heaven, and the cup of the wine of the fierceness of His wrath is passed to it?

v. 6. "Render unto her even as she rendered, and double unto her the double according to her works: in the cup which she mingled, mingle unto her double." Who is to "render unto her, even as she rendered"? Surely not "my people," the saints, for the Lord had forbidden them to execute such vengeance (Rom. 12:17, 19). Probably the ones called to carry out the execution as retaliators are those of 17:16f., in whose heart God had put the disposition to do His mind. As this spiritual Babylon had rendered, so now it would be rendered unto her. She was responsible for woe and destruction in the earth; now that same woe and destruction would fall upon her. As she had sown, so would she reap. The saints exiled in ancient Babylon had cried out, "O daughters of Babylon, that art to be destroyed, Happy shall he be that rewardeth thee as thou hast served us" (Ps. 137:8). Jeremiah said of the same ancient captor, "It is the vengeance of Jehovah: take vengeance upon her; as she hath done, do unto her" (Jer. 50:15, 29).

Although there were some crimes in the Old Testament law that demanded double indemnity (Exod. 22:4, 7, 9), it is doubtful if the exhortation to "double unto her the double" indicates twice the punishment that the crime merited or called for. This expression, "the double," occurs numerous times in writings of the prophets: Isaiah said of Judah, "she hath received of Jehovah's hand double for her sins" (Isa. 40:2); and in their joy over deliverance from their enemies, it was said, "Ye shall have double; and instead of dishonor they shall rejoice in their portion: therefore in their land they shall possess double; everlasting joy shall be upon them" (Isa. 61:7; cf. Jer. 16:18; 17:18; Zech. 9:12). The idea expressed by the phrase indicates a balancing of the scales; on the one hand, punishment commensurate with guilt, and on the other, joy in proportion to the shame and dishonor commuted. The measure of Babylon's sin was the measure of her punishment.

"In the cup which she mingled, mingle unto her double"; that which she had prepared for and passed to others and by which she had made them drunken (v. 3), would now be hers. In the cup of "the wine of the wrath of her fornication" which she had given to the nations, there would be mingled a commensurate measure of "the wine of the fierceness of his [God's] wrath" (16:19). It would be a judgment to balance the scales: iniquity on one side of the scales and judgment on the other.

v. 7. *"How much soever she glorified herself, and waxed wanton, so much give her of torment and mourning: for she saith in her heart, I sit a queen, and am no widow, and shall in no wise see mourning."* This confirms the thought indicated in verse 6, "How much soever... so much give." The judgment is to be compatible with the sin; the scales of justice are balanced. In her arrogance the harlot had glorified herself and grown wanton, living luxuriously on the delicacies of earth (v. 3). Jeremiah pointed out that this had been the sin of ancient Babylon who had "sinned against Jehovah" (Jer. 50:14), striving against Him (v. 24), "for she hath been proud against Jehovah, against the Holy One of Israel" (v. 29). She had oppressed God's people (v. 33); Babylon was "a land of graven images, and they are mad over idols" (v. 38). Does not this adequately describe Rome, the harlot of John's vision, the enemy of God's people? Now comes the retribution: torment is meted out to her who is the cause, and mourning comes as the consequence.

To her self-glorification and wantonness, the harlot Babylon added arrogant boasting and pride. She said in her heart, she boasted within herself: (1) "I sit a queen, (2) and am no widow, and (3) shall in no wise see mourning." She was indeed no widow, but a harlot with many illicit lovers. Further, she boasted that she would not see the very thing God said she would see. David had long since sung, "Thine eyes are upon the haughty, that thou mayest bring them down" (II Sam. 22:28). And Solomon had said, "When pride cometh, then cometh shame" (Prov. 11:2); also, "Pride goeth before destruction, and a haughty spirit before a fall" (16:18); and again, "A man's pride shall bring him low; but he that is of a lowly spirit shall obtain honor"

(29:23). The harlot's boast is reminiscent of the boasting of old Babylon who said, "I shall be mistress for ever... I am and there is none besides me; I shall not sit as a widow, neither shall I know the loss of children" (Isa. 47:7f.). Jehovah charged Tyre with having made a similar boast, saying, "Because thy heart is lifted up, and thou hast said, I am a god, I sit in the seat of God, in the midst of the seas; yet thou art man, and not God, though thou didst set thy heart as the heart of God" (Ezek. 28:2). Each of these boasting harlots of ancient times had been brought low, coming to naught at Jehovah's hand; and so would the present Babylon, and all that would come after.

v. 8. *"Therefore in one day shall her plagues come, death, and mourning, and famine; and she shall be utterly burned with fire; for strong is the Lord God who judged her."* "Therefore" introduces the consequence of the harlot's boast, which revealed her character. Because of her vaunting, these plagues would come suddenly upon her. Isaiah's description of Babylon and her arrogant vainglory seems still to be in the prophet's mind: "But these two things shall come upon thee in a moment in one day, the loss of children, and widowhood; in their full measure shall they come upon thee" (Isa. 47:9; cf. also Ezekiel on Tyre, Ezek. 26:16). However, as Alford aptly suggests, "The judgments here are more fearful: death, for her scorn of the prospect of widowhood; mourning, for her inordinate rebelling; famine, for her abundance" (p. 716). Where affluence and gaiety once held sway these three (death, mourning, and famine) would now prevail. The end comes to the great city, followed by mourning over the death and famine from the economic collapse, for "she shall be utterly burned with fire"—totally destroyed (17:16). The guarantee of this end rests on the character and power of God, "for strong is the Lord God who judged her." The God who can create can surely control, for even "the weakness of God is stronger than men" (I Cor. 1:25).

LAMENT OF THE EARTHLINGS OVER BABYLON
vv. 9-19

vv. 9–10. *"And the kings of the earth, who committed fornication and lived wantonly with her, shall weep and wail over her, when they look upon the smoke of her burning, standing afar off for the fear of her torment, saying, Woe, woe, the great city, Babylon, the strong city! for in one hour is thy judgment come."* The earth-dwellers who looked to the harlot city for their trade and wealth are thrown into consternation and weeping at the burning of the prostitute. The mourners fall into three categories: the kings (vv. 9-10), the merchants (vv. 11-17a.), and the shipmasters and seamen (vv. 17b.-19). The petty kings and great ones of the empire who had enjoyed wealth, luxury, and pleasure through their whoring with the harlot, weep at her destruction—even though they hated her. They weep (*klaiō*), giving vent to loud expressions of grief, and wail (*kaptō*), beating their breasts as a token of anguish because of her fall. Helplessly they look upon the smoke of her burning, but keep themselves at a distance. They dare not draw too near because they fear the torment; they console themselves with empty lamentation and mourning. Like so much of the world with selfish sorrows and tears, these kings mourn their own loss, not because Babylon herself has fallen.

"Woe, woe," is an interjection of grief for "the great city, Babylon, the strong city." It was great as the world counts greatness, and strong enough to withstand a forcible assault, but it was no match for the Lord God who judged her. As in 17:12, "one hour" indicates brevity and suddenness—in a brief moment her judgment had come.

vv. 11-13. "*And the merchants of the earth weep and mourn over her, for no man buyeth their merchandise any more; merchandise of gold, and silver, and precious stone, and pearls, and fine linen, and purple, and silk, and scarlet; and all thyine wood, and every vessel of ivory, and every vessel made of most precious wood, and of brass, and iron, and marble; and cinnamon, and spice, and incense, and ointment, and frankincense, and wine, and oil, and fine flour, and wheat, and cattle, and sheep; and merchandise of horses and chariots and slaves; and souls of men.*" The merchandise described in these verses is analogous to or modeled after Ezekiel's description of the fall of Tyre, which the student should pause and read (Ezek. 26:1—28:19). The merchants (introduced, v. 3) follow the kings in their lamentation; their cause for weeping is even more selfish than that of the kings, for their source of revenue and riches is now gone. "Merchants" (from *emporos*) indicates wholesalers rather than retailers or petty merchants.

"Merchandise" (from *gomos*) occurs only here (vv. 11, 12) and in Acts 21:3, and in each instance it refers to the burden or cargo of a ship. These merchants were put in the position of having cargo and nowhere to sell it. Rome was the center of trade; roads from all countries of the world led to the great emporia of trade at Ostia, the chief seaport of the city, and Puteoli, the seaport for cargos of grain. No doubt "the merchants of the earth" may be extended to include all who traffic heavily in a corrupt or anti-Christian spirit.

In verse 12 there follows a list of the items of merchandise which consists primarily of the luxuries of life. Only a few of these require special attention. Purple and scarlet were the colors of royalty and luxury, and were the colors in which the harlot was arrayed (17:4). Silk came from the far east, probably China, indicating the extent of Roman trade. Tacitus says that in the days of Tiberius two men introduced a measure in the senate, in which "it was decided that vessels of solid gold should not be made for the serving of food, and that men should not disgrace themselves with silken cloth from the east" (*Annals* 2:33 [p. 70]). Of course this situation changed with the passing of time, giving way to the excessive luxury which contributed to Rome's downfall. Thyine wood was an aromatic wood of beautiful texture, imported from North Africa and prized for its aroma and as a resource for making fine furniture. "Every vessel," or article, made from ivory would include either boxes or small sculptures or ivory inlaid furniture of larger size. The "most precious wood" of which vessels were made is not known.

In verse 13 it is thought that the cinnamon came from south China rather than from Ceylon. It was known to the Jews as early as the exodus from Egypt, being used by them in making incense and perfume. Probably they learned of it in the land of their bondage (Exod. 30:23; Prov. 7:17; Song of Sol. 4:14). "And spice" (from *amōmon*), was a spice from India, from which was made a perfume or ointment popular with the Romans. "And incense, and ointment, and frankincense," all went to satiate the senses of the luxury-loving Romans. Many of the items of food listed next were used for the finest banquets of wealthy Romans, and for sacrifices to the gods. "And merchandise of horses and chariots and slaves," went to satisfy the vanity of the worldly empire. The word "horse" occurs fifteen times in the

Apocalypse; in this instance the importing and exporting of horses for military use seems to be indicated, for the Roman military included cavalry (cf. Acts 23:23, 32). However, these may have been horses to draw the wagons or carriages that are introduced next. The chariot (*rhedē*) denotes a four-wheeled wagon or carriage, while a second word (*harma*, 9:9; Acts 8:28, 29, 38) indicates a two-wheeled war chariot. Slaves (*sōmatōn*, literally, "bodies"), and souls (*psuchos*, literally, "lives") of men, may mean, "slaves, even the lives of men." The slave market was widespread throughout the empire. Slaves were a household commodity, being used in all aspects of social life and as gladiators in the arena for the amusement of a depraved people.

v. 14. "And the fruits which thy soul lusted after are gone from thee, and all things that were dainty and sumptuous are perished from thee, and men shall find them no more at all." This verse, and the ones just commented on, clearly indicate that this harlot is not a religious symbol but a representation of worldliness and lust. However, it is certainly true that the worldly ones in the church who lose sight of the true relationship to God, and lust after the things of the flesh, will suffer along with the world. The word *opōra*, translated "fruit," occurs only here in the New Testament and means ripe or juicy fruit which is found in the late summer or fall of the year. At that season, when the harlot lusts for the ripe fruit to fall into her mouth as in time past, she will find that it is gone from her.

That which was dainty (*liparos*, found only here in Scripture) was rich, luxurious, and costly. It was also "sumptuous," from *lampros*, meaning bright and shiny, radiant; in this case it means living in splendor. Probably before the seer's mind are the choice foods and the furniture and clothing of splendor with which Babylon, the harlot, adorned herself. These are perished and gone for ever; never again shall she live as in the past. What about the United States, which has been a land of plenty and great abundance? It has taken much for granted, wasting and squandering its resources. Is it approaching a time when it shall reach for the great abundance bestowed upon it by God, and find it gone for ever? It is doubtful if there is any other consequence.

v. 15. "The merchants of these things, who were made rich by her, shall stand afar off for the fear of her torment, weeping and mourning." John next returns to the merchants described in verse 11. As with the kings, so with the merchants: they were interested only in the gain derived from their fornication with the harlot. These also stood afar off, helpless to save and fearful of intervening; they could only weep and mourn. And as it was with the kings, their grief is selfish; they mourn because of their own loss.

v. 16. *"Saying, Woe, woe, the great city, she that was arrayed in fine linen and purple and scarlet, and decked with gold and precious stone and pearl!"* The lamentation of the merchants is similar to that of the kings, but with this difference: the kings saw her as both the great and "the strong city" (v. 11). To them she was impregnable, indestructible, destined to endure; the merchants saw her as "the great city," clothed in splendor and ruling in luxury—a continuing market for their merchandise. Their description of Babylon is harmonious with the description in 17:4, confirming again the identity of the two. She is arrayed and "gilded" with all that the merchants have to sell (v. 12), and by which her seductiveness was enhanced. With her fall their market is gone, causing their grief.

v. 17. *"For in one hour so great riches is made desolate. And every shipmaster, and every one that saileth any whither, and mariners, and as many as gain their living by sea, stood afar off."* The suddenness of Babylon's collapse (v. 10) is again emphasized. Several new groups are introduced: "every shipmaster" (the word is used only here and Acts 27:11) describe the pilots or helmsmen, the sailing masters of the ship. Next are those who travel in ships, whether as passengers or those who accompany their cargo. The mariners or seamen (from *nautic*, translated "sailors" in Acts 27:27, 30), those who operate the ships, are the next category. And finally, as many as "work the sea" (a literal translation of the Greek), describe those whose living comes from the sea, including shipbuilders, fishermen, or divers for pearls. All nautical life, industry, and trade are affected by the fall of the great city. As did the kings and merchants, so these also stand afar off (See Ezek. 27:27 for a similar description). In 13:1 the sea is a symbol for the mass of society generally. But in this instance the sea appears to be the lanes of commerce by which the great city was supplied with luxuries gathered from all parts of the world.

v. 18. *"And cried out as they looked upon the smoke of her burning, saying, What city is like the great city?"* As the smoke of her burning billowed heavenward, it left a heavy pall over the empire. The seamen and shipmasters ask, "What city is like the great city?" There was none to compare with her. In the same way the people had lamented over Tyre, saying, "Who is there like Tyre, like her that is brought to silence in the midst of the sea?" (Ezek. 27:32).

v. 19. "And they cast dust on their heads, and cried, weeping and mourning, saying, Woe, woe, the great city, wherein all that had their ships in the sea were made rich by reason of her costliness! for in one hour is she made desolate." The casting of dust upon one's head had long been a symbol of grief and lamentation among the orientals (cf. Job 2:12). A similar demonstration had been made over Tyre's fall; as seamen lament, and "cause their voice to be heard over thee [Tyre], and shall cry bitterly, and shall cast up dust upon their heads" (Ezek. 27:30). The seamen add their cry, "Woe, woe," to that of the kings (v. 10) and merchants (v. 15). But as Barclay observes, "There is something almost pathetic in all these laments," for they lament not over the fall of Rome, but over that "wherein all that had their ships in the sea were made rich by reason of her costliness! for in one hour is she made desolate." Their grief was in truth selfish; they were thinking of themselves, not of the destruction of Rome.

Trade and commerce of themselves are not wicked; they are good when used for the welfare of humanity. However, when used for selfish luxury and the gratifying of fleshly lusts, they become unrighteous, profane, and wicked. As Blackwood so aptly said of Tyre, "Like the uprooted vine that generated the self-consuming fire (Ezek. 19:14), a culture that worships commercial success will strike the sparks that ultimately will burn it to ashes" (Blackwood, p. 186).

THE VOICE OF REJOICING
v. 20

v. 20. "Rejoice over her, thou heaven, and ye saints, and ye apostles, and ye prophets; for God hath judged your judgment on her." In the midst of the mourning, wailing, and lamentation of the earth-dwellers over the fall of this spiritual Babylon, there is an exhortation to the people of God to rejoice. This is not an expression of glee over the fall of a great city or people, but a rejoicing over the defeat of evil and the victory of righteousness. In this instance to rejoice is to make merry because of gladness (cf. Luke 15:23, 24, 29, 32). The earth-dwellers made merry over the death of the two witnesses (11:10), but the tables have been turned. The heavens and they that dwell in them had been called upon to rejoice at the casting down of Satan, although woe would be the fate of the sea and earth (12:12). That woe upon the earth and sea had now been experienced and judged.

The interest of the heavens continues, and they now rejoice with the saints in their victory. Included in the rejoicing are saints, apostles, and prophets, in contrast to the mourning of kings, merchants, and seamen. These who rejoice had together fought a bitter battle against the enemy. The apostles are not mentioned with the prophets in 16:6 and 18:24, where the blood of saints and prophets is said to have been poured out in slaughter. God has now pronounced their judgment upon the harlot; that is, he has rendered judgment on their behalf— "God has imposed on her the sentence she passed on you" (Caird, p. 238. cf. also Deut. 19:16–19). The church has been avenged upon her great enemy and rival, the world, and justice has been fully rendered to that great destroyer of mankind.

THE SILENCE OF THE TOMB
vv. 21-24

v. 21. "And a strong angel took up a stone as it were a great millstone and cast it into the sea, saying, Thus with a mighty fall shall Babylon, the great city, be cast down, and shall be found no more at all." The rejoicing of heaven and the saints over God's judgment against Babylon is followed by a symbolic act, representing the complete and final judgment against the harlot-city. This is the third time "a strong angel" has been mentioned; there was one at the introduction of the sealed scroll (5:2) and another at the presentation of the little scroll (10:1). Someone has called this third angel "the angel of the consummation." The stone which the angel hurled into the sea, is "as it were, a great millstone," which stands in contrast to the small hand mill operated by women. As a millstone cast to the bottom of the sea, never to be seen again, shall Babylon be cast down, to be "found no more at all." Though on a grander scale, this scene is reminiscent of Jeremiah's instruction to Seraiah to read the words of Babylon's judgment in the ears of the people, then to tie a stone to the scroll "and cast it into the midst of the Euphrates: and thou shalt say, Thus shall Babylon sink, and shall not rise again because of the evil that I will bring upon her" (Jer. 51:61–64). The destruction of the imperial city of John's day would be as complete as was that of the ancient Babylon in Jeremiah's time.

v. 22. *"And the voice of harpers and minstrels and flute-players and trumpeters shall be heard no more at all in thee; and no craftsman, of whatsoever craft, shall be found any more at all in thee; and the voice of a mill shall be heard no more at all in thee."* John emphasizes the silence and inactivity of the harlot city as he is shown five aspects of normal life now completely extinct. All is as quiet and motionless as ancient Babylon and the tomb in which the millstone lies buried.

(1) The sound of musical instruments, symbols of joy and gladness (Luke 15:25), of revelry (Amos 6:5–7), or, as in the Old Testament, associated with religious services (II Chron. 29:25), is now silenced. The word *phōnē* (voice) is most often used of the human or a heavenly voice; but it is also used of "the voice" or sound of the wind (John 3:8), "the sound of a trumpet" (Matt. 24:31), and "the voice" of musical instruments (I Cor. 14:7f.). So here the voice or sound of the musicians—harpers, flute players, and trumpeters—seems to be the sound of the instruments themselves, and not the singing of the players. However, the word "minstrel" (from *mousikos*) denoted one "devoted to and skilled in the arts sacred to the muses; skilled in music" (Thayer), and may have included other instruments and also singers.

(2) "And no craftsman of whatsoever craft, shall be found any more at all in thee," for all business has vanished with the fall of Babylon. Forever gone is the whirr of the loom, the ring of the anvil, the resounding echo of the hammer, the shouts of animal-drivers and the voice of hawkers announcing their wares.

(3) "And the voice of the mill," so essential to the sustaining of life as the grain for bread is ground, "shall be heard no more at all in thee." All business life of the once thriving metropolis is now stilled and deathlike; it is as silent as the tomb.

v. 23. *"And the light of a lamp shall shine no more at all in thee; and the voice of the bridegroom and of the bride shall be heard no more at all in thee: for thy merchants were the princes of the earth; for with thy sorcery were all the nations deceived."*

(4) There seems to be no evidence that the streets of ancient Rome were lighted after dark, but the houses of the wealthy seem to have been abundantly illuminated. Tacitus describes one of Nero's extravagant banquets on a specially built raft for Agrippa's lake, then adds, "As darkness approached, all the adjacent grove and surrounding buildings resounded with song, and shone brilliantly with lights" (*Annals* 15.37 [p. 376]). He also says that in persecuting Christians, some were "doomed to the flames, and burnt to serve as a nightly illumination, when the daylight expired. Nero offered his gardens for the spectacle... while he mingled with the people in the dress of a charioteer or stood aloft on a car" (Annals 15.44 [p. 381]). Not only shall the candlelight in the homes of the poor, "shine no more at all" in the great city but also the lights and extravaganzas of the rich shall be extinguished for ever.

(5) And finally, the merriment of the wedding festival, with its music, song, and torches of the night celebration, shall be heard and seen no more, for the harlot city is dead and the silence of the tomb enshrines her.

The seer next offers two reasons for the desolation which had come upon this modern Babylon: (1) Her merchants had made the accumulation of wealth and its luxuries their goal in life. In doing this they had provided themselves with incentive to deception and avarice for the harlot's greatness. (2) And with her sorceries—deceptions—the harlot had caused all the earth to drink of the cup of the wine of her fornication. She had deceived, enticed, and seduced by her magic wiles and influence to bring all under her power. Sweet makes a pertinent evaluation of her misuse of influence and wealth when he says, "Babylon has been submerged in her own greatness, for her greatness has been used to bewitch and mislead the world, and not to raise and purify it." After using her power, influence, and material wealth to an evil end, "all nations had learnt to adopt her false standards of life and worship" (p. 241). This criticism could also be made of the United States; through America's traffic with the world during the past few decades, the peoples of earth have adopted her false standards and worship of the material instead of being raised and purified.

v. 24. *"And in her was found the blood of prophets and of saints, and of all that have been slain upon the earth."* Immediately we think of the blood of the saints that had been poured out in the arenas of Rome and her provinces to satiate the blood-thirst of the heathen. But John's summary seems to go far beyond this. Since Rome is a spiritual symbol, representing the world of lust and seduction, his statement, "all that have been slain upon the earth," takes on an enlarged meaning. For it was in this world-city that all God's people, from Adam to the present, have been killed. Some had been slain by those of the world who had received the mark of the beast and had worshiped his image, pouring out the blood of saints and prophets (16:2, 6). But apart from this there was also that great host who had succumbed to the harlot's wiles, and who, through their own weakness and uncrucified lust, had fallen dead at her feet. And now, through the cumulation of guilt, her fall has come. Chapters 17 and 18 set forth the subtlety of Satan's appeal to the flesh, emphasizing the uncertainty of riches and the ruinous end of worldly lust. John's exhortation and warning are eminently appropriate at this point, "Love not the world, neither the things that are in the world. . . . For all that is in the world, the lust of the flesh and the lust of the eyes and the vainglory of life, is not of the Father, but is of the world. And the world passeth away, and the lust thereof: but he that doeth the will of God abideth for ever" (I John 2:15-17).

CHAPTER 19

Victory

HALLELUJAHS OF VICTORY
vv. 1-10

The first ten verses of this chapter conclude the theme of the harlot's fall and judgment (chaps. 17, 18), and should be included as a part of that section. Several times John has introduced a future event, then detailed the actual happening later; for example, the fall of Babylon was first mentioned in an angel's message (14:8), but occurred and was related afterward (chap. 18). Heaven and the saints had been exhorted to rejoice over the harlot's fall in 18:20, whereas the active rejoicing is now portrayed in the great outbursts of hallelujahs over the triumph and victory of righteousness and the defeat and destruction of evil.

vv. 1, 2. *"After these things I heard as it were a great voice of a great multitude in heaven, saying, Hallelujah; Salvation, and glory, and power, belong to our God: for true and righteous are his judgments; for he hath judged the great harlot, her that corrupted the earth with her fornication, and he hath avenged the blood of his servants at her hand."* "After these things" focuses attention on the events which followed the revealing of the harlot and her seductive wiles (chap. 17) and the judgment which befell her (chap. 18). The rejoicing stands in bold contrast to the helpless weeping and wailing of the kings, merchants, and mariners who mourned the fall and destruction of the great harlot city. The first voice John heard is that of "a great multitude in heaven," which probably was the voice of the victorious multitude that had triumphed in the great tribulation and was before the throne singing the praise of God and the Lamb (7:9ff.). Those in the multitude now respond to the charge, given them in 18:20, to rejoice in the judgment rendered unto Babylon on their behalf.

"Hallelujah," occurring in the New Testament only in this scene (vv. 1, 3, 4, 6), is a transliteration of the Hebrew phrase, "Praise ye Jah [Jehovah]." It occurs at the beginning and at the conclusion of

373

numerous psalms, commencing with Psalm 104. The multitude in Revelation gives praise unto God for "*the* salvation, and *the* glory, and *the* power"; in the original the definite article appears before each noun, thereby giving to each a definitive emphasis (cf. 12:10). "The salvation" is that which God has provided for the redeemed; "the glory" ascribes honor and praise to Him for salvation; and "the power" acknowledges the mighty strength and omnipotence by which He rules His universe. He is able to save His own and to bring the world opposition to nought. These "belong to *our* God," thus identifying the multitude as a united body in Him.

Hoti, "for" or "because" introduces cause or reason for the praise: "for true and righteous are thy judgments," they are genuine and just, proceeding from and based upon the character of God (cf. 15:3; 16:7). A second reason is offered: "for he hath judged the great harlot." Thus the righteous and just character of God, who executed the judgment, and the nature of the judgment itself, form the basis of their rejoicing. This judgment was introduced at and continued from the message of the several angels (14:7f.), and it had now been executed. The harlot's crime was that she had "corrupted the earth with her fornication." To corrupt (from *phtheirō*) means to destroy by bringing to a state of moral decay, effected by "the lusts of deceit" (Eph. 4:22). A form of the same word is used in 11:18 and is translated "destroy": the time came "to destroy them that destroy the earth."

The earth, the whole realm of the unregenerated, had been affected by the power of lust by which the harlot deceived and enticed to moral decay. The souls underneath the altar, who had been "slain for the word of God, and for the testimony which they held," had cried for an avenging of their blood upon them that dwell on the earth (6:9f.). These were probably part of the great multitude coming out of the great tribulation and were among those before the throne (7:14f.). In this true and righteous judgment "He hath avenged the blood of his servants at her hand," the blood of those beneath the altar. The petition of the martyrs beneath the altar is now answered and their cause is vindicated. The world of lust and deceit has received its death blow.

v. 3. "*And a second time they say, Hallelujah. And her smoke goeth up for ever and ever.*" With this second hallelujah, the multitude concluded the shout of praise as they had begun it. As suggested above, a number of the psalms begin and end with "Praise ye Jehovah," or "Hallelujah." Miriam had introduced this pattern as she began her psalm of praise, saying, "I will sing unto Jehovah," and concluded it with an exhortation to the people, "Sing ye to Jehovah" (Exod. 15:1, 21).

As the smoke of the torment of those who worship the beast and his image goes up for ever and ever (14:10f.), so also ascends the smoke of the destroyed Babylon (see comments, 14:11; also cf. 18:9), whose destruction is complete and final; never again shall she arise to taunt and destroy.

v. 4. "And the four and twenty elders and the four living creatures fell down and worshipped God that sitteth on the throne, saying, Amen; Hallelujah." A second group, the twenty-four elders and the four living creatures, add their expression of homage to Him who sits on the throne as they fall prostrate before Him shouting, "Hallelujah!" At the last mention of these in the second group (14:3) they were before the throne (see comments, 4:4, 6, 8). From the time the angels were given the seven bowls of wrath, no one was able to enter the sanctuary of Jehovah's presence until the seven plagues were completed (15:8). These had been finished (16:17), and now again the throne and those who stand before it come into view. The marvelous creatures and elders before the throne can add only their "Amen" (Be it so!) and their "Hallelujah" to what is being said.

v. 5. "And a voice came forth from the throne, saying, Give praise to our God, all ye his servants, ye that fear him, the small and the great." As on several other occasions, the voice from the throne is anonymous. It is neither God nor Christ, for the call is to give praise to "our God." Although Christ included Himself with men as the Son of man and is not ashamed to call the redeemed His brethren (Heb. 2:11f.), He is distinctly different from all men. His relation to God and men is emphasized throughout the Gospels; it was "my Father and your Father," and "my God and your God" (John 20:17).

The throne, from which the voice came, symbolized the majesty and power of Him who sat upon it. The address is to "his servants," His bondservants or slaves who had been purchased unto Him. Except for Moses (15:3), the Old Testament prophets (10:7; 11:18), and those who shall serve Him beyond the judgment (22:3), whenever God's servants are mentioned in this book, they are upon the earth. It was to them that John was to show the revelation of the things shortly to come to pass (1:1; 22:6); they were the ones threatened by the teaching of Jezebel in Thyatira (2:20), and the ones sealed upon the earth (7:3). From this it may be concluded that the exhortation of the voice is to the church on earth, all who fear His name, with no class or intellectual distinctions, "the small and the great." If this is true then the three groups who shout the hallelujahs are (1) the redeemed in heaven, (2) the living creatures and elders, and (3) the saints on earth.

v. 6. "*And I heard as it were the voice of a great multitude, and as the voice of many waters, and as the voice of mighty thunders, saying, Hallelujah: for the Lord our God, the Almighty, reigneth.*" John never lets his readers lose sight of the fact that what is seen and heard is in a vision; this is emphasized by the word *as*. The voice was *as* the tremendous cry of a great multitude, which was *as* the awesome roar of a mighty tumbling cataract, *as* the peal of rolling thunder with its vibrations and reverberations. Those in the multitude add their hallelujahs to the shout of the redeemed in heaven, the living creatures, the elders, and the saints on earth. The Lord has been praised because of His judgment of the harlot and the avenging of the saints (v. 2); now He is praised for His glorious reign. He is "the Almighty," a word which occurs ten times in the New Testament, once in II Corinthians 6:18 (a quotation from the Old Testament) and nine times in Revelation. The word denotes sovereignty over all creation (see comments, 4:8). In spite of all the opposing forces, God is always in control over His universe. Through His infinite power and might He has exercised these in bringing to pass His divine will and purpose.

v. 7. "*Let us rejoice and be exceeding glad, and let us give the glory unto him: for the marriage of the Lamb is come, and his wife hath made herself ready.*" Two women have already been introduced: the radiant woman (chap. 12) and the harlot (chap. 17). Now a third is designated the wife of the Lamb. She is the radiant woman under this new symbol, and her appearance gives fresh cause for rejoicing. With the removal of the harlot, the great enemy and rival of the church, the marriage of the Lamb has come; therefore let the saints "rejoice and be exceeding glad." This phrase occurs only one other time in Scripture, which these rejoicing seem to have in mind. When Jesus told His disciples of persecutions and false reproaches which would come against them, He said, "Rejoice, and be exceeding glad: for great is your reward in heaven" (Matt. 5:12). These are entering into that joy and gladness promised by their Lord as they anticipate the coming event. In the midst of this rejoicing, the redeemed acknowledge the source of their blessing as the object of their praise. "And let us give the glory unto him," for it was through His sovereignty and complete control of His universe that their victory had been won.

In the Old Testament the relation of Jehovah to His people is often referred to as a marriage or as a husband and wife relationship (Hos. 2; Isa. 50:1; Jer. 2:32; Ezek. 16, et al.). It is quite natural, therefore, that the close relation of Christ and the church should be expressed in this same sacred analogy. However, understanding of this passage rests upon an understanding of the Hebrew custom of betrothal and marriage. Mary, who had been "betrothed to Joseph," was with child by the Holy Spirit "before they came together" (Matt. 1:18); but Joseph was told, "Fear not to take unto thee Mary thy wife" (v. 20). Wherefore Joseph obeyed the Lord's command, "and took unto him his wife" (v. 24). The word "betrothed" (from *mnesteuō*, which occurs only here and in Luke 1:27; 2:5), means "to be promised in marriage, to be betrothed" (Thayer), "to become engaged" (A. & G.). From the Hebrew point of view being engaged or promised in marriage was much more sacred and binding than in our society. Although they had not come together, Mary was called Joseph's wife in her period of betrothal. The custom of a marriage feast is set forth in Jesus' parable of the king who gave such a feast for his son (Matt. 22:1-14); the time lapse between the arrangement for marriage and the wedding feast itself is indicated in the parable of the ten virgins (Matt. 25:1-13).

It is clearly revealed in Scripture that the church's relationship to Christ is that of a wife (Eph. 5:22ff.; Rom. 7:4), but in the same way that Mary was betrothed to Joseph before they came together (Matt. 1:18). Objection to this view may be offered on the ground of Paul's statement that we are joined to Christ "that we may bring forth fruit to God" (Rom. 7:4). This objection assumes that the fruit is offspring, which the text does not support. As Whiteside observes, "Verse 6 shows that the bearing of fruit is done in serving God in newness of the spirit." It is the fruit of righteousness (cf. Rom. 6:20-22; Gal.

5:22). Paul wrote, "I espoused you to one husband, that I might present you as a pure virgin to Christ" (II Cor. 11:2); and Christ gave Himself up for the church, that He might present it "to himself a glorious church" (Eph. 5:27). The word espoused (from *armoxō*) means "to join, to fit together... or betroth, to give one in marriage to any one" (Thayer). So then, when viewed in light of the Hebrew custom of marriage, the church is now espoused or betrothed to Christ as His wife, as was Mary to Joseph, preparing herself for the marriage supper which is to come (v. 9).

v. 8. *"And it was given unto her that she should array herself in fine linen, bright and pure: for the fine linen is the righteous acts of the saints."* The phrase "it was given unto her," occurs over and over in the book (some twenty times) and indicates that God has given the saints the power and responsibility to make proper preparation. Even so, the church's response is voluntary. The attire of the wife is presented in sharp contrast to that of the harlot. The harlot is arrayed in all the gaudy, sensuous apparel of the world, intending to seduce by worldly splendor; the wife is to array herself "in fine linen, bright and pure." "Fine linen" (*bussinos*) occurs only in Revelation (see comments, 15:6). Bright (*lampros*) and pure (*katharos*) indicate that the fine linen is shining, radiant, and clean, "not having spot or wrinkle or any such thing, but... holy and without blemish" (Eph. 5:27); "for the fine linen is the righteous acts of the saints." The white robe is not Christ's righteousness imputed to the saints, but their own righteous acts and life in Him; the individual saints thus combine to make up the bride. In the parable of the wedding feast prepared by the king, the man who came in without a wedding garment was without excuse for his appearance and was therefore speechless (Matt. 22:12). In Christ God has made provision for the bride's attire, "For we are his workmanship, created in Christ Jesus for good works, which God afore prepared that we should walk in them" (Eph. 2:10). These righteous works or acts involve the whole of the saints' spirit, conduct, and life by which they develop the character that God demands.

v. 9. *"And he saith unto me, Write, Blessed are they that are bidden to the marriage supper of the Lamb. And he saith unto me, These are true words of God."* The speaker's identity is once again undisclosed. He instructs John to write, and the fourth beatitude follows. Some think the speaker is the angel who invited the apostle to come and see the judgment of the harlot (17:1), or the angel who had announced the fall of Babylon (18:1ff.). Others think he is either the unidentified voice from heaven (18:4), or from the throne (19:5). Since a voice from heaven instructed John to write the beatitude concerning those who die in the Lord (14:13), it is possible that the present voice is the one from the throne. This voice called upon the servants to give praise to God (v. 5), and thus in this beatitude is advancing a step further. The ones bidden to the marriage supper are those called by the gospel into fellowship with Christ (I Cor. 1:9; II Thess. 2:14; see comments, 14:6f.); it follows that the bride is composed of the individual guests who respond to the invitation of the gospel.

The supper or wedding scene itself is not described. As the seer had introduced the fall of Babylon in 14:8, but reserved the description of the fall to chapter 18, so here the Lord speaks of the feast as if it is taking place, but reserves the revealing of the actual occasion until chapter 21. The speaker concludes, saying, "These are true words of God"; they are absolutely genuine and can be relied upon. The speaker is not only referring to the beatitude just spoken, but is also placing the seal of divine assurance upon the entire section, 17:1—19:9, where a climax of the book is reached. The word is a true word; but this does not mean that one must look for literalism in the fulfillment, for, as Swete points out, apocalyptic visions have their own method of expression and laws of fulfillment.

v. 10. *"And I fell down before his feet to worship him. And he saith unto me, See thou do it not: I am a fellow-servant with thee and with thy brethren that hold the testimony of Jesus: worship God: for the testimony of Jesus is the spirit of prophecy."* We are surprised at John's action in response to the speaker's words. Was John confused as to who the speaker was, thinking possibly it was Christ Himself? Or was he so overwhelmed by the awesomeness of the whole scene that impulsively he fell at the speaker's feet as an act of homage? Surely he would not have willfully worshiped an angel; there must be some other explanation. Writers have proposed both views suggested above, but there is no definite answer to the question—though something can be learned from the use God made of the incident. The speaker responded, "See thou do it not," an emphatic negative. Surprisingly, John repeated the act at the conclusion of the complete revelation (22:8f.); and again he is told, "Do it not." It might be concluded that as the seer had been fighting idolatry so vigorously, God is revealing the subtlety of mistaken identity of the true object of worship and of truth. By these two occasions He is warning the church against idolatry's insidiousness, that it be on guard from within lest the worship of things other than God lead the saints astray.

The speaker offers a valid reason for not accepting worship when he announces that he is a fellow-servant (*sundoulos*, "fellow-slave") with John and with his brethren that hold the testimony of Jesus. Those underneath the altar were identified as fellow-servants with others who were yet to be killed (6:11). The speaker is not only a fellow-servant with John, but also with his "brethren who hold the testimony of Jesus" (cf. 12:17). This reasoning led Lenski to suggest the possibility that the speaker is one of God's saints now on the throne with Jesus (3:21), and can speak from the throne, exhorting the church to praise God (19:5), thus identifying himself with John (p. 546). The point merits consideration. The testimony of Jesus is that truth to which He bore witness (John 18:37), which was the word given to Him from God (John 8:28; 12:47; 14:24; Rev. 1:1, et al.). This testimony borne by Him must be held faithfully by all disciples.

"Worship God," is a terse command reminiscent of Jesus' reply to Satan, "Thou shall worship the Lord thy God, and him only shalt thou serve" (Matt. 4:10). Of course Jesus is also to be worshiped, for He, too, is God, and accepted worship as God (John 9:35-38). "For the testimony of Jesus is the spirit of prophecy"; that is, the testimony of Jesus is the life-principle of prophecy. Although it is true that the testimony of Jesus is the spirit of all prophecy previous to John's, here the phrase has likely reference only to the prophecy of this book; He is its very breath of life (cf. 1:3; 22:18).

THE WARRIOR-KING: DEFEAT OF THE TWO BEASTS
vv. 11–21

Though the harlot has been destroyed, there remain the two great enemies of God and man: the beast and false prophet along with their leader, Satan. Their destruction is now at hand. The enemies of God and His church were introduced in the visions in the following order: Satan (chap. 12), the beast out of the sea and the beast out of the earth (chap. 13), and the harlot (chap. 17). Their defeat and destruction are now revealed in reverse order: the harlot (chap. 18), the beast and the false prophet (chap. 19), and finally, Satan himself (chap. 20). Since they all stood together, they now must fall together. Satan is the only personal being in the group; the two beasts and the harlot are symbolic personifications of anti-God power, false religion, and seductive lusts of the flesh, the instrumentalities used by Satan in the war against God and His kingdom. The scene described in this section reveals the warrior-king as He conducts the war against His enemies, engaging them in a decisive battle. This is not a description of Jesus' "second" or final coming, but of the victorious war against the forces that have been under discussion.

A. The Warrior-King Revealed, vv. 11-16

v. 11. "*And I saw the heaven opened; and behold, a white horse, and he that sat thereon called Faithful and True; and in righteousness he doth judge and make war.*" Early in his visions John saw "a door opened in heaven" through which he had been caught up to behold the heavenly scene (4:1); later "there was opened the temple of God that is in heaven," that he might behold the ark of God's covenant (11:19); afterward "the temple of the tabernacle of the testimony in heaven was opened," from which came the seven angels with the seven bowls of wrath (15:5). Now John beholds the entire heaven opened so that the warrior-king and His army might be seen as they emerge to do battle with Satan's forces. The rider of the white horse can be none other than Christ, for this is clearly revealed in His name, "Faithful and True" (see comments, 1:5; 3:14). As God's faithful and true witness He has given to man a complete revelation of the Father, of truth, and of His divine purpose; and now not a jot nor tittle of that word or purpose shall fail: all shall come to pass (Matt. 24:35; I Peter 1:25).

Some writers interpret the white horse and its rider (introduced at 6:2) to have been victorious militarism. But there is no valid reason for making the first horse and rider symbolic of imperial militarism and this second the Christ. He is the rider in both instances, though in the two visions He is seen under different circumstances and with different objectives. In the earlier vision the rider wore a victory crown (*stephanos*), symbolic of victory over Satan and death. Following that victory He went forth in the gospel "conquering and to conquer" (6:2), to conquer the souls of men, making them citizens of His kingdom (see comments). Now He is seen in a different role, as in righteousness He judges and makes war against all who would hinder His purpose and destroy His kingdom; He brings each enemy to defeat and destruction. The horse's color, white, indicates purity and holiness; the rider's judgment is in righteousness, as are all His judgments (Rom. 2:5; Rev. 15:3; 16:7; 19:2). In His final appearance Jesus will come to judge and reward, not to wage war with His enemies. Therefore the judgment and battle in this vision are against the enemy forces in time, not at the end of time.

v. 12. *"And his eyes are a flame of fire, and upon his head are many diadems; and he hath a name written which no one knoweth but he himself."* "His eyes are a flame of fire" further identifies the rider as the Son of man (cf. 1:14; 2:18), who looks with burning penetration into the hearts of His enemies. He judges not the outward appearance of men but has a clear insight into character. "On his head are many diadems," or royal bands, symbols of royalty and sovereign rule (for *diadem*, see comments, 12:3). Satan wore seven diadems and the sea-beast wore ten, whereas Jesus wears "many," a great number, indicating the broad, unlimited extent of His rule.

Much has been written about "his name written which no one knoweth but he himself," but any effort to determine what the name is remains futile. One's name stands for all that he is, and only he can know his true self. The overcomer is given a new name, "which no one knoweth but he that receiveth it" (2:17). The angel that wrestled with Jacob left his name unrevealed to the patriarch (Gen. 32:29), as did the angel to Manoah (Judg. 13:18). The name may possibly indicate the inner relationship of Jesus to the Father and to redemption and victory, a relationship beyond our comprehension but known to Himself, "for no one knoweth the Son save the Father" (Matt. 11:27). Swete offers an excellent summary of the matter when he says, "Notwithstanding the dogmatic helps which the church offers, the mind fails to grasp the inmost significance of the Person of Christ, which eludes all efforts to bring it within the terms of human knowledge. Only the Son of God can understand the mystery of His own Being" (p. 252).

v. 13. *"And he is arrayed in a garment sprinkled with blood: and his name is called The Word of God."* The rider is further described as being "arrayed in a garment sprinkled with blood." Some of the older authorities render, "dipped in blood," but probably "sprinkled" is preferable. Because the treading of the winepress by the king-judge does not occur until verse 15, the question is raised whether John intends to give two accounts of the same event (v. 13 and v. 15), and if not, why does this description precede the active treading of the winepress? Several proposals have been offered in explanation of the blood-sprinkled garment being introduced before the account of the winepress: (1) "It is possible that there is here a reference to the blood of Christ himself, which he shed in his warfare with Satan" (Plummer); (2) "The Rider bears on his garment the indelible traces of the death of his followers, just as he bears on his body the indelible marks of his own passion (1:7; cf. John 20:20-27)" (Caird); (3) the phrase "makes us think of the blood of Christ shed in expiation: the Saviour is the Judge, John 5:27" (Lenski). A more probable explanation is offered below.

Already a gory judgment has been described in which the winepress was trodden outside the city and blood covered the land (14:20). The scene depicted here of the blood-sprinkled garment is reminiscent of the one in which Jehovah was returning from Bozrah with His garments stained with blood. In response to the question posed, "Wherefore art thou red in thine apparel, and thy garments like him that treadeth in the winevat?" Jehovah replied, "I have trodden the winepress alone.... I trod them in mine anger, and trampled them in my wrath; and their lifeblood is sprinkled upon my garments, and I have stained all my raiment" (Isa. 63:1-6; cf. also Joel 3:9-13). His garment was sprinkled with His enemies' blood when He tread the winepress. This parallel leads to the conclusion that the blood sprinkled upon the Rider's garment is that of His enemies and not His own or that of His own people who had died for His cause. In spite of the problem raised over the separation of the two phrases, the explanation based on Isaiah 63 is preferable because the theme of the chapter is war and judgment, not redemption *per se*.

"And his name is called The Word of God." This name is recorded only by John. In his Gospel John looks back to the incarnation, as "the Word" which was with God in the beginning "became flesh" (John 1:1, 14); and in his first epistle John refers to the Lord as "the Word of life," which He is to all at present (I John 1:1). In Revelation John looks to the destruction of evil forces at that time, and ultimately to the end of time. As "The Word of God," Jesus is the ultimate revelation of God and of His will; He is the guarantee that God's purpose will be achieved.

v. 14. "*And the armies which are in heaven followed him upon white horses, clothed in fine linen, white and pure.*" An army (*strateuma*) may be of any size, from a small detachment of soldiers serving as a bodyguard (Acts 23:10, 27) to a massive company of "twice ten thousand times ten thousand" (9:16). The "armies which are in heaven" (plural) is "the army" (singular) engaged in the war (19:19). Two views are suggested of the armies in the heaven: First, they are the great host of heavenly beings who minister unto Jehovah (Dan. 7:10). Jesus said that He could call more than twelve legions of them to His aid (Matt. 27:53); He will bring them with Him when He comes in judgment (Matt. 25:31; Mark 8:38; Luke 9:26; II Thess. 1:7).

A second view is that these are the victorious saints whom the Lord leads in the defeat and overthrow of His enemies. It was said that they who would overcome would be arrayed in white garments (3:5); the martyrs underneath the altar each had a white robe (6:11); and those standing before the throne, who had come out of the great tribulation, were also arrayed in white robes (7:9, 14). As was the bride who had prepared herself for the marriage (v. 8), these of the army who follow Him are arrayed in "fine linen" (*bussinos*) which is white and pure, indicating identity with those mentioned above.

Furthermore, the war now to be fought is not at His final coming, for there is to be no war then; all will be over. It is the war introduced earlier, though not described (16:14–16). It seems therefore that this army is the "called and chosen and faithful" who overcome with the king (17:14). The picture symbolizes a divine judgment and a spiritual war directed from heaven, led by a heavenly warrior-king. It is fought by a host of pure and faithful warriors, whose citizenship is in heaven (Phil. 3:20), and whose names are written there (Luke 10:20)—the faithful saints of God.

v. 15. "*And out of his mouth proceedeth a sharp sword, that with it he should smite the nations: and he shall rule them with a rod of iron: and he treadeth the winepress of the fierceness of the wrath of God, the Almighty.*" The sharp sword which proceeds out of His mouth is not the word of the gospel by which men are converted, but the sword or word of judgment. This sword out of His mouth was a characteristic description of the glorified Christ (1:16; [2:12]). With it He would make war against the unfaithful in the church (2:16), and in a far greater judgment he would smite the heathen nations and their idolatry. His rule over the nations with a rod of iron fulfilled the prediction of the psalmist, "Thou shalt break them with a rod of iron; thou shalt dash them in pieces like a potter's vessel" (Ps. 2:9). It also fulfilled Isaiah's prophecy, "And he shall smite the earth with the rod of his mouth" (Isa. 11:4), and the vision of the birth and rule of the man child (12:5). The three—armies, sword, and rod—are punitive in their nature, destroying by divine judgment, reducing to chaff, burning, and carrying away (Dan. 2:35; 7:9–12). The treading of the winepress has been introduced earlier, indicating a full and terrible judgment (see comments, 14:19f.). Isaiah 63:1–6 and Joel 3:12–14 serve as a basis for interpretation of the winepress as a severe judgment and of the blood-sprinkled garment of the king (v. 13).

Since the worshipers of the beast and his image and the harlot Babylon would have to drink the wine of the wrath of God (14:10; 16:19), the treading of the winepress of His wrath may well symbolize the preparing of that wine which they must drink. In either case, whether it symbolizes the judgment itself or the preparation of the wine of His wrath which they must drink, a terrible destructive judgment is indicated. It is the warrior-king who judges, makes war, and treads the winepress of the wrath of God the Almighty, indicating His complete sovereignty in all realms (see comments, 4:8).

v. 16. "*And he hath on his garment and on his thigh a name written,* KING OF KINGS, AND LORD OF LORDS." The Lord has a name known only to Himself, and is known to the saints as "Faithful and True" and the "Word of God"; but to all, friend or enemy, He is known as "King of Kings, and Lord of Lords," "the ruler of the kings of the earth" (1:5), for He is conqueror of all. This title is assigned to the Lamb in 17:14, and here is given in transposed order, but there is no apparent significance to this change. Just how this name was "on his garment and on his thigh" is not clear; probably it appeared on that part of His war garment which covered the thigh. In any event, the point is that it was in a conspicuous place where it could be clearly seen and recognized by all.

B. The Angel's call to "The Great Supper of God," vv. 17-18

vv. 17, 18. "And I saw an angel standing in the sun; and he cried with a loud voice, saying to all the birds that fly in mid heaven, Come and be gathered together unto the great supper of God; that ye may eat the flesh of kings, and the flesh of captains, and the flesh of mighty men, and the flesh of horses and of them that sit thereon, and the flesh of all men, both free and bond, and small and great." The hour of decision has come! In the great battle between the faith and paganism, the victory of the Lamb is to be complete and final. A lone angel (Greek, "one angel") stands "in the sun," a place suiting the importance of his mission, where he can be clearly seen and heard by all. His loud voice cries to all carrion-eating birds of mid-heaven to come and be filled at the supper which God provides (for comments on "mid heaven," see 14:6). Similar pictures of gory sacrificial meals occur frequently in the Old Testament prophets (cf. Isa. 34:6; Jer. 46:10; Ezek. 39:17-20). This one stands in contrast to the marriage supper of the Lamb (v. 9). To interpret this scene literally is to completely miss the purpose of the book; the picture is a vivid symbolic portrayal of the defeat of the Lamb's enemies. The war and the victory are spiritual, as defeat comes to the spiritual forces of evil.

The symbolism finds a parallel in Ezekiel's vision of God's destruction of Gog and Magog, the heathen forces of old, which were antagonistic to God, His people, and His purpose (Ezek. 38—39; for a fuller discussion, see comments, 20:7-10). Ezekiel was to call "birds of every sort" and "every beast of the field" to Jehovah's sacrifice of the heathen. At His table these were to "eat the flesh of the mighty, and drink the blood" of horses, mighty men, and men of war (Ezek. 39:17-20). The supper of John's vision was comprised of (1) "the flesh of kings, and the flesh of captains"—*chiliarchs*, military leaders who were over a thousand men; (2) "the flesh of mighty men," the great of earth, and of horses and horsemen; and (3) "the flesh of all men, both free and bond, the small and great." In this war the devil recruits from every walk of life; he has some of all these of earth in his army. There are no barriers or limitations except righteousness. There is no middle ground; every one is either on one side or the other in this conflict. "He that is not with me is against me; and he that gathereth not with me scattereth" (Matt. 12:30). One group is destined for victory, the other for destruction in the lake of fire.

C. The Decisive Battle and Defeat of Evil, vv. 19-21

v. 19. "And I saw the beast, and the kings of the earth, and their armies, gathered together to make war against Him that sat upon the horse, and against His army." The beast is the great heathen world power of that day, the Roman Empire, which dominated the world and oppressed the saints (13:1-10). In league with the dragon and the false prophet, the beast had called the kings of the world together to the great decisive battle of Har-Magedon (16:13-16). These kings aligned themselves with the beast to make war against the Lamb and His followers (17:12-14), but no battle was described. For the third time these are revealed with their armies (plural) to make war against the warrior-king and His army (singular), but again no battle; only the outcome is described. It seems clear that we have now come to the actual battle of Har-Magedon which is fought to decide who is the King of Kings—Christ, or world-caesars and potentates.

v. 20. "And the beast was taken, and with him the false prophet that wrought the signs in his sight, wherewith he deceived them that had received the mark of the beast and them that worshipped his image: they two were cast alive into the lake of fire that burneth with brimstone." The battle still is not described; only results are announced. The false prophet is the beast that came up out of the earth; he is associated with, backed by, and used by the beast out of the sea (13:11-18). The signs wrought in the sight of the sea-beast to deceive the heathen worshipers

(13:13f.; 19:20) and cause them to be identified (marked) as emperor worshipers (13:16f.; 14:9, 11; 16:2; 19:20; 20:4) confirm that the false prophet and the earth-beast are the same. These "two were cast alive into the lake of fire that burneth with brimstone," where the harlot had already met her fate, being "utterly burned with fire" (17:16; 18:8, 9, 18; for "brimstone," see comments, 9:17).

Because of the expression, "cast alive," some writers have concluded that these two are literally individuals who will appear in person before the end of time. But this does not necessarily follow; for "being cast alive into the lake" indicates that up to the actual time when they were cast into the lake of brimstone and were brought to final destruction by His mighty power and judgment, these two personified forces of political and spiritual power were actively fighting against the Lamb. The Roman Empire and emperor worship backed by the imperial power were now brought to a final and complete end, never to rise again.

v. 21. *"And the rest were killed with the sword of him that sat upon the horse, even the sword which came forth out of his mouth: and all the birds were filled with their flesh."* "The rest" are the kings and their hosts of individuals who make up the armies of verse 19. These are destined to be tormented in the lake of fire and brimstone (14:9f.), but they are not cast there until the final judgment (20:15). These were slain by the sword of Him who sat upon the white horse, even by a judgment from the King.

The victory is won, and the defeat of the beast and his ally, the false prophet, is complete. The Roman power and the paganism which it supported are now destroyed forever. The vision of Daniel is fulfilled (Dan. 7:11), and in this defeat and destruction is revealed the destiny of all such powers that should ever arise to fight against God and His kingdom. This is God's guarantee of victory to the saints who lived then and to all who would come after them, even until the end of time. "And all the birds were filled with their flesh" completes the symbolism of verses 17–18. Not a vestige of the anti-Christian forces was left; the destruction was complete. The sword of truth and judgment prevailed over the sword of political force and human wisdom in false worship.

CHAPTER 20

The Thousand Years and the Final Judgment

THE THOUSAND YEARS
vv. 1-10

This section is composed of seven parts, each beginning with, "And I saw" (19:11, 17, 19; 20:1, 4, 11; 21:1). In the battle of Har-Magedon the beast and the false prophet were cast into the lake of fire that burns with brimstone (19:19-21). With the defeat of these two and the destruction of the harlot, Satan has lost his allies. What becomes of him and the victory of the saints is the chief subject of 20:1-10, rather than the "thousand years," which usually receives the emphasis.

From the early centuries of Christianity this passage has been used as the basis for various theories of a thousand year reign of Christ on earth. For a brief but excellent summary of the history of millenarianism and four specific theories based on the passage, see Albertus Pieters (pp. 278-311). The general theory, with variations among different schools, is briefly this: Christ will come in the first phase of his return to earth (called "the rapture"), and at this time the righteous dead will be raised, the living saints will be changed and both will be caught up in the air to meet the Lord. Then will come the marriage feast of the Lamb, during which there will be great tribulation on earth. After the wedding He and the bride, the church, will then complete the return to earth (called "the revelation,") where Christ will set up His kingdom, sit on David's throne and reign from Jerusalem for a literal thousand years—the millennium. According to some, the Jews will be converted and return to Palestine, Old Testament worship will be restored (with modifications) and there will be on earth an idealistic life which will continue for the definite period of one thousand years. At the end of this millenium Satan will be loosed for a short time and make a last furious effort to destroy the Lord's people and work. This will be followed by the resurrection of the wicked dead (for the righteous dead will have been raised at the beginning of the thousand years). The judgment will occur and the eternal destinies of heaven or hell will be meted.

The theory must read into the passage (vv. 1-10) all that it claims to draw from it, for the following are not mentioned in the text: (1) the second coming of Christ, (2) a bodily resurrection, (3) a reign of Christ on earth, (4) the literal throne of David, (5) Jerusalem of Palestine, (6) conversion of the Jews, or (7) the church on earth. A theory that rests on a passage of Scripture in which not one of its peculiar tenets of doctrine is found cannot be true!

Briefly summarized, the passage deals with the binding of Satan, who is cast into the abyss for a thousand years during which time he cannot deceive the nations. At the end of this time he is loosed for a little season (vv. 1-3). Thrones are set, and upon them the martyrs sit with those who held the faith during the period of oppression by the beast. These shall reign with Christ during the thousand years; this is the first resurrection (vv. 4-6). When the thousand years are over, Satan is freed from his prison, gathers new allies, Gog and Magog, and comes against the camp of the saints; but fire comes down out of heaven and devours these new helpers. The scene closes as Satan is cast into the lake of fire where the beast and false prophet are already. His ultimate end has come (vv. 7-10). This scene is followed by the final judgment and the end of the present age (vv. 11-15).

v. 1. "And I saw an angel coming down out of heaven, having the key of the abyss and a great chain in his hand." Some writers identify this angel as Christ; however, this cannot be correct, for in Revelation Christ never appears as an angel (see comments, 10:1). Rather, angels are His servants, ministering to the divine will. Christ is always the Lamb of God, the King of Kings, who rules and judges from the throne of Jehovah, carrying out the Father's purpose. The angel of the vision had the key to the abyss, the bottomless pit; and in his hand was a strong chain with which to bind Satan. In an earlier vision John saw a fallen star who was given the key to the pit of the abyss and the power to open it and let loose upon earth the terrible smoke out of which emerged the scourge of locusts (see comments, 9:1-3). That key is now in the hand of this angel who has power to close and seal the abyss which had been opened.

The key and chain are not literal. Each is a symbol conveying ideas as have other symbols throughout this book. The key symbolizes power to bind (see comments, 1:18); the chain symbolizes that by which Satan is bound. With the loss of his allies and the victory of the saints under Christ, Satan is bound; that is, his power is severely curtailed. No longer can he control the nations as he once controlled them, nor can he control a man against his will.

v. 2. "And he laid hold on the dragon, the old serpent, which is the Devil and Satan, and bound him for a thousand years." The four names by which the great deceiver of the whole world was called in 12:9 are repeated here. As a dragon, he is strong and ferocious; as the old serpent, he is the cunning deceiver, who from Eden has beguiled with his craftiness (II Cor. 11:3); as the devil, he has been the accuser and slanderer, the malignant enemy of God and man; and as Satan, he is the adversary, opponent and antagonist of all that is good. The thousand years during which Satan is bound must be interpreted symbolically, as are other numbers in the book. This number is a complete number which stands for an indeterminate but full period of time (cf. Job 9:3; 33:23; Ps. 50:10; 90:4; Eccles. 6:6; 7:28; II Peter 3:8). The binding of Satan does not render him absolutely helpless or unable to operate; for he continues to be exceedingly active. He walks about as a roaring lion, seeking whom he may devour (I Peter 5:8); but his activity is limited, as a dog chained to a wire between two trees. He can operate only within the limited distance between the trees, and to the length of the chain from side to side. In this binding, Satan is divinely restrained from reestablishing control over nations.

v. 3. "And cast him into the abyss, and shut it, and sealed it over him, that he should deceive the nations no more, until the thousand years should be finished: after this he must be loosed for a little time." Having bound Satan, the angel with the key to the abyss cast him into the pit, shut it, and sealed it over him. The abyss was the place dreaded by the demons, and apparently was their proper place of habitation (Luke 8:31). The sealing of the abyss is reminiscent of the tomb of Jesus which was sealed that it might not be tampered with and the body stolen (Matt. 27:66). Also the book in the hand of God was "close sealed with seven seals," safeguarding its content (5:1). The purpose of casting the devil into the abyss was not punitive, for his punishment comes later (v. 10); but it was preventive. He is now restrained from deceiving the nations, trapping and controlling them as he did before Jesus came, for his power and the power of paganism are now broken. The abyss is not final; for when the appointed period is finished, Satan is to be loosed for a little time (see comments, vv. 7-9). The period of this "little time" is not to be confused with the "short time" of 12:12, for they are different periods; one is before and one follows the thousand years.

In order to understand more clearly the scene before us, it will be helpful at this point to bring certain events and periods introduced earlier in the book into proper focus: (1) The holy city was to be trodden under foot forty-two months (11:2); (2) the witnesses were to prophesy under persecution twelve hundred sixty days (11:3); (3) the radiant woman was to be in the wilderness, protected from Satan and cared for by God and the Lamb, twelve hundred sixty days (12:6), or "time, times and a half a time," three and a half years (12:14); (4) the beast with authority to persecute and blaspheme would continue his unholy work forty-two months (13:5: cf. Dan. 7:25). This period was the same for each and was interpreted to be the period of the Roman persecution (see comments, 13:5). In two previous visions God said (1) to the saints beneath the altar "that they should rest yet for a little time, until their fellow-servants also and their brethren, who should be killed even as they were, should have fulfilled their course" (6:11); and (2) following the casting down of Satan, He said, "he [the devil] knowing that he hath but a short time" (12:12).

These expressions of a period of time, the three and a half years of persecution, the "little time" of the martyrs, and "the short time" of Satan are the same and are now fulfilled. The Roman persecution as it backed paganism is at an end; the devil is cast into the abyss, no longer to deceive the nations as once he did; the saints' death for the Word of God is avenged and vindicated as they now sit upon thrones, reigning with Christ (vv. 4-6). This leads to the conclusion that the thousand years symbolizes that period of victory beginning with Constantine, when Roman persecution ended, and continuing until some time before the Lord's return when Satan will be loosed from his present restraint.

v. 4. *"And I saw thrones, and they sat upon them, and judgment was given unto them: and I saw the souls of them that had been beheaded for the testimony of Jesus, and for the word of God, and such as worshipped not the beast, neither his image, and received not the mark upon their forehead and upon their hand; and they lived, and reigned with Christ a thousand years.*" Several questions confront us here: (1) What thrones are seen by the apostle? (2) What is the judgment given unto them? (3) Who are these souls that reign with him? In answer to the first, it may be observed that the word throne (*thronos*) indicates "the seat of office or chair of state," whether of a king or of a judge; by metonymy it refers to kingly power or royalty, speaking of one who holds dominion or exercises authority (Vine; Thayer). "Throne" is used to refer to (1) God's throne (Acts 7:49; Rev. 4:2, et al.), (2) Christ's throne (Heb. 1:8f.; Rev. 3:21), (3) the throne of David on which Christ now sits (Luke 1:32; Acts 2:30), (4) thrones of judgment occupied by the apostles in the present dispensation (Matt. 19:28; Luke 22:30), (5) the elders' thrones (4:4; 11:16), (6) the throne of judgment (20:11), (7) the throne of grace (Heb. 4:16), (8) Satan's throne, the seat of paganism (2:13), (9) the throne of the dragon (13:2), (10) the throne which Satan gave to the beast (13:2), hence his throne (16:10), (11) the throne of princes or rulers (Luke 1:52), and (12) the thrones before us in verse 4.

In answer to the second question, the judgment is that rendered against Satan on behalf of the saints. Such a judgment on their behalf had been executed against the harlot as she was burned with fire (18:20). Now judgment is executed against the beast and false prophet as they are cast into the lake of fire, and against the dragon as he is cast into the abyss (cf. Dan. 7:21f. and comments, 11:18). As these had been cruel and relentless enemies, persecutors, and seducers of the church, so now on behalf of the saints, judgment is executed against them.

John himself answers the third question. He saw upon the thrones the souls—not bodies—of two groups: (1) the souls of "*them that had been beheaded for the testimony of Jesus, and for the word of God.*" These were martyrs who had offered their lives in sacrifice. To behead (from *pelekizō*) is a strong word, occurring only here in the New Testament, and means "to cut with an axe" (From *pelekus*, an axe), hence, beheaded with an axe or two-edged hatchet. (2) The second group is "*such as worshipped not the beast, neither his image, and* received not the mark upon their forehead and upon their hand" (cf. 13:16-19). Somehow these had escaped death, but they had possessed the same spirit as those who had been put to death. They refused to yield to the beast's demands, being willing to die rather than deny the faith; for "they loved not their life even unto death" (12:11), but providentially had been spared from being beheaded. In John's vision he saw the souls who sat upon the thrones, sharing the rule of Christ's victory for a thousand years, the full and complete period of time in the mind and purpose of God.

This does not exclude all the faithful who have lived since that time from sharing with Him in his reign, for saints who partake of His grace and gift of righteousness, "reign in life through" Him (Rom. 5:17), even those purchased with His blood who "reign upon the earth" (Rev. 5:9f.). But these latter ones are not those portrayed in the vision; we are not in the picture.

v. 5. "*The rest of the dead lived not until the thousand years should be finished. This is the first resurrection.*" It seems clear that those expositors err who find in either of these verses (vv. 3, 4) a resurrection of the body. The vision portrays the victory of the martyrs underneath the altar, whose "little time" is finished, whose cry has been answered, and whose victory is symbolized as a resurrection and as being seated on thrones. Christ's victory was manifested and exemplified in His resurrection and His being seated on His throne which stands as a symbol of His total triumph. The figure is not new; Old Testament prophets pictured Judah's and Israel's triumph over idolatry and Assyrian and Babylonian captivity as a resurrection, a return from the dead (Isa. 26:19; Hos. 13:14; Ezek. 37:1-14).

"The rest of the dead" who live not until the thousand years are finished are not the dead awaiting a bodily resurrection. As the cause for which the martyrs had died is symbolized by a resurrection, so "the rest," those killed with the sword of Christ in their war on behalf of the beast and paganism (19:21), shall experience a resurrection of their cause in the revived effort of Satan which will come toward the end of time through new allies, Gog and Magog (vv. 7-9).

v. 6. "*Blessed and holy is he that hath part in the first resurrection: over these the second death hath no power; but they shall be priests of God and of Christ, and shall reign with him a thousand years.*" This is the fifth of the seven "blesseds" pronounced in the book; the word indicates a heavenly joy, being blissfully complete. In 14:13, the Lord pronounces this happiness upon those who die in the Lord (see comments, 14:13). Here that blissful completeness is again pronounced with the added commendation that they are holy who are now completely and finally separated from sin and its blighted surroundings. The pronouncement "blessed and holy" is upon him who had part in the first resurrection, which has been interpreted as the victory of the cause and principles to which he was faithful under the most trying circumstances, even unto death.

Three grand rewards follow this announcement, one negative and two positive: (1) "Over these the second death hath no power." To the church at Smyrna the Lord had written, "He that overcometh shall not be hurt of the second death" (2:11). This leads to the conclusion that they who have part in the first resurrection are those who overcome, for the second death has power over neither. The "second death" is explained below as "the lake of fire" (v. 14; 21:8). (2) "They shall be priests of God and of Christ." Earlier John said that Jesus made the saints to be "a kingdom, to be priests unto his God and Father" (1:6), who "reign upon the earth" (5:10), whom Peter called "a holy" and "a royal priesthood," who offer spiritual sacrifices unto God (I Peter 2:5, 9). Although 5:10 does not have the same focus as this passage, evidently the saints' function as priests continues in some unrevealed manner of service. (3) "[They] shall reign with him a thousand years." This indicates that, as the priestly function, the reign which began with Christ here continues in the victory and triumph achieved through Him. Other than reigning with Him through this victory and triumph, nothing more is known about the reign.

v. 7. "And when the thousand years are finished, Satan shall be loosed out of his prison." Though freed at the end of the thousand years, Satan's attitude toward Christ and the saints shows no change. He remains the inveterate and relentless enemy of God and His people. This loosing was introduced in verse 3, and is "for a little time." As the three and a half years of the beast's triumph had been but "a short time" for Satan's unrestrained work in comparison to the time of the saints' victory, (12:12; 13:5; see above, v. 3), so also the time of his release will be short in comparison to the period of victory which was not accomplished. We can only suggest as to where or in what way Satan was loosed. The victors on thrones were those who overcame; and those who overcame did so by the blood of the Lamb, by holding fast the word of their testimony, and loving not their life even unto death (12:11). In the spirit of this faithfulness they bound Satan by overcoming him. When such a spirit and loyal devotion to the principles and cause of Christ no longer distinguish God's people, the restraining power is gone; Satan is loosed once more.

v. 8. "And shall come forth to deceive the nations which are in the four corners of the earth, Gog and Magog, to gather them together to the war: the number of whom is as the sand of the sea." Satan changes his tactics; he no longer works through one great imperial power, backing a crass form of religion such as emperor worship. But as it had been from the beginning, deception continues to be his means of control: "He shall come forth to deceive the nations which are in the four corners of the earth." No longer relying upon one great power, he now gathers his forces from all sources, from nations in all quarters of the earth; the host is numberless. His battle may be another Har-Magedon, a decisive battle, but it is not the battle of 16:14–16; that one had long since been fought (19:19–21). This is a continuation of the same war that has been raging through the centuries, but it is a new battle.

The world from which Satan draws his new forces is Gog and Magog. An interpretation of "Gog and Magog" must depend upon Ezekiel's prophecy, chapters 38—39. "Gog, of the land of Magog," was the prince of countries to the north (38:2f.), the east, west, and south (38:5). He would command a great horde with which he would invade and cover the land of Israel (38:6–9). His eye would be upon the spoil of the land to take it for himself (38:10–13). He would continue even into the "latter days"—the Messianic period (38:16)—but he would be utterly destroyed, buried in defeat, as the birds would gorge on the carcasses of his forces (chap. 39).

Many questionable theories have been built upon the Gog and Magog of John's vision. Some say the scene points to a great physical battle to be fought in Palestine at some future date with Russia, the United States, and other nations participating. Unfortunately for the theory, God through Ezekiel explains who the Gog and Magog are.

397 THE THOUSAND YEARS AND THE FINAL JUDGMENT 20:9

"Thus saith the Lord Jehovah: Art thou he of whom I spake in old time by my servants the prophets of Israel, that prophesied in those days for many years that I would bring thee against them?" (38:17). God said that He had spoken of Gog's coming, but no prophet ever named Gog or Magog. Yet the prophets foretold over and over of the heathen enemies who would come against Israel and who would be defeated and destroyed by His hand. Therefore we conclude that Gog of the land of Magog symbolized all the heathen enemies of God's people from the time of the prophets to the Roman Empire, all who sought to thwart His purpose and to destroy His king. The seer now prophesies that toward the end of time there would be a horde gathered and led by Satan in a final furious effort to destroy the church.

Far from a physical conflict, this battle will be a moral and spiritual one. Satan's Gog and Magog symbolize such forces and agencies as atheism, humanism, communism, materialism, astrology, and all manner of false and perverted religions. Gog and Magog also represent such forces as anarchy (rebellion against all principles and standards of truth); corruption in government and business; immorality with its decay of home, lack of natural affection and devotion to children; sodomy; alcoholism; and total abandonment to a base and sordid life of the flesh. Satan will use the anti-God, immoral standards and practices that he is using today, but probably to a more intense and flagrant degree. Gog and Magog do not gather around a conference table and offer themselves to the devil in a nefarious pact; but being deceived, they are drawn to him as were the kings of old.

v. 9. "*And they went up over the breadth of the earth, and compassed the camp of the saints about, and the beloved city: and fire came down out of heaven, and devoured them.*" If millenarians are correct in their view, then their millennium ends in total disaster. All Satan has to do is make an appearance, and the nations (whose identity are not specified by the theorists) rally around him in great numbers from the four corners of the earth, ready to come up against "the camp of the saints" and their beloved city.

The word "camp" (from *parembolē*) is used in the New Testament as a military term. It occurs six times in Acts, where it is translated "castle," meaning the barracks or headquarters of the Roman soldiers (Acts 21:34, 37; 22:24; 23:10, 16, 32), once as "armies of aliens" (Heb.

11:34), twice with reference to the camp of Israel (Heb. 13:11, 13), and once in Revelation. The "camp of the saints" would be the barracks of God's faithful army. The "beloved city" is the "heavenly Jerusalem," the spiritual Zion, the church (Heb. 12:22f.); the two terms suggest different aspects of the same group, the church of the Lord. These are still the objects of Satan's rage. But as God brought Ezekiel's Gog of Magog to an end by His judgment, so He brings this last enemy to an end. Whenever and wherever the battle and whatever be the nature of its enemies, the church can be assured that in all ages and at all times God will fight for His own and give them victory.

v. 10. *"And the devil that deceived them was cast into the lake of fire and brimstone, where are also the beast and the false prophet; and they shall be tormented day and night for ever and ever."* The devil, man's great deceiver from the beginning, now reaches his final doom and eternal end. First, he was cast down to the earth (12:9), then into the pit of the abyss (20:3), and now into the lake of fire and brimstone, his ultimate end. His destruction has been gradual, but long-since determined in the mind of God, for the lake was prepared for him and his own (Matt. 25:41, 46). He now shares the lot of his allies—the beast, the false prophet, and the harlot.

It should be observed that "they shall be tormented day and night for ever and ever." Torment (from *basanizō*) conveys the idea of torture, severe distress, and pain of body and mind. The torment of the locusts "was as the torment of a scorpion, when it striketh a man" (9:5); and those who worshiped the beast would be tormented with fire and brimstone, and the smoke of their torment would ascend for ever and ever (14:10f.). And now the devil and his former helpers suffer the torment of the lake of fire and brimstone for ever and ever.

There are many who question the eternal duration of this torment, but these must explain away biblical teaching. Jesus said that at the judgment those on His left hand would be told, "Depart from me, ye cursed, into the eternal fire prepared for the devil and his angels ... and these shall go away into eternal punishment; but the righteous into eternal life" (Matt. 25:41, 46). Both the punishment and the life are eternal. In Revelation it is said of these two groups that those before the throne "serve him day and night" (7:15), and the wicked "have no rest day or night" (14:11), and that with the devil they are tormented (25:41, 46), a torment which is "day and night, for ever and ever." There is no day there, for it is "outer darkness" (Matt. 22:13; 25:30). Since the day is in heaven and the night in hell, and since the one group serves Him day and night while the other group is tormented night and day, it follows that the night endures as long as the day. But since God is the light of the eternal day, the day (and, consequently, the night) will never end. The period of this torment, "for ever and ever," is the same in duration as God, for He lives "for ever and ever" (4:9). If there shall be total annihilation of the devil and the wicked it is not revealed.

THE FINAL JUDGMENT
vv. 11-15

Thus far in the book several scenes of judgment have been described, but none depicted the final judgment. There was a judgment of the nations on behalf of the saints (11:18), one of those who poured out the blood of the saints (16:5), one of the harlot (18:8; 19:2), and one of the beast and the false prophet (19:11-21); but all of these pertained to the period of Roman rule. John now brings the final judgment into view, at which point there is the passing of the present order and the resurrection and judgment of all who have lived upon the earth. God judges nations and forces of wickedness during time, but people await this great final judgment for their reward or sentence.

Sometimes the question is raised as to why there will be a judgment if the individual knows from death what his state is and what his destiny will be. Although the thoughts, words, and deeds of life are all open for inspection at the judgment, it appears that the occasion is primarily one of meting rewards to the righteous and executing punishment to the wicked (see comments, v. 12).

v. 11. *"And I saw a great white throne, and him that sat upon it, from whose face the earth and the heaven fled away; and there was found no place for them."* John introduces this portion of his vision as he does each phase of the section with the phrase, "And I saw." He sees in vision the great throne of judgment. As the throne of God, it is great in distinction from all other thrones that have appeared previously; it surpasses them all. Its sparkling white color indicates purity, holiness, and righteousness which characterize all His judgments, for all are blameless (16:7; 19:2).

Does John see God the Almighty on the throne, or is it Christ the Lamb? All judgments of the book have been ascribed to God the Almighty (16:5, 7; 18:8, 20; 19:2); but it was the Word of God, the King of Kings who came forth to judge and to make war (19:11). Jesus said that the Father had given all judgment unto the Son (John 5:22, 27), and that it was He who would sit on the throne at the final judgment (Matt. 25:31ff.). The idea that God judges, and yet Christ judges, should present no problem; for Jesus taught that He and the Father are one—one in Godhood, purpose, and work (John 10:30; 14:10). Later Paul taught that God's judgment would be carried out through Jesus Christ (Acts 17:31; Rom. 2:16). The judgment seat is "the judgment-seat of God" (Rom. 14:10, ASV) and it is "the judgment-seat of Christ" (II Cor. 5:10). Christ sat down on the throne of the Father (3:21), which is "the throne of God and the Lamb" (22:1). The explanation of the judgment by God and Christ is offered by Paul when he said, "In [that] day... God shall judge the secrets of men, according to my gospel, by Jesus Christ" (Rom. 2:16). We conclude that it is Christ whom John beheld on the throne executing judgment on behalf of the Father. It may be suggested that as Christ went forth on a white horse to conquer (6:2), and to make war against His enemies (19:11), so now He is on the white throne to judge all men.

"From whose face the earth and the heaven fled away." As the islands had vanished or disappeared from the divine presence at the pouring out of the seventh bowl (16:20), so now both earth and heaven flee from His face as He appears to judge, "and there was found no place for them." It has been abundantly foretold that heaven and earth will pass away. The writer of Hebrews quoted the psalmist who said of the earth and heavens, "They shall perish" as a garment, and be changed (Heb. 1:11f.; cf. Ps. 102:25-27). Peter said that the heavens would pass away with a great noise, the elements would be dissolved with fervent heat, "and the earth and the works that are therein shall be burned up" (II Peter 3:10). John sees this taking place at the coming of Christ in judgment, as the present order passes away.

THE THOUSAND YEARS AND THE FINAL JUDGMENT 20:12

v. 12. "And I saw the dead, the great and the small, standing before the throne; and books were opened: and another book was opened, which is the book of life: and the dead were judged out of the things which were written in the books, according to their works." This scene presupposes the resurrection of all human beings that have lived and died from Adam until the end of time. Jesus assured His listeners that "the hour cometh, in which all that are in their tombs shall hear his voice, and shall come forth" (John 5:28f.; cf. Acts 24:15). The tombs from which these shall come forth are not limited to rock-hewn sepulchers, but include whatever graves hold the dust of the dead, whether it be vaults, or decayed boxes beneath the ground. All will be raised to stand before this throne of judgment.

"And the books were opened" is reminiscent of Daniel 7:10, where "the books [plural] were opened" in the judgment of the fourth great beast who was judged, slain, and burned. This suggests that the books contained the record of the beast's character and deeds. In comparison to "the books" which were opened at the judgment of the beast, there was "the book" (singular) in which was found written those that would be delivered (Dan. 12:1). These are not literal books in which angels have written the actions, words, and thoughts of each individual; for, as someone has said, each person writes his own book. The books symbolize the divine record of the lives and deeds of all who have lived. Pieters has well expressed it: "The books evidently stand for the omniscience of God the Judge, to whom nothing is unknown, and by whom nothing is forgotten" (p. 313), except what He wills to forget (Heb. 8:12).

"The book of life," or God's book, is referred to many times in Scripture (Exod. 32:32f.; Ps. 69:28; Isa. 4:3; Mal. 3:16; Luke 10:20; Phil. 4:3; Rev. 3:5; 13:8; 17:8; 21:27; see comments, 3:5; 13:8). It is God's roll of the faithful in His city of Zion, those who were redeemed by the blood of the Lamb and have continued "in the faith, grounded and stedfast, and not moved away from the hope of the gospel" (Col. 1:23). John writes, "And the dead were judged out of the things which were written in the books, according to their works." This is not a judgment of the wicked only, "For we must *all* be made manifest before the judgment-seat of Christ; that each one may receive the things done in the body, according to what he hath done, whether it be good or bad"

(II Cor. 5:10). Each receives his reward or execution: "And these [the wicked] shall go away into eternal punishment: but the righteous into eternal life" (Matt. 25:46).

v. 13. *"And the sea gave up the dead that were in it; and death and Hades gave up the dead that were in them: and they were judged every man according to their works."* Because of the Jewish emphasis on proper burial of the dead and fear of possible calamity if this was not done, some have concluded that John speaks of the literal sea. According to this view, the seer is emphasizing the fact that even the sea gives up its dead; these are not lost to God's sight. However, to be consistent with the plan of the book, the sea should be considered symbolically. In commenting on 13:1, it was pointed out that John refers to the sea both literally and figuratively, but in 13:1 he uses the sea as a symbol of the mass of human society out of which emerge upheavals and governments (see comments, 13:1). This mass of humanity must also stand before the judgment with those who have died, for Jesus is ordained of God "to be the Judge of the living and the dead" (Acts 10:42; see also II Tim. 4:1; I Peter 4:5). Also included in this group are the saints who will be living when He comes (I Thess. 4:16f.; I Cor. 15:51f.).

"And death and Hades gave up the dead that were in them." These two have been the captors of humanity from the beginning. Death claims the body when the spirit leaves it (James 2:26), whether the body be left to decay in the sea or on the earth. Hades, "the unseen," claims the spirit (Acts 2:27, 31; see comments, 1:18). In the resurrection, the spirit and body of both the wicked and righteous will be reunited (I Cor. 15:52ff.; I Thess. 4:13ff.; I John 3:1-3). The specific nature of the resurrected body of the wicked is discussed nowhere in Scripture; it is simply said that all shall be raised, the just and the unjust (Acts 24:15; John 5:28). Among the wicked will be those of Tyre, Sodom, and Nineveh (Matt. 11:22, 24; 12:41), who will appear in a body of some form (Matt. 5:29f.; 10:28; 18:8f.). When Jesus ascended to heaven with the keys of death and Hades, "He led captivity captive" (Eph. 4:8). That which had held men captive, including these two, was now a captive under His power.

"And they were judged every man according to their works." As Ecclesiastes 13:14 says, "For God will bring every work into judgment, with every hidden thing, whether it be good or whether it be evil"; for "all things are naked and laid open before the eyes of him with whom we have to do" (Heb. 4:13). This is truly a sobering thought.

v. 14. "And death and Hades were cast into the lake of fire. This is the second death, even the lake of fire." Each time the word Hades occurs in the book it is associated with death; these two rode together (6:8), and now they end together. Death, the last enemy to be destroyed (I Cor. 15:26), is now cast into the lake of fire. The second death, here described as the lake of fire, was introduced earlier: "He that overcometh shall not be hurt of the second death" (2:11); those that overcome had part in the first resurrection (20:6). Thus far the harlot, the beast, the false prophet, Satan, and now death and Hades, have been brought to their end in the lake of fire.

v. 15. "And if any was not found written in the book of life, he was cast into the lake of fire." There remains only one group to be dealt with: those not found written in the book of life. These would be "the rest" who had fought with the beast and false prophet against the Lord, those who had been slain with the sword out of His mouth (19:21), those who had rallied about Satan in his last effort to destroy the camp of the saints (20:9), and all others who, in their indifference to the Lord, had not taken a stand for Him, or had turned away from Him (Heb. 10:26, 31). The defeat of Satan and his forces against God and truth is total—complete and final. Of this second death, Alford writes, "As there is a second higher life, so there is also a second and deeper death. And as after that life there is no more death, so after that death there is no more life" (pp. 735f.).

CHAPTER 21
The Eternal Glory

To most believers the next section of the book, 21:1—22:5, is a portrayal of heaven, the glorious home of the soul beyond the judgment. Through the centuries this concept has comforted the hearts of millions during times of trial, tragedy, and death of loved ones. Today (aside from millenarian views) two views are usually held with respect to the vision. One is that the city described is the victorious church as God considers it today, purged and purified by the tribulation through which it has passed. A second view is that the vision portrays the church at home with God in final glory beyond the judgment. Though it is true that the faithful church is glorious in the Lord's eyes, and in this vision is seen blessings present throughout the history of God's people, yet after considering the evidence for both views, the latter seems to be the correct one.

In the series of visions beginning in chapter twelve, the seer beheld the birth of the man child; the assault on the church by the dragon's agents; the trials of the church; the waging of the great war; the destruction of the harlot city, the beast, and false prophet; the final conflict with Satan and his destruction; the passing of the present order; the final judgment of mankind; and the punishment of the wicked. From this arrangement of the visions it is logical that the next scene in order would portray the final glory of the church as it comes to rest with God beyond time. This appears to be the design of the revelation before us. Heaven could be no more than is revealed symbolically in this picture of perfect fellowship with God, safety, security, and abundance in the glorious city desscribed by everything that is precious and priceless.

"ALL THINGS NEW"
vv. 1-8

v. 1. *"And I saw a new heaven and a new earth: for the first heaven and the first earth are passed away; and the sea is no more."* At the appearing of the Lord in judgment, the heaven and earth had fled away, signifying the passing of the present order (20:11). In their stead John sees a new heavenly order. "And the sea is no more." According to the interpretation of "the sea" assumed earlier, this phrase indicates the removal or passing of the body of society, the great sea in which the restless upheavals of men have cast up their mire as the nations rage against God (see comments, 13:1; 20:13; and cf. Isa. 57:20).

The concept of a new heaven and earth at the passing of a former one is not strange to Bible students. Isaiah had described the consequence of Jehovah's indignation against the heathen nations as the melting of their mountains with blood, and the "mouldering away" of their heavens, being rolled together as a scroll, fading away as leaves from a vine or fig tree (Isa. 34:3f.). Jehovah's own nation would suffer a similar fate, for "the heavens shall vanish away like smoke, and the earth shall wax old as doth a garment," which pointed to the passing of the old Jewish national system (Isa. 51:4-6). In their stead, Jehovah would "plant the heavens, and lay the foundations of the earth, and say unto Zion, Thou art my people" (v. 16), which pointed to the new spiritual Zion under the Messiah—the present dispensation.

This passing of the old order and instituting a new one is more clearly announced by Isaiah in chapter 65. Jehovah says that the former troubles are forgotten, being hid from His eyes; they shall not be remembered, nor come into mind (vv. 16f.)—they shall have passed away. In the place of the old God says, "I create new heavens and a new earth," in which He shall rejoice in Jerusalem and His people, and they shall rejoice in Him (vv. 17-19). It is evident from the remainder of the chapter that the Lord is speaking of the new order under Christ in contrast to the old under the law; "they shall not hurt nor destroy in all my holy mountain" (v. 25), which is Zion of Messiah's rule (Isa. 2:2-4). Isaiah was not writing of the new heaven and new earth of John's vision but of the new creation and order under Christ—the present dispensation. This new order of the new covenant would remain, and in it the seed and name would likewise remain; worship and victory would not cease (Isa. 66:22-24). The New Testament system is composed of new creatures (II Cor. 5:17; Gal. 6:15), involving a new divine creation which is "after God" (Eph. 2:10; 4:24).

A careful study of Peter's account of a new heaven and new earth (II Peter 3) reveals a striking parallel to that which John describes. Each points to the judgment and destruction of ungodly men (II Peter 3:7; Rev. 20:13), and the passing of the present heaven and earth (II Peter 3:10; Rev. 20:11) before the coming of the new heaven and new earth (II Peter 3:13; Rev. 21:1). Peter and John were both writing of the final judgment and what should follow, rather than of the church today, purged and purified by suffering. Isaiah wrote of the passing of the old Jewish order and the inauguration of the new under Christ, whereas both Peter and John wrote of the passing of the new state of which Isaiah wrote and the introduction of the final and eternal order beyond the judgment.

v. 2. *"And I saw the holy city, new Jerusalem, coming down out of heaven from God, made ready as a bride adorned for her husband."* This "new Jerusalem" is new (*kainos*) in kind, superior to that which preceded it. As the present order has its holy city, Jerusalem (Gal. 4:26; Heb. 12:22), so also does the new heaven and new earth have a new city, holy and heavenly, befitting such a spiritual creation. The fact that it comes down out of heaven manifests its divine origin, for "all things are of God" (II Cor. 5:18) that pertain to the spiritual and eternal. This is the city searched for by the patriarchs of old, "which hath the foundations, whose builder and maker is God" (Heb. 11:10), and for which we seek, an abiding city "which is to come" (Heb. 13:14). He who overcomes is related to this city in his present citizenship (see comments, 3:12). The city is arrayed in bridal splendor, having "been made ready as a bride adorned for her husband" (19:8). She is now to be presented to the Lord in glory, without spot or wrinkle or blemish or any such thing (Eph. 5:25–27). Her true beauty and glory are described below (vv. 9ff.).

v. 3. *"And I heard a great voice out of the throne saying, Behold, the tabernacle of God is with men, and he shall dwell with them, and they shall be his peoples, and God himself shall be with them, and be their God."* The voice from the throne is not identified; it may belong to the unknown speaker of 16:17 or 19:5, or it may be that of Christ or God. Whoever the speaker is, his voice expresses God's message to those addressed. John brings together a number of symbols familiar to Bible students. The church is a bride, a sanctuary, a family, a body of individuals. Twice the tabernacle in heaven has been in view (13:6; 15:5); the word means a tent or booth, a lodging or dwelling place. The verb (*skēnoō*) means to dwell or abide; "the Word became flesh, and dwelt [tabernacled] among us, and we beheld his glory" (John 1:14). The Old Covenant tabernacle, constructed according to the divine pattern and the dwelling place of God's glory among the people (Exod. 40:16–34), pointed to the new, "which the Lord pitched, not man" (Heb. 8:2; 9:11), and where God dwells in the spirit (Eph. 2:21f.). The development of God's presence among His people now reaches its zenith as He dwells or tabernacles with them in His heavenly fellowship.

Although "peoples" (plural) usually refers to the heathen, here it is said, "And they shall be his peoples." The same unusual plural occurs of "nations" in 21:24, 26; 22:2, and has been the basis on which some writers conclude that 20:1—22:5 describes the church now; but this does not necessarily follow. Isaiah said, "All nations shall flow unto it [the mountain of Jehovah]; and many peoples" shall come unto it (Isa. 2:2f.). The seer also said that the redeemed are of every people and nation (5:9), and that he saw a multitude "out of every nation" and of "all tribes and peoples" standing before the throne (7:9). These are now with God and He with them. So the "peoples" simply describe His people from among all the peoples of earth who now share a perfect fellowship with God.

v. 4. "And he shall wipe away every tear from their eyes; and death shall be no more; neither shall there be mourning, nor crying, nor pain, any more: the first things are passed away." The old heaven and earth have passed away; and with their going went also everything that marred life on earth as God would have had it: the fruit of sin, death, and its consequences. The bliss of being with God is described by five negatives: no tears, no death, no mourning, no crying, and no pain; for "the first things are passed away." These are no more, because sin which caused them is no more; sin and death are swallowed up in victory.

v. 5. "And he that sitteth on the throne said, Behold, I make all things new. And he saith, Write: for these words are faithful and true." Again it is difficult to determine who speaks, whether God or Christ. It could be either, for both sit upon the throne (3:21); and Christ acts for the Father, carrying out His purpose as set forth in the sealed roll (5:7). In contrast to things which are removed, all things are now made new.

As when one becomes a new creature in Christ, "the old things [of his former character and life] are passed away" and "are become new" (II Cor. 5:17), so now, the things of the old order are passed away, and all things are made new. The grandeur of the "all things made new" will surely surpass and exceed anything that our imaginations can conceive. Again John is instructed to write, for these words are faithful and true, bearing the signature of God Himself. The things to be written probably include the whole of verses 1-8, for a message of such stupendous import and assurance must be preserved for all mankind for all time.

v. 6. *"And he said unto me, They are come to pass. I am the Alpha and the Omega, the beginning and the end. I will give unto him that is athirst of the fountain of the water of life freely."* It seems that as in 1:8 (see comments) where Jehovah is the speaker, that it is also He who speaks here; however, one cannot be dogmatic at this point, for near the close of the book Jesus makes the same claim (22:13). The scheme of redemption and its revelation originate and terminate with God. As "the beginning and the end," He created and He determines the objective and consequence of all things planned and brought forth. In the Old Testament He repeatedly claimed to be the sole Deity, "the first and the last," and that beside Him there is no God (Isa. 41:4; 43:10; 44:6; 48:12). This claim is verified by the fulfilling and consummation of His purpose in Christ, for only an infinite being could have so accurately foretold and carried out such a plan. As God through Jesus had provided the life-sustaining spiritual water in this present dispensation (John 4:10; 7:37), and as the Shepherd had guided those coming out of the great tribulation unto fountains of water of life (7:17, see comments), so now fresh assurance is given that there would be abundance of the water of life in this relationship, for a great river of it shall flow from the throne of God and the Lamb (22:1). Nothing will be lacking in the complete fullness and realization of all spiritual desires of the glorified soul in heaven.

v. 7. *"He that overcometh shall inherit these things; and I will be his God, and he shall be my son."* In each of the seven letters to the churches the Lord promised a reward to him that overcomes (2:7, 11, 17, 26; 3:5, 12, 21) even as He overcame (3:21; 5:5). The saint would conquer by the blood of the Lamb, by the word of his testimony and by loving not his life even unto death (12:11). Now to each who prevails is given the assurance that he shall inherit these blessings of the new earth. To inherit (*klēronomeō*) is "to receive by lot; especially to receive as an inheritance; obtain by right of inheritance" (Thayer).

Now fulfilled are those "exceeding great promises" by which the Christian has been sustained in life: that he "shall inherit everlasting life" (Matt. 19:29), "shall inherit salvation" (Heb. 1:14), and shall "inherit a blessing" (I Peter 3:9). Now he has heard the King say, "Come ye blessed of my Father, inherit the kingdom prepared for you from the foundation of the world" (Matt. 25:34). Along with the glorious presence of God, the immunities from death, sorrows, and griefs, and the abundance of water to refresh and satisfy every desire of the soul, God adds, "And I will be his God, and he shall be my son." Here is assurance of an eternal relationship with God, like that of a son receiving the inheritance which has been guaranteed to him (Eph. 1:14).

v. 8. *"But for the fearful, and unbelieving, and abominable, and murderers, and fornicators, and sorcerers, and idolaters, and all liars, their part shall be in the lake that burneth with fire and brimstone; which is the second death."* In sharp contrast to the inheritance of the righteous, the Lord now describes the character and destiny of the wicked. This serves as a warning to those who are living, for after death it is too late to make any correction of life. "The fearful" are the cowardly and timid, those who in fear shrink back: in these God has no pleasure (Heb. 10:38f.), for in His army there is no place for cowards. The "unbelieving" are those who have betrayed the trust committed to them (cf. Luke 12:46); by their lives and conduct they have denied the Lord. The "abominable" are those who become morally or spiritually foul, who make themselves abhorred; these partake of the harlot's cup of abominations, "even the unclean things of her fornication" (17:4), which include all the unnatural vices of paganism and idolatry. "Murderers" are those who willfully and maliciously take life unlawfully. This lack of respect for life has been punishable by death from the days of Noah (Gen. 9:6), under the law (Exod. 21:12), and under the present dispensation (Rom. 13:4). "Fornicators," translated "whoremongers" in the KJV, are the sexually immoral. This sin was exceedingly prevalent among the pagan people, as it is today in modern society. It was condemned and warned against repeatedly in the New Testament writings (see Rom. 13:13; I Cor. 5:9ff.; 6:9-11; Gal. 5:19, 21; Eph. 5:3-5; Col. 3:5f.; et al.). A "sorcerer" is one devoted to magical arts, especially a user of drugs, potions, spells, and enchantments to bring others under his power (Vine). Astrologers and prognosticators, peddlers of various narcotics, and false teachers who claim to have miraculous powers and thereby bring the unwary under their control, are no less sorcerers than those of John's day. "Idolaters" are worshipers of false gods, whether visible idols or invisible mental images. A Christian may in weakness succumb to such worship (I Cor. 5:11; 6:9) by eating and drinking (I Cor. 10:7, 21), or by covetousness, wherein he becomes a worshiper of mammon (Eph. 5:5). "All liars," includes those who practice all that is deceitful or false, whether in word or by silence, by deed or intimation. Ananias and Sapphira lied to God and the Lord struck them dead, thereby leaving for all time a strong warning of His abhorrence of a lie and of its inevitable punishment. In contrast to the saints' heavenly inheritance, these suffer the second death in the lake that burns with fire and brimstone.

THE NEW JERUSALEM
vv. 9-27

v. 9. "And there came one of the seven angels who had the seven bowls, who were laden with the seven last plagues; and he spake with me, saying, Come hither, I will show thee the bride, the wife of the Lamb." The discussion of the Lamb's bride and His marriage, which was introduced earlier (19:7f.), is now resumed in greater detail. It is not clear whether this is the same angel who showed John the judgment of the great harlot (17:1), or one of the remaining six. The similarity of the two phrases, "Come hither, I will show thee the judgment of the great harlot," and, "Come hither, I will show thee the bride, the wife of the Lamb," suggests that it was the same angel in each instance; but it could have been otherwise. The judgment of the harlot and the marriage of the bride are set forth in clear and vivid contrast, as have been the seductive lusts of the one and the beauty and holiness of the other; each has been represented by strong symbols.

v. 10. "And he carried me away in the Spirit to a mountain great and high, and showed me the holy city Jerusalem, coming down out of heaven from God." As when the angel appeared to John to show him the judgment of the harlot, John wrote "he carried me away in Spirit" (17:3, the definite article was omitted), so again he is carried away "in Spirit." But instead of being transported to a desolate wilderness where he was shown a harlot full of names of blasphemy, he is taken to a high mountain. In a former vision John looked to see "the Lion that is of the tribe of Judah, the Root of David," but instead saw "a Lamb standing" (5:5f.). So now, instead of seeing a beautiful woman attired in bridal garments as would be expected, he is shown "the holy city Jerusalem, coming down out of heaven from God." As the harlot was symbolized by a great city, the bride is signified by a holy city. It was from "a very high mountain" that Ezekiel was shown "as it were the frame of a city," the spiritual Jerusalem, the church, which was to come (Ezek. 40:2). John now sees that city, the church, in its final glory at home with God and the Lamb.

The precise phrase, "new Jerusalem," occurs only twice in Scripture, both times in Revelation (3:12; 21:2). "The holy city" occurs three times (11:2; 21:2; 22:19), and "the beloved city" once (20:9). It is now called "the holy city Jerusalem," not "great" as in the KJV. The "great city" is applied nine times to the harlot city Babylon, the world city (for occurrences of the phrase, see 11:8). One is great, the subject of the wrath of God; the other is holy and beloved, the object of His favor. As he introduced the new eternal order, John said he saw the holy city, the new Jerusalem, "coming down out of heaven from God" (v. 2). Does he now see this vision a second time, or does he repeat himself that he might give a detailed description of the majestic vision of the new city? The latter seems to be the correct view. The emphasis rests on two truths: the city is holy, and it is from God, that is, divine in its origin and nature (see comments, v. 2). Like the gospel, it is not according to man, it is not from beneath, and it is not human in any respect (Gal. 1:11f.). It comes from God.

A. Exterior of the City, vv. 11-21

It must again be borne in mind that John is describing visions and is dealing with symbols. There has been set forth the great dragon, a radiant woman, a great beast with seven heads and ten horns, another beast with two horns and a dragon-like voice, bowls of wrath, a great harlot, a decisive battle, a spiritual resurrection, a thousand years, and a lake of fire. None of these are to be interpreted literally, but they do represent actual spiritual entities, forces, and conflicts.

So it is in this passage. In considering the description of the holy city, it must be continually borne in mind that this is a vision in which is set forth a majestic symbol of a great spiritual reality. Literally there never was, is not now, and never will be such a city; but there certainly will be that which the city symbolizes, for God has declared it.

v. 11. *"Having the glory of God: her light was like unto a stone most precious, as it were a jasper stone, clear as crystal."* The emphatic thought here is that this city is made glorious by the glory of God which fills it. God's glory filled the tabernacle in the wilderness (Exod. 40:34), the temple erected by Solomon (I Kings 8:11), and the church, the spiritual temple of the New Testament, as He makes it His dwelling place in the Spirit (Eph. 2:22; 3:21). So now, His glory in its completeness fills the holy city. Her light (*phōstēr*, "luminary, a light-giving body," occurring only here and in Phil. 2:15) is as a brilliant, sparkling, flashing diamond with every facet reflecting and expressing the glory of God. The jasper stone, the diamond, and the sardius, a ruby-red stone, were used to describe the splendor of Him who sat on the throne (see comments, 4:3). However, the sardius is not included here, for all judgments are passed; and the jasper, absolutely flawless and as clear as crystal, expresses the perfect illumination of the holy city.

vv. 12, 13. *"Having a wall great and high; having twelve gates, and at the gates twelve angels; and names written thereon, which are the names of the twelve tribes of the children of Israel: on the east were three gates; and on the north three gates; and on the south three gates; and on the west three gates."* The theme introduced at verse 2 is now resumed. In John's day no city could endure without a strong wall for protection. In this vision the wall is not necessary as a protection against assault from without, for all enemies are now destroyed; but the wall completes the symbolic picture of absolute and perfect security of those within the city and of their complete and unassailable fellowship with God. Though the wall is great and high, its height is not specified (see comments, v. 17). The wall has gates or portals (three on each of the four sides), and large gate towers such as were built into the city walls of that day.

Ezekiel's city likewise had three gates on each side; but in Ezekiel's vision the gates were "egresses," exits through which each tribe went out to possess its inheritance (Ezek. 48:30-35). In John's vision the gates are portals of entrance, identified with the twelve tribes of Israel and by which each enters the city. Since the city is the church in its final glory beyond the judgment, and not the church at present, the angels cannot symbolize protection; for there are no foes to assail, all having been abolished. Inasmuch as angels sustained a continuous interest in the development of God's plan of redemption (I Peter 1:12) and served as ministering spirits (Heb. 1:14), keeping the faithful in the way and bearing them up lest they dash their feet against stones (Ps. 91:11f.), it is probable that these twelve at the gates symbolize the completed work of angelic ministering servants.

v. 14. "*And the wall of the city had twelve foundations, and on them twelve names of the twelve apostles of the Lamb.*" The twelve foundations are twelve huge stones (vv. 19f.) bearing the names of the twelve apostles. With gates bearing the names of the twelve tribes and the foundation stones bearing the names of the twelve apostles, the churches of the Old and New Covenants are thus united into one, bringing all redeemed into one eternal home (see comments, 12:1; cf. also Heb. 9:15; 11:40). It is futile to try to decide which of the apostles is omitted in the number, Matthias or Paul, for both are included. Twelve symbolizes the full number of the apostles who serve the Lamb, just as twelve indicates the full number of the tribes of Israel. The apostles laid the foundation of the church (Eph. 2:20; I Cor. 3:10), carried out the Great Commission by preaching the gospel to all the world (Mark 16:15f.; Col. 1:23), and sat upon twelve thrones judging the twelve tribes of Israel by the same word (Matt. 29:18).

v. 15. "*And he that spake with me had for a measure a golden reed to measure the city, and the gates thereof, and the wall thereof.*" In John's earlier vision of measuring the temple, the seer was given an ordinary reed like a rod and told to measure the sanctuary, its altar, and worshipers. This was interpreted to be the church of the present age (see comments, 11:1). But the heavenly city must be measured by an angel, apparently the one who had called John to see the holy city (vv. 9f).

Unlike the reed used by John, this one is golden, befitting the majesty and glory of the heavenly tabernacle or sanctuary which is identified later as the eternal one. The angel is to measure the city, the gates, and the wall.

v. 16. "*And the city lieth foursquare, and the length thereof is as great as the breadth: and he measured the city with the reed, twelve thousand furlongs: the length and the breadth and the height thereof are equal.*" The size of the city staggers the imagination, which is probably what God intended; for who can comprehend the greatness of the city of God? The wall was twelve thousand furlongs in each direction, suggesting twelve, the perfect religious number, multiplied by a thousand, the full or complete number. A furlong is an eighth of a mile; therefore, the city was revealed as a great cube, fifteen hundred miles in length, breadth, and height. This may remind us of the holy of holies of the wilderness tabernacle which is estimated to have been a cube of 10 × 10 × 10 cubits, although the exact dimensions are nowhere stated. However, the "oracle," or holy of holies in Solomon's temple is said to have measured 20 × 20 × 20 cubits and to have been overlaid with gold (I Kings 6:20). The size and shape of the measured city symbolizes a great and marvelous holy place into which the faithful priests of earth will eventually enter and in which they will offer an eternal sacrifice of praise to their God. Under the Old Covenant only the priests could enter into the holy place, and only the high priest could go into the holy of holies. In the present sanctuary, the church, the priests of Christ serve in the holy place, and the High Priest, Christ Jesus, in the most holy. But in this final sanctuary the priests will serve in the holy of holies ever before their God. The number of spiritual Israel was numbered by twelves, so now the final home of these is measured by twelves.

v. 17. "*And he measured the wall thereof, a hundred and forty and four cubits, according to the measure of a man, that is, of an angel.*" The wall also is measured by twelves; but instead of furlongs, the measurement is by cubits. A cubit is between eighteen and twenty-one inches long, determined by the distance of the arm from the elbow to the end of the middle finger. Thus the wall measures about 218 feet. It is uncertain whether this indicates the thickness of the wall about the city or the height of the wall. If it is the height of the surrounding wall, it would be only a marker in comparison to the city itself. If it is the thickness of the wall of the city, the ratio would be one-inch thickness compared to three thousand feet in height, which is completely out of proportion. Probably the writer intends to give only the height of the wall about the city, allowing its comparative insignificance to emphasize the lack of future need of a defensive wall. The real significance of the number in comparison to the size of the city is unknown. The measure "according to a man, that is, of an angel," is that it is a measure understood by man, one in common use by men, but in the hands of an angel.

v. 18. *"And the building of the wall thereof was jasper: and the city was pure gold, like unto pure glass."* The splendor and glory of this description far exceeds the powers of the imagination. Paul's words describing the mystery of the gospel, "Things which eye saw not, and ear heard not, and which entered not into the heart of man, whatsoever things God prepared for them that love him" (I Cor. 2:9; cf. Isa. 64:4), could likewise be said of that which God has in store for those who are prepared for it. The building (*endōmēsis*, used only here in the New Testament) of the wall probably indicates either the material of its structure, or possibly that it was inlaid with sparkling diamonds. The city itself was pure gold, but gold unfamiliar to us, for it too sparkled as pure polished glass.

vv. 19, 20. *"The foundations of the wall of the city were adorned with all manner of precious stones. The first foundation was jasper; the second, sapphire; the third, chalcedony; the fourth, emerald; the fifth, sardonyx; the sixth, sardius; the seventh, chrysolite; the eighth, beryl; the ninth, topaz; the tenth, chrysoprase; the eleventh, jacinth; the twelfth, amethyst."* Naming the most precious stones known to the world at that time (some of which cannot be identified today), the seer now returns to give a fuller description of the foundations. Eight of the stones named in John's vision appear on the breastplate of the high priest (Exod. 28:17–20), but even the identity of some of these is questionable.

(1) Jasper is thought to be the diamond, the most precious of all stones (cf. 4:3; 21:11, 18). (2) Sapphire (*lapis lazuli*, margin) is a stone of various shades of blue, and ranks next to the diamond in hardness (Vine). (3) Chalcedony, a green carbonate of copper, is found in the

mines of Chalcedon (Plummer). (4) Emerald is probably the emerald of our day, but it could be some other green stone. (5) The sardonyx was a stone highly valued as a cameo setting; it was a kind of onyx in which the white was broken by layers of red or brown (Swete). (6) Sardius was a stone of two special varieties, one a yellowish brown, the other a transparent red (Vine). In this instance it is probably the red variety (see comments, 4:3). (7) Crysolite, whose identity is uncertain, was probably a yellow beryl or gold-colored jasper. (8) Beryl, which is a sea-green color, has much in common with the emerald. (9) Topaz was a stone held in high esteem in Pliny's time for its green tints (*I.S.B.E.*), but it possibly was of a yellow color (Vine). (1) Crysoprase was akin to the beryl, but of a paler color (Swete). (11) Jacinth (sapphire, margin) is probably the sapphire, a precious stone of transparent rich blue color. (12) Amethyst is a stone whose color nearly approaches wine, a purplish red.

There are many uncertainties in the identities and colors of a number of these stones, for names have changed through the centuries. But the exquisite beauty of such a city with these foundation stones is not lost; God seeks to impress upon us the splendor of being a part of that glorious city.

v. 21. *"And the twelve gates were twelve pearls; each one of the several gates was of one pearl: and the street of the city was pure gold, as it were transparent glass."* John resumes his discussion of the gates (v. 12), describing each gate or gate tower as made of one huge, massive pearl. As do many today, the ancients esteemed pearls, which were often highly lustrous; white or variously colored. The street (*plateia*, singular), has caused problems for many readers, since a single street—even though symbolic—seems out of proportion in a city of such magnitude. Different writers have given various explanations to the passage. Caird suggests that "in the Septuagint the word is commonly used collectively or generically, much as in English we use the phrase, 'in the street' without implying that there is only one" (p. 278). Alford says, "And the street (generic: the street material)" (p. 743), and Lenski suggests that avenue or street refers to that of each portal (p. 642). Plummer holds a similar view; "'the street' is not merely one street, but the whole collective material of which the streets are composed" (p. 513). Probably the streets leading from each gate are joined together to make up one street. Since the vision is of a great symbol, whatever the view or explanation one may hold, we can accept the idea of unity; all portals admit and lead to Him who is the central figure.

The gold, like that of verse 18, is unlike any known to us; for it is as transparent glass, transcending the beauty of any metal known on earth. The beholders of the great harlot city cried as they beheld her burning, "What city is like the great city?" (18:18). In her class there was none like her. And so shall the beholder of this city say, To what shall we compare such a city? It is as incomparable as the God from whom it comes. Isaiah issued the following challenge to the people of his day, "To whom then will ye liken God? or what likeness will ye compare unto him?" (Isa. 40:18). There was no one or any likeness to which to make a comparison. And so might John challenge the whole creation, "To what will ye liken this city? or to what will you compare it?" The answer is that there is nothing in the universe with which it can be compared.

B. Interior of the City, vv. 22-27

v. 22. "And I saw no temple therein: for the Lord God the Almighty, and the Lamb, are the temple thereof." From the splendor of its exterior, the seer directs attention to the glory of its interior. The whole of this majestic city is one grand sanctuary (*naos*), which already has been indicated (v. 16). There could not be another within it, for the great God Almighty, and the Lamb, the perpetual sacrifice, are there. The glory of God's being and presence fills the city. The promise of 3:12 is now completely fulfilled; those who have overcome are permanent worshipers within the sanctuary of the divine presence.

v. 23. "And the city hath no need for the sun, neither of the moon, to shine upon it: for the glory of God did lighten it, and the lamp thereof is the Lamb." From the beginning, God's residence among His people has been developed step by step, each concept of His presence being progressively greater. His glory, which the Jews call "the Shekinah," filled the tabernacle and temple. His glory is in the church by His Spirit (see comments, v. 11), and now that glory is full and complete as He and the Lamb fill the new temple. And as there is no need for a temple, so there is no need for any created light, either sun or moon;

for the source of all light, God and the Lamb, now fill the new Jerusalem of the new heaven and new earth.

v. 24. *"And the nations shall walk amidst the light thereof: and the kings of the earth bring their glory into it."* Beginning at 6:15 and extending throughout the remainder of the book, the kings, those who are in league with Satan and who stand in opposition to the Lamb, are finally destroyed (19:18–21). But as is pointed out in verse 3 (see comments), the "peoples" and "nations" in the holy city are those whom the Lord called, redeemed, and made His own from among all groups in the earth (5:9; 7:9). Isaiah had said, "And nations shall come to thy light [the light is the Lord and His glory], and kings to the brightness of thy rising" (Isa. 60:3; cf. 52:15). When that light appeared in the person of Jesus Christ, men from every nation came to it. Since all civil kingdoms and political kings have come to an end, there are none to challenge or share God's glory; whatever glory these had possessed or claimed is now laid at the feet of Him who is Almighty.

v. 25. *"And the gates thereof shall in no wise be shut by day (for there shall be no night there)."* In the same context in which Isaiah pointed out that nations and kings would come to the light, he also said, "Thy gates also shall be open continually; they shall not be shut day nor night; that men may bring unto thee the wealth of the nations" (60:11). The gates of God's city under Christ have always been open to all who would enter. This admission and acceptance of all who would come reveals clearly the mercy and grace of God bestowed in love upon any person of any nation. But Isaiah continued, "For that nation and kingdom that will not serve thee shall perish; yea, those nations shall be utterly wasted" (v. 12). Those who would enter had come in, and those who would be destroyed had now been destroyed. The Master of the house had risen up and shut the door (Luke 13:25); the gospel opportunity was now past. Since all enemies had now been cast into the lake of fire, there was no occasion to shut the gates, in the way the city gates of the world had been shut at night. Further, there is no night in the celestial city; there is one eternal day, for God and the Lamb are its light.

v. 26. *"And they shall bring the glory and the honor of the nations into it."* All the glory and the honor sought or achieved by these redeemed out of the nations shall be brought into the city. When we consider that which is outside the city, we realize that all glory and honor is to be found in the spiritual city of God; only dishonor and shame are to be found outside of it.

v. 27. "And there shall in no wise enter into it anything unclean, or he that maketh an abomination and a lie: but only they that are written in the Lamb's book of life." "When the saints go marching in," led by their King and Savior, to take up their eternal life and work with Him, only those fitted for such a life shall enter. "There shall in no wise [emphatically, assuredly] enter in anything that is unclean," that is, anything defiled, impure or polluted. Neither shall there enter anyone who makes or does an abomination and a lie, specifically an idolater (see comments, v. 8). All that is contrary to the holiness that God demands and all who live after such a standard shall be outside. Only those that are written in the Lamb's book of life shall enter into the city (see comments, 20:12).

CHAPTER 22
The New Jerusalem, Continued

C. Its Life, vv. 1-5

The description of the holy city set forth in chapter 21 continues through the first five verses of chapter 22. The external grandeur of the city and its internal glory made up of those who dwell in it have been presented. The blessedness of the life of that city is now revealed.

A close relationship between these verses and the first few chapters of Genesis is readily apparent. In Eden there was a garden, a river, the tree of life, man's disobedience and separation from these, a curse pronounced on the serpent, the soil and indirectly, upon man, for it brought death and separation from God. In the city of God, the eternal Eden of the redeemed, there is the river of water of life, the tree of life, the absence of a curse, and a perfect and full fellowship of the redeemed with God. What was lost in Eden is now fully restored; God's purpose is achieved.

v. 1. "*And he showed me a river of water of life, bright as crystal, proceeding out of the throne of God and of the Lamb.*" Although these verses are a continuation of the previous chapter, the phrase "and he showed me" indicates a break. With this same phrase the vision of the Lamb's bride, the new Jerusalem, had been introduced (21:9). The expressions "living water" (John 4:10, 11; 7:38) and "water of life" (Rev. 7:17; 21:6; 22:1, 17) are peculiar to John's New Testament writings. Though they differ from each other slightly in the Greek, as indicated in the translation, both expressions probably have the same meaning. The living water that Jesus offered the woman at Jacob's well was from this river which flowed from the eternal throne. The question might be raised whether the phrase "water of life" signifies "water possessing life-giving powers, water which restores, refreshes, supports life" (Plummer, p. 545), or "water that *is* life, zōe, the very life or life essence," a whole river of it (Lenski). The answer may elude us, but it is certainly the river of water of life that sustains life in its fullness.

"Bright as crystal" (*krustallos*, rock-crystal, A. & G.), occurring only here and in 4:6, emphasizes the sparkling purity and beauty of the stream. Unlike the streams of earth, polluted and corrupted by Satanic interference, becoming as wormwood (8:10f.), bringing judgment and death (16:4-7), this river is the essence of purity and life.

The source of the river is clearly revealed, "proceeding out of the throne of God and of the Lamb," the fountainhead of all life; but no reference is made to its mouth, for it has no end. This is the first time the expression, "throne of God and of the Lamb" has occurred. Until now it has been, "him that sitteth on the throne, and the Lamb" (5:13; 6:16; 7:10) and the Lamb "in the midst of [or before] the throne" (5:6; 7:17). The idea of a joint occupancy of the throne by God and the Lamb has, however, been implied throughout the book. Jesus speaks of sitting down on His and the Father's throne (3:21); John sees Jesus "caught up unto God, and unto his throne" (12:5); and the seer beholds Christ sitting on the great white throne of judgment, which is certainly God's throne. As the kingdom is Christ's and God's (Eph. 5:5), so also is the throne theirs.

John's vision of the river is similar to that of Ezekiel's, but with important differences (cf. Ezek. 47:1-12). In Ezekiel's vision the waters issued from the threshold of the house (temple), flowed eastward toward the Dead Sea, increasing in breadth and depth as it flowed onward. Its waters were for the healing of the salt waters of the sea, providing fish in abundance; on either side of the river grew every tree for food. In John's vision the river flows out of the throne of God and the Lamb, continues beside or in the midst of the street, and has no designated termination. It sustains life or is life. Common to both visions are the trees on either side of the river. In Ezekiel's vision the trees provide fruit and leaves for food and healing, and in John's vision they provide the food of eternal life and leaves for healing of the nations. In similar visions, Joel (3:18) and Zechariah (14:8) also saw rivers from God. The message of these Old Testament prophets looked to the spiritual kingdom under the Messiah, but John's vision points to the consummation of that kingdom in heaven.

v. 2. *"In the midst of the street thereof. And on this side of the river and on that was the tree of life, bearing twelve manner of fruits, yielding its fruit every month: and the leaves of the tree were for the healing of the nations."* "In the midst of the street thereof" belongs to verse one; it completes the sentence. Again, "the street" is used collectively, representing all the avenues from the twelve gates which extend through the city. The picture is difficult to visualize but it seems that in the midst of the streets, viewed collectively as one, the river flows alongside with trees on its banks. The tree of life, singular, "on this side of the river and on that," indicates that "tree" is used collectively, as is "street," to represent all the trees that lined the river. The vision pictures a beautiful park with golden streets, rivers of crystal pure water flowing through it, and banks and avenues lined with trees for fruit and leaves for healing. Of course, the whole picture is symbolic.

The precise phrase, "tree of life," indicating fullness of life, occurs twice in Genesis (2:9; 3:22), referring to the tree placed in Eden that if man would eat of it he would be immortal. But when man sinned, the tree was taken away, lest he should eat of it and in his sinful condition live forever. What a blessing that it was removed; for, with the tree gone, immortality in sin was made impossible. Man must now find his eternal life in a different tree, the one on which the Savior was hanged (Acts 5:30; 10:39; 13:29; Gal. 3:13; I Peter 2:24). The phrase, "tree of life," occurs three times in the Book of Proverbs: wisdom is said to be a tree of life (3:18), as is also the fruit of the righteous (11:30; cf. 12:28), and "a gentle tongue" (15:4). These three deepen the moral and spiritual life of the individual. "Tree of life" occurs often in Jewish apocalyptic writings and in pagan mythology, but the concept is distorted. However, such writings testify to an original divine source of the idea.

In John's vision, that which was lost in Adam's paradise is gained in Christ's city of God. Jesus promised all who would overcome that they would eat of the tree of life in the paradise of God (2:7). Now in their victory this is realized. Instead of "twelve manner of fruits" (ASV and KJV), the marginal reading of the ASV "twelve crops of fruit" is preferable, suggesting constant and perfect abundance. It appears that the tree produces only one kind of fruit, the fruit of life, as the river flows with one kind of water, the water of life. Life—abundance of life—seems to be the theme of this section; for we have the book of life, the river of the water of life, and the tree of life. The leaves are included in the symbol; they are for the healing of the nations. All that we possess of life, the provision for life, and the spiritual healing of all nations comes from God—He is the source of all life. The vision reveals that the life we now have comes from heaven, and the final perfection of God's purpose is consummated in heaven.

v. 3. *"And there shall be no curse any more: and the throne of God and of the Lamb shall be therein: and his servants shall serve him."* Again we are reminded of Eden, where the curse was pronounced first upon the serpent (Gen. 3:14), then upon the ground (v. 17), and indirectly upon Adam and Eve (vv. 16 -19). Later a curse was placed upon Cain because of his sin of murder (Gen. 4:11). Another was placed upon all who would curse Abraham or his posterity through whom the seed would come (Gen. 12:3; 27:29). Further, this pronouncement was carried over into the law as God cursed those of His people who would disregard and violate His law (Deut. 27:15-26; 28:15-68). In each instance the curse was the judicial pronouncement of an appointed penalty because of the violation of divine law. In some instances to curse meant to abhor, to detest utterly, therefore to devote to destruction. Under the gospel the curse of the law was taken away, for Christ became a curse for those under it (Gal. 3:13). To the Jerusalem to which we have come (Heb. 12:22) it was promised, "And men shall dwell therein, and there shall be no more curse, but Jerusalem shall dwell safely" (Zech. 14:11).

All that is subject to the curse in time will be abolished in the heavenly city, for the throne of God and the Lamb is in the midst of it; and nothing accursed can abide in the presence of that throne and its occupants. In that glorious state His servants will serve Him with a perfect service. What that service will be is one of the mysteries of God yet to be revealed. It is sufficient for His saints to know that it will be a glorious, uninterrupted service for which the whole of time and the sacrifice of Christ have prepared us.

v. 4. *"And they shall see his face; and his name shall be on their foreheads."* To behold God face to face, something man has never done, will be the reward of faithful devotion to Him in this life. This universal desire of the human soul to see God was expressed by Philip when he said, "Lord, show us the Father, and it sufficeth us" (John 14:8). This yearning is now fulfilled as the redeemed behold His face. Some think the face here beheld is the face of the Lamb rather than that of the Father, but it appears that it is the face of God, for John had written, "Beloved, now are we children of God, and it is not yet made manifest what we shall be. We know that, if he shall be manifested, we shall be like him; for we shall see him even as he is" (I John 3:2). Also, His name was to have been written upon the one who should overcome (Rev. 3:12), and the servants of God were to have been sealed on their foreheads (7:3). On the other hand, those standing on Mount Zion had the name of the Lamb and of His Father written on their foreheads (14:1)—so, that which is before the seer's view may be indeterminable. In the light of John 14:7-9; I John 3:1-3, and the passages alluded to, it seems that God is the one spoken of, for the Lamb has redeemed the saints and brought them unto the Father. These who have His name, behold His face, and serve Him, stand in contrast to those who received the mark of the beast (13:16), who were to drink the cup of God's wrath (14:10), and were now in the lake of fire.

v. 5. "*And there shall be night no more; and they need no light of lamp, neither light of sun; for the Lord God shall give them light: and they shall reign for ever and ever.*" John repeats what was said earlier, that there is no need for lamp or sun (see comments, 21:23, 25). The thought has developed from walking in the midst of the light (21:24), to serving in the light (22:3), and now, to reigning in that light. The reign is now extended from the thousand years with Him during this age (see 20:4), to a reign "for ever and ever," ages without end. These reigned with Him upon the earth (5:10) and in life (Rom. 5:17); but this reign is one that is not limited by time. It shall not cease. Here is further evidence that Revelation 21:1—22:5 refers to the eternal glory, and not to the present age.

CONCLUSION: THE DIVINE WITNESS
vv. 6-21

The curtain has fallen on history and time—both are swallowed up in eternity. The glory of the vision is now finished, and John is left with the angel who has shown him the things which were shortly to come to pass. In the long conflict with Satan and his forces the church has emerged victorious, and in the last vision it was seen at home with

425　　THE NEW JERUSALEM, CONTINUED　　22:6

God. Trials are forgotten in the joy of being in the Father's presence. Ezekiel, forerunner of John in divine apocalyptic visions, had faced the storm of Judah's suffering in Babylon's fierce world conquest. However, as he looked into the storm, he had seen God in it, redeeming a remnant. So also John had faced the fury of Rome's long persecution of the saints and had seen God on His throne giving victory to His faithful ones.

Three things remain to be added: (1) the signature of God and the Son as witnesses to the vision, (2) a few exhortations to those to whom the book was addressed, and (3) an earnest exhortation to the Lord to come. In matters involving life or death, every word had to be established by two or more witnesses (cf. 11:3; see also Deut. 19:15; Matt. 18:16; II Cor. 13:1; I Tim. 5:19). The nature and content of the entire vision was such that it demanded the witness of God and Christ. This done, the book closes with a fitting climax and conclusion to the whole revelation of God to man.

v. 6. *"And he said unto me, These words are faithful and true: and the Lord, the God of the spirits of the prophets, sent his angel to show unto his servants the things which must shortly come to pass."* Throughout this section it is difficult to determine who is speaking. In this instance is the speaker the angel of 21:9, 15, and 22:1, or the angel God had sent to give the revelation to John (1:1; 22:16), or Jesus Himself? The similarity of this verse to 1:1 leads to the conclusion that the speaker is the angel to whom the Lord gave the commission at the first. This angel may be representative of all the angels who have appeared in the book. In this phase of the revelation he represents the eternal Father who now gives His witness to the divine origin of the book's content. Jesus was designated as the "faithful and true witness" (3:14), and "Faithful and True" as He judged and made war (19:11). Now, through the angel, the Father endorses both Christ and the message as He says, "These words," the words of the entire revelation, "are faithful and true." "The Lord, the God of the spirits of the prophets," is not only the Father of the spirits of us all (Heb. 12:9), but through the centuries He has endued the spirits of the prophets with His Spirit to speak and reveal His message to His people (Deut. 18:18; II Peter 1:21; Acts 1:16; and cf. I Peter 1:11).

The eternal God who had inspired the prophets had likewise sent

His angel to show to His true bondservants the things that would "shortly come to pass." The affirmation, "These words are faithful and true," is therefore God's testimony to the things revealed. "Which must shortly come to pass" (shortly, *en tachi* from *tacheōs*, 1:1; 22:6; see comments, 1:1), indicates "speedily" or with speed (Luke 18:8), "quickly" (Acts 12:7; 22:18), "shortly" (Acts 25:4; Rom. 16:20). The reference is to the conflict developed in the book; hence, in a brief time the events of that conflict would come to pass.

v. 7. *"And behold, I come quickly. Blessed is he that keepeth the words of the prophecy of this book."* "Behold" is an imperative, bidding the reader or hearer to give serious attention to what is said. "I am coming quickly" (*tachu*, from *tachus*), signifies an action executed speedily or swiftly (cf. Matt. 5:25; 28:7f.; John 11:29). But who speaks? Are these the words of God who would come in the person of Christ, or are they the words of Jesus, parenthetically (Swete) declaring His speedy coming? Commentators are divided over the answer; probably we can never decide definitely. However, we know that God came in Christ doing His redemptive work (John 14:10; II Cor. 5:19f.) and will come in Him with the angels at the end of time (I Thess. 4:14; Titus 2:13). It would not be amiss, therefore, to conclude that God is the speaker, declaring that in Christ He will come speedily to His needy saints. Whether it is God speaking of His coming in Christ or if it is Christ speaking, it is certain that the one who comes is Jesus. He uses the same word (*tachu*) of His swift coming to the churches (2:16 [v. 5 in some mss.]; 3:11) and in this chapter repeats the promise of a speedy coming (vv. 12, 20).

A sixth beatitude announces a blessing upon him who keeps "the words of the prophecy of this book." This repeats the principle set forth in the first beatitude, "Blessed is he that readeth, and they that hear... and keep the things that are written" in the prophecy (1:3). To keep (from *tēreō*) is to observe, fulfill, pay attention to (A. & G.; see also v. 9). The third "blessed" was pronounced upon him "that watcheth and keepeth his garments" (16:15). One keeps his garments as he keeps the words of the prophecy. One must be both a diligent student and a devout observer of what God says. The command to write (1:11, 19) is now carried out.

vv. 8, 9. *"And I John am he that heard and saw these things. And when I heard and saw, I fell down to worship before the feet of the angel that showed me these things. And he saith unto me, See thou do it not: I am a fellow-servant with thee and with thy brethren the prophets, and with them that keep the words of this book: worship God."* In this concluding section both the Father and the Son testify to the authenticity of the revelation. Although it would seem that man could add nothing to such witness, John adds his testimony, saying, "And I John am he that heard and saw these things." John vouches for a true record of what he saw and heard; God testifies to the divine origin, inspiration, and truth of all these things. The apostle had added a similar testimony to the veracity of his Gospel (John 19:35).

It is surprising that so shortly after John had been reproved for worshiping an angel that he would again commit the same error (see comments, 19:10). Possibly John was overcome because the angel stood so near to God in revealing His testimony; however no one knows why he responded as he did. But let us not be too critical of John; for when a person brings to one of us the glorious gospel, points us to the Lamb and makes life and heaven real to us, we are prone to give him reverence beyond his due, though he is merely a man and nothing more than a servant (I Cor. 3:5). Even angels are just fellow-servants with God's faithful prophets and servants who keep or hold sacred His word. The divine command is, Worship God; for all adoration, praise, and devotion belong to Him.

v. 10. *"And he saith unto me, Seal not up the words of the prophecy of this book; for the time is at hand."* Apparently the speaker who now instructs John to seal not up the words of the prophecy is the angel before whom John had prostrated himself (v. 8). A "sealed" book is one beyond the comprehension of uninitiated persons. When John heard the voice of the seven thunders he was told to "seal up the things which the seven thunders uttered" (10:4), and so we cannot know what they were. Daniel was instructed to shut up the vision he had seen and the words he had heard, for they pertained to the end of Hebrew history (Dan. 8:26; 10:14; 12:4, 9). But John's prophecy was not to be sealed up, "for the time is at hand"; the events of its revelation were not in the distant future but were for the immediate period. The book was to be sent to the churches at that time, (1:11), and its content made applicable to all churches (22:16). Its message was to be made known, its warnings were to be heeded, and its hearers encouraged by the divine assurance of victory.

v. 11. "*He that is unrighteous, let him do unrighteousness still: and he that is filthy, let him be made filthy still: and he that is righteous, let him do righteousness still: and he that is holy, let him be made holy still.*" The speaker of verse 10 continues. In the Gospel of John, chapter 3, the Master divided the world into two groups, believers and unbelievers (v. 18), who love the light or the darkness (v. 19), and who either continue the practice of evil or "do the truth" (vv. 20f.). So here the speaker separates society into two groups, the unrighteous and filthy and the righteous and holy. Each individual chooses the class in which he is identified. One's actions grow out of the basic character he develops or makes for himself. As he chooses his course he persists in traveling that path. He either practices sin, sinking deeper into his unrighteousness and moral defilement, or he seeks righteousness, rising higher and higher in holiness.

The word "still" or "yet more" (*eti*) "indicates the permanent character, condition, and destiny of the unrighteous and filthy" (Vine). Paul summed up sin's development when he said, "Evil men and impostors shall wax worse and worse, deceiving and being deceived" (II Tim. 3:13). The righteous and holy person will develop a permanent character, for in his righteousness he is set apart for holiness. He follows his Lord, "the Holy and Righteous One" (Acts 3:14), going on to perfection (Heb. 6:1; II Cor. 7:1). One either grows in grace and stature as a Christian or sinks deeper into hardness and indifference as a sinner; there is no standing still. Let the sinner beware, lest when "the Master has risen up and shut to the door" he find himself on the outside, knocking for entrance, but finding none (Luke 13:25–27). There is a point of no return (Heb. 6:4–6).

v. 12. "*Behold, I come quickly; and my reward is with me, to render to each man according as his work is.*" The immediacy and swiftness of the Lord's coming is given special emphasis in this section: "the things which must shortly come to pass" (v. 6), "Behold, I come quickly" (v. 7), "for the time is at hand" (v. 10), and "I come quickly" (vv. 12, 20). Since the book was not sealed, for the time was at hand, the passages do not refer to the Lord's second or final coming, for that was not at hand (II Thess. 2:1f.). "Reward" (*misthos*), which means primarily pay or wages, occurs only twice in this book, here and in 11:18, where the reward of the prophets and servants is mentioned (see comments). The pay may be for work done (Matt. 20:8; John 4:36), wages held back (James 5:4), money paid for treachery (Acts 1:18), or for wrongdoing (II Peter 2:15). It may also indicate recompense given for the moral quality of an action, such as reward in heaven (Matt. 6:2-4, 5-6, 16-18), or reward for wrongdoing (II Peter 2:13). Rewards will be according to the promises of the Lord and according to the work—the whole life— of the individual. The present passage may refer to the reward rendered to good and bad men at any coming of the Lord and also to the reward rendered to each at His final coming. Since the reward is to be given according to works, we should not embrace a superficial or false concept of grace which displaces works, lest anyone be found wanting when He comes (Matt. 16:27; Mark 13:34; Rom. 2:6; Rev. 2:23; 20:12f.).

v. 13. *"I am the Alpha and the Omega, the first and the last, the beginning and the end."* The phrase "Alpha and Omega" has occurred twice previously, and in each instance it was a title ascribed to the Father (1:8; 21:6). The phrase expresses the completeness of God and all His purposes. Likewise the expression, "the first and the last" (*ho prōtos kai ho eschatos*) has appeared twice, and in each instance it was claimed by Christ (1:17; 2:8), indicating His eternal being (see comments, 1:17). In former times Jehovah declared that He was the first and that He would be with the last (Isa. 41:4), before whom there was no God (Isa. 43:10; 44:6; 48:12); thus Christ identifies Himself with absolute deity. The speaker makes a third claim; He is "the beginning and the end" (*he archē kai to telos*; cf. 21:6; 22:13, in 1:8 the phrase is omitted in better mss.). The "beginning" (*archē*) indicates the first person in a series, one of foremost authority, one by whom all things commence (cf. Isa. 40:14, 25).

Although God the Father has claimed all three of these qualities for Himself, it is evident that in this instance it is Jesus who speaks. He is hereby identifying Himself with the Father in completeness of godhood, in eternal being, and in divine authority. He was with God in the beginning (John 1:1), is the beginning of the creation of God (Rev. 3:14), is the one by whom all things created were brought forth (Col. 1:16), and has had all authority delegated to Him (Matt. 28:18). God purposed and predetermined all things and their ultimate destiny, and this purpose is carried out by Christ (Rom. 16:25ff.; Eph. 1:9-11; John 5:22).

v. 14. "Blessed are they that wash their robes, that they may have the right to come to the tree of life, and may enter in by the gates into the city." This is the seventh and final beatitude occurring in the book. The American Standard Version has adopted the above reading over the King James Version's "Blessed are they that do his commandments," and is recognized by recent scholarship as more probably correct. These are they who, in the blood of the Lamb, wash their robes from the filth of the world (cf. v. 11). By the blood of Jesus we are loosed from our sins (1:5), purchased unto God (5:9), and have our robes, or lives, made white (7:14). This verse speaks of those who accept martyrdom or have the spirit and character of one willing to die for the Lord (12:11; 20:4). Such have "authority over" the tree of life; they have the right to partake of it, and they possess the credentials which permit them to enter by the gates into the city. The tree of life (see v. 2) was promised to those who would overcome (2:7) through the blood (12:11); they are thereby admitted into the eternal city.

v. 15. "Without are the dogs, and the sorcerers, and the fornicators, and the murderers, and the idolaters, and every one that loveth and maketh a lie." Again the Lord sets forth in strong contrast those who would inherit the things prepared for the redeemed, and those who would be cast into the lake that burns with fire and brimstone (21:7f.). The blessed ones enter into the celestial city (v. 14), whereas the filthy are doomed to the lake of fire. Those without are the dogs, here used to describe the immoral, the prostitutes and sodomites (homosexuals, Deut. 23:17f.), the vicious (Ps. 22:16; Phil. 3:2), the moral scavengers whose howl distresses and vexes the righteous (Ps. 59:6f.; II Peter 2:7f.), and those who wallow in filth (II Peter 2:22). "Dogs" probably describe the abominable of 21:8 (see comments) and the filthy of 22:11. The list repeats the character traits of those cast into the lake of fire, except for "the fearful and unbelieving" of the former passage. "All liars" of 21:8 is further enlarged upon to include "every one who loveth and maketh a lie." These walk in darkness; they lie, and "do not the truth" (I John 1:6), having "pleasure in unrighteousness" (II Thess. 2:12). A man acts out of love. If he loves truth, he will seek for and walk in it; if he loves a lie, he will have no problem finding and walking in it. Each man walks after that which he loves.

v. 16. *"I Jesus have sent mine angel to testify unto you these things for the churches. I am the root and the offspring of David, the bright, the morning star."* Since the revelation was given to Jesus Christ by the Father to show unto His servants by His angel (1:1), and since Jesus claimed the same eternal attributes as the Father (v. 13), He can say that it is He who sends His angel to testify these things for (or, over) the churches. Nowhere does John identify the church in the way that Paul does (Eph. 1:22f.; Col. 1:18, et al.), but represents it as a female arrayed in light (chap. 12), as a glorious city, a bride adorned for her husband (chaps. 19, 21, 22), and as "the churches," which include all the brethren.

Jesus here adds His testimony to that of the Father, making twofold the divine witness to the truth of the book. In addition to the above claim (v. 13), He now affirms His human relationship. What the angel had claimed for the Lord as "the root of David," worthy to open the book (see comments, 5:5), Jesus, using His human name (Matt. 1:21), now claims for Himself. In one of the seven letters He claimed to have the "key of David," the power to open and to shut, the authority to rule over the promised realm of David (3:7). As the root and offspring of David He fulfills the ancient hope of Israel that a descendant of David would rule on the throne of David (II Sam. 7:12–16; Ps. 132:11; Isa. 11:1, 10 [cf. Rom. 15:12]; 53:2; Jer. 23:5; Ezek. 34:24; 37:24f.). Furthermore, the phrase indicates that He is the beginning and the end, the total fulfillment of all that God promised through the prophets. In Him is realized the ideal and ultimate purpose of God.

To the church in Thyatira Jesus promised that He would give the morning star to whoever would overcome (2:28, see comments). A prophet had long ago declared that out of Jacob would come forth a star, a scepter (symbol of royalty) that would smite His enemies, breaking the sons of tumult (Num. 24:17). Jesus now declares that He is that star, "the bright, the morning star," who, as the offspring of David, has conquered His enemies. And as the morning star, He heralds the approach of eternal day.

v. 17. "And the Spirit and the bride say, Come. And he that heareth, let him say, Come. And he that is athirst, let him come: he that will, let him take the water of life freely." This is the Spirit that inspired prophets and apostles, and that the churches were to hear; for in each of the seven letters occurs the exhortation, "He that hath an ear, let him hear what the Spirit saith to the churches" (chaps. 2, 3). In chapter 12 it was pointed out that the woman symbolized spiritual Zion; but when she went into the wilderness she was the church, whose seed (in the symbol) was warred against by the dragon. So here, the bride symbolizes the church, and "he that heareth" the individual members. Wherefore the Spirit, the bride (the church), and the individual members combine their voices to say, "Come."

Is the exhortation to come addressed to Jesus or to those who are thirsty? It is more likely that the address is to the Lord Jesus, who said, "Behold, I come quickly" (v. 12). However, it is certainly true that the Spirit, through the Word of God, and the saints, God's instruments for declaring the Word, are to urge all to come. Those who yearn for a higher life, a spiritual life fed from the fountain of eternal life, are now urged to come and drink freely of the water of life. In anticipation of the enlarged Zion under the new covenant of peace, Isaiah had cried, "ho, every one that thirsteth, come ye to the waters, and he that hath no money; come ye, buy, and eat; yea, come, buy wine and milk without money and without price" (Isa. 55:1). The final call is now being made, the water is being offered free for the taking; the invitation is warm and cordial, but each must come willingly. He who comes and drinks of this water shall not thirst again (John 6:35).

vv. 18, 19. "I testify unto every man that heareth the words of the prophecy of this book, If any man shall add unto them, God shall add unto him the plagues which are written in this book: and if any man shall take away from the words of the book of this prophecy, God shall take away his part from the tree of life, and out of the holy city, which are written in this book." Jesus continues to speak. This book is to be accepted as Scripture. It has the stamp of God (v. 6) and of Jesus (v. 16), with the added testimony of John that he had heard and seen these things which he had written (v. 8). Now is added a warning from the Lord Himself that the prophecy of this book is not to be tampered with, either by deleting from, adding to, or changing it. A similar command and warning had been given concerning the law (Deut. 4:2; 12:32; Prov. 30:5f.) and the gospel (Gal. 1:6–9). God's spiritual and moral truth must be neither altered nor perverted; it must be faithfully handed on from one generation to another. The principle applies to all the Word of God, but here Jesus is speaking particularly of this book, the Revelation. To add to the book is to incur the wrath of God and receive the plagues written therein—those of the trumpets, the bowls, and the lake of fire. Anyone taking from the words of the prophecy will have his name blotted from the book of life and his right to the tree of life and the blessings of the eternal city removed.

The words of the prophecy are the thoughts, principles, judgments, and messages of the book. The Lord is not speaking of an honest error in judgment and interpretation, even though this is serious. Rather He condemns the presumptuous and all who manifest a careless or flippant attitude toward the Word. As Lenski intimates, this makes writing about the book a serious and sublime matter to be pursued with the deepest of reverence for God and His truth.

v. 20. "*He who testifieth these things saith, Yea: I come quickly. Amen: come, Lord Jesus.*" Jesus, not John, is the true author of this book. He now adds His final word of testimony which is in response to the call of the Spirit, the bride, and the faithful and loyal saints, who say, "Come." That response is, "Yea, I come quickly." Through the centuries He has come as He said He would, in swift retribution (2:5, 16) and in response to the needs of His saints (3:11). In answer to the cry of both suffering and joyous saints, He has responded with assurances that when the time is ripe for His final coming, He will come to gather His saints unto Himself and His Father. To this John responds, echoing the urgent cry of all faithful hearts, "Amen: Come, Lord Jesus."

v. 21. "*The grace of the Lord Jesus be with the saints. Amen.*" The word "grace" (*charis*) occurs only twice in this book, once at the beginning, "Grace to you and peace," from God, the seven Spirits, and from Jesus Christ (1:4f.), and now at the very end of the prophecy. This is a fitting benediction pronounced upon the saints of God who were facing the vicissitudes, hardships, and suffering of persecution.

The grace of the Lord Jesus involves His gracious favor and constant good will, which provides for every need in every hour. Only one word remains to be said: Amen—be it so!

A CLOSING WORD

As the vision fades from our view and the last word spoken echoes in our souls, our hearts are wrapped in awe at the majestic sight and sounds which we have beheld and to which we have listened. Surely our faith in God and His Christ has been strengthened, our hope for victory and heaven made more precious, our love for the spiritual and eternal made to abound beyond all previous measure, our will given a permanent determination to succeed, and our whole aim and goal of life become more fixed.

Now that we have advanced with John from glory to glory in this drama of spiritual history, conflict, and victory, we feel that we are more than excited spectators of a divine cinema—we are a part of the drama! We continue to share with those early Christians the pressures of political power and intrigue, the subtlety of false religious appeal through human wisdom, philosophy, and tradition, and the seduction of the world of lust. Also we share with them the strength, power, and help that come from our heavenly Father through faith in the blood of the Lamb. And we shall share with them the eternal reward of victory and an inheritance in God's celestial city as the bride of the Lamb. And so with the voice of all creation, let us join the song as they sing:

> Unto him that sitteth on the throne,
> and unto the Lamb, be the blessing,
> and the honor, and the glory,
> and the dominion, for ever and ever.

Bibliography

HISTORICAL BACKGROUND

Angus, S. *The Religious Quest of the Graeco-Roman World.* New York: Charles Scribner's Sons, 1929.
Ante-Nicene Fathers. American reprint of the Edinburgh edition. 10 vols. New York: Charles Scribner's Sons, 1903.
Barrett, C. K. *The New Testament Background: Selected Documents.* New York: Harper and Row, 1961.
Cambridge Ancient History. Cambridge: University Press, 1952, 1954.
Cochrane, Charles Norris. *Christianity and Classical Culture.* New York: Galaxy, 1959.
Coleman-Norton, P. R. *Roman State and the Christian Church,* vol. III. London: S. P. C. K., 1966.
Daniel-Rops, Henri. *The Church of Apostles and Martyrs,* vol. I. Garden City, New York: Image, 1962.
Ducheshe, Louis. *Early History of the Christian Church.* London: John Murray, 1909.
Eusebius. *Ecclesiastical History.* Translated by Christian Frederick Cruse. 9th ed., New York: Sanford and Swords, 1850.
Frend, W. H. C. *Martyrdom and Persecution in the Early Church.* Oxford: Basil Blackwell, 1965.
Gibbon, Edward. *The Decline and Fall of the Roman Empire.* 5 vols. Notes by H. H. Milman. Philadelphia: Henry Coates & Co., 1845.
Glover, T. R. *The Conflict of Religion in the Early Roman Empire.* London: Methueh & Co., 1909.
International Standard Bible Encyclopaedia. 5 vols. James Orr, ed. Chicago: Howard-Severance Co., 1937.
Josephus, Flavius. *The Works of Josephus.* Translated by William Wheaton. Philadelphia: The John C. Winston Press, n.d.
Kidd, B. J. *A History of the Church,* vol. I. Oxford: Clarendon Press, 1922.

Kraeling, Emil G. *Bible Atlas.* New York: Rand McNally and Co., 1965.

Mattingly, Harold. *Christianity in the Roman Empire.* New York: W. W. Norton and Co., 1967.

Pliny. *Letters and Panegyricus.* Translated by Betty Radice. 2 vols. Cambridge: Harvard University Press, 1969.

Ramsay, William M. *The Church in the Roman Empire Before A.D. 70.* 5th ed. London: Hodder and Stoughton, 1897.

———. *The Letters to the Seven Churches of Asia.* Grand Rapids: Baker Book House, reprint, 1963.

Richardson, Cyril C., trans. and ed. *Early Christian Fathers.* New York: Macmillan Co., 1970.

Rostovtzeff, M. *Rome.* Translated by J. D. Duff. New York: Oxford University Press, 1960.

Schaff, Philip. *History of the Christian Church.* 8 vols. New York: Charles Scribner's Sons, 1887.

Seutonius, Gaius. *The Twelve Caesars.* Translated by Robert Graves. Baltimore: Penguin Books, 1957.

Severy, Merle, ed. *Greece and Rome, Builders of Our World.* Washington: National Geographic Society, 1971.

Stevenson, J. *A New Eusebius.* London: S. P. C. K., 1963.

Tacitus. *The Annals of Imperial Rome.* Translated by Michael Grant. Baltimore: Penguin Books, 1968.

———. *The Complete Works of Tacitus.* Translated by Alfred John Church and William Brodribb. New York: Random House, 1942.

Weiss, Bernhard. *A Manual of Introduction to the New Testament.* 2 vols. New York: Funk and Wagnalls, 1889.

WORD STUDIES AND DICTIONARIES

Arndt, William F., and Gingrich, F. Wilbur. *A Greek-English Lexicon of the New Testament.* Chicago: University of Chicago Press, 1952.

Baker's Dictionary of Theology. Grand Rapids: Baker Book House, 1960.

Berry, George R. *A New Testament Interlinear, Greek-English.* Grand Rapids: Zondervan, 1952.
Englishmen's Greek Concordance of the New Testament. 9th ed. London: Samuel Bagster and Sons, 1908.
Hastings, James. *Dictionary of the New Testament.* 4 vols. Grand Rapids: Baker Book House (reprint), 1973.
Thayer, Henry J. *Greek-English Lexicon of the New Testament.* Grand Rapids: Baker Book House, 1977.
The Greek New Testament. New York: American Bible Society, 2d ed., 1968.
Vine, W. E. *Expository Dictionary of New Testament Words.* 4 vols. London: Oliphants, 1946.

COMMENTARIES

Alford, Henry. *The Greek Testament.* 4th ed. 4 vols. London: Rivington's, 1871.
Barclay, William. *The Revelation of St. John.* 2 vols. Edinburgh: Saint Andrew Press, 1961.
Barnes, Albert. *Notes on the New Testament: Book of Revelation.* Grand Rapids: Baker Book House (reprint), 1961.
Blackwood, Andrew W., Jr. *Ezekiel, Prophecy of Hope.* Grand Rapids: Baker Book House, 1965.
Caird, C. B. *The Revelation of St. John the Divine.* New York: Harper and Row, 1966.
Delitzch, Franz. *Commentary on Isaiah.* Grand Rapids: William B. Eerdmans (reprint), 1950.
―――. *Commentary on the Psalms.* Grand Rapids: William B. Eerdmans (reprint), 1950.
Hendriksen, William. *More Than Conquerors.* Grand Rapids: Baker Book House, 1944.
Hinds, John T. *Commentary on the Book of Revelation.* Nashville: Gospel Advocate, 1951.
Jenkins, Ferrell. *The Old Testament in the Book of Revelation.* Marion, Ind.: Cogdill Foundation Publications, 1972.

Lenski, R. C. H. *Interpretation of St. John's Revelation.* Columbus: Wartburg Press, 1957.

MacDonald, James M. *The Life and Writings of St. John.* New York: Scribner, Armstrong and Co., 1877.

Milligan, William. *The Book of Revelation.* New York: A. C. Armstrong and Son, 1889.

Moffatt, James. *The Revelation of St. John the Divine.* The Expositor's Greek Testament (5 vols). Grand Rapids: William B. Eerdmans (reprint), n.d.

Pieters, Albertus. *The Lamb, The Woman and The Dragon.* Grand Rapids: The Church Press, 1946.

Plummer, Alfred. *Revelation: Pulpit Commentary.* New York: Funk and Wagnalls Co., n.d.

Roberson, C. H. *Studies in the Revelation.* Fort Worth: The Manney Co., 1957.

Swete, Henry Barclay. *Apocalypse of St. John.* Grand Rapids: William B. Eerdmans (reprint), 1951.

Summers, Ray. *Worthy is the Lamb.* Nashville: Broadman Press, 1951.

Tenney, Merrill C. *Interpreting Revelation.* Grand Rapids: William B. Eerdmans, 1957.

Thompson, W. S. *Comments on the Revelation.* Privately published, n.d.

Trench, R. C. *Epistles to Seven Churches in Asia.* New York: Charles Scribner and Co., 1872.

Wallace, Foy E., Jr. *The Book of Revelation.* Nashville: Foy E. Wallace, Jr. Publications, 1966.

Westcott, B. F. *The Epistle to the Hebrews.* Grand Rapids: William B. Eerdmans (reprint), 1950.

Whiteside, R. L. *Paul's Letters to the Saints at Rome.* (Clifton, Texas: Mrs. C. R. Nichol, 1945.

Wishart, Charles Frederick. *The Book of Day.* New York: Oxford University Press, 1935.